JOSEPH HAYDN

JOSEPH HAYDN

HIS ART, TIMES, AND GLORY

BY

H. E. JACOB

GREENWOOD PRESS, PUBLISHERS
WESTPORT, CONNECTICUT

Originally published in 1950
by Rinehart & Company, Inc., New York & Toronto

Reprinted with the permission
of Holt, Rinehart and Winston, Inc., New York

First Greenwood Reprinting 1971

Library of Congress Catalogue Card Number 76-138591

SBN 8371-5792-7

Printed in the United States of America

To

the everpresent

HELENE ANGEL

Her Life:

Creative Wisdom—Love—and Light—

and Melody

FOREWORD

"HAYDN," Sir Donald Tovey once pointed out to his students, "means a century in itself. For, with his life and his art, he filled the gap between the Bachs and Schubert . . ."

What an awe-inspiring fact it is that an individual could with his left arm reach to the realm of Johann Sebastian Bach, and with his right arm almost to the beginnings of the romantic era! Haydn's main achievement, then, was perhaps his longevity—and this is not meant in jest. For his longevity alone explains both the slow-maturing perfection of his work and his amazing rise to the peaks of an uncommon glory.

Even Beethoven was not sure which he ought to admire more in Haydn: the works or the life. Lying on his deathbed, Beethoven scanned a picture of Haydn's birthplace, given to him by Johann Nepomuk Hummel. "How is this possible," he exclaimed; "how could so great a man spring from this barn?"

Haydn, Mozart, Beethoven. Yes, everyone knows that they form the immortal triad of classic music. But ninety persons in a hundred erroneously conceive of them only in terms of succession. This misapprehension necessarily leads to other errors. Haydn, especially, could not have been merely the *precursor* of Mozart, because he outlived Mozart by almost twenty years, and when Haydn died in 1809 Beethoven had already completed almost two-thirds of his life. It is more accurate to consider the three as *contemporaries*—and this, properly considered, means that the Haydn disparagingly referred to as "the old man to whom the two others were more or less indebted" was a figment of the imagination.

Tovey, the rediscoverer of Haydn in our century, jokingly demanded capital punishment for everyone who used the epithet "Papa Haydn." Tovey would not have made this remark had he known that Haydn himself adopted this professional title when he was about thirty-five (it was a custom taken over from the world of the stage), to indicate that he would watch over the musicians of his band *like a father*. But it is strange indeed that for more than one hundred years the most vigorous of all composers has been pictured as a pitifully weak old man. Concurrent with this misunderstanding of his personality, Haydn's music remained, during that long period, an unknown continent.

The author of this book set out to explore that continent some fifteen years ago, and he will not presume to say that he or any of the other explorers have penetrated to the heart of it. He has been able to follow the trails they blazed a good part of the way, but—in all modesty and with due gratitude to them—it must be said that he has had to blaze some of his own. He is, for example, convinced that the life and character of Haydn—that ordered life and pedestrian character—have always been somehow more amazing than the music—because that character and life were the inexhaustible source of the music. Moreover, the author is convinced that Haydn's life, recorded in countless touching stories as well as in the amusing collection of his misspelled notebooks and letters, cannot be separated from his music. They explain, they interpret, each other. In speaking of Haydn's music it is necessary to recount—not separately, but simultaneously, in an essentially contrapuntal style—the life as well, and vice versa. Sometimes the leading voice speaks of "music," but it speaks just as often of "life."

The subtitle of this book on Haydn is concerned with his art, times, and glory. Why his "times"? All the writers on Haydn insist that the master was an extremely humble man. But, in fact, he was not always humble; his naïveté was genuine; he was able to employ it as a tool for raising his standard of living. Consequently, he was profoundly influenced by the political, economic and—although he scarcely ever opened a book—the philosophical trends of his century. And in turn he influenced *them,* as we shall see, to a truly astonishing degree.

So much for his "times." And what about "art"? Well, now, elements other than musical enter into the works of Haydn. His music often extends into the adjacent realms of poetry and, even more distinctly, of painting. Thirdly, this book, for the first time, describes the story of Haydn's glory—a glory that often went astray and that was increased even as the result of mistakes—the strangest of mistakes in politics and philosophy.

Haydn, Mozart, Beethoven. In the end Haydn had to pay dearly for the fact that, during his lifetime, his contemporaries elevated his music far above that of his two companions.

But in the Tiergarten at Berlin stands (or stood?) a monument that speaks the truth. The statues of the three immortals gaze out to three sides and stand on the same level. None towers above the others.

H. E. J.

CONTENTS

BOOK SIX

THE CLOUDY NIGHT

ILLUSTRATIONS

Book One

THE MORNING OF A MAN

In the history of music no chapter is more important than that filled by the lifework of Joseph Haydn.

SIR DONALD TOVEY

CHILD OF A LANDSCAPE

One summer's day in the year 1736 a poor Austrian peasant went to his barn to let in his cow, which was waiting patiently outside. It was his one and only cow. But he stopped short as he heard unmistakable sounds of mooing and the trampling of straw coming from inside his barn. The Devil himself must have duplicated his cow, he thought, and in mortal fear he crossed himself and fled.

The peasant fetched the village priest to search the barn. But instead of finding some emissary of the Evil One, the priest came across a four-year-old child who was playing cow. The child's name was Joseph Haydn. Perhaps the small boy actually fancied himself a cow, for in his village of Rohrau on the border of Lower Austria and Hungary the animals were unquestionably in the majority. Throughout his early childhood Haydn absorbed their warmth and affection; he watched the Burgenland cows slobbering water from the trough beside the sleepy, squeaking Hungarian draw-well. Here also the geese clustered to snap at the bees humming by. The thatched roofs of the quiet village rustled in springtime when a whirling flock of storks settled on them.

The child grasped the acoustic language of nature at an early age, and the sensory experiences of his childhood became part of his very being. None of the great composers of the past had been either huntsman or peasant; they would never have been able to distinguish between the squelching, sucking sound of a duck's tread and the patter of an approaching dog. This Haydn could do. As a boy he was a past master at sound mimicry, and such mimicry fills *The Creation,* which he wrote at the age of sixty-five. The very words, "By heavy beasts the ground is trod," sung to the notes of the bassoon and contra-bassoon, conjure up the vivid fantasy that man is vastly outnumbered on this earth.

It was a sleepy land in which Joseph Haydn was born. Not that it lacked energy, but it was without fire, without temperament. Its character is not what is conventionally considered "Austrian"; it has none of that particular beauty which characterizes the mountain country west of Vienna. Haydn was a lowlander; there is no evidence that he was even acquainted with the towering Alps and the other true beauties of Austria. At the age of nineteen he went on a pilgrimage to the shrine of the Virgin at Mariazell, but no trace of this journey can be found in his works. In his music we find no sign that he was aware of the gleaming, gem-like chain of lakes that stretch out toward Bavaria or of the mountainous torrents that foam through Innsbruck.

Burgenland is more fruitful than the rest of Austria. It is fertile farmland whose flat contours are broken only by a few low chains of hills, the Rosalie and Leitha Mountains, from which came the shell-limestone that was used to build many of Vienna's palaces. The landscape does not charm those who are not very much at home there. But even a puddle can reflect the rainbow. "Nature is in essence always beautiful," says Werfel in one of his novels. It was in this landscape that Haydn first felt the sun, the wind, and the stars. It was his motherland, and he always preferred it to any other landscape on earth.

A strange guest has found shelter in this landscape: The Neusiedlersee. This lake is an alien indeed; it seems to belong rather to the steppes of Asia than to this western country. It is shallow—so shallow that sometimes it would not wet a man's ankle, but it is of enormous extent. The farther shore of the lake cannot be seen with the naked eye. It is surrounded by a belt of reeds inhabited by flocks of strange birds. (The very name of Haydn's birthplace—Rohrau—means "field of reeds.") By the shores of this lake Haydn, as a boy, probably whittled pipes of Pan, and listened to the harsh voice of the herons. Here, as a grown man, he hunted and fished. The gleam and the sunlit radiance of the lake return again and again in his symphonies.

However, what secretly ties the people of the Burgenland to their homeland is the vine. Their wine is sweeter than other Austrian wines; it has a Hungarian bouquet and resembles Tokay. It is the wine that saves the East Austrians from the "dullness" of their race; at grape-gathering time they are transformed. In that immortal work of his old age, *The Seasons,* Joseph Haydn created a memorial to the wine.

Countless features in Haydn's music are of peasant origin. The "great peace" in all his works is the peace of the peasant's life. Haydn's love for nature is not like that of a romantic poet who demands of nature that it stimulate his feelings. It is, rather, a love for "law." To him, landscape is the firmly established and permanent factor in the change of the seasons; it is the object of human activity and of the peasant's tenacity. The people whom Haydn describes in his works and with whom he dwelt lived in an eternal alliance with nature. For that reason he was free from the unrest which the romantics worshipped, and he hated chance.

Haydn did not leave East Austria before his sixtieth year! Up to that time he knew nothing of the world except Burgenland and Vienna—but he was not discontented with this narrow horizon. We must think of his art as that of a most deliberate pilgrim who contentedly settles down and begins painting the landscape. Any more impetuous course would have struck him as rash. He, who so rarely engaged in dispute, could on occasion speak sharply against a premature "interruption" in composition and against a too rapid "throwing in of new themes." The composer ought rather, he declared, "expatiate on and sustain the old ones." That is the classical view of art, and in this respect Haydn differed sharply from the later composers.

Nevertheless, in another sense he influenced all the composers who followed him. There was one element of unrest that even a man like Haydn could not banish from his musical landscape—on the contrary, he actually cherished it. Fields and houses are fixed; water and fire are tamed in Haydn's music; but the *air* remains untamed and untamable. Haydn's works are full of grandiose atmospheric changes. He is the first modern to incorporate into his music tempests and thunderstorms; in fact, the slightest barometric changes. In Haydn as in no other great composer, we can sense the variety of the air, of the winds. At forty he composed a famous storm-choral for his Biblical oratorium *Il ritorno di Tobia.* And at sixty he wrote in London (in 1792) a cantata, *The Storm,* to the words:

Hark! the wild uproar of the winds, and hark
Hell's Genius roams the regions of the dark;
And thund'ring swells the horrors of the main:
From cloud to cloud the Moon affrighted flies,
Now darken'd, and now flashing through her skies—
Alas! bless'd calm, return, return again.

The music-lovers of London praised Haydn's palette and declared that no other composer had portrayed the raging of the winds so realistically as he. But Haydn was a man of peace and calm, and he modulated the wild tumult in G-minor to a tranquil andante in G-major.

In all these works the memories of his earliest childhood played their part: Recollections of Burgenland which, open to the East, was lashed by storms that were like the hordes of mounted Tartars whose advance had broken against the foothills of the Austrian alps. Haydn's depictions of weather, in his music, had an influence that reached far beyond his own century. They affected Beethoven's *Pastoral Symphony* and Rossini's *Overture to William Tell,* and established a tradition in which Weber and Wagner later worked.

THE CARRIAGE MAKERS

ALTHOUGH Haydn's music always "walked in peasant shoon," he himself was not a peasant's son. This is probably the second most important fact in his life.

He was the child of an artisan, as was his father, born in 1699, and his grandfather before him. Perhaps his great-grandfather had also been an artisan. The workshop of Father Matthias Haydn resounded to the cheerful blows of the hammer. The rhythm of the forge has more than once been the inspirer of good music, as we know not only from Johannes Brahms's beautiful song, but, above all, from the immortal notes of Master Handel's *Harmonious Blacksmith*. D'Alembert, chief of the French aestheticians, even went so far as to assert that smiths were the discoverers of rhythm.

But Haydn's forefathers were something more than smiths. For centuries they had all been cartwrights—that is to say, they practised a trade which is basic to civilization, for the wagon was requisite before society could emerge from a primitive state in which agriculture was very rudimentary. The cartwright was more than a peasant and considered himself a good deal better.

Was Wheelwright Haydn aware, as he looked out the door of his workshop, of the tremendous progress that had been made in his trade during the past century? In his days as a journeyman Matthias Haydn had traveled far—as far, it is said, as Frankfurt-on-the-Main—and had seen much. Certainly, a great deal had been done for the comfort of noblemen and burghers since the days when Louis Quatorze rode into Paris in a "coach that hung on saddlegirths." The court carriages of his successor, gold-embossed and upholstered on the inside with silks and brocades, their boxes swaying as gently as a sedan chair, had become miracles of elegance. Even the ordinary traveler in western countries now rode far more comfortably, in coaches with springs that softened every jolt. But it is doubtful that, for all his traveling, Matthias Haydn knew very much about these innovations. He may well have considered as altogether fabulous the story that an Austrian archduchess had been driven across half of Europe in a glass bridal coach to meet her bridegroom.

Nevertheless, when Matthias Haydn stepped to the front of his house and looked out on the highroad, he was sharp enough to know what vehicle it was that plunged toward him out of a cloud of dust—whether it was a Polish "droccke," a "pirutsch," or a Bohemian stagecoach. At such times he was touched by the longing to build such magnificent carriages himself—perhaps one of those new French "diligences" which were so fast that they could race from Paris to Lyons in two days.

But even with his simpler trade, Master Matthias Haydn was kept busy. The tiny village of Rohrau in which he lived belonged to the family of Count Harrach, and frequently a merry company assembled at the count's castle. On such occasions hunting coaches were used—very long, narrow, open vehicles that were called "sausages." On a narrow, upholstered bench the hunters sat one behind the other, their muskets in their right hands, their left hands holding the hunter's horn to their lips. At other times the count's men were sent flying off to Vienna or Pressburg, and all these activities at the castle kept Wheelwright Haydn busy with orders.

Joseph Haydn's father was not one to be sympathetic to innovation. The good old family carriages of the seventeenth century suited his tastes. They gave long service and remained in the possession of children and children's children, needing only to be newly upholstered from time to time. His character has been described in a merry apprentice's song about a man who made a cart that would serve him both as a carriage for his wedding journey and a hearse for his funeral. The rhythm of the song was beaten out with hammers:

> His car himself he did provide
> To stand in double stead:
> That it should carry him alive
> And bury him when dead.
> Heigh doune, derry!
> Heigh doune derry, derry doune!

As often as young Joseph Haydn could, he played around the coach-house which held the new and the old carriages. Never did he have the opportunity to take a ride inside such a carriage—but that was no matter. A real artisan cared little for the excitement of travel, but much for the construction of the vehicle itself; the sensible distribution of seats was an important problem. Neither too much nor too little was the rule, and this the wheelwright's son soon grasped. He also grasped the fact that a good artisan had to have the qualities of a physician. When the coachman took his seat upon the box, the box was covered with a hammer-cloth, for it concealed hammer, nails, pincers, rope and other remedies for broken wheels and shivered panels; accidents were common in the days of poor paving and worse lighting, when sewers were left open at night while undergoing repairs, and no light but a farthing candle in a dirty lantern was placed by them to give notice of danger to the speeding coachman.

For generations the safety of men was entrusted to such carriages, and they had to be very strong; yet they also had to be light and easy to handle. In the end, every carriage sooner or later reached its grave—a fact that probably gave rise in Matthias Haydn to such quizzical thoughts as Oliver Wendell Holmes expressed:

> "And that's the reason beyond doubt:
> A chaise breaks down, but it doesn't wear out."

But the most important thing on a carriage is the wheel. How much dignity is in a wheel! And it was no small experience for the child Haydn when he saw a wheel, tested and found good, placed, for the first time, on the axle and finally rotating faster and faster. Even as a man he glorified the memory of these revolving and humming wheels—in the first bars of his First Symphony—and, more than a half of a century later, he could not help incorporating the music of the same whirring wheels in one of his latest works, in the famous spinning chamber music of the "Seasons."

Haydn never lost the childhood impressions gathered in his father's workshop; he regarded himself, first and foremost, as a craftsman. When he was sixty-three and had already become famous throughout Europe, he was questioned by some customs officials on the Austro-Bavarian frontier about his profession.

"Ich bin ein Tonsetzer," Haydn replied, truthfully. In German the word "ton" can mean either "tune" or "clay," and the official mistook Haydn for a potter, a worker in clay.

"Yes, I am a potter," Haydn answered, quite seriously. And pointing to his servant, Elssler, beside him, he added, "and this is my apprentice." He could never consider it degrading to be taken for an artisan. His forefathers had been artisans for a far longer time than he himself had been a composer. To grasp the essential dignity of the man, we need only imagine Beethoven in such a situation—how he would have stormed and raged at the insult! Even Bach and Handel would solemnly have shaken the locks of their heavy wigs, in pitying contempt.

COUSIN SCHOOLMASTER

HAYDN's father was entitled to hang outside his workshop a shield showing a golden ball against a red field emblazoned with three silver ostrich feathers. This was Count Harrach's coat-of-arms. Forebears of the Harrach family, members of Bohemia's ancient nobility, had inherited the castle and village of Rohrau two hundred years before Joseph's birth. Young Haydn early learned the meaning of servility, when his father bowed his head to the ground in the presence of His Most Noble Lord. His mother before her marriage had been a cook in the lord's castle and had instilled in her son a lifelong taste for good food—but it was a taste that was seldom satisfied until the great composer came of age. During the most important years of his development Haydn often went hungry.

Of Haydn's mother, Maria, we know little beyond the fact that she bore twelve children. Six of them died early—the death rate was high in those times when elementary hygiene was unknown. Joseph Haydn, born on March 31, 1732 (or perhaps on April 1; unwilling to be an "April fool" he stubbornly denied this), was the oldest surviving child. His full baptismal name was Franz Joseph.

The mother's maiden name was Koller. This meant in German a soldier's leather jerkin. A more likely derivation of the word is from the Slavic *kolar,* which means "wheelwright." Perhaps Matthias had chosen his wife from a family in which, as in his own, the wheelwright's trade once was hereditary.

It is clear from the church records that Matthias was descended from German-speaking people, but the mother's name may possibly have been Germanized. The village of Rohrau was, in Haydn's time, also called Trstnik, and had a large number of Croat inhabitants. Just twenty years ago the population census of Burgenland showed, in addition to the 227,435 Germans, 115,554 Hungarians and 42,013 Croats—in other words, every sixth person acknowledged himself a

Croat. When Haydn was a child the proportion may well have been even more favorable to the Croats.

Haydn's father was musical; he played simple songs on his "harp," and at the age of five the child could sing these songs quite well to his accompaniment. Undoubtedly, the father played German tunes. But when little Joseph sat on his father's lap at the tavern, he also heard Croat songs, the melancholy-merry rounds that the people loved. The poor sheaf-binders and the itinerant scissors-grinders also sang Slavic melodies and songs. The little Haydn's ear eagerly absorbed them. Mozart's famous remark that he never forgot a single note he had ever heard was true of Haydn as well. He had "a memory like a pincers."

But, previously, he had to exercise his memory on far unpleasanter things than on German or Croat tavern ditties. For now the time had come for young Haydn to attend school. It is not definitely known whether there was a schoolmaster in Rohrau. Most of the inhabitants could not read or write. In any case, the Haydn family recalled that in the little town of Hainburg on the Danube, with whose citizens the Haydns had old ties of kinship, there was a "Cousin Schoolmaster," Johann Matthias Frankh, who was the pride of all his relatives. Frankh was a "magister" of the type that the great German humorist, Jean Paul, has described—mercurially active, ready with his ferrule, a good-natured thunderer who did a hundred things that had no connection with teaching. In short, Frankh was an indefatigable *paterfamilias*. In later years the composer perpetuated the memory of his character in a few humorous and pedantic bars of the symphony known as "The Schoolmaster Symphony" (No. 55).

So it was that the child sat in a carriage for the first time, and rode away from his home to a strange town. It was a glorious summer morning. The larks darted exuberantly about in the sky, a loud humming filled the air as with the beat of drums, and there were a multitude of things for a little boy to look at in wonderment. First he rode by the ancient town of Petronell, whose Roman name was planted so strangely in this Hungarian plain. As he approached closer, the name hardened into stone—framed against the pale-blue sky there stood a Roman triumphal arch, still magnificent in ruin, a relic of past ways of life. In this vicinity the Roman town of Carnuntum had stood, itself a little Rome, and its temples, palaces and theaters had been reflected in the Danube. Here the great Emperor Marcus Aurelius had lived in his camp and had written his wise and justly famous book, the *Meditations*. He was not a Christian, but his grave and sober philosophy, his stoicism, enhanced by manliness and pathos, have won for him the devotion of Christians.

The carriage was driven on through the medieval town of Deutsch-Altenburg where a Gothic cathedral looked down upon them from a hill. This was the road down which the widow of Siegfried, the murdered legendary king, had traveled when she went eastward from the Rhine to become the wife of Attila, King of the Huns. A fort built by the Huns, with ring-walls and tower, had stood on the ridge above the Danube like a segment of Asia transported into Europe; it had witnessed the journeys and battles of the *Nibelungenlied*.

It was through such a landscape that the Haydns' child rattled along for a whole day, until the town of Hainburg appeared before him at twilight. He passed through the Vienna Gate, where the marks of the bullets and bolts of the infidels still commemorated the Turkish wars, and rode into the Ungargasse, where Cousin Schoolmaster lived. The cheese and sausages which had been sent as a first payment for his schooling were unpacked, and little Joseph was led to his new home.

The main attraction of Hainburg, as far as the child's family was concerned, was that Frankh was also a musician. In addition to performing his duties as schoolmaster, he supplied the church music for the little town. He himself played the organ, and directed a chorus and a small orchestra consisting of strings, horns, and percussion. In addition, the schoolmaster—an old document informs us—was required to "train the boys to act as acolytes and, with the aid of two paid assistant teachers, to instruct them in singing and music in general, also in reading, writing, and arithmetic, and especially to teach the schoolchildren Christian decorum and honesty and the proper manner of praying."

In the first and the third tasks Johann Matthias Frankh acquitted himself well. Haydn learned the elements of music from him, reading notes and singing, and he also received a good many admonishments to behave decorously and honestly as a good Christian. But the second task, instruction in the elements of worldly knowledge, Frankh and his assistant teachers did not fulfil very well. Perhaps they themselves were not overly learned. In any case, Haydn never learned to write in German without mistakes. He was certainly not proud of this, for he lived in a century when culture and knowledge counted for a great deal. (Goethe, as a boy, had a fluent command of four languages.) Haydn was no barbarian; he was not the "all brawn and no brains" type who ranted about "blood and soil" and looked down in misguided romanticism on "scribbling intellectualism." On the contrary, throughout his life he was respectful of those who were better educated than he. But as a boy he was unable, even with the best will in the world, to acquire the elements of book-learning, and later, life put other demands upon him.

It may be said in extenuation of Frankh that at that time the grammar-school education of Austrian Germans was at its lowest level. This was true not only of the lower classes, but of the higher circles as well. The aristocrats who spoke fluent Italian and French had difficulty in couching a sentence in correct German. When the Saxon poet Gottsched visited the Empress Maria Theresa, in 1749, she, blushing, said to him: "I ought to be ashamed to converse in German with the master of the German language; we Austrians speak very poorly." Whereupon the visitor gallantly assured the monarch that no such reproach could be addressed to her—a compliment which, as it happened, was deserved. But the great majority of Austrians did not speak the Empress's German; they were unable to agree on either a consistent dialect or an accepted high German.

At any rate, Joseph Haydn received at Hainburg more instruction in music than was common for boys of his age. In addition to learning singing and musical notation, he soon began to learn piano and violin playing. At the age of six he served as an acolyte at mass, and he swung on the ropes to ring the church bells. In his old age Haydn told his biographer: "Almighty God, Whom alone I must thank for immeasurable grace, so lightened for me the task of learning music that by the time I was six I had the boldness to sing masses in the church choir and to play a little on the piano and the violin." And seventy years after his sojourn with the schoolmaster he passed favorable judgment on his cousin Frankh: "Even in my grave I shall continue to be grateful to this man for urging me to undertake so many various activities, although I received more cuffs than food in the course of them." And he showed his appreciation by remembering Frankh's descendants in his will.

The boy soon became painfully aware (as he later recounted) of the untidiness of the schoolmaster's home. His father had accustomed young Haydn to the strictest cleanliness. But in Hainburg "uncleanliness was master, and although I was very conceited about my own little person I could not prevent traces of the general dirtiness from becoming visible on my clothes now and then, and this shamed me most deeply . . . I looked a little urchin." Haydn could never endure carelessness or dirt; even as an old man he dressed "as if he expected visitors any moment." In this respect his external appearance was symbolic of his inner conscientiousness.

In other respects, Haydn at that time was inclined to be an urchin. He mistook noise for music, tussled violently with the instruments, snapped his violin bow and expanded his lungs to the point of bursting when he blew the trumpet. Every healthy child loves fortissimi; lyrical joy in pianissimo is something that comes with maturity.

Shortly before the Festival of St. Florian in June the kettledrummer of Frankh's orchestra died suddenly. Frankh promptly ordered Joseph Haydn to substitute for him. With characteristic exuberance, Joseph practiced on a flour tub that was generally used for baking bread. He tied a cloth tightly across it, for a drumhead. Then he ran through the town in a cloud of flour dust and had to be caught and cleaned up before he could take his place in the saint's-day procession. But he strode confidently along amid the gaily dressed crowds, and hammered away very well with a real drumstick on a real drum. It is very Austrian, this anecdote; the same sort of thing might well have happened in the lives of another musician, such as Bruckner or Schubert.

And then Fate entered the aloofness of this provincial town—fate in the shape of a tall, imposing, but friendly man whose wig, pigtail, side-curls, jabot and high collar gave him the appearance of an army officer. He was Court and Cathedral *Kapellmeister* Johann Georg Reutter, of Vienna. And in a sense he *was* a recruiting officer; he was looking for "recruits of song," by which he meant choir-boys for his choir in St. Stephen's Cathedral. Accompanied by his host and friend, Pastor Palm of Hainburg, Reutter attended a performance in the church, and heard "by chance the weak but pleasing voice of the seven-year-old boy."

He sent for the boy at once. Accompanied by his cousin, Schoolmaster Frankh, Joseph went to the parsonage and sang for Reutter. The Cathedral kapellmeister made a few smiling remarks of praise, and said a number of other things that the child did not understand.

Near the guest's elbow stood a plate of dark-red cherries. Haydn's eyes widened; as usual, he was hungry. He stared at the fruit and forgot about everything else. Reutter held a cherry in two fingers, and waved it before the boy's nose. "Can you sing a trill, too?" he teased. Haydn understood the pantomime; if he said "yes" he would receive the fruit as a reward.

"A trill? No," the boy answered, honestly. "Not even my cousin Herr Frankh can do that."

Only Italians, or people who had studied Heaven only knew what subtleties, could manage such things, the boy thought. But Reutter shook his head. "Now, look, here's how it's done," he said, and stood up. He trilled to the best of his ability. Joseph closed his eyes, and tried to imitate him. At first he could not, but after a few tries he succeeded. The pastor and the schoolmaster held their breaths as if to lend their own strength to little Joseph.

When he had finished his trill, he opened his eyes. And he found that in his right hand were not only a dozen cherries, but there was a gold piece in his left—an earnest of his employment as a "recruit of song."

"Bravo! You must stay with me," Reutter exclaimed. "If your parents are willing, you'll come to sing in the choir at Vienna next year."

THE WORLD OF ST. STEPHEN'S CATHEDRAL

WERE the parents willing?

Matthias Haydn was, undoubtedly, perfectly content. The master wheelwright had a house full of children. If the eldest were sent to Vienna it would mean that for years little Joseph would support himself by his singing—an economic fact to be reckoned with.

Joseph's mother probably felt otherwise—but was she allowed to feel at all? Work, unending work, was her lot. In house and kitchen, in the fields, in the barn and in their small vineyard, she labored six days of the week. It was only on Sundays that Mother Haydn could have put her black velvet bodice over her homespun blouse, tied her black apron around her waist and her blue-and-red kerchief under the chin, and gone to speak to her pastor.

This pastor was a Croat by the name of Selescovic. We don't know his answer when Maria Haydn confided her doubts to him. The only thing we know for sure is that, on an autumn day in 1740, the eight-year-old child rode into Vienna.

This journey was a very different one from the ride to Hainburg. Even in the middle ages the first sight of Vienna had taken away the breath of strangers. Ever since, a great deal of progress had been made. The city had become a mosaic of incomparable beauty in stone, broken everywhere by bands of greenery and gleaming ponds. Great architects had studied in Italy to learn how baroque Vienna, the imperial city, deserved to be built. And now those architects—Burnachini and Hildebrandt, and, above all, the great Fischer von Erlach—were surpassing the cities of the South.

When little Joseph rode into Vienna from the east, he saw at once three palaces: The two Belvedere Palaces which had been built for Prince Eugene, and the Schwarzenberg Palace. How could a child help thinking that the Emperor must certainly live in one of these? But, had he expressed his thought, he would have been informed that all this splendor did not approach that of the Emperor's dwelling. And that if the magnificences of Trautson, Auersperg, Schoenburg, and Lichnowsky were all heaped one upon the other, they would not reach the Emperor's boot! What kind of city was this, where even the middle-class houses looked like stone jewel boxes? Everywhere were naked giants, and nymphs that bore portals, balconies, and windows on their heads; there were cornucopias, figurines of children, baskets of fruit, helmets filled to the brim with flowers and pearls. . . .

What a stage this was, on which living men moved about! No theater in the world could equal it—and yet it was all real life! Was German spoken here? Perhaps, but the streets also resounded with shouts in Italian. Great lords in their gorgeous carriages came from Bohemia; Polish noblemen who had business at the friendly court of Vienna passed into the city surrounded by their flocks of servants and armed guards. There were merchants from Bavaria and Swabia, shipping agents, traders in textiles and wine. There were turbaned Moors and Asiatics. Turkish carpets were bought by the rich and promptly hung out of the windows. The Hungarian guard of honor, dressed in silver helmets, tiger skins and furred dolmans, rode slowly through the Inner City. It was, in fact, impossible to ride fast, so cheerfully tumultuous and crowded were the streets. And how much food these people ate! They had ample money to pay for it. Aeneas Piccolomini, a Pope and a great litterateur of the fifteenth century, wrote: "It is hard to believe the amount of food that is daily brought into the city. Carts filled with eggs and crabs arrive; bread, meat, fish, and poultry are supplied from the countryside in enormous quantities. And of all these vast provisions, none remains by evening to be bought."

Poor Joseph—it was really nothing but a stageset that he saw! Very quickly it was snatched from his sight. For he had not been invited to come to Vienna, but to the choir-house of St. Stephen's Cathedral. His destination was the environs of a structure which he had seen long before the city itself became visible, for the Cathedral towered against the horizon like a delicate needle of stone. His service began, and was to last for nine years.

Cathedral Kapellmeister Georg Reutter, who at that time was only thirty-two years old, lived in the choir-house, a four-story dwelling house opposite the cathedral. The choir-boys boarded with him. The city paid for their board and education. In the choir-house the boys were taught reading, writing, arithmetic, religion and Latin, and, in addition, they were given lessons in singing, violin, and piano. But the major part of their day was taken up by hard work in the cathedral. They had duties to perform at high masses, vigils, vespers, and memorial masses, as well as at baptisms and funeral services within the cathedral. They were without doubt overstrained, and they were not fed well enough at their boarding-school.

Reutter had married the daughter of Heinrich Holzhauser, the former court-music director, and his wife, Therese, had been a singer of note. However, Therese Reutter paid little attention to her husband's pupils. In consequence, Haydn was motherless during the most important years of his childhood although (like Bruckner) he was very strongly attached to his mother. Certain islands of dryness and loneliness in his music testify to this unhappy circumstance.

Haydn's true master during those years was the cathedral. For him it was a strange world, steeped in traditions ancient beyond his comprehension. When the gigantic portal of St. Stephen's Cathedral was erected, about the year 1250, it was felt even at that time to be "old." The frieze along its sides, which portrayed the dangers that threatened both priests and laity, had probably been thought "obscure and scarcely comprehensible," even in those days. And now Haydn the choir-boy, a child of ten, of twelve, of fourteen, wandered about amid the stone flora and fauna of this ancient world, without truly understanding it. He walked shyly down the vast, main aisle of the cathedral, where bright light never fell. It was a night illuminated by burning candles—as if God could be worshipped only at night.

The organ was a triumph of Renaissance art, lightening the gloom. Here Heinrich Isaak of Flanders had sat, as well as Paul Hofhaimer, the old Cathedral Kapellmeister Fux, and young Reutter's own father.

But otherwise it was a gloomy, Gothic world that surrounded the young boy. Everywhere, on all sides, were reminders of death. The edifice always smelled of damp wreaths, placed there to hide the scent of corpses, for adjoining the cathedral was the sexton's house.

To be sure, Joseph came from an environment in which death was regarded with no undue awe. A peasant culture, unlike the culture of cities, is accustomed to the processes of growth and decay. Nevertheless, this overemphasis upon death, pervading the ecclesiastical atmosphere, was something that could be expected to produce a reaction in the child. He might have become melancholy, nervous and anxiety-ridden. But just the opposite reaction took place: Haydn became an even more exuberant child than he had been. Although he lived for nine years in this shrouded world of the cathedral, he did not let the somberness come any closer to him than was necessary for the exercise of his duties.

This fact is so amazing and is such testimony to the soundness of his instincts that we must dwell upon it. Haydn was pious—a very pious man, indeed, who even in old age would still say, unabashedly: "When my composing doesn't go well, I tell a few rosaries; then the rest comes easily." And yet he was a son of the eighteenth century, when all classes shared in a natural antipathy to the Middle Ages. In Haydn's music there is no trace of that medieval world, no trace of the stone gutters, the pointed arches, the flying buttresses, the waterspouts, and the gargoyles that, taken all together, made for the dark Gothic atmosphere of the cathedral. Gloom was not congenial to his nature. Haydn had no need of fear in order to approach closer to his God. He found Him manifested in this earthly existence, in the daylight world.

That was precisely what his age required of him. We cannot doubt that about 1740 St. Stephen's Cathedral was somewhat embarrassing to many of the devout. The baroque age, which was already tending toward rococo, conceived its cathedrals in a different fashion from that of St. Stephen's. It filled its churches with a secular piety that smacked of the salon and even of coquetry. The type of the genial Italian and French abbé was everywhere coming into prominence in the Catholic Church, and replacing the cruder German priest. Vienna was no exception, and gradually it became customary at the chief church festivals to use by preference those parts of the cathedral to which there could be given a contemporary tone by means of modish additions to the existing structure. The theater, too, with all its paraphernalia, forced its way into the cathedral.

And thus, the compositions that Haydn was later to write for the church were not pointed and not overcast with mystical shadows; they did not spire upward to the dimness of great heights. Rather they were expansive, joyous, full of the sky's blues and the sunset's purples and the harvest's yellows. What Haydn learned during the years he spent in the choir-house was the grammar of writing masses, the century-old syntax of musical worship. But the spirit and the flesh of his music were different. Round clouds of angels hover above his

Great Organ Mass of 1766; he enlivens the texts with coloraturas:

Even his *Stabat Mater* is impregnated with the sweetness of the grape, with a Correggio-like warmth that is almost too gracious for the somber subject-matter. Only one of his compositions is infused with really profound tragedy, *The Seven Words of the Saviour on the Cross.* But even about this there is nothing Gothic. It is not the breath of the other world that chills us, but the human tragedy; we suffer for the Son of Man and thirst with Him when He is athirst. The somberness of this piece is Spanish. A Spanish grandee ordered it, and Haydn piously accommodated him.

It was particularly fortunate for the development of the fourteen-year-old boy that Georg Reutter was also a composer, and that he was Court Kapellmeister as well as Cathedral Kapellmeister. Often he would be writing a pantomime or an operetta that some noble dilettante at the Imperial Court wished to see performed. Thus, the spirit of the Court penetrated into the cathedral and secular artistic influences merged with the ecclesiastical ones. In fact, they were very much interwoven. Reutter could not compose a mass without employing trumpets and drums very vigorously. The English writer, Charles Burney, who was traveling on the continent at the time, wondered at Reutter's masses. He exclaimed at "how much noise they really made" (he would not credit them with being anything but a great deal of noise). And the Empress Maria Theresa once remarked, after a mass which had sounded, to her ears, much too light-hearted for a sacred composition, "But my dear Reutter, I imagined I heard the tramp of horses." Whereupon the quick-witted composer replied: "When I wrote that in four-quarter time I was thinking of the court equipage, which I should be happy to have the use of." The empress laughingly granted the ingenious petition. And from that time on his compotion was called the "White-Horse Mass." Above the score the composer wrote: *"Quadrupedante putrem sonitu quatit ungula campum."* ("In four-quarter time the hoof strikes the yielding soil of the field.")

Reutter had his fifteen boys take part in secular festivals, and this apparently provided important additional income for him. He lent his group to noble houses, where their crystal-clear voices embellished levees and soirées. The director often had to use his baton as a whipping-cane, for the boys were apt to become rough and knock bass viols and music-stands about. On these occasions the boys had only one interest: What is there to eat? Where is the kitchen; where is the pantry? For years they were so hungry that they vied with one another for engagements to sing at the profane orgies staged by the nobility. As soon as their concert was over, they would swarm into the baronial larders like rats. They were frequently routed from the premises by attendants, but not until their faces were smeared beyond recognition with dripping and chocolate.

Little Haydn was more savage than all the rest. He was a boisterous, obstreperous child. While the empress's summer palace of Schoenbrunn was being built, he clambered about the scaffolding, shouting merrily or chirpingly mimicking birds. She had him hauled down and whipped—probably because she feared for his neck.

It was during these years, between 1740 and 1760, that Jean Jacques Rousseau was working on his novel dealing with education, *Emile*. Rousseau wrote: "Keep the child dependent on things only. Let his wishes meet with physical obstacles only, or the punishment which results from his own actions. Such lessons will be recalled when the same circumstances occur again. It is enough to prevent him from wrongdoing without forbidding him to do wrong. Experience or lack of power should take the place of dogma." Evidently the empress had another view of the matter. Such an attitude would have seemed criminal to her. "I am a mother," she was wont to say. "It is my duty to prevent."

Her own son, Crown Prince Joseph, could not be whipped, of course. One day, however, the empress was so annoyed at something he had done that she ordered one of her waiting women to punish the boy. The woman shrank back in horror. "Thrash a Hapsburg!" she exclaimed. "Such a thing has never been done."

"Do you, then," the empress asked with gay mockery, "find the results so admirable?"

THE EMPRESS

THE empress was not only a woman; she was a little wonder of the world.

The first of the wonders ascribed to her was that the man who was her husband could not be the emperor—he was the Duke Francis Stephen of Lorraine—so that she herself had to take over the functions of an emperor. This was the source of most of the complications in her life, and of her greatness as well.

In October, 1740, in the fall of the same year in which Joseph Haydn was taken into the choir-house, Maria Theresa's father, the Emperor Charles VI, had died. There began a new order of things.

The vast empire was left in the hands of an inexperienced young woman—an empire as intricate as an ancient tapestry, preciously worked with threads of silver and gold but also full of raveled and rent spots that would have to be mended. The German empire consisted of three hundred portions, some secular, some ecclesiastical; it was peopled with princes, classes, and free cities, which at times fought energetically against one another. Incorporated in the empire were Belgium, Northern Italy and Central Italy, Bohemia, Hungary, and part of the Balkans. The subjects of Maria Theresa spoke so many languages that they could not understand one another. And yet it was her task to bring order out of confusion, to assign each person to the place in which he would be most useful to the empire.

Her enemies took it for granted that no woman could control such manifold factors. Frederick the Great of Prussia fell upon her dominions, and took Silesia from her. The "evil masculine principle" rose up against her, who was the "mother." But in the midst of all misfortunes Maria Theresa succeeded in being loved by her people and by the rest of the world, to which she gave the example of a model wife and mother. She bore her husband sixteen children—and the secret of her art of government consisted, perhaps, in applying her maternal spirit to the dealings with the lands under her sway.

Sixteen confinements! And scarcely were her labors over, when she was not yet out of bed, documents and memoranda from her Chancellor, Kaunitz, ministerial business and dispatches from the theater of war, were thrust upon her. Her physician, Guerardus van Swieten, could shield her only with difficulty. All around her bed of state sounded the clash of arms and the tinkle of chamber music, programs for the improvement of her country and the world, theatricals, operas —incessant activity of all kinds. And yet she remained beautiful to old age, with her blue eyes, her gleaming teeth and her high and majestic brow.

Music was a tradition in her family. A century before her accession to the throne her ancestors had been composers. Emperor Ferdinand III (1637-1657), Leopold I (1658-1705), Joseph I (1705-1711) and Charles VI (1711-1740) had all written music. Maria Theresa herself, a splendid singer in her younger years, did not compose, but she became a generous patroness of music. "Insofar as the age was proud," Hofmansthal wrote, "it was proud without stiffness and hardness. Haydn, Gluck, and Mozart gave perfect expression to the temper of the age and are synonymous with it."

So they were. And yet it is sad to note—so imperfect are all human relationships—that none of the three was precisely fortunate in his relationship with the empress. After fine and fruitful years of composing operas the great Gluck finally went to Paris, where his "heroic ideals" of the stage were better understood than they were among the unheroic Viennese. And when Mozart tried to obtain employment under Archduke Ferdinand, son of the empress, the careful and thrifty "mother of her country" gently dissuaded her son from employing him. "You ask me about taking into your service the young Salzburg musician. I do not know in what capacity, but I believe that you have no need for a composer or for useless people. If, however, it would give you pleasure, I do not wish to prevent you, but . . ." Useless people! Unquestionably, Maria Theresa had nothing against Mozart in particular. As a child he had sat on her lap, and he had played the piano at court. It was dull thrift alone that made the empress advise her son against employing Mozart. "He has, besides, a large family," she noted in her letter. It was really no more than the temporarily unmotherly whim of a mother who, visiting the nursery, suddenly decided that some of the dolls seemed too expensive. Yet the consequences of this rejection were tragic indeed. What development might have been Mozart's had he been given the position!

Haydn—who was, even more than the two other musicians, a creation of the Theresian age—also suffered harm from a whim of the empress. A stupid but crucial criticism on her part robbed him of his livelihood as a choir-boy, without offering him any other prospects.

The empress knew him very well, because he had sung not only in the choir but in the boy's chorus that supplied dinner music at Schoenbrunn. At this time Haydn was eighteen—too old for a soprano—and his voice had changed. As Dies tells it: "This fine voice, by whose aid the boy had so often dined heartily, suddenly betrayed him; it broke and wavered between two tones." The empress had a sensitive ear. In jest—or perhaps in earnest—she remarked to Kapellmeister Reutter: "That choir boy, Joseph Haydn, does not sing; he croaks like a pheasant." That was hint enough for Reutter. He already had another Haydn in his choir, Joseph's younger brother, Michael, whom Father Matthias Haydn had recently brought from Rohrau to the choir-house. Michael's soprano was clear as a bell. The empress herself had made him a present of twenty-four ducats for his solo performance at the festival in honor of St. Leopold. Joseph was no longer needed. For the sake of decency, Reutter waited for a pretext. He soon found one when Haydn snatched up a pair of scissors and cut off a fellow pupil's pigtail. The kapellmeister punished the boy for this "wanton outrage" with a few blows of the ferrule over his hand, and with expulsion from the choir-house where he had lived for nine years.

VIENNA BOHEME

"HELPLESS, without money, possessing only three shabby shirts and a worn-out jacket, the nineteen-year-old boy stepped out into a world he did not know." Thus writes the chronicler to whom Haydn in old age told the story of his life. Where was he to turn? Not a soul troubled himself about the boy. But the framework of his character was firm. His lower-class origins soon proved to be his good fortune. The comfortable life in the choir of St. Stephen's had never, in fact, been very comfortable; it had been a frail span flung across the abyss of poverty and hunger. There young Haydn had had the privilege of singing to devout churchgoers and to the court and the nobility. Now that the span broke, he fell far. Several very hard years began for him. "For eight years I had to drag out a thoroughly wretched life," he later recounted. And he added, "Many a genius is spoiled prematurely by earning his bread by miserable work."

It is to the credit of his strength of will that he nevertheless remained a musician. He might have gone home and asked his father to take him in as an apprentice wheelwright. Probably it was his pride that forbade this step. His mother, who sympathized acutely with him, earnestly advised him in a letter to prepare himself for the priesthood. This seemed to her a logical continuation of his life; after a youth spent as a choir boy it would be only natural for him to turn monk, she thought. Haydn's view of the matter was somewhat different; he wondered whether it might not be a good idea to enter a monastic order, so that for once he might get enough to eat. He rejected this idea. After all, he could teach! He knew a good deal about composing; for years he had been practicing the singing of masses, and to Georg Reutter's amazement he had written an entire "Salve Regina" for twelve voices, although it would have better suited his limited abilities had he been content with two voices. Still, he was skilled in the piano and the violin. If only he were not repeatedly embarrassed by the sad state of his wardrobe! In his shabby clothes he could scarcely enter society.

During the early stages of his "bohemian" life it was not rare for Haydn to sleep in the open air, but later he had the good fortune to meet an old acquaintance, while he was searching for lodgings. This was the tenor, Johann Michael Spangler. The latter was himself not very well off, but, although he had a wife and a child, he invited Haydn to share his home temporarily. It was high time that Haydn had a roof over his head, for winter was already far advanced.

When the first snows of Christmastide fell—we may well imagine that Haydn thought of something very white in C-major, a memory of his home in Rohrau—the impulse to travel awoke in him. He did not, however, want to go home to Burgenland; he thought rather of making a pilgrimage to Mariazell in the Steiermark. He joined up with a group of pilgrims who shared their food with him, and in their company he traveled for many days until he reached the cathedral of Mariazell. He went to the director of the cathedral choir and offered his services. "I was formerly a choir boy at St. Stephen's," he said.

"Out of the question," the good pater responded harshly. "I've seen too many of you beggarly rascals from Vienna who claim to be choir boys. But when it comes to performance you can't sing a note correctly."

The next day, when the mass began, Haydn secretly climbed up into the choir loft. With a pleading look, he pressed his last few pennies into the soloist's hand, and snatched the music sheet from him. Before the surprised boy could do anything about it, Haydn was sight-singing the solo part in a fine, tenor voice; he was now twenty years old and his change of voice was complete. The monks listened in astonishment, and at its completion praised the performance. The prior himself invited Haydn to dine, and kept him at the monastery for eight days. When Haydn left he was given food and money for his journey.

When he returned to Vienna, Haydn found that the Spangler family had increased. It was no longer possible for the young man to live in the tiny apartment. He would have to find another place, and earn money quickly. Fortunately, the season came to his aid. The snow was melting, music was awakening. Birds were already perching on the bare shrubs, and the musicians of the streets and parks were tuning up their instruments. This city, which fed so many songbirds, would also provide Haydn with a livelihood of sorts. A person who could play an instrument was never quite without resources. In eighteenth-century Vienna, music had a higher status than it had in any of the other great cities of the world. It was the constant accompaniment to the life of all classes, from the nobility to the proletariat.

The cause of this almost mad hunger for music in the Viennese has been much discussed. In the seventeenth century Vienna was visited by the Black Death; a large part of the population died. The rest fiddled and sang and drank the good light wine, because slight drunkenness was considered a protection against the plague. The hero of the period was a man named Augustin, who is the hero of the cynical song: *"Ach du lieber Augustin, alles ist hin!"* One night this Augustin, fell drunk, into a grave filled with the corpses of plague victims. He slept off his drunk, and climbed out in the morning as if nothing had happened. The tale became a symbol for the Viennese populace—wine and song would triumph over death in any form.

That was in 1679. In reality, the joy of the Viennese in music and song was much older. In 1540, when Wolfgang Schmelzl, a Swabian versifier, toured Vienna, he observed something that he considered remarkable enough to preserve in verse that still breathes the quaint, stiff flavor of the age of the *Meistersinger:*

> Before all folk I praise this town.
> Here many singers are and fiddlers play,
> Here is good company and all are gay:
> Many musicians and many an instrument,
> I know not how many bows are bent.

Vienna is the crossroads of Europe, where North and South and East and West meet. The consequence is a kind of whirlwind of peoples and cultures and moods from which *music* is generated. Any kind of music. Since Haydn could play the violin, we must assume that he fiddled in smoke-filled taverns, among draymen and petty traders who wanted music with their food and drink. The next day he might be paid by a better-class citizen who was entertaining his friends or wished to present a pretty lady with a serenade. For eight months of the year Vienna rang with serenades and nocturnes, since its climate permits spending evenings in the open air from March to October. After October, music went indoors, along with the new wine.

The *alla fresca* music that was played in the streets and parks was guided by its own laws. Flutes, oboes, violins, clarinets and lutes were the instruments used. The relationship of open-air music to music performed in a room is approximately that of an outdoor mural to a picture in a frame. Out of doors the music must be firmer and cruder, so that the wind cannot dispel it; on the other hand, open-air music lacks one distinct advantage of indoor music in that there are no walls to act as sounding boards.

Viennese serenade music—whose great master Mozart later became—had a wide variety of forms at its disposal: the *Staendchen,* the divertissement, the cassation, brass-band music, and, above all, dinner music. (Georg Reutter's symphonies were *servizio di tavola;* they were of necessity very loud, in order to be heard above the rattle of dishes.) The trimmings, the instruments, the occasions, might change, but in all cases it was occasional music, no matter how ennobled it might be. When, for example, Mozart wrote a serenade for four bands which were to be placed at four spots in a park and would play to and through one another, there was an architectonic idea behind this curious feat; he conceived of crowds which would be constantly moving around among these four orchestras. When he entitled one of the loveliest pieces of music he ever wrote *Eine kleine Nachtmusik,* it was done out of a precise knowledge of the way in which darkness influenced the music. When heavy masses of leaves and low-hanging stars form the background for a nocturne, it does not sound the same as it does by day.

It was rarely however, that a nocturne was performed by a large orchestra—because the performance was too expensive. To praise a lady three instruments were, after all, quite sufficient—two strings and a wind instrument formed a pleasantly intimate trio. A fourth and a fifth instrument could be added, but they were not essential. One feature was, however, quite definite: the serenade had to be "portable," which meant that the heavy bass viol had to stay at home. This fact had a definite effect upon the art of composing. The music became lighter and less academic. The problem of thoroughbass was eliminated. The older aestheticians had contended that no music could exist which did not rest upon a fundamental bass—that it would collapse or slide around like a house built on soft sand. But the new sort of music proved to be quite sturdy, although gracious. It seemed to float; it was not, like seventeenth-century music, bound by the attraction of gravity.

We cannot doubt that Haydn himself wrote many such nocturnes on order, for people's name-days, for lovers, or even for the simple pleasure it gave him to make music under a starry sky. These pieces were never printed, and so they have been lost. But examples from the work of other composers give us an approximate idea of what they were like. The expression "divertissement" (in Itálian, *divertimento*) meant "diversion." As Rousseau explained it in his *Complete Dictionary of Music,* it was a musical fragment in an opera: "An importunate diversion, which the author had inserted to divide the action of some interesting moment, and which the actors and spectators, the former seated, the latter standing, have the patience to see and listen to." It was, then, a highly inartistic "insertion" which stood in no relationship whatsoever to the dramatic subject of the action.

In the case of street music, however, it was quite a different matter. For there the *whole* was a *divertimento;* it was a diversion, indeed. As soon as this importunate music was heard in the street, even if it were at three o'clock in the morning, men and women rushed to their windows and out on their balconies. No one was angry, and everyone listened attentively. Nor was Mozart angry when, some thirty years later, he unexpectedly was serenaded at his name day with his own music by six poor devils of street musicians in the middle of the night.

The first and the last movements of such a serenade were marches, which were to represent the approach and the departure of the musicians. In between were dance forms (usually minuets), and the center, the solid kernel of the piece, was the actual serenade, the wooing. This concentric form corresponded to the spirit of rococo. "It may be compared to the radial layout of a French park," remarks the musicologist Mersmann, "or to the five-winged structure of a castle, around the core of which the more airy courtiers' houses are placed, like the minuets around the serenade, and toward which broad avenues lined with marble statuary lead, like the introductory movement and the finale."

One noteworthy night Haydn was plying the bow in front of a house near the Kaerntner Gate, where a theater was located. This happened during the second year of his "bohemian" life, in the fall of 1751, after a long period of too little food and too little sleep. The house was owned by a man named Anton Dirks, a maker of beaded embroidery. But the serenade was not addressed to the owner's wife; it was for Frau Franziska Kurz, the wife of a famous man, theater director, clown, and idol of the Viennese, known as "*Bernardon.*"

"Who thought up the lovely serenade? Whom ought we to thank?" the couple called from the balcony. And when Haydn stepped forward they said, "Come right up, my dear fellow."

THE KING OF THE CLOWNS

Haydn saw before him a man with a high brow and of impressive bearing, in whose face intelligent eyes sparkled cheerfully. From the corners of those eyes the wrinkles of laughter ran to his temples. "Want to compose an opera for me?" Director Kurz asked, in his thickest Viennese dialect. "I just finished knocking the book together."

Haydn was bewildered. What sort of opera was it, he inquired politely. As a matter of fact, he had never heard an opera, and had made only rare visits to the theater to see plays.

"Oh, a regular *Bernardoniade,*" Kurz said. That was his name for pieces in which he himself played the principal role, that of the popular favorite "Bernardon" whose character was that of a saucy servant. "Sit down at the piano there and let's hear a storm at sea. That can't be much of a job, I shouldn't think. "Bernardon" has fallen into the water and tries to save himself by swimming."

Haydn was still more bewildered. How was he to express in music something he had never seen? On his way to England some forty years later, on New Year's Day, 1791, he saw for the first time the sea —the "monstrous beast" with its "vast and turbulent waves." He remembered then the shock he had felt when Theater Director Kurz asked him to compose a storm at sea.

Kurz meanwhile was becoming impatient. He had a servant bring up two chairs, stretched himself full length over them, and began making the movements of swimming. "There, don't you see how I swim?" At last Haydn caught the rhythm: An irregular forward thrust, represented by a dotted note followed by several eighth notes. The movements of the arms were different from those of the legs. The music expressed farce, jest, humorous despair, as if "Bernardon" had really fallen into the water.

"Fine, fine!" the director exclaimed, wiping the perspiration from his brow. "You'll write my *opera buffa.* Here, take the book home with you." He promised Haydn twenty-five ducats, admonished him to work fast, and hurried him out of the house.

So the man wanted to have an *opera buffa?* His was the sheerest kind of effrontery. Haydn at nineteen scarcely knew what such an opera was—and Kurz-Bernardon in his Kaerntner Gate Theater had scarcely one actor who could sing an aria decently. The music would, therefore, have to consist chiefly of instrumental accompaniment to a number of more or less farcical situations. Before he reached the bottom of the stairs, Haydn opened the libretto, and at first could make nothing of it. But then he went home and sat down at the piano to compose.

Who was the man who had hired him? After his fashion, Director Kurz was a genius. We can take our choice as to what we wish to consider the most astonishing feature of the man—his profound culture, his intimate knowledge of Molière, Shakespeare, Goldoni and the best of the modern French, English, and Italian dramatists, or the cynicism with which he betrayed them all. For no one had so low an opinion of the public as Kurz. His concept of the theater was not pure showmanship alone; rather, he wanted deliberately to make mock of great art and all it stood for. Anything that was not pure spectacle became the object of his parodies.

Born in Vienna in 1718, Kurz was—as was his predecessor Prehauser—playwright, director and actor, in one. He set a tone for the popular plays of Vienna which lasted for more than a hundred years. His countless plays were either fairy pantomimes or animal plays. The fairy play was based on the age-old longing of men to exercise faculties that nature had not bestowed upon them: To conjure up power, money and success, to ruin enemies; to fix the limbs of animals on men by enchantment; to put beasts into a sack, drown them, burn them. This sort of primitive drama existed in classic antiquity, and such wish-dreams of spellbinding naturally occurred also in the works of Shakespeare and of modern dramatists. But in these it is in a sublimated form. When Prospero weaves spells in *The Tempest,* he does so as a representative of a moral order. In the Viennese popular drama such things remained crude raw material, and afforded pleasure in enchantment for its own sake.

The second class of plays, which was often combined with the first, were the animal pieces. Here the parts were played either by animals in fact or by actors wearing animal masks. There was an incredible number of such plays. Shakespeare's *A Midsummer Night's Dream,* which had been known in Vienna for more than a hundred years, wielded an incalculable influence on these plays; but all the philosophy and nobility as well as the iambics of Shakespeare were dropped. The scenes with the ass's head were imitated, but they became, in the hands of the Viennese playwrights, pure meaningless farce. Apparently, the public simply wanted to see animals and to hear their roaring and cackling. In one piece by Josef Kurz, birds were suddenly released from a pie and flew out among the audience. In another, *Harlequin's Birth,* a huge egg lay on the stage. It opened, and Kurz's own children emerged, riding on cocks. Kurz's greatest disciple, Schikaneder, the librettist of *The Magic Flute,* later forced Mozart to introduce into his opera the scene in which Prince Tamino enchants the beasts. This scene is, to be sure, intended to be taken in a philosophical sense—music conquers the passions—but the masks produce so comical an effect that the scene almost always evokes great hilarity. Even in our time Gustav Mahler, the great conductor, regularly had to stop, at this point, the performance in the Viennese State Opera for a couple of moments. His shoulders shook with laughter, when he saw, from the dirigent's pulpit, the well-known actors transformed in beasts . . .

The Empress Maria Theresa, too, loved laughter; and so, at first, she seemed inclined to favor Kurz's-Bernardon's productions and the popular "raw" comedy. But after a while she cooled toward them. Another element entered. The artistic policy of the Viennese court favored the great Italians and Gluck, in the field of opera. The court was also trying to establish serious drama of the German type. Both efforts met with the determined resistance of the masses of the Viennese public, who clung to their popular theater. Considerable friction developed between the "popular party" and the "aristocratic tastes." In the center of this conflict stood always Josef Kurz, whose improvisations attracted the public far more than did operas with mythological subjects or the type of moralizing drama represented in the eighteenth century by Lessing.

In all of the popular farcical plays there was an undercurrent of anti-philosophy. The things the court, the middle class and the savants were interested in could not be found in the popular drama. Those things were, in fact, rejected outright. Instead of politics, noble deeds, wisdom, art, and religion, the popular art portrayed only the instinct for sex and, perhaps, gluttony. For example, a man of peasant build would appear on the stage in a green hat and would indulge in the following verses:

The beasts all seek and hope to find
A female of their proper kind.
The bull the gentle cow doth sue
And sings Moo Moo! Moo Moo!
The lion roars, the poodle yaps,
The sparrow peeps, the turtle snaps,
The frog pursues his lady fair
And cries Quare Quare! Quare Quare!

That noble animal, the buck
Leaps over stiles and runs through muck
To catch the doe and make a pair
And cries Meah Meah! Meah Meah!
The bear growls after his own sweet,
The rat desires his helpmeet,
Before his queen the tomcat bows
And everywhere Meows! Meows!

The hog wants *her* to share his slough
And runs after his wife, the sow.
He touches snouts and is not coy
And says: Oi Oi! Oi Oi!
Even the ass pricks up his ears,
Stands in his stable dropping tears;
When his beloved is not there
He weeps Eeyare Eeyare!

Therefore when my sweeheart's away
Why wonder that I am not gay
And that I too cry out for woe
And pant: Oh Oh! Oh Oh!
My sweet, my helpmeet, dearest love
Cannot you hear your mate, your dove?
Answer me with your sweetest coo:
"Harlequin: Goo Goo! Goo Goo!"

There was in this the "kindly miasma of the beasts"—to use a phrase of Thomas Mann. And that pleased the public. Haydn, too, liked it. It lured him, reminded him mysteriously of his youth in the country, of the warm fragrance of the stables, of the animal basis upon which, in the final analysis, man's existence is founded. Alongside his workshop his father had a barnyard. Even according to the most recent census of the Burgenland there were one and a half cattle for every human being.

Haydn probably did not notice at all the polemical element in Josef Kurz's verses, the blasphemy against all "higher interests" (or, to speak in terms of Mozart's *Magic Flute,* the victory of Papageno's world over that of Prince Tamino). Haydn, without giving the matter much thought, simply felt at home in this realm of beasts.

THE CROOKED DEVIL

The libretto that Kurz had given him was that of a transformation and enchantment farce, rather than of an animal play. Its name was *The Crooked Devil,* and it was a version, after a fashion, of the French novel by Le Sage, *Le diable boiteux.* In addition to motifs from the novel, there was a large number of the familiar, comic situations. There was a doctor of medicine, Arnoldus, a miserly old man who wanted to marry his young ward (as in Rossini's *Barber* and Donizetti's *Don Pasquale*). The ward, Fiametta, refuses his suit. She would rather accept "the devil's help" than marry the old man. "The devil will do it!" exclaims the devil Asmodi, who appears in the background.

In the next scene Arnoldus, the infatuated old man, is advised by his own kinsfolk against marrying so young a woman. But he does not take their advice, and publicly embraces her. Now the devil himself steps in. In a succession of ludicrous scenes, he cures the old man of his desire to take a young wife. He shows him how bad all women are. By magic, the devil transports him to another Italian city. There, as they are walking in the street, they see "Bernardon," the servant, who complains, "My wife has disappeared." A friend, the servant Leopold, shows him a house where he will find her. They knock at the door. Fiametta appears first as a Bolognese doctor, then as Punchinello, then as Pantaloon and Harlequin. In each of her disguises she sings an aria in another Italian dialect. Finally Leopold tears the mask from her face and "Bernardon" recognizes his own wife. He wants to stab her, but she runs away. The betrayed husband bewails his fate, and warns all against the faithlessness of womankind. "Well," the devil asks Arnoldus, "what do you think of 'Bernardon's' fate?" The doctor, perspiring with sympathy, assures the devil that he is already cured of his infatuation. He will never marry, he declares—neither Fiametta nor any other shameless woman. This is the cue for all of his relatives to appear and rejoice, since their inheritance will now be much larger. Arnoldus proves his nobility by bestowing publicly twelve thousand gulden on "Bernardon" in compensation for his having to put up with so wicked a wife. "Bernardon," deeply moved, thanks the doctor. Now he will be able to live happily. Fiametta, too, forgets her part, and gratefully kisses the old man's hands; all they lacked was money. Arnoldus becomes suspicious. What is going on? Has he been tricked? The devil replies, "Possibly!" But is it not true that only like and like belong together? The chorus sings its assent to this sentiment, and everyone marches off rejoicing.

Finis comediae! All very well—but why did Haydn have to compose a storm at sea and imitate in music "Bernardon's" motions while swimming? Apparently no one fell into the water. We seem to have forgotten something! This two-act *opera buffa* also contains an intermezzo which takes place in a kind of America. "Bernardon," the servant, suffered shipwreck on a remote island, swam to shore and met islanders, some of whom wanted to eat him and others to make him their god. (We know from Indian folklore that these two fates were not mutually exclusive.) "Bernardon" and his companions would have got on very well together if a woman's coquetry had not again placed them in grave danger. This time the islanders decided to eat all of them. At this critical juncture, while the savages are heating the pot, there is a blast of trumpets and a Dutch war fleet appears. There is a battle, the Indians flee, and the shipwrecked men are rescued. Amid shouts of joy and a concluding march, all sail off in the ships.

This intermezzo, a pantomime with musical underscoring, was apparently intended also to illustrate the faithlessness of woman. What other link it had to the main part of the opera we can no longer fully understand. Perhaps the public had to recover from the first act before it witnessed the second. Perhaps it was charmed by the appearance of children in this pantomime—and Josef Kurz's own children, no less. (He had a good many of them; he himself was very happily married.)

How did Haydn react to this potpourri? Shall we assume that he tossed the libretto aside as soon as he had read it? Quite the contrary. For the first act he wrote a duet and eleven arias, and closed with a rousing finale. For the pantomime he wrote the storm music and a military march. We no longer know exactly what he did for the second act, for the nineteen-year-old's first music for the theater has been lost, although it has long been sought. Perhaps it lay for two hundred years in some garret in Vienna. When the Russians took

Vienna by storm in 1945 a good many old houses were burned to the ground, and it seems hardly likely that the music will ever be found. It is unfortunate, for the history of music has probably lost some very amusing material. For Haydn had no idea—could not possibly have had any idea—how to write an aria!

After completing his work in all haste, he took the music to Kurz in order to get his twenty-five ducats. At first the maid did not want to let him in. The director "was working." We can imagine Haydn's astonishment when he looked through the glass door and saw "Bernardon" sitting before a mirror grimacing and gesticulating. "That was the way 'Bernardon' practiced," his biographer, Griesinger, recounts. In the mirror Kurz caught sight of the dumbstruck Haydn waiting outside. He hastily went over the score, was delighted with it and paid him twenty-four ducats. (What happened to the extra ducat we do not know.) Then he feverishly began studying the parts, together with his wife, who was to play Fiametta. He himself was playing "Bernardon"; Asmodi, the devil, was to be played by his brother-in-law. Frau Franziska Kurz must have been an accomplished singer. Unlike Haydn, she spoke Italian fluently, which enabled her to reproduce the tangled roles of the second act—to the joy of the public, which laughed uproariously, though it did not understand a word.

Shortly after Easter, 1751, the announcements appeared: *"The Crooked Devil.* An *opera comique* in two acts, together with a child pantomime as intermezzo: Harlequin in America. All written by *Josef Kurz.* The music both of the *opera comique* and of the pantomime has been composed by *Herr Joseph Haydn."*

The opera was a tremendous hit. All the actors were called out for repeated bows; the children were showered with candy. Haydn, too, reveled in good fortune. A future career as conductor and composer for Kurz's theater seemed assured to him. But then, after the second performance, the police intervened and banned the play "on account of grave slander of living persons." Kurz was fined and even threatened with imprisonment if he did not mend his ways.

What had happened? For a long time the world could only conjecture. About 1800, however, Goethe's friend Bertuch wrote down the curious story and stated his conviction that the offended person had been an Italian. Presumably the Italian must have been a member of the art faction at court, which then held sway. One member of that faction was Count Durazzo who in 1752 took over the direction of the court opera and theater.

The Crooked Devil had been banned only the year before. We do not know whether it was Durazzo who was insulted in the *ad lib* parts of the farce and in Fiametta's dialectal gibberish. The satire might equally have been directed against some other Italian who was connected with the Imperial Opera. Kurz-Bernardon and his company were constantly at war with the "foreign opera," and on this point the Empress Maria Theresa was very sensitive. Maintaining the opera cost her a good deal of money, and, moreover, her ambitions and her artistic convictions were on the side of the Italian artists.

THE DOMINANCE OF ITALIAN OPERA

From all sides young Haydn heard the *opera seria* being laughed at and reviled. What, exactly, was this "serious opera"?

The classic Italian opera was originated by one of the greatest musical geniuses of the ages, Claudio Monteverdi, of Cremona. Monteverdi (1567-1643) had mustered together all the musical developments of his age—all the vocal, instrumental, ecclesiastical and secular forms—and had powerfully forged them into the *opera seria.* His successors and disciples, the Cavallis, Carissimis and Cestis, made of the structure a stronghold whose walls soon circumscribed the entire musical world. Italian opera attained a supremacy which was to last for centuries. Everywhere, in Paris, Vienna, Dresden, Amsterdam, Saint Petersburg, and Stockholm, Italian composers and conductors ruled. Not since the days of the *Imperium Romanum* had such unity of taste, such artistic homogeneity, been aimed at or enforced. Characteristically, England alone revolted, and successfully. Whether justly or unjustly, Protestant England scented popishness in the Italian opera, and soon rebutted it with a national opera of its own, whose great originator was Henry Purcell (1657-1695).

One is led to wonder how so dubious an art form as the opera could achieve world dominion. Even at its outset the opera had hosts of enemies. Some held that the text was too much the slave of the music, the requirements of the music forcing the drama into illogical channels, stretching it out and saddling the actors with senseless repetitions. Musical expression, they urged, was much more complicated and leisurely than thought; notes were slower than words, and for that reason they could not be harnessed together. This, it was argued, was the "hereditary taint of opera." Others came to precisely the opposite conclusion: That the music was intolerably burdened by intellectual conflicts, by didactic historical matter, symbolic actions and mythological events which did not at all require music. In the three hundred and fifty years during which the opera has persisted, every new operatic reform—introduced by Metastasio, Gluck, Calzabigi, Mozart, Weber, Wagner, or Verdi—tilted the balance one way or the other, toward purer music or purer drama; but no permanent peace with the "species as such" has ever been established. Perhaps the opera is not an art form at all. But it is a rare stroke of good fortune, like genius itself.

"Gluck" wrote Josef von Sonnenfels, the official aesthetician of Maria Theresa's epoch, "is the Sophocles of music. For that reason the limits of all national music are too narrow for him. Out of Italian, French, and German music, out of the music of all nations, he has created a music that is his own . . . If musical tones could be made visible, Gluck's phrases would possess the most beautifully fashioned forms."

These words were not written before 1768. But as early as 1750 anyone who was opposed to Gluck's initial experiments was opposed to the development of the art itself. And that was precisely the position taken by Viennese popular taste. The "popular party" would have none of the *opera seria,* the aristocrats' opera. The thousands of theatergoers who were devotees of Josef Kurz and young Haydn, too, laughed at the serious opera. But what was the root of this mockery?

The Italians' *opera seria* used no bass voices (though the *opera buffa* did), for bass singing was considered ugly. It is a little hard for us to imagine, but the paternal element that we associate with the bass voice—the noisy rounds of jovial groups of men, and the note of wisdom and dignity that is expressed by the low, bass voice of a Sarastro —all these were taboo in this "serious opera." Everything was transposed to the most ethereal heights. The *opera seria* was a world of tenors, altos, and sopranos. This in itself was not important. But Italian opera—and Viennese opera, as well—was sung chiefly by eunuchs.

We may well wonder at this. If the Italian concept of beauty ruled out deep voices in the interest of a "cloudless tone," why were not the roles entrusted to female singers only? Why, in particular, were the roles of lovers and heroes always assigned to eunuchs? The reason was that all contemporary music lovers unanimously agreed that women could not sing so beautifully. "The voice of the eunuch," Max Arend writes, "is distinct from that of women; it is sharper; its breath range is greater because of the greater chest expansion; it has a masculine timbre. The eunuch is an artistically stylized man. That is something that no longer exists today—that can no longer exist—

and yet it cannot be condemned artistically. In those days the institution of the *castrati* offered a unique aesthetic opportunity which was highly valued by the masters of music, including Gluck." And so, for reasons of art, the role of Gluck's "Orpheus," that "heroic exponent of connubial love," was sung by a eunuch.

And it was this feature that became the butt of Viennese mockery. The Viennese masses did not go to the opera at all, but the ushers or the cloakroom attendants who came from their own stratum of society told them about it: There, on the stage, men sang who were not men at all! All of the Viennese—and not only the lower classes—gossiped about the fact that there existed in Italy "artificial voice factories." That this is so is indicated by the story that is told about Haydn. Several of his biographers and friends—Pleyel, Framery, Le Breton among them—say that at the time the young man's voice broke and he feared he might lose his place in the choir of St. Stephen's, Reutter suggested to Haydn that a means existed "not only to restore his voice, but to increase its range, flexibility, and mellifluousness." Reutter would have simply needed to point to the court chorus, where a dozen eunuchs were employed.

Various versions of the tale are given: That Father Matthias Haydn was informed by Reutter in good time and his consent asked for, or that he heard about the matter as already a *fait accompli*. In any case, he hurried from Rohrau to Vienna, by chance found his son lying in bed, and blurted out: "Sepperl, does anything hurt you? Can't you walk any more?" He was overjoyed—according to the sources—to have come in time to save his son from the knife, and warned him that he would not hear of anything of the kind—"in which decision a eunuch who happened to be present expressed full agreement."

The whole story is, of course, sheer invention. The operation in question was illegal in Austria and was subject to severe penalties (as it was in France and England). To take up the career of a eunuch a man had to be a native Italian.

Young Haydn undoubtedly classed himself among the "true Viennese" who objected to the "foreign vanities" of Italian opera. He surely would have refused to believe it had someone prophesied that within less than twenty years he himself would be behaving like an Italian and writing Italian operas.

After the banning of *The Crooked Devil,* Josef Kurz probably apologized to the censor, who at the time, or shortly later, was Sonnenfels, one of Maria Theresa's favorites. He acted out of real sincerity and often, in his reports, inveighed against the "absurd ideas, the repulsive, filthy jokes and the immoral insinuations" of the popular theater. For some time extemporizing on the stage had been expressly forbidden. Every play had to be presented to the censor in manuscript or in printed form, and no *ad libbing* was allowable. (At one time Sonnenfels mentioned in a report "A kind of howling rendered musically which accompanied a shameful text." Let us hope he was not referring to something of Haydn's!)

Director Kurz took his revenge for these restrictions by presenting only classical plays. But how he presented them! In Lessing's *Miss Sara Sampson* he and his actors maliciously burlesqued the lines to such an extent that the most serious passages in this sentimental tear-jerker produced roars of laughter, and a tremendous scandal was the result. The same was done with *The Earl of Essex;* the public greeted with hoots and howls the political and emotional entanglements of Queen Elizabeth. At this point the authorities at last intervened, and Kurz was deprived of his license. In the year 1753, to the great discontent of the Viennese populace, he had to leave Vienna. With him went his wife, his sister Monika, his brother-in-law, and his numerous children. He was departing, it was announced, on an "extensive tour."

With the going of Kurz-Bernardon, Haydn lost his patron, and was, possibly, saved from a rather considerable danger. Haydn had a strong streak of the "parodist," "the prestidigitator with sounds"; both phrases were later applied to him. We shall see how he played around with his themes even in his most serious symphonies. No other composer used so many "mock reprises," jests of modulation, and surprise effects; his gravest efforts are tinged with humor. Had he remained a theater musician and a composer for Kurz-Bernardon, writing music to accompany fairy plays and animal pieces, he would have lacked any counterpoise to this impulse, and might well have ruined himself. As it was, all that remained with him of this youthful sin was a lasting love for the marionette theater with which he became acquainted during this period. (Kurz occasionally gave public performances of puppet plays.) Later, Haydn wrote marionette music for his Prince, Nicholas von Esterhazy; this was composed in a humorous-melancholy mood and a fine rococo style which was much admired.

ST. MICHAEL'S HOUSE

SOME houses are the embodiment of destiny. Such a fateful house was "old St. Michael's house," in which Haydn had been lodging for some time.

It was situated near St. Michael's Church, above the cabbage-market, and was a fine tenement house of several stories, in the top floor of which the young man occupied a sloping-roofed, wretched attic. From the adjacent gutter the rain poured in; in the winter, snow entered through the cracks in the roof and, as our sources recount, "Haydn awoke soaked and covered with snow." Only his marvelous constitution preserved him from illness. But he looked upon this creaking dwelling as a paradise because there was a piano in it—an old, worm-eaten box which some tenant had banished to the attic. Here Haydn studied music. His neighbors were, at various times, a printer's apprentice, a tender of fires, a music copyist, a lackey, and a cook—common people like himself who were far beneath "society" but who were accustomed to serve their betters.

How had Haydn come to this house? Remarkably enough, at this time he not only had this "flat," but some ready money as well. Something strange had happened. In our merciless world he had found a man who had lent him 150 gulden, without interest and for an indefinite time. This man was the market magistrate, Anton Buchholtz, who lived in the house of "The Golden Crab." This man, whose business it was to adjudicate crass disputes of everyday life—the price of apples or the weight of geese—had taken a liking to the tall, clumsy youth with his grave face in which Buchholtz somehow sensed immortality.

By taking only one meal a day, a thrifty person could live a fairly long time on 150 gulden. (Haydn paid the money back, and half a century later he remembered Buchholtz's granddaughter in his will.) But eating was not what mattered; musical texts were far more important—not the latest and most expensive works, of course, but second-hand music, old music, was what he bought. If he wanted to be a composer—and that was his sole desire!—he must know what the state of music was. He had to be acquainted with the course that the ship had pursued the day before; he had "to be able to read its log." This he could learn from musical texts, although it would have been better for him had he been able to hear of its history from living human beings who knew more than he did.

At that point the house intervened and, in its role of destiny, arranged it so that one day Haydn encountered another man on the stairs. The man, who was coming downstairs as Joseph was going up, stood still for a moment. And this man was the court poet, Pietro Metastasio.

Haydn had occasionally looked pensively out of his dormer window and had seen not only the square below, crowded with carriages, but the Burgtheater across the way, where the great Gluck had first won acclaim. Three years before, on May 14, 1749, Gluck's operatic fortune had begun. On that day, the name day of the empress, he had produced his *Semiramis* in which he and the author of his libretto, Metastasio, had paid homage to Maria Theresa. Haydn had, of course, often heard the poet's name, but he had not known that this celebrity and he lived in the same house.

Classical drama observed the rule of the three unities—of place, of action, of time. In St. Michael's house this rule once more prevailed. We must picture the house in cross-section. In the attic lived Haydn; in the middle the great Metastasio; and the ground floor was actually occupied by Princess Esterhazy, the mother of Haydn's future master.

And now these two men stood confronting each other, and the great man, in his embroidered jacket, buckle shoes and fawn-colored waistcoat, condescendingly asked the shabby young man who he was and where he was going. Haydn replied that he was a *musikus* and that he lived here in the house. In this wise they fell into conversation. Metastasio could scarcely have concealed his disgust with that wretched fellow, "Bernardon," that "aberration of Viennese taste" and "despiser of all sacredness and beauty." Probably he also expressed astonishment that anyone should sell his talent to this clown and plebeian. There must be other ways for a young musician to earn his living!

Haydn listened respectfully. For this man was a messenger from that other world in which people did not say "west wind" but "Zephyr," not "north wind" but "Boreas," and referred not to "wisdom," but to "Minerva." The name Metastasio itself was probably a pseudonym and meant "master of transformation." And indeed, everything was transformed when such an Italian poet—who was called "the greatest of his age"—stretched out the magic wand of his word. Even the city of Vienna was transformed. Where Pietro Metastasio went, Vienna became an Italian city. The etiquette he prescribed was followed by the court and the empress. When he condescended to speak German, as he now did to Haydn, it was merely a whim.

Haydn could not possibly have had any conception of the real significance of Pietro Metastasio. He did not know that the librettos which Metastasio was writing for all the prominent musicians of the age were holding all Europe spellbound by their choice of subjects alone. For Metastasio introduced upon the stage all of classical history, its symbolism, its tyrants, kings, loving women, and sacrificial deeds. In so doing, he dictated to the composers, the singers, and the orchestra. Thus, the high society of the age thrilled with self-esteem when it saw itself portrayed on the operatic stage in gaudy colors, heard its chivalry celebrated with fine phrases concerning flashing swords and sweet revenge. However, a certain amount of misinterpretation existed in these classical parables. Some minor potentate might take himself for the Emperor Titus; or, Gluck and Metastasio could celebrate Maria Theresa as Semiramis when the empress had nothing in common with a Semiramis; she was far more sociable, humorous, and humane than the ancient oriental tyrant queen.

Since Haydn was not aware of Metastasio's true significance, he was also ignorant of the poet's faults. In reality, the classicism of which Metastasio was an exponent was of a low order. He lived in a gallant age, and he considered himself obliged to smuggle gallantry into all the classic themes with which he dealt. The role of love was ridiculously exaggerated in his operas. Caesar, and Alexander, with the fate of the world in their hands, lose their heart to a woman. Virtue, wisdom, bravery—all the qualities that a scene before were praised to the skies—were suddenly tossed upon the ground, to be trodden by some female's dainty shoe. Haydn, the son of a country artisan, knew perfectly well that things were different in the real world.

But now this was not at issue. Almost at the moment of his meeting with Metastasio, an event took place which opened to him far-reaching prospects. With a kind of peasant cunning he snatched at the offer, just as he had acquiesced at once when Metastasio's polar opposite, Josef Kurz, had requested him to write a harlequin opera. Metastasio asked Haydn to play for him on the piano, and he seemed satisfied with the young man's performance. He mentioned the name of Pórpora, a well-known composer who was giving singing lessons to a girl in this very house. Would Haydn be willing to accompany the old gentleman on the piano during these lessons? He might also, incidentally, teach the piano to the girl. What was his pay to be? *Free board!*

Haydn was informed that the pupil was a nine-year-old Spanish girl, Marianne de Martinez, the daughter of the master of ceremonies attached to the staff of the papal nuncio in Vienna. Metastasio, a bachelor, had long been sharing the apartment of her parents. Haydn surmised that the father was a very influential figure. Perhaps that was why Pórpora, a composer famous throughout Europe, was willing to give singing lessons to little Marianne. At any rate, Haydn snatched at the offer. For a full three years he taught Marianne to play the piano. Those years were the first carefree ones which he had ever experienced, and they made another man of him. But the chief thing about this period was his relationship with Niccolo Pórpora.

Pórpora, who, like Pergolesi, was one of the most prominent masters of the Neapolitan operatic style, was born in 1686. By his genius the secular aria was perfected. The strength and sweetness of this music must inevitably have moved Haydn profoundly, for the young man (as so often happens) had scoffed at something with which he had no acquaintance. He could not have known Italian music, because he had never had the money to buy a ticket to the opera. At Maria Theresa's court festivals, of course, there were occasional performances by opera singers; but at the time he had attended these, the country lad was far too young to appreciate such music. Now, as an adult, he heard real aria singing for the first time. This was the music of which Madame de Staël later admiringly wrote: *"Qui n'a pas entendu le chant italien ne peut avoir l'idée de la musique. Les voix, en Italie, ont cette mollesse et cette douceur qui rappelle et le parfum des fleurs et la pureté du ciel."* * But she added:

* "Whoever has not heard Italian singing can have no conception of music. In Italy voices possess a mellowness and sweetness that is reminiscent both of the perfume of flowers and the purity of heaven."

"La nature a destiné cette musique pour ce climat: l'une est comme un reflêt de l'autre." * What Madame de Staël, the Frenchwoman, understood, was self-evident to Haydn as a German—*outside* of Italy the psychological climate was unfavorable to Italian music. Had he not comprehended this, he could scarcely have become, as he later did, the master of German realism.

But it does not matter what Haydn felt in his heart of hearts about Maestro Pórpora's art. He wanted to rise; that alone was important. He must possess himself of the advantages that these Italians possessed. And so the diminutive, temperamental old man became his teacher. Probably what happened was that Haydn showed Pórpora his compositions, upon which Pórpora commented tersely and contemptuously—for the pieces were full of crude errors. Probably no regular instruction (for which the student could not, after all, pay) took place for more than half a year. Nevertheless, Haydn learned. In his old age Haydn declared: "I wrote diligently, but without firm foundation, until I had the good fortune to learn the true fundamentals of composition from the famous Signor Pórpora." We know also that Haydn was also charged with a valet's duties; he had to look after Pórpora's extensive wardrobe, to polish his shoes and to keep his snuffbox filled. The old gentleman was exacting and irritable. "There was no lack of *Asino! Birbante!* and pokes in the ribs; but I accepted it all because I was learning from Pórpora much of singing, composition and the Italian language." This latter was the most important. Haydn was learning Italian—the world-language of music—and this in itself helped to propel him upward. If he succeeded in learning by observation of Pórpora how to write operas, Italian operas in the accepted style (whether or not he liked it), he might one day enter that society in which music, and *good* music, was taken as a matter of course.

* "Nature has destined this music for the climate of the land; the one is like a reflection of the other."

THE NORTH GERMANS

WHAT was the state of music at the time? Nowhere could the field be surveyed better than in Vienna, situated midway between north and south. From there it was exactly as far to Leipsic as to Venice, no farther to Berlin than to Florence, as far to Hamburg as to Rome and Naples.

Working at night, seated at the desk or at the piano, Haydn could choose either direction. It does him credit that he decided in favor of the North German masters; for it indicates his desire to set up a counterpoise. After hearing Italian spoken or sung all day long, he turned his compass needle to the north, at night. He began studying the great works of the Bach family—not so much those of Johann Sebastian as of Carl Philipp Emanuel, the great father's great son.

With the death of Johann Sebastian Bach four years before, in 1750, a door had slammed shut, and the echo was heard for a long time. A whole epoch had come to its end, an epoch which Bach had magnificently dominated. Not that he had been loved or that his aspirations had been understood. The greatest scientific work he left to posterity, *The Art of the Fugue,* had had only thirty purchasers by 1756. Certainly, Haydn was not one of them, but probably only because a copy was too expensive. On the other hand, he already owned a number of works by North Germans, and in these he studied Bach's manner, counterpoint, and the nature of the fugue. In addition to the Austrian work, *Gradus ad Parnassum,* we find among his books the most ponderous compendiums of technical and intellectual matters written by German contemporaries like Mattheson, Marpurg, and Kellner. To balance these there was only a single Italian book, Carissimi's *Rules of Singing.* All these books from Haydn's library were preserved, after his death, by Prince Esterhazy, and it is touching to see how thoroughly used the books are—virtually read to pieces. They are covered with marginal notes in an awkward hand; these annotations reveal a student who did not learn easily. Sometimes the flyleaves served for writing out laundry lists. In one of the books by Mattheson we find the entry: Shirts 8, ties 6, handkerchiefs 9. Each of the three German words is misspelled. Poor Haydn never learned to write German correctly. On the other hand, he knew Italian well—which was at the moment more important for his future—and he also knew ecclesiastical and musical Latin. Above all, however, he had a capacity for unflagging industry. What others could not learn from expensive teachers, he learned by himself.

During his years as a choir boy Haydn had, of course, had ample practice in the *singing* of fugues. But it was from Marpurg's *Treatise on the Art of the Fugue* that he learned, more thoroughly than he had ever done before, what a fugue really *was*. Certainly it was the strangest of forms, begotten of mathematics and the ear. Several centuries before, in the age of the Renaissance, composers and aristocratic gentlemen had invented a social game, a *ludus cacciae,* a hunting game. A fox, so to speak, had been sprung and a hound set to pursue it. The one wildly fleeing, the other hotly pursuing, the pair had rushed along, teasing and deceiving each other as they ran, and the whole affair was called *fuga,* a flight. The Austrian Haydn might well have imagined, with cheerful disrespect, that this was all there was to the writing of fugues. But he was, nevertheless, impressed by the fact that men had not abandoned this game. From decade to decade they had made the rules harder—how queer men were in their activities and their amusements!

And that man Johann Sebastian Bach! What an ear he had had, what profound insight, and what an understanding of art! His countless fugues began with the subject's being sung alone by the first voice. (This initial theme was called the *dux,* the leader.) Immediately afterward a second voice replied. This was the *comes,* the companion, or answer. It ran along a few beats behind the leader. Then the leader turned around. As if it did not wish to be caught, it started another subject as a *foil,* the so-called counter-subject, in a rhythmically pregnant counterpoint. Now a third voice enters; it is conceived of as a reinforcement of the first, and the fourth voice reinforces the second. They run along together. This unique course of the subject through all the voices—Haydn learned—was called the "first development of the fugue." In the further developments the voices exchanged positions, paraded inversions and modulated to strange keys. How confusing it was! Why this questioning and answering, this game of hunter and hunted who could never catch each other because the hunter modulated to the dominant when the prey remained in the tonic, and, vice versa, when the hunter modulated back, the fleeing prey had reached the key of the dominant. There is breathless excitement when they seem to have caught up with each other after all in the *stretto,* in which they scurry along side by side and so fast that they almost seem to unite, only to part again. But what in the world was it all about? There were simple, double, and triple fugues, fugues on melodic and rhythmical transformations of the subject, fugues in double counterpoint, fugues of the octave, the decima, the duodecima; fugues that were veritable towers, story upon story built up to the clouds, and fugues that were put head downward. It was enough to make one dizzy! And the frantic speed with which these organ-born creations moved! Haydn set his teeth. "I must understand it and respect it, but I'll never write one myself," he may well have murmured to himself. For the tension in listening was no longer psychic but scientific; it verged on curiosity. One kind of fugal writing was called *ricercata*—a search. What was being searched for—the solution of a problem in arithmetic, a mathematical miracle in the realm of tone? Why? Should not music rather be like "the songs the people sing at evening?"

What was so strange about Bach, however, was the fact that the devices which led others to dryness never parched the springs of his inspiration. In this no one could imitate him. In spite of imposing rules, everything he wrote was fragrant, remained fresh and sweetly flowing. His inventive powers could conquer the most rigid of his principles.

But no one could go further than he. Where was music to begin afresh? Bach's own son and heir apparent, Carl Philipp Emanuel, supplied the answer. With an ease which even today, two centuries afterward, arouses our astonishment, he created a new music, virtually from the day of his father's death. With calm self-assurance and matter-of-factness, as if no other course could be thought of, he proclaimed the dominion of *melody.* "It seems to me that music must chiefly touch the heart," he wrote. His piano concertos strove to achieve, as he himself declared, "singability." This was a revolutionary idea. He tore down the "prison of polyphony" and wrote a three- or two-voiced phrase in which he achieved the most intimate effects and portrayed the most delicate psychological nuances. Probably the first of his works that Haydn saw was a volume of piano sonatas. The younger Bach's important book of the year 1753, the *Essay on the True Manner of Playing the Clavier,* came into his hands. In this book there are many remarkable sentences about the soul and meaning of music and the legitimacy of improvisation, without which any art must remain rigid.

Haydn supplemented the study of Carl Philipp Emanuel Bach by that of other composers, and at this period of his life the men who influenced his work were all North Germans. (To compensate for this, he, in his turn, influenced the North German Brahms, who out of his love for Haydn wrote his *Variations on a Theme by Haydn.*) Among these North German musicians were the Brothers Graun of Berlin, Telemann, of Hamburg, and, above all, Johann Joachim Quantz, author of the famous flute sonatas, and instructor of Frederick the Great. The cool, spiritualized, rather melancholy instrument—whose music was like the very embodiment of the rational, anti-passionate spirit of the "Age of Enlightenment"—strongly appealed to Haydn.

There was, indeed, so very much that Joseph Haydn could learn from the North German school. In the Italians he never found the pensive half-tints, the shadings of mood, the twilit look of landscapes. Pórpora and Metastasio, with their musical flourishes and their rhetoric about the "chariot of Phoebus," could not understand such things. The glaring sun of Italy conditioned their colors and tones. Theirs was the music of the full morning, the noonday, the deep night. But among the North German masters, water, earth and air were not so precisely divided the one from the other; delicate, diffuse colors could be seen; the mists of woods and heaths rose into the atmosphere. Such nuances were climatically more akin to Haydn, struck him as more true to life, than the Italians' fulsome art. Both the blur and the tenderness of the tones seemed to him a reminder of home. Those North German composers had never seen Rohrau—but on the nights when he played over their music or read their notes, he felt them as friendly and neighborly.

BAD MANNERSDORF

WHEN summer came, the ambassador of the Republic of Venice to the Austrian court, Pietro Correr, left Vienna to wilt in the heat of summer while he himself went to the country. He did not go alone. In another carriage, dressed in silks, with her Viennese female companion beside her and with coachman and footman in front, sat his mistress. Behind this carriage came the baggage-cart, heaped with trunks and hat-boxes. The intellectual appurtenances rode behind the baggage: Wilhelmine's singing teacher, the seventy-year-old Pórpora, the "Patriarch of melody," the famous composer of the *Hesperian Gardens* and of *Dido Abandoned by Aeneas.* Beside Pórpora sat his factotum, Joseph Haydn. But this time Haydn was not Pórpora's servant; he was co-tutor to Wilhelmine. His salary was six ducats a month, and he had the right to eat at His Excellency's table. All this represented a great advancement.

They were bound for Bad Mannersdorf. Soon they saw in the twilight the tree-shaded gardens set amid vineyards, promenades, and bath-houses. The spa servants ran up to the carriages and opened the doors.

Mannersdorf had become a popular spa since the Empress Maria Theresa had chosen the place for the site of a summer castle. Along the park paths Archduke Josef and his older sisters rolled hoops. They knocked shuttlecocks about under the summer sky, and often butterflies would blunder into the game and pay dearly for their folly.

The spa was visited by many noble families. During the day it was often very hot; at this far eastern extreme of Austria a searing Hungarian sun could be felt. On such occasions people lolled in hammocks and did nothing but wait for the courier who arrived once a day, in yellow waistcoat and white sleeves; he blew his horn, snapped his whip, and brought news from the capital.

Evenings the guests visited one another in the villas, which were half hidden among the hills. Music rang out under the moon, the fragrance of the honeysuckle pervaded the air, a violin sonata, accompanied by piano and flute, filled the gardens; and, whenever the music stopped for a moment, full orchestras of nightingales could be heard singing in the woods. Later, the noble ladies and gentlemen went out into the gardens, drank wine, ate iced confections, and sat at tables illuminated by flickering, globed candles. Etiquette relaxed—and the amazed Haydn might find himself sitting at the same table with the Prince of Hildburghausen, a great patron of music. Conversation in society was in Italian, a language of which Haydn already had an excellent command. But we may well imagine that he spoke little in the company of so many lords and ladies. It was only when the conversation turned to his art that he talked without shyness.

During his sojourn at Mannersdorf, Haydn made the acquaintance of the violinist and composer Dittersdorf, and, above all, of Gluck, who came from Vienna in a coach of state, to remain a few days. The great composer, it is said, told Haydn at the time that he ought to go to Italy to finish his education. Haydn listened to him with amazement. This was due not to Gluck's advice, but to his person. This famous man, whose musical accomplishments were the talk of the world, who was as much at home in Paris and Venice as he was in Vienna, was the son of a Bavarian innkeeper. And yet he associated with counts and princes as if he were their peer. Would Haydn ever attain to this? He perceived, in any case, that music could obliterate class differences to an astonishing extent. During the performance of a trio in which a prince played the first violin, a burgher the viola and an artisan's son the piano, a kind of comradeship was engendered—although it might not necessarily last beyond the performance. For the first time, Haydn observed that musical ability was a coin of the realm with which recognition by high society could be purchased. When he accompanied on the piano the famous singer, Signora Tramontani-Tesi and when later Baron von Fuernberg discussed technical questions with the two of them, he was something other than the son of Master Wheelwright Haydn.

Nevertheless, he was the wheelwright's son. When he sat by the Leitha River on such a summer day, he might well have thought, as Schubert later did in his *Schoene Muellerin:* "Whither?" For the river, in its downward course, led, by a few hours' journey, to Bruck, and from there it was not far to Rohrau. And so, one day, Haydn paid a visit home. He was accompanied by his "little brother," Michael, who was now seventeen and had almost outgrown his position as choir boy. Michael was also a composer; he was an excellent organist and a first-rate Latin student who gave promise of getting on well in life.

The two brothers went on foot for a whole day. Everything they passed had a homelike aspect. The cows by the stream turned toward them and looked at them out of large, shining eyes whose peacefulness was peculiar to cows of this district. "Did you wonder," the younger brother asked, "what happened to the ducats I earned for singing at the last festival? I sent them home; father had lost a cow at the time." Joseph flushed. What a good son Michael was—certainly much better than he himself, who was interested only in his music! His own life, of course, was harder; he had no choir-house where his needs were looked after. Tutoring was an uncertain livelihood; the pupils changed too frequently. At the moment he was worrying whether his two pupils in music theory, Abundus Mykisch and Kimmerling, both incipient clerics, would remain loyal to him while he was off enjoying a summer vacation. Hard upon this thought, he burst into laughter. What an impertinence it was for him to teach theory at all, the very subject that he himself had to cudgel his brains to understand! But perhaps the old Latin saw was right: *Docendo discimus,* "By teaching we ourselves learn."

The straw-roofed parental home seemed to have shrunk. This was only natural; the two boys had grown larger. But the same sunset was reflected in the same puddle in the yard; the well remembered swallows shot up out of the eaves, and a stork flapped its wings on the church tower. The wheelwright, kindly, grave, unchanged, confronted them. In honor of the two musicians, the father took out his harp and began, as he had done in former days, to sing a peasant song and to pluck the strings in a frail, little minuet. As he played he kept a sharp eye on his two sons, to see that they showed the proper respect. At last, Michael, the younger, ventured an objection; his father had played a false note, he said. The father repeated the note. Joseph attempted to mediate; it was probably the fault of the instrument that the note was off. "My harp is a fine instrument!" Father Matthias exclaimed angrily, thrusting it aside. "If you don't like my playing, you're a pair of asses." Meanwhile, a flaxen-haired little brother named Johann Evangelist had come into the house. Joseph and Michael had never seen him before. The little one promptly declared that he, too, wanted to be a musician. At this point, Mother Haydn approached with black bread, eggs, ham and country wine, and this put an end to the quarreling. She looked old and worn out, although she was only forty-five. She wore her black Sunday dress in honor of her sons, but her face was more drawn than usual. The sons did not notice this.

The following February, word reached Vienna that she was dead. A year later Father Haydn married again. No one could blame him for this. The house was full of children. The workshop needed a mistress, the farm a worker. Life on the land is hard, and leaves little time for sentimentalities.

We do not know what tears Joseph Haydn may have shed over his mother. He must have known, however, that it had been a sorrow to her to see her son still without his place in life. Undoubtedly, her mother's eye had seen that his clothes were better than they had been, and that he now associated with fine gentlemen. But was that any assurance of a happy future? She recognized his genius and was secretly proud of it—but was not life more secure for the man who had a farm or a wheelwright's shop, or—if he must live in the city—a grocery store?

A place in life! Managed properly, music could feed its practitioner, too. Many noble Austriar houses possessed their own orchestras, with paid directors. The musicians consisted partly of servants, partly of Viennese artisans who played voluntarily in the orchestra, and partly of the nobles themselves. The kapellmeister who knit the orchestra together could live on his salary—and it was soon to be Haydn's turn to procure such a position. His reputation was already spreading; a Countess Thun, in Vienna, praised his first attempts at writing clavier sonatas, and a music publisher had already begun pirating these early compositions. But even more important for him became the patronage of a Baron von Fuernberg whom he had met in Mannersdorf.

The baron invited the young composer to his estate of Weinzierl, with a small castle in the vicinity of Melk, west of Vienna. Here the mists of the Danube mingle all year long with the fragrance of the wine-grapes that are planted everywhere in the neighborhood. Here Haydn spent several summers, and the four wings of the castle resounded with music all day long, to the very tops of the turrets and gables.

The music was performed by four persons, the village pastor, the master's bailiff, Albrechtsberger, the cellist, and young Haydn. Naturally, they played quartets. We may demur at asserting that it was this chance circumstance that produced a whole new category of music. Yet so it was. Had there been three or five players they would have played trios or quintets. As it was, they devoted themselves to quartets.

Ambition, calling, a craftsman's pleasure in his trade—all these elements combined in Haydn's creative life. One day he surprised Baron von Fuernberg with a four-voiced composition for strings that he himself had written. It was his first quartet, B-major in six-quarter time.

Brimming over with *joie de vivre* and bubbling with cheerfulness, it races along quite simply: After the first subject the second follows without further modulation in the key of the dominant. A final bar, and the first part is finished. In the second part there is a middle movement group using motifs from the first part which are treated cautiously and briefly. The third movement is a minuet, the fourth an *adagio cantabile* in which the first violin takes the lead. (Music must sing, Haydn had learned from Carl Philipp Emanuel Bach.) The fifth movement is another minuet.

Baron von Fuernberg was delighted. What most amazed him was the exactitude with which Haydn, in his composition, made allowances for the idiosyncrasies of each player. Ordinarily, such considerations were applied only to compositions for the voice; writing instrumental music with such precision was something new. To Haydn, however, it seemed quite natural. He early realized that the playing of quartets was a highly personal affair, and that, as he put it, he must "write to suit the peculiarities of particular men." His ear had a knowledge of his subject, just as his father, the artisan, had all his life had the technique of the wheelwright in his fingers. Music, too, was an object for personal use.

Was Haydn proud of his artistic creation? A witness of that memorable evening in the castle of Weinzierl informs us that the young composer was extremely confused. The witness was a Prussian prisoner of war, a Major Weirach, who happened to be present. (In those humanitarian days prisoners who were held in the vicinity could be invited to a concert sponsored by an Austrian nobleman!) Weirach later recounted, "The young man was modest to the point of timidity, and although everyone present was delighted by his composition, could not be convinced that his work deserved to be at all known in the world of music." This exaggerated modesty, however, passed away within a few days. As the earth after a thunderstorm, he began steaming with fertility, and produced quartet after quartet. Soon there were six, then twelve, then eighteen—the famous first eighteen quartets which, when printed, were everywhere received with plaudits. Or, rather, not quite everywhere. Haydn had his first experience with those carping critics who were not to be silenced until his death; they declared that he "debased music to comical trifling, and made a travesty of grave matters." As C.F.W. Pohl says, it was prophesied not only that he was headed for a rapid intellectual decline, but that he was "wanting in all serious ambitions."

There was a reason for this. These critics had sharp ears; they could already hear in these early works something new and menacing. They detected the popular songs that the lower-class Haydn, disguised in rococo silken vest and powdered peruke, smuggled into the castles of the nobility. The middle class—in fact, the whole of the Third Estate—stepped forth in Haydn's music, in the motifs at the roots of his subjects. (Johann Strauss the Elder was later accused of debasing music because he borrowed themes from Beethoven and Weber and used them for dance music, "waltzed them, so to speak; the practice is similar to that of present-day jazz.) In music there is no lasting barrier between high and low; from time to time a democratic leveling takes place.

With Haydn, it was the reverse of this process. He took the jocose rogues' songs and the vulgar tavern chanties that he had picked up in his Bohemian days—in short, he took "low" music—and he worked them over and ennobled them. This was his musical mission. Why, we may ask, did this mission have to be assigned to Joseph Haydn?

Because it could have been assigned to no other composer.

HOW THE POPULAR SONG BECAME SOCIALLY PRESENTABLE

AT THE age of twenty-five, Haydn wrote his first string quartets; at twenty-eight his first symphony. But during this period, between 1755 and 1760, a remarkable, liberating struggle was launched in English, French, and German literature. Germany's intellectual life exhibited it most markedly, perhaps. This rebellion was directed against the relics of the seventeenth, the baroque century, which had reduced art to a "servant of scholarship," but it attacked also its own century, the century of gallantry, which considered art merely a sportive adjunct to rococo social life. Music, in particular, was to the early eighteenth century a pretty ornament, an aid to elegant living—like a powder box, a toilette mirror, an agate table.

Haydn's art led the way in reintroducing genuine feeling into music. First, his work was opposed to learned polyphony; second, just because of Haydn's petty-bourgeois origins, his music was antagonistic to the pure salon music of France. Haydn fought in the realm of music the same battle that J. G. Herder conducted in literature.

Herder, a native of Eastern Germany, was twelve years younger than Haydn. He, too, was twenty-eight when he first placed a mark upon his times with an epoch-making essay. The lyric, Herder wrote, must be rescued; all over Europe it had been laced into "a corset of weakness, falsehood, and artificiality" and was upon the point of suffocating. Help was to be looked for in the simple and grand popular art of the past. "Among the Scythians, Slavs, Wends, Bohemians, Russians, Swedes, and Poles there are still traces of our ancestors' footprints," he wrote. "If care were taken to search out old national songs, we should penetrate deeply into our ancestors' poetic mode of thought, which often produced poetry of equal rank with the splendid British ballads, the Spanish romances, the songs of the isolated Norwegians. Among these national songs we might well include Lithuanian *dainos*, Cossack *dummi* and Peruvian and American songs."

In other words, although Herder was himself a highly nationalistic German, he placed equal value upon the artistic gift of all nations and all peoples. But what he was seeking was, he stressed, the old, anonymous poetry which was not derived from any individual personality—a poetry which must be free, as he put it, of "the vanities of authorship." He longed to see contemporary lyricism simplified, treating of simpler matters and casting off "the oppressive ornament which has by now become virtually compulsory with us."

Translated into musical terms, Herder's ambitions were those of Haydn. We cannot assume that Haydn was acquainted with the younger man's efforts, and especially with his later essay, *On German Art and Character* (for Haydn was no reader of books), but Herder's sentiments were in the air. On the other hand, Herder was very musical and well acquainted with Haydn's work; the latter's *Seven Last Words of the Saviour on the Cross* seemed to him the profoundest work of contemporary music. He sensed that Haydn's cause was his own: now that the contrapuntal manner and the polyphonic style of Johann Sebastian Bach lay in the past, music had to return to the people. The people must be the teachers—the servant girl who sang as she hung out the wash, the street-crier who melodically offered his vegetables.

This was the reason for young Haydn's listening to the voices of the people. Since Croats happened to be the folk nearest at hand, he gladly took his inspiration from them. Spaniards, Eskimos, or Patagonians would have served him equally well, had he lived among them. In 1759, when he went to Lukavec and Pilsen, he wandered through the neighborhood to listen to Bohemian folk songs. In Eisenstadt he eavesdropped on the gypsies. In London, at the age of sixty, he lost no time studying Scottish songs and making them the basis of his compositions. However, he could not become a slave to Croat music, because he was by nature a composer in the major mode. In spite of his use of numerous Slavic themes, there is in his work a hard core of brightness which is completely at variance with the melancholy minor mood of Slavic music. The precipitate shifts of tempo of Slavic song were utterly alien to him. Haydn was the personification of German character and German "steadiness." To understand what Haydn was *not,* we need merely to see how Antonin Dvořák treated the well-known German folk song: *Ach, wie ist's möglich dann* ("Oh, it could never be possible!"), with a few chords and syncopation transforming it into the passionate Czech style of his *"Slavonic Dances."* It sounds like a variation, but the structure and the emotional tone of the music have been completely changed.

In regard to Haydn's borrowings, however, this must be said: His vast production, which ran the whole range of the art of music, could not possibly have been based everywhere on his own invention. In all conscience, he invented enough, but the treatment of his subjects, the "dressing of the stone," was of greater importance to this artisan-genius than sheer originality. Since he wished the people to speak in his music, he let the people collaborate in its production. And in his turn, Haydn influenced the *German* folk song. Besides the *Austrian Imperial Hymn,* probably no theme of Haydn's is so well known as that of the andante of the *Surprise Symphony:*

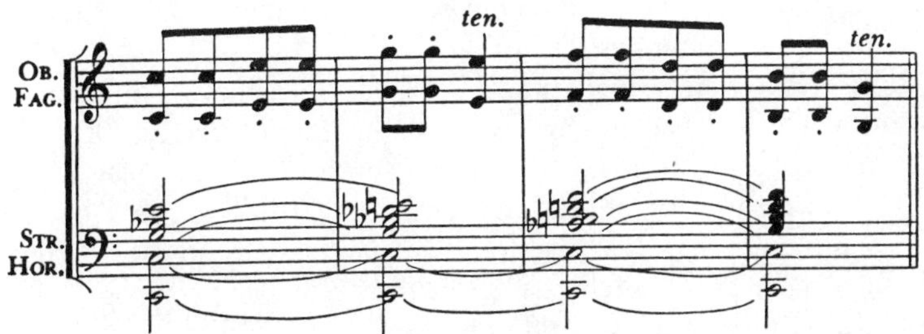

This theme is identical, note for note, with the German folk song: "Going my way through the street I saw the black cherries dangling."

However, Haydn did not exaggerate the importance of the folk song. Such immoderate remarks as Herder's, "Poetry and savagery are not necessarily opposites; I consider as healthfully savage those folk who move freely and have not yet had their emotional life shattered," would never have been accepted by Haydn. Like Goethe, he remained a true child of his eighteenth century—a moderate.

WITH COUNT MORZIN

THE best that Baron von Fuernberg could do for his protégé was to recommend him to someone else. A great Bohemian aristocrat, Count Maximilian Morzin, now hired Haydn as his musical director, at a salary of 200 gulden, with free room and food and wine at the employees' table. In winter he composed and conducted in Vienna, in summer on the count's estate in Pilsen.

It was certainly high time for Haydn to achieve a measure of security. He had had to pay dearly for his former liberty. Often his day had been eighteen hours long. At sunrise he would play the violin at an early mass; in the forenoon he might have organ rehearsals in some count's chapel; at noon he gave piano lessons; in the afternoon he sang tenor at a church service; in the evening he composed. This frightful burden of work could not go on indefinitely.

But Haydn's "bohemian" days were not quite over. Fate still held him at a distance, and struck a brief *Auftakt* before the actual theme of his manhood years was heard. However, the theme was not yet struck while he remained with the Morzin family.

During this brief relationship, Haydn seems to have dealt mostly with the count's son. The orchestra that Haydn directed was composed of fifteen members. That was fairly large for a private orchestra. With its aid, the composer performed the requisite dinner music, evening concerts, string trios, quartets, and *divertimenti* for guests. The aim of such performances was to outdo the musical fare to be had at the houses of other counts and princes. Music in those days was as much an affair of vanity as clothes, gems, and expensive journeys—even for those who were utterly inept musically. Snobbery played a great part, although there was also a great deal of genuine love for the art.

The important thing for Haydn was that he had at his disposal an orchestra with which he could experiment. It was during this period that he wrote the F-major octet for two French horns, two English horns, two violins and two bassoons, which exploited the possibilities for orchestral color in the contrast between strings and woodwinds, in a manner that was new for Haydn.

Haydn's contract stipulated that he assume his summer duties in Bohemia, after the winter in Vienna. The war with Prussia was still going on. But the great battle of Kolin in 1757 had again cleared the enemy out of Bohemia. Frederick the Great's armies had been temporarily driven back to Prussian soil. When the young kapellmeister produced music in the castle of Lukavec, the pleasant sounds would not be drowned out by the boom of the cannon in Silesia.

This manor-house, in the vicinity of Pilsen, stood in the midst of a rococo park. The summer life in the country may well have been as lazy and sleepy as Joseph von Eichendorff later described it in his *Life of the German Nobility at the Close of the Eighteenth Century* —visits to neighboring estates, small banquets, balls in the dark gardens, and *obbligato* fireworks. On the long, hot afternoons "the naughty little princelings sat in the cherry trees and tossed pits at their bored sisters who stood looking over the garden fences, hoping to espy the plumed hat of some cavalry officer emerge from the distant greenery. From the farmyard, meanwhile, sounded the chattering of the sparrows, the gobbling of the turkey-cocks and the monotonous beat of the threshers."

Haydn loved to stroll through the neighboring woods. He had never been addicted to sitting over manuscripts; in spite of his prodigious industry, he was very fond of the outdoors. Probably, on many a misty September morning he rode out behind the count and countess. He listened to the tones of hunting horns, and perhaps it was here that the first germinal ideas for his hunting symphony, *La Chasse* (No. 73) sprouted, though it was not to be completed until twenty years later. In the presto finale of that symphony are contained all the sights and sensations he must have felt during that country summer. There are the six-eight time of the stepping horses (*see next page*), the brassy glitter of the sun, and the plunges into the underbrush where sharp twigs scratch the hunter's face. Then there comes the slow fading away as the hunt disappears into the mists, the dying voices of the hounds—the *perdendosi* that was to be revived again half a century later by the romantics. In Haydn we hear anticipations of the fifths in Schumann's hunting sequences, Weber's horns, and Mendelssohn's nostalgic yearnings.

He did not, however, put into his hunting symphony one event

VL.
VLA.
VC.

VL.
cresc.
f
cresc.
f
VLA.
cresc.
f
VC.
cresc.
f
CB.
cresc.
f

of those days, his fall from a horse in 1759. This accident spoiled his pleasure in riding—perhaps the sport was, after all, the exclusive pursuit of high-born gentlemen. In any case, Haydn never again mounted a horse.

He did, however, later recount another "accident" that occurred at this time. It happened to him at the piano, while he was accompanying the mistress of the house while she sang. In order to see the notes better, the countess stooped over him, and her fichu fell open, revealing her breasts. "This was the first time I had ever been accorded such a sight; it confused me, I stopped playing, and my fingers remained numb upon the keys. 'What's the matter, Haydn,' the countess exclaimed, 'what are you doing?' 'But, my gracious lady,' I replied, 'who could help losing his composure?' "

THE KELLER SISTERS

Haydn was twenty-eight years old, and as yet had never touched a woman. This is strange—so much so that we must linger a while to consider the matter.

Haydn was, into old age, a thoroughly healthy man. Everyone who met him described him as powerful in build. We know of no childhood sicknesses. There is no account of any trace of youthful melancholy, such as characterized the early days of other artists. On the contrary, we hear only of pranks. Even when his belly was empty, his mind was bursting with wanton good spirits.

There is, for example, the story of how the nineteen-year-old Joseph one night snatched a chestnut vender's iron stove, hitched it behind a cart, and with a pair of horses dragged the clanging, noisy stove through Vienna's streets. Perhaps this story is fictitious, since it was told seventy years later, and in almost the same phrases, about Johann Strauss senior. There is, however, another story which is quite true: Haydn posted several musicians in the *Tiefer Graben* in Vienna (the exact spot is to this day pointed out to tourists), placed another band on the bridge opposite, and had them play to one another, serenade-fashion. Only the two bands played altogether different pieces, producing, to Haydn's delight, a burlesque of a serenade. The fearful din brought the police to the scene, but Haydn succeeded in escaping. The other musicians were caught and made to pay a fine.

Almost anything would set off this spirit of youthful wildness. Sometimes the provocation was his early fame. Once he was walking at night through the streets of Vienna, accompanied by Dittersdorf, when he heard one of his own minuets being played in a tavern. He entered, and asked what was being played. "It's by Haydn," the violinist said, and went right on. "Well," Haydn said, shrugging his shoulders, "that's the stinkiest minuet I ever heard." The fiddler, his musician's pride offended, raised his bow and was about to hit Haydn over the head with it. Dittersdorf had to pull him away, to prevent a brawl.

But with women Haydn remained shy. Shall we assume that he did not need them? No; naturally, he needed them just as much as did any other healthy man. Or was it a matter of lacking time to synchronize his own musical development with the pursuit of a sweetheart? It is strange how many musicians, in their old age, excused their failures in this realm with the apology that they had no time. We recall the hoary-bearded Brahms murmuring to himself one day, after a female admirer had extolled his C-major piano trio, "After all, I am only a poor, unmarried man." It was a curious mingling of artistic and human timidity that had made an eternal bachelor out of a man who in his youth was blessed with an almost angelic beauty. "At the time when I should have most liked to marry, my works were hissed in the concert room" he said to his friend I. V. Widmann "and I could not have borne being pitied by my wife."

Bruckner, for different reasons, suffered a similar fate. His rather clumsy, peasant character, his lack of education, and his absolute devotion to music alone, are apparent links with Haydn. He offered the same dubious excuse as Brahms: "My dear friend, I have no time. I must get on with my Fourth Symphony." Perhaps, as Decsey says, in avoiding marriage Bruckner really wanted to avoid the "loss of energy and the peril of dispersing his efforts." Interestingly enough, it was principally the great erotic music of Wagner's *Tannhaeuser* and *Tristan* which stimulated Bruckner's creativity; but he poured this spiritual and sensual fire into the great forms of Catholic ritual. He himself recognized only one kind of eroticism, the love of God, and the sermons on chastity and sinfulness remained with him during his whole life. In this there is no parallel between him and Haydn, who never for a moment considered women as something forbidden. His shyness as a young man had other causes.

While Bruckner's life seems to be related to Freud's theory that attachment to the mother (the earthly or the heavenly mother) hinders attachments to other women, Haydn's predicament seems to require an Adlerian interpretation. Haydn, who, unlike Mozart, manifested no trace of early maturity, no sign of having been a child prodigy—who, in fact, did not show a spark of true genius before his thirtieth year—had an inferiority complex toward "grown-ups." And he considered every woman grown up. He would never have ventured toward a woman any such timid hypocrisy or clumsy familiarity as Bruckner exhibited when he wooed a lady by sending her the gift of a prayer-book or, at other times, offered to ladies snuff from his snuffbox. Haydn had taste, and never overstepped the limits of propriety. He was afraid to make advances because he was unattractive, or considered himself so. Later, he spoke of his appearance as that of a *brutto ritratto;* his body was stocky but crude. Although his eyes sparkled with liveliness and warmth, his face was disfigured by pockmarks; his complexion, moreover, was too dark a brown for the taste of salon ladies. His lower lip and jaw were too protruding; as a result of a polyp inherited from his mother the lower part of his nose was swollen. He did not look at all like an artist. His was a very earthy face, indeed, and, generally, he did not make a particularly good impression upon his aristocratic patronesses. When Countess Thun, who thought very highly of his compositions, first met him, she asked: "Are you *really* Haydn?"

Things changed in his later life. With the passage of years and increasing success, Haydn's self-confidence rose considerably. His face changed correspondingly; his brow and eyes took on a dignified look; his sincere cordiality won the hearts of women. While Bruckner's art did not affect them, and, indeed, was not directed toward them, it was quite the reverse with Haydn. He wrote his music, not for the church, but for the household, and women were the rulers of the household. Once Haydn said, "anyone can see by the look of me that I mean well by everybody." There is no doubt that women saw this. Perhaps the only woman who did not was his own wife. But that was not his fault —or his fault to a limited extent only. He should not have married her.

We have seen that Haydn's masculinity developed uncommonly late; at the age of eighteen he was still singing soprano! For the following ten years, while he lived in the midst of the loosest sort of Viennese "bohemians," he had no mistress. When, at the age of twenty-eight, he was at last assailed by love, he was overcome as more experienced men might not have been. It happened at the home of a barber to whose daughter he was giving piano lessons.

This barber, Johann Peter Keller, had done Haydn a good many favors during the musician's years of wretchedness and poverty. We must not imagine the barber's scale of life as necessarily lowly. As a maker of perukes he had a highly respected business. The age of rococo expended more care upon the coiffure than any other. "The wig is the man," was a favorite saying of the day, and not only in aristocratic circles. And let us not mistakenly imagine that one powdered wig looked like every other. A Parisian or Viennese barber studied his patron carefully before he set to work creating a peruke.

Ever since Louis XIV had introduced, in 1673, the majestic fashion of the *allongé* wig into the world of the courts, a flood of new hair styles had swamped Europe, the hairbag, the bobtail-wig, the pigtail, and countless other variations. Each social group adopted its special peruke. Councillors, scholars, and clerics would not wear the same hairdo as army men, civil servants, or merchants. Mountains of powder had to be poured on wigs and natural hair, and the trade of the hair stylist flourished as never before.

Every sort of craft was of interest to Haydn, and so he was interested in the fine artistry of such a craftsman as Johann Peter Keller. Wig-making remotely resembled tailoring, for not only the shears but the tape-measure was employed. The shape of the head and brow and the natural inclination of the hair had to be taken into account. Persons with high brows were treated differently from those with broad skulls or with fat necks; for bald-headed men, the wig had to be so skillfully shaped that it seemed to be worn on top of a proper head of hair.

Haydn spent many of his free hours in Keller's workshop, which was enlivened by cheerful Viennese gossip and skillful manual work. The master had apprentices, of course, and his two pretty daughters also helped with the work. Haydn fell in love with the younger daughter. We do not know what she looked like; Haydn never spoke of that, nor do we know for certain whether or not she loved him. After several weeks, during which she seemed to respond to his ardor, she declared, to his dismay, that she could not marry him. She felt herself to be a "bride of Christ," and planned to enter a convent. Perhaps her cleric brother, later Father Eduard of Graz, encouraged this decision. In any case, her father was amazed and distressed, and Haydn was inconsolable. For the first time in his life he had fallen in love—and had been so swiftly rejected.

The traces of this love did not show immediately in his art, as similar experiences were to be manifested with painful distinctness in the work of Schubert or Beethoven. What we should not forget, is that Haydn's was, by and large, a cooler temperament. The artisans from whom he had sprung had no patience with excessive emotionalism. Ten more years were to pass before Haydn's art advanced into the realm of more delicate feelings, before he became, for a fleeting while, one of the great sentimentalists in music.

A principal cause was the fact that Haydn did not then have the time to turn his sorrow to creative uses. He committed the fateful error that Mozart later repeated; he married the other daughter. Actually, he did not love her at all. He married her out of a kind of conservatism, because she was the nun's sister, because he loved the atmosphere in which his pleas and his sweetheart's replies had been spoken. The father also had a hand in the game, for he was unwilling to let Count Morzin's musical director, a man with an important office and a good livelihood, slip quite out of his hands. Father Keller played the same part as did Mozart's mother-in-law when she talked him into taking Constance, since the younger sister whom he loved had married another.

Mozart was careless about his own life, but he was not inexperienced with women. Haydn was wholly inexperienced—but, on the other hand, was very prudent in his own matters. It is more surprising in his case that he married the wrong woman than that Mozart did. But this time his peasant shrewdness deserted him, and he did not react with that healthy carefulness and absence of haste that usually characterized his behavior. Without considering what he was doing, he fell into the trap—and made two persons unhappy.

Whereas Constance Mozart was always considered charming, no one has ever said a good word about Maria Anna Aloysia Haydn. "According to the most credible witnesses," wrote a friend of Haydn, the painter Dies, in 1810, "Anna Aloysia was a shrewish and jealous woman, incapable of reflection." And Pohl, the most comprehensive biographer of Haydn, called her "an unendurable, quarrelsome and heartless woman, spendthrift and bigoted in the bargain—a scolding Xantippe." Haydn did not always put up with her patiently. On occasion he took vigorous action against her, and to others he spoke of her in terms of the utmost contempt. Nevertheless, he was united to her for forty-one years without separation, except for the years he spent in London—and those were the happiest of his life. Worst of all for Haydn was the fact that the marriage remained childless, for he worshipped children, as Brahms did. To him a house without heirs was empty.

Let us not inquire into Anna Aloysia's views on her great husband's music. We need only remember the resigned words that Mozart spoke a few weeks before his death, when he went with Constance Mozart to a performance of *The Magic Flute,* "In her case what will probably happen will be that she will see the opera, but not hear it." Sadly enough, all the time that Haydn was married to the wrong woman, the right one was still living, with the convent name of Josepha; she died after Anna Aloysia. But at that time Haydn was a very old man indeed. Even at the age of seventy-five his youthful mistake was still painful to him. Once he led Baillot, a famous French violinist, through the portrait gallery in his home. He paused in the corridor, gripped his guest's arm and, pointing to a portrait, said (Haydn usually spoke Italian to illustrious guests): *"E la mia moglie; m'ha ben fatto arrabbiare!"* ("This is my wife; she often infuriated me.")

But we anticipate. At present it is November 26, 1760, and we are in Saint Stephen's Cathedral. Outside a Viennese fog envelops the streets; one can scarcely see a few yards ahead. The head and shoulders of the great cathedral cannot be distinguished; the Gothic tower which afforded Haydn, as a child, his first glimpse of Vienna is now invisible. Candles are lit; the priest murmurs. Haydn, standing beside his bride, sees the stony landscape where he spent his boyhood as a singer. Is not this present marriage of his a reasonable one, close to boyhood, one that will find favor in the sight of God?

Present at the ceremony are, besides the barber Keller, a few bridesmaids with flowers in their hands (it is unfortunate that wedding flowers in November are exactly like those that go into funeral wreaths); the master stonemason Karl Schunko, and the market magistrate Anton Buchholtz, the philanthropist who had lent money to the young Haydn. During the ceremony Haydn had only one real concern: What would the Morzin family say? As with any other musician employed by the count, he was forbidden to marry without written permission.

But the next weeks were to show that Haydn had been right to follow his own initiative. The count's financial status, long shaky, collapsed. The family had to cut down expenditures, sell several of its estates, and dissolve the orchestra. Haydn would have been thrown out on the street had not a tremendous stroke of luck, such as he had already experienced more than once, immediately altered his fortunes for the better. A far richer and more powerful noble house than Morzin's offered to hire him—the Esterhazys, one of the mightiest families in Europe. He at once accepted the offer of the reigning prince, Paul Anton. Together with his wife he moved to Eisenstadt, the capital of Burgenland and of the "Esterhazy realm." (It only began there, for it extended deep into Hungary.) Rohrau was only a few hours from Eisenstadt. From there he could visit his father. Haydn was returning to the land of his childhood.

When he left Vienna, he did not know that he was departing for a full thirty years, during which time he was to return to the city only on brief visits, a few weeks out of every year, and never as his own master. Would he have agreed had he known that he was to stay away from Vienna for a whole generation of human life?

Haydn himself answered the question. "From then on," he later recounted, "I was retained as kapellmeister by His Highness Prince Esterhazy, *in whose service I wish to live and die.*"

Book Two

LABORIOUS FORENOON

Haydn's reform of the symphony is one of the greatest miracles of art of any age.

GUIDO ADLER

A CONTRACT AND ITS CONSEQUENCES

NOTHING has done more harm to Haydn's reputation than Richard Wagner's verdict: "Haydn was and remained an imperial lackey, providing, as a musician, for the entertainment of his splendor-loving master. He was submissive and humble, and therefore the peace possible to a kindly, serene disposition remained with him till a ripe old age."

This pronouncement is so devastating because, sociologically speaking, it is not untrue. Haydn, indeed, did compromise, and by eschewing poverty, forfeited his freedom. And, of course, Wagner is right in seeing an attendant loss of initiative. Since Haydn was not working for the "open market," he was bound to select the conventional techniques that were recognized in palace and court. It was incumbent upon him to devote his talents to pleasing one individual and his entourage—whose tastes, however, were on a high plane. Yet, could he have composed one hundred and four symphonies had he not been shielded from poverty?

What Wagner did not recognize (and what, in fact, has seldom been recognized) was a certain dialectic trait in Haydn's character which enabled him for thirty years to preserve his inner freedom while submitting to outward servitude. Haydn's renowned "simplicity" was actually the product of conflicting instincts and convictions. Though his education was limited, the composer inclined to mingle Stoic and Epicurean elements, and this rational synthesis was the well-spring of much of his energy. Indeed, beneath his docile surface Haydn was capable of astonishing sentiments. Wagner might well have been astounded had he known that Haydn's "boundless respect for the aristocrats" did not hinder him from setting to music Lessing's disrespectful—in fact, venomous—canon:

TO A NOBLE BLOCKHEAD

This is indeed a noble ass,
In lineage older than us all.
His forebears brayed ere Adam was.

Haydn, the flunkey, achieved a much more independent character than did many a son of the nineteenth century.

Wagner, who prized outward liberty above all else, preferred not to see how composers of his day were placed at the mercy of both their public and their publishers. Was Verdi free when, after his successes, he was again and again constrained to produce variations of the same pattern of Italian grand opera to give to the tyrannical Milanese public? Goethe, who had personally met Esterhazy, described him as "lively, devoid of arrogance or wounding coldness." The kindly patronage of such a man, in whose livery a genius like Haydn found it pleasant to live and work, was beyond the comprehension of Wagner, who was linked in a highly questionable friendship to an insane patron, King Louis II of Bavaria. The relationship existing between Haydn and the princely family of Esterhazy was certainly one of service and not friendship. Haydn was a court official who ranked no higher than the master of the stables or the keeper of the silver—but he did not have to put up with tyranny.

The text of the contract was, it must be said, unique. There probably has not been, either before or after Haydn, a single genius who would have signed his name to such an agreement. Let us see what was demanded of him:

> 1. Seeing that the kapellmeister at Eisenstadt, by name Gregorius Werner, having devoted many years of true and faithful service to the princely house, is now on account of his great age and infirmities unfit to perform the duties incumbent upon him, therefore the said Gregorius Werner, in consideration of his long services, shall retain the post of kapellmeister, and the said Joseph Haydn as vice-kapellmeister shall, as far as regards the music of the choir, be subordinate to the kapellmeister and receive his instructions. But in everything else relating to musical performances, and in all that concerns the orchestra, the vice-kapellmeister shall have the sole direction.
>
> 2. The said Joseph Haydn shall be considered and treated as a member of the household. Therefore, His Serene Highness graciously trusts that he will conduct himself as becomes an honorable official of a princely house. He must be temperate, not showing himself overbearing toward his musicians, but mild and lenient, straightforward and composed. It is especially to be observed that when the orchestra shall be summoned to perform before company, the vice-kapellmeister and all the musicians shall appear in uniform, and the said Joseph Haydn shall take care that

he and all members of his orchestra follow the prescribed rule, and appear in white stockings, white linen, powdered, and either with a pig-tail or a tie-wig.

3. Seeing that the other musicians are referred for directions to the said vice-kapellmeister, therefore he should take the more care to conduct himself in an exemplary manner, abstaining from undue familiarity, and from vulgarity in eating, drinking, and conversation, not dispensing with the respect due to him, but acting uprightly and influencing his subordinates to preserve such harmony as is becoming in them, remembering how displeasing the consequences of any discord or dispute would be to His Serene Highness.

4. The said vice-kapellmeister shall be under an obligation to compose such music as his Serene Highness may command, and neither to communicate such compositions to any other person, nor to allow them to be copied, but to retain them for the absolute use of His Highness, and not to compose anything for any other person without the knowledge and permission of His Highness.

5. The said Joseph Haydn shall appear in the antechamber daily, before and after midday, and inquire whether His Highness is pleased to order a performance of the orchestra. After receipt of his orders he shall communicate them to the other musicians, and shall take care to be punctual at the appointed time, and to ensure punctuality in his subordinates, making a note of those who arrive late or absent themselves altogether.

6. Should any quarrel or cause of complaint arise, the vice-kapellmeister shall endeavour to arrange it, in order that His Serene Highness may not be incommoded with trifling disputes: but should any more serious difficulty occur, which the said Joseph Haydn is unable to set right, His Serene Highness must then be respectfully called upon to decide the matter.

7. The said vice-kapellmeister shall take careful charge of all music and musical instruments, and shall be responsible for any injury that may occur to them from carelessness or neglect.

8. The said Joseph Haydn shall be obliged to instruct the female vocalists, in order that they may not forget in the country what they have been taught with much trouble and expense in Vienna, and, as the said vice-kapellmeister is proficient on various instruments, he shall take care to practise himself on all that he is acquainted with.

9. A copy of this agreement and instructions shall be given to the said vice-kapellmeister and to his subordinates, in order that he may be able to hold them to their obligations therein laid down.

10. It is considered unnecessary to detail the services required of the said Joseph Haydn more particularly, since His Serene Highness is

pleased to hope that he will of his own free will strictly observe not only these regulations but all others that may from time to time be made by His Highness, and that he will place the orchestra on such a footing, and in such good order, that he may bring honor upon himself and deserve the further favor of the prince his master, who thus confides in his zeal and discretion.

11. A salary of 400 florins to be received quarterly is hereby bestowed upon the said vice-kapellmeister by His Serene Highness.

12. In addition, the said Joseph Haydn shall have board at the officers' table, or half a gulden a day in lieu thereof.

13. Finally, this agreement shall hold good for at least three years from May 1st, 1761, with the further condition that if at the conclusion of this term the said Joseph Haydn shall desire to leave the service, he shall notify his intention to His Highness half a year beforehand.

14. His Serene Highness undertakes to keep Joseph Haydn in his service during this time, and should he be satisfied with him, he may look forward to being appointed kapellmeister. This, however, must not be understood to deprive His Serene Highness of the freedom to dismiss the said Joseph Haydn at the expiration of the term, should he see fit to do so.

Duplicate copies of this document shall be executed and exchanged.
Given at Vienna this first day of May, 1761.

What made Haydn accept such a contract? Only the acute fear of poverty and the conviction that it would not only ruin his life, but would submerge his music, too. Haydn put himself into a position which assumed complete control of his life, day and night. Yet he did not shrink from the stipulation—and how right he was!—that he should compose only such music as His Serene Highness might command. Probably Haydn imagined that he would have the last word in matters of taste. But could he be so certain of that? The close of Paragraph 4 was likely to be of far graver consequence. If the prince intended to enforce the provision that Haydn's new compositions were to be made available to no one else and that they were not to be copied, but were to be reserved exclusively for His Serene Highness, then Haydn should have felt compelled to reject the contract, for his profession's sake. For by its terms his music was withheld from all the rest of Europe, and even from Austria and Germany.

That Haydn nevertheless consented to go to Eisenstadt is proof of his knowledge of human beings and of circumstances. He must have reasoned that the Esterhazy family, who were expending on a kapellmeister the unusual annual salary of 1,600 gulden, would soon be eager to make their musical director well known throughout Europe. When highly placed foreign guests were delighted by Haydn's music, would the Esterhazys actually refuse to let them have copies? And the way from foreign noblemen to foreign publishers would not be very long. If Haydn's published compositions bore the inscription, "Kapellmeister to His Highness Prince Esterhazy," the prince's egoism would certainly be satisfied. We may well assume that the master foresaw this eventuality; he had a peasant's shrewdness in all that concerned his art.

Nevertheless, no "modern" man—no post-Beethoven musician, that is—would have signed such a contract. Or, if he were constrained to do so, he would have done his utmost to sabotage the contract from within. He might compose the desired music for the prince's household, but some day he would also attempt to break the conditions holding him dependent and to give the whole arrangement the semblance of a voluntary one. Above all, the modern man would seek to establish social equality with his employer. This much, he would feel, he "owed to music."

Haydn had a different view of the matter. It was precisely for the sake of his creative life, which alone concerned him, that he did not engage in a hopeless struggle for social equality (which, in any case, was not accorded to the artist until after the French Revolution). There is nevertheless an unquestionable note of pride in the words he spoke to Griesinger in his old age: "I have had converse with emperors, kings and many great lords, and have heard many flattering praises from them; but I do not wish to live on a familiar footing with such persons and prefer people of my own class." It would be wholly wrong to read humility into these words; they express rather a real pride of class, that same artisan's pride that is expressed by the musician Miller in Schiller's *Love and Intrigue.*

The artist of the nineteenth and the twentieth centuries has chosen absolute freedom. He has not desired what Haydn desired and what Mozart vainly longed for, a secure position with a rich and generous employer—though, to be sure, the latter element was a matter of luck. Since Beethoven, artists have chosen merciless competition, the nerve-wracking, soul-destroying struggle for bread and appreciation. Such a pattern prohibits the "fabulous" productivity that was Haydn's.

Which type is the happier? There are no more noble lords who hire great artists body and soul. A Hungarian writer, Gabriel Tolnai, in 1939 challenged the descendant of Esterhazy with the question, "What are you doing for art?" And the American composer Aaron Copland wrote in 1940 that American radio stations ought "to undertake the role of the musically enlightened nobility of the eighteenth century who vied with one another for the services of the best composers of their day, for no better reason than the entertainment of their guests and their own greater glory . . . Is it sheer daydreaming to ask that each of our three largest networks employ ten men each as regular staff composers, very much in the way that Prince Esterhazy employed Haydn?"

THE KINGDOM OF ESTERHAZY AND NICHOLAS THE SPLENDID

No MAP will reveal a "kingdom of Esterhazy" lying between Austria and Hungary. Yet that kingdom really existed, for the Esterhazys were the richest landowners in Hungary and wielded, in politics and in economics, vast influence.

As the position of the Hapsburgs in the Holy Roman Empire proper became weaker, support forthcoming from the Hungarian magnates became proportionately more important. Not all of these Hungarians stood by the Hapsburgs, however. The Hungarian petty nobility were nationalistic, and saw no reason why the Hungarian king should be identical with the German kaiser whose capital lay in remote Vienna and who seldom could speak a word of Hungarian. It was only the highest aristocracy in Hungary who were internationally minded and therefore favorably inclined toward the Hapsburgs. For the Austrian Hapsburgs were themselves international; they reigned, as need be, after a Spanish, Italian, German, or Bohemian fashion—or rather, since they denied the principle of nationality, they reigned as cosmopolitans.

The Hapsburgs often had difficulties to overcome, and it must be accounted as one of their principal advantages that the Esterhazys remained loyal to them. The founder of the Esterhazy family fortune was Nicholas I (1582-1645), who acquired legendary wealth by marrying into the Magocsy family, by fighting the Turks (who had overrun the greater part of Hungary), and, at another time, by making agreements with them. Nicholas was only a count, but his son Paul (1635-1713) received the title of prince from the Emperor Leopold I. This Esterhazy was one of the first to take up the collector's mania of the baroque age. He collected weapons, old paintings, silverwork in his old castle of Forchtenstein. He also was a lover of the theater with which he had become acquainted as a Jesuit pupil and shone himself in women's rôles, such as that of Judith with the head of Holofernes.

Moreover, he also wrote sacral compositions which he published, two years before his death, with the inscription: "Dedicated to the Christ Child."

It was Paul's grandson, Paul Anton, who engaged Haydn. Paul Anton was no longer the lord of a feudal stronghold, but a city man who made the little town of Eisenstadt his actual residence. He was a typical *grand seigneur* of the rococo age. He played both the violin and the cello; testimony to his interest in music can be seen to this day in the scores of the music of foreign masters which he amassed in Milan, Rome, and Naples. He also maintained a small army of his own, and twice he placed at the disposal of Maria Theresa an entire regiment of hussars, gratis. He was a versatile man, and demanded versatility in his vice-kapellmeister, who was director, composer, magistrate, overseer, teacher and tutor all in one—not a little was required of Haydn.

The prince must have had a high personal regard for Haydn, to have entrusted him with so many duties. And we must remember the elegance and suavity of tone of the "slave contract." It is therefore quite out of the question that the prince's first meeting with Haydn took place as the French later described it. According to the French story, after hearing Haydn's music the prince shouted: *"Quoi! La musique est de ce Maure? Eh bien, Maure, de ce moment tu es à mon service. Comment t'appelles tu?"* * To which Haydn, it is alleged, responded meekly: "Joseph Haydn." The French of the Napoleonic age fabricated this story to illustrate Haydn's amazing rise from so low a station. In reality the first meeting was neither so dramatic, nor was the Esterhazy manner so tasteless.

In 1764 Haydn might have given notice. But the occasion did not arise, for before the contract terminated Prince Paul Anton died, and his brother Nicholas became master of the vast Esterhazy possessions. When he took over the domain he found Haydn already there, and not only as an item in his inventory of servants, but also—and in human terms this was far more important—as someone who was already respected within the band.

The new master who rode into Eisenstadt on May 17, 1762, had already acquired fourfold fame as a soldier, diplomat, patron of art, and spendthrift. There was, however, scarcely anything soldierly

* "What's that? This Moor wrote the music? Very well, Moor, from now on you're in my service. What's your name?"

about his appearance. He was frail of frame; his eyes were large but deep-set within a small face. Nicholas gave one the impression of a man who is not particularly healthy, but who attempts to stress his soundness of body by practicing the equestrian arts. His military exploits were undoubtedly of this compensatory nature. As commander of a regiment of hussars, he had fought, five years before, in the victorious battle of Kolin which freed Bohemia of her foes. Under the famous Field Marshal Hadik he had swept northward and participated in the taking of Berlin (which, however, was held for a short time only). But the retiring army left the Prussian munitions factories in ruins.

Nicholas's services as a diplomat for Empress Maria Theresa were more important than his feats as a soldier. At a time when everything depended on Austria's winning friends abroad, he had represented the imperial court in several South European countries. In Italy, Nicholas became acquainted with the "Medicean ideal"—the accumulation of power and wealth to be used for the benefit of art and artists. He began to speak of himself as if he were a Renaissance prince sadly out of place in his rococo age. All that his brother and his sister-in-law had accomplished at Eisenstadt seemed far too scanty to him. His dissatisfaction could be seen in his eyes as he rode abroad and his people bowed low before him.

Haydn celebrated the arrival of his new master with three tone-paintings. Just at this time, a beginning was being made, timidly, of calling such compositions "symphonies." These three of Haydn were entitled *Le Matin, Le Midi, Le Soir*. In them he showed, splendidly, everything he could do. The introductory adagio set forth a miniature sunrise in music, the sparkling of the dew, and the fresh morning air; in the slow middle movement was a humorous parody of a singing lesson: *Do-re-mi-fa-sol.* (As we know, under the contract Haydn also had to function as a singing teacher.) In *Le Midi* he reproduced a noonday siesta in rich Italian colors; the Italians themselves later compared Haydn with Tintoretto. As in the music of the Neapolitan Corelli, an ensemble of two violins and a cello contrasted with the other voices. The sinfonietta *Le Soir* was an especially felicitous piece of work. First comes the cheerful main subject, buzzing up like a swarm of gnats

and twittering from instrument to instrument with its subsidiary themes. In the andante in C-major the horns are silent; the bassoon alone speaks up, and the world is colored a rich purple; the day is over, the violins sing their evensong. Then, with a sudden assault that is typical Haydn, there begins a frenzied presto: the tempest. First the violins in sixteenth figures underline the sultriness of the air; quarter notes divided by eighth-note rests (a device Rossini later made use of in the overture to *William Tell*) indicate the first gusts of wind. Then the flutes strew bluish-white zigzag darts of lightning over the landscape, and then comes the *tutti* of the strings; in fortissimo thirty-second notes the masses of air race along, diminishing and again increasing, until the storm has blown itself out, and night descends peacefully.

Would the new master understand this music? He was seventeen years older than Haydn. Would he sense the musical aspirations of the composer and make them his own—or would he clip Joseph Haydn's wings by making dilettante demands upon him? Apparently Nicholas was satisfied. Immediately after his arrival he raised his vice-kapellmeister's quarterly salary from 400 to 600 gulden. Was this the mark of the "spendthrift"? Such *pourboires* did not, at any rate, impoverish Hungary's richest landowner. For he owned twenty-one castles, sixty marketplaces, two hundred and seven dairy farms and manor farms, and four hundred and fourteen villages with all the peasants who inhabited them. His annual income amounted to some 1,800,000 gulden. The salaries he paid out came to no more than 40,000 gulden.

Although the court was nominally in mourning for the deceased prince, the very first weeks of the new era were marked by showy banquets and festive balls. Perhaps Nicholas Esterhazy agreed with the principle expressed in Hofmannsthal's lines, "Festivity and rejoicing accompany the life of kings even when they mourn and hold their funerals." Perhaps Nicholas was unwilling to mourn at all because, in his presence, he ceded no rights to death. At any rate, there were resplendent fireworks; for weeks costly inventions of the pyrotechnical art blazed the new master's initials in the night sky. Music necessarily accompanied these displays. And such things interested Haydn; they stimulated his love of experiment, his joy in the primitive. The great Handel before him had also written fireworks music, and, later Richard Wagner, in 1849, looking down from the Kreuzkirche upon burning Dresden, probably found the motif for the "magic fire music" that he later wrote.

For weeks Haydn scarcely put off his blue musician's frock coat with its richly embroidered collar and silver trimming. But since the Prince was also a theater enthusiast, the kapellmeister sometimes was permitted a breathing spell. Italian comedians were brought to Eisenstadt; with furious speed a stage was set up in the conservatory attached to the palace park, and the famous painter, Le Bon, came posthaste from Paris to paint the sets. The backdrops were still damp when Haydn and his musicians entered the theater to provide accompaniment for two comic operas, *La Marchesa Nepola* and *Sganarello.*

Nicholas had made many changes in the band and had greatly expanded it. He supplemented the old instruments by expensive novelties from Italy; in addition, he set up a library of music which was to surpass in extent the library of the Vienna Opera. As first violinist he appointed Luigi Tomasini of Pesaro, where Rossini was later born, and decades of co-operation with this great virtuoso were to deepen Haydn's knowledge of the possibilities of the instrument, for he himself was not more than a fair violinist.

Naturally, Prince Nicholas, who had grown up in the musico-theatrical tradition of the early eighteenth century, at once required Haydn to produce an opera of his own. He would have fallen into disfavor with the prince if he had proved unable to comply. So he produced *Acide,* a routine Italian opera that recounted the love of Acis and Galatea and the handsome swain's murder by the giant Polyphemus. It was one more of the innumerable theatrical productions in the style of the *opera seria* and had no special merit. But the prince liked it.

In the winter Nicholas the Splendid moved for a few weeks to his palace in Vienna, taking with him his entire musical retinue. Haydn was, to be sure, not a free man and had no more right to leave the house without permission than had the other servants; but at the palace festivals cultured Vienna paid him a respect that showed how far he had come from his former status. For now he belonged to the household of a prince, and that redounded to the credit of his music.

Nicholas had always traveled a great deal, and his stay in Eisenstadt, plus a few weeks in Vienna, could not satiate his love of the world and of public appearances. But the year 1764 had arrived, a great year for the prince. In 1763 the empress had concluded the peace of Hubertusburg with her enemy, Frederick of Prussia. As Gottfried August Buerger's famous ballad, in Rossetti's translation, described it:

> The empress and the king
> With ceaseless quarrel tired
> At length relaxed the stubborn hate
> Which rivalry inspired
> And the martial throng with laugh and song,
> Spoke of their homes as they rode along,
> And clank, clank, clank! came every rank,
> With the trumpet sound that rose and sank.

A great war had been fought; the principles of the matriarchal state and of the Prussian paternal state, embodied in the persons of the two protagonists, had fought almost to the point of mutual annihilation. In the end, neither had actually won. However, Maria Theresa had been forced to renounce Silesia for all time. In order to compensate for this loss of prestige, in 1764, in the free city of Frankfurt (the coronation city of the German emperors) she organized a grand political celebration at which she appointed her son Joseph, who was twenty-four years old, co-ruler with herself, and had him crowned as "King of Germany."

Nicholas Esterhazy traveled to this grand celebration, bringing the congratulations of Hungary and of Bohemia as well, for he possessed vast estates there also. Goethe, as a boy of fifteen, was one of those who witnessed this celebration, and in his autobiography he wrote with reminiscent appreciation of Esterhazy's "fairy empire" and described how the title representative of Hungary and Bohemia had had an entire quarter of Frankfurt illuminated in order to honor the young emperor. Goethe marvelled at

> the great esplanade of lime-trees with its portal glowing in many-colored lights, and in the background a still more splendid prospect. Among the trees stood pyramids of light and globes upon glowing pedestals; from one tree to the next were stretched gleaming garlands from which candelabra hung, swinging in the air.

Meanwhile, the people dined at Nicholas's expense; roasts, sausages, beer, and wine were distributed among the populace of Frankfurt.

On this journey Nicholas went not only to Frankfurt, but also to Paris. This proved to be a step of fateful significance. Perhaps Esterhazy's inclination toward diplomacy led him to Paris; perhaps, also, he undertook some mission for the empress, some special embassy to the court of Louis XV. Since the end of the Seven Years' War and the semi-reconciliation with Prussia, it had become necessary to strengthen the alliance with France. Perhaps, too, Nicholas merely wished to visit the French Esterhazys, his cousins of the family who had fled from Hungary in 1706. Now they were great lords in France. But whatever it was that led him to Paris, everything else dwindled when he beheld the architectural glories of Versailles.

He stood and looked in amazement. What a palace! Out of a small hunting castle Jules Hardouin-Mansart, an architect of genius, had created for Louis XIV *the* triumph of absolutism. Graceful as a lioness at rest, the middle part of the castle crouched and looked into the dark-green park peopled with stone gods and nymphs whose rustling garments were frozen into marble. The manner in which the famous landscape architect Lenôtre had co-ordinated trees and stonework in the park was a source of unending pleasure. Within the palace itself every yard of wall space displayed a painting or arrangements of silks; there were innumerable wood carvings and Chinese tapestries; every corner was habitated by some masterpiece of sculpture, some chalcedony urn, or alabaster table. Each of these rooms and great halls contrived to be both as intimate as an intrigue and as majestic as a royal ceremony. There were an orangery and a gallery of mirrors that had not their like anywhere; the cascading stairways were admirably designed for easy ascent and descent; there was a palace theater and there was a chapel which seemed to have been built less in honor of God than of the earthly prince who had created this wonder of art.

When Nicholas rode home, he brought from France a wagon-train of *objets d'art*—furniture, rugs, paintings, and objects set with precious gems. Moreover, he carried in his mind's eye a vision of the palace of Versailles. He saw it day and night, down to such details as the wrought-iron grating which surrounded the *place d'armes*. Architects accompanied him. He had decided to create a Versailles in the midst of the Hungarian plain.

It was a mad undertaking, a whim that could have had no practical justification, for Nicholas already had his palace in Eisenstadt; there he could "govern" his people at his leisure. Where lay the sense of going into the wilderness, many days' travel from any center of population, to erect a copy of Versailles? Frederick the Great had, at any rate, built Sans Souci close to Potsdam, and Maria Theresa had placed her Schoenbrunn on the outskirts of Vienna. But Nicholas was of another mind. At the southern end of the Neusiedlersee, in a wholly inhospitable neighborhood beset with malaria and swamp fevers, lay the tiny hunting castle of Süttör. Only gamekeepers or ornithologists inhabited the place, for great flocks of herons and bitterns had taken advantage of the solitude and for decades had built their nests there. Only once or twice a year did the Esterhazys and their invited friends disturb the birds by hunting parties. But now all was changed overnight. At the prince's command, tens of thousands of workers and peasant serfs assembled; engineers supervised the draining of the marshy soil and saw to the laying of firm foundations for a palace. Only eighteen months after the first spadeful of earth was turned, the palace stood there, a Fata Morgana. Travelers who chanced upon the place stood still and gaped, believing they saw a mirage. There never had been a castle at this spot—and why should there be one now? There were no people at all here, no nearby town, scarcely more than a few tiny villages. The scattered population of the vicinity consisted of fishermen and shepherds. Who could be inhabiting this palace, and whom would the noble masters have for company?

Yet company would not be lacking. Invitations went out to all quarters of the continent. The palace, which the noble builder had named for his own family "Esterhaz," could hold hundreds of guests in addition to the host of servants. "I can match the emperor in everything," Nicholas used to say, and this was an understatement, for Maria Theresa and her son, the co-regent, lived quite frugally. It was rare in Vienna for two hundred to be served at table; in Esterhaz this happened almost every day.

Greedily the master of Esterhaz drank in the flatteries of all Europe. It was said that ten million gulden had been expended on the palace. Since Nicholas the Splendid did not have to pay for labor—the laborers were his own serfs!—this vast sum had been spent chiefly on materials: on the black lacquer panels from Japan decorated with landscapes in gilt; on the gallery of Italian and Dutch paintings; on the hall of clocks which contained such surprises as a clock "from which on the hour a golden bird emerged and whistled a tune." There were candelabra of quartz, and a splendid library of eight thousand expensively bound books. And every day the mail coach brought the latest novelties from all over Europe.

The main attraction was the opera house, which was the midpoint for a radiating group of avenues lined with chestnut trees. The opera house seated an audience of five hundred. Its boxes had anterooms furnished with mirrors, clocks, and fireplaces. Alas for these anterooms! In one of them, years later, the fire started which destroyed the entire palace; today we know of its splendor from hearsay only. There was a daily performance of an Italian *opera seria* or *buffa*. Often, too, performances of German dramas were given or (when there were visitors from France, whom the prince preferred above all) works of the Parisian literary masters. After the French ambassador, Prince Rohan de Guéméné, had been guided by his host through the hall of mirrors, had admired the ceiling frescos and the marionette theater, whose walls were set with seashells and precious stones, he pronounced the historic words: "This is the only place in Europe where I have found Versailles recreated." Nicholas was delighted by this praise; champagne poured freely, rockets shot into the air, music sang jubilantly.

The music? It is not without concern that we envision Master Haydn among this illustrious company. In Vienna his gifts had almost been quenched by poverty; was he to be smothered here in wealth? Fortunately for the kapellmeister, Nicholas Esterhazy, who apparently was so bent upon fame and public acknowledgment of his merits, had a dual nature. There was in him an inclination toward solitude which, twenty-five years later, after the death of his wife, was to grow into melancholia. Like so many other great lords, he loved chamber music. It served him as a sweet antidote to the loud turmoil and the obligations of hospitality. For days—even for weeks—at a time, he closeted himself with Haydn, to play his favorite instrument. This was the barytone, a now forgotten stringed instrument in the class of the viola da gamba, which was handled as is the cello. Its tone was deep yet dry, and of a silvery evanescence—a true rococo instrument which could express a delicate sadness and a muted gladness. Technically, its peculiar feature was that it was plucked far more than are modern stringed instruments. In addition to six or seven strings running over the fingerboard, there were some fourteen strings that went under the fingerboard and could not be reached by the bow. When the top strings were bowed, these lower strings vibrated sympathetically and thus altered the color of the sound; moreover, they could be plucked with the left hand, giving an effect like that of a guitar; contemporary taste considered this operation highly important, and it occasionally influenced the composer's manner.

The barytone was usually played in trios with a viola and a cello. In order to satisfy the prince's passionate love for it, Haydn wrote many barytone trios, in the course of the years. Fifty would have been a goodly number, but the actual figure was one hundred and sixty-nine. For Nicholas was insatiable in his demand for such trios; once, when Haydn did not supply enough of them, he wrote an ungracious letter to his kapellmeister admonishing that veritable prodigy of industry to be more diligent! (This, by the way, was the only disharmony that ever occurred between the prince and the composer.)

It is immaterial whether or not Haydn liked to compose for the barytone. Not only did he never tire of writing any kind of music, but he would have redoubled his labors had he been asked to do so. He was one who would have gladly married Leah to win his Rachel. The work that alone concerned him, the work that was his life's mission and which he had already conceived in his mind with a thoroughness shared by none of his contemporaries, was the symphony.

THE INVENTION OF THE SYMPHONY

HISTORICAL evidence shows that the symphony originated in the theater. It is an offshoot of the overture. Originally, the symphony was nothing more than the overture itself. "Sinfonia," wrote the Frankfurt musicologist, Martin Heinrich Fuhrmann, in 1706, "is the name given to a harmony that is played by instruments before the voices begin." In Naples, Rome, or Munich, when people went to the opera, pure instrumental music lasting ten minutes or so prepared them for the acting and the singing. It was a kind of apéritif to make the ear receptive for the grand musical banquet. It was a kind of music that had to be slight in order not to overburden the appetite.

When this sort of music began to assert its independence, it did not forget its obligations to the theater. It subsisted on the left-overs of the stage. The early symphonies bustled along—usually in three movements—always brilliant and full of dramatic excitement, ariose, according to the contrasts which were sung or represented by the characters in the theater. Any slowing of tempo or increase of profundity would have been denounced as boring.

There were thousands of overtures. Born of the love of the baroque age for festivities—going to the theater was, for example, a festive occasion, an opportunity for display—they grew in popularity from the seventeenth to the eighteenth century. In the latter century these instrumental forms were joined by the *concerto grosso,* a form of instrumental music whose inventors had realized that the instruments could serve another purpose besides that of introducing an opera. *Concerto grosso* signified "grand competition"; the form, most successfully developed by Handel, was a competition among the instruments, and behind it was the idea of bravura. The players and their instruments attempted to "combat" one another and win a kind of "victory." Essentially, then, it was the opposite of what we feel a symphony to be, for symphony means "consonance."

Overture and concerto had not yet merged when they were joined by the *orchestral suite.* The suite was indiscriminately favored by all. In castle and court it delighted the nobles; as street music it gratified burghers and lovers. As we have seen from Haydn's street serenades, it was usually divided into five parts; the first and fifth were swift and joyful, the second and fourth were minuets, and only the third was a slow movement in which the composer could show real musicianship.

These three forms—the suite, the *concerto grosso* and the overture—were taken up by a man of genius in Mannheim, Germany, about 1740, and molded into one; and out of this synthesis something entirely new arose, the modern symphony. The innovator was a Bohemian, Johann Stamitz, who lived at the court of the Count Palatine, Karl Theodor. With singular vision Stamitz foresaw that the new form would one day become the "queen of music" and would win over the opera-going public. It must be possible, he thought, without the aid of singers or of a stage, to express by pure instrumental music all that could be expressed in an opera. "Stamitz makes the instruments sing so," an admirer wrote, "that one forgets that such things as voices exist." And Charles Burney, the Englishman who had been friendly with Handel, ventured to dub Stamitz a "second Shakespeare." "As the genius of the one summed up the whole of nature," he wrote, "so the other, without deviating from nature, brought art farther than anyone before him had done."

Stamitz's manner of composing has such a kinship to Haydn's style that we must pause awhile to consider it. Both had taken from Carl Philipp Emanuel Bach the logic of the sonata form and had developed it instrumentally. In Stamitz's allegro movements there first appears a resolute principal subject; the second subject, Mennicke remarks, "is introspective and of delicate structure; it opposes to the stiff, masculine character of the principal subject the delicate sensibility of woman." Thus the thematic structure remains dualistic. In the development Master Stamitz turned away from the structure of the exposition and worked only with fragments, so that he often produced the impression of renouncing his themes. This, however, is no more than the famous "Haydn effect," in which, during an apparent digression, the listener is made to wait in suspense for the return of the original subjects. The modern quality of Stamitz's work is best exemplified by his clever use of dynamic nuances. The effect ascribed to Beethoven of a rising melodic phrase which, when it reaches its rhythmic center of gravity, does not go on into the expected forte, but instead subsides into piano, was anticipated by Stamitz.

The Mannheim composer demonstrated his brilliancy in the structure of his orchestra also. If the symphony were to outdo the opera in the eyes and the ears of the public, it would have to use a monster orchestra—and that was what Stamitz did use. In 1756 the Mannheim orchestra possessed ten first violins and ten second violins, four violas, four violoncelli, two bass-viols, two oboes, two flutes, two bassoons, four horns, and two kettledrums. Such a volume of instruments had never yet been heard; with it the composer could achieve effects of bravura and of intimate chamber music at which Europe was to marvel as it had hitherto marveled only at the vocal feats of eunuchs and female singers. It was something entirely new for the music of the concert hall to be praised in the same high terms as the opera. The "Mannheim crescendo" and the "Mannheim diminuendo," which rose to a zenith or fell to a nadir over dozens of bars, became æsthetics concepts. The Swabian poet, Daniel Schubart, who was also a good musician, declared that no other orchestra in the world surpassed that of Mannheim. "Its forte is thunderous, its crescendo like a cataract, its diminuendo a crystalline stream lapping over the rocks in the distance, its piano a spring breeze. The wind instruments are all used just as they should be used; they raise and carry or fill and animate the tempest of the violins." Tempest of violins! The emotionality of this phrase, coined by Daniel Schubart, should not strike us as unusual. For nothing could more adequately denote the value of Stamitz's style.

He had just begun to be a "symphonist of emotion" when he died in 1756; he was not yet forty. Who was the genius to carry on his work? In Vienna similar tendencies were prevalent, but the noblemen who paid for music were reluctant to sacrifice the ornate and amusing for the sake of a new emotionality and subjectivity; the populace, with its liking for crudity and superficiality, was even less so inclined. Moreover, there was a third institution opposed to the symphony—the mass. Ecclesiastical music was at that time not austere, but secular and glittering, and as such it detracted from the trend toward this new form, which was boldly laying claim to be a complete work of art. The talented Viennese composers of symphonies, Matthias Monn and Wagenseil, encountered many difficulties.

But Haydn found little trouble. Far from the world's business, wholly unaffected by the whims of a Viennese or a Mannheim public, he could experiment as if there were no public at all. "No one about me could torment me and make me doubt myself, and so I could not help becoming original," he said later. "As director of an orchestra I could make experiments; I could observe what evoked the impression and what weakened it; and thus I could improve, add, take away and venture what I would."

Haydn did, of course, have an excellent amateur public, Prince Nicholas Esterhazy and his guests of the moment. And he was fortunate in that all these people (whether out of real understanding or chiefly out of snobbery) praised everything he wrote. He composed under contract, of course—but even in retrospect we scarcely wish to think what the alternative might have been had he rebelled against the contract and all its terms. We are grateful that such was not the outcome of his "enslavement." For Haydn had in mind something entirely different from light entertainment for the prince. He was concerned with the symphony as an art form and with the soul of music.

When Haydn took possession of the symphony in order to reform it, he stripped it of the last relics of its theatrical origins. Every memory that the symphony had ever been allied with the drama was obliterated. This statement would seem to be contradicted by his introduction of symphonic material into the intermezzos which he had to write for the prince's theater (such as the music to the comedy *Il Distratto*). Actually, this proves only that the theater music which Haydn wrote to order was not always very theatrical. For he was a thoroughly epic artist; all his symphonies are epic in character.

In a symphony, he decided, there must be no *action,* but solely *narration.* The instruments were not to act out a drama; they were to narrate, to weave a tale. No musician before Haydn's time developed so sovereign a command of the technique of story-telling, of the tricks of "interrupting," of introducing a "new thread" or an "episode." Seventeen years after Haydn's death the French composer Henri Berton wrote (although he was not, significantly, a symphonist himself, but an operatic composer): *"Avec quel art Haydn sait établir un motif, le presenter sur toutes ses faces, l'abandonner un moment, et le faire reparaître en suite avec un nouveau charme."* * Berton actually sug-

* "With what artistry Haydn contrives to establish a theme, to present it in all its facets, to abandon it for a moment, and then to bring it back with a novel charm."

gested that "Haydn's symphonic principles be applied to the opera." (Though this would have been a mistake.)

The dramatic and the epic styles are fundamentally different. Haydn's symphonic structure is Homeric; it moves along with a restrained energy, like a sweeping series of hexameters. And even where this music is very fast, the presto movements do not give the feeling of presto. The sensibility of an epic artist and the gesturing of a narrator are so prevalent throughout Haydn's work that even his fastest *tempi* are felt as somewhat deliberate. ("Deliberate" was his favorite word.)

The full force of this "narrator's gesturing" can be measured by the disparity between the music of Haydn and of Mozart and the symphonies of Beethoven. The Romantic writer, E. T. A. Hoffmann, heard in Beethoven's instrumental music "unappeasable unrest . . . continuous, ever-mounting thrusting and surging." This was certainly revolt against the objectivity and "orderly narrative tone" of Haydn. After Beethoven had learned from Haydn everything there was to learn, he shifted ground and overthrew the Haydn type of symphony because it was no longer suitable for him. In the beginning, however, this did not mean that Beethoven made the symphony once more a vehicle of the drama. For he, too, knew that the symphony was not designed to express the dialectic nature of a play. Beethoven's great innovation upon the work of Haydn consisted rather in the fact that the symphonies of his maturity were *subjective* narrations in whose tormented emotions the listener participated. Later on Beethoven reversed this technique once more. In his last symphony, the Ninth, narrative and epic character are absent; what exists is the dramatic situation, charged with electricity which at any moment may discharge in new and more thunderous blasts.

Haydn, however, remained objective and never permitted himself to color a tonal narrative with too much subjectivity—or, at least, not for any considerable space. When the orchestral instruments converse among themselves, the conversation remains on an epic plane, although there is still in it a touch of the slight rococo comedy, of Goldoni and other Venetians. With Haydn all agitation is resolved; he is an epic singer "who wishes to give men a foretaste of the uncontentious joys of Paradise."

This he accomplished, and the pleasure he took in striving toward that goal accounts for his marvelous fertility, which is indeed one of the greatest miracles of art. So unbelievably rich is the harvest of his works, one is forced to imagine that every year had for him four springs, sixteen summers and thirty-two autumns. He wrote one hundred and four symphonies—forty in the seventeen-sixties, thirty in the seventies, twenty in the eighties and, in the early nineties, in London, an additional twelve.

The decreases in quantity indicate that he made the problems of conception and composition increasingly difficult for himself, thus fortifying the challenge. Still, there was incredible productivity. Beethoven wrote nine symphonies. He lived to be only half the age of Haydn. That means that he might have written eighteen, if the symphony had had for him the same attraction as it had for his teacher. But therein lay the difference between the two. The tremendous psychic energy with which Beethoven freighted his symphonies might perhaps be discharged nine times, but certainly could not fill one hundred and four works of tranquil narrative art.

But neither the symphonies of Beethoven nor those of any other composer would have been possible without Haydn's reform of the form.

THE SYMPHONIC CONTINENT

To STEP into the symphonic world of Haydn is to enter a continent of music, a great land mass in which every sort of life exists in every imaginable variation, every stage of development, species, and form. It is a life that seems to have sprung directly from the hand of God; virginal, with the morning dew still upon it; unsullied and merry; woods, shrubs, meadows, and brooks, all ringing with the glad cries of birds and beasts; sunlit cornfields in which the scythe hisses softly; breezes that gently ruffle the bright foliage and the darker evergreen masses covering distant hills, and that produce constant changes of color. It is an ideal landscape, lacking only high mountains and the ocean. But there is no lack of evening mists, of the solemnity of the starlit night, and of the certainty that dawn will come again. All this is unmistakably Haydnesque. His music is that of a healthier, more vigorous elder brother of Mozart's.

The basic stuff of Haydn's symphonies, however, is not simply melody but the manipulation of subjects and motifs. At first hesitantly, but later consciously, Haydn obeyed the artistic principle of "not writing down a single note which does not emerge of itself from the working out." This is an austere ideal, intensely formalistic. It seems to contravene the free exercise of imagination and invention. But the opposition is only apparent, for it is the conjunction of imagination with this severity which produced the characteristic tone of Haydn's style.

How long did it take Haydn to develop this typical style of his? The problem has puzzled his lovers, who are many. Haydn made his greatest discoveries in his old age, when Mozart was already dead. The hardships besetting his youthful life were partly responsible for his slow growth in artistry; but I believe that the leisureliness with which the "real Haydn" developed was due to another cause: The secret biological awareness that he had eight decades to live. He had no need for haste.

Although up to his thirty-fifth year Haydn manifested none or very few of the traits of original genius, that by no means implies that his production until then was merely imitative. Haydn was not an eclectic; rather, he was an incessant experimenter who assembled all the known techniques before him and asked himself, "What shall I use today for this specific purpose?" Such is not the manner of an imitator, but of a researcher, of a man who is always learning. And for the most part he learned from himself!

Hermann Kretzschmar has emphasized the fact that only in composing the symphonies of the middle period did the principle of working with motifs occur to Haydn, and Adolf Sandberger has made the same observation about the master's quartets. In reality, Haydn had much earlier insights into the course of his reforms, although he did not invariably pursue that direction. At any rate, Georg Schuenemann has correctly pointed out that there is much more in common between the young and the old Haydn than is generally assumed. Just as we find the air of youthful insouciance in his later symphonies, so we also often find strict working-out of motifs in the early ones. *Nec natura nec Haydn faciunt saltus*—"neither nature nor Haydn proceed by leaps." Both "develop."

Let us see how Haydn develops: For example, in the finale of his eleventh symphony he has the rather simple subject:

What does he do with this theme? The wheelwright's son dissects it, in truly artisan fashion, into its smallest components, and obtains from each fragment new material for construction. We can count no less than nine fragments which he uses as motifs (*see next page*).

Schuenemann justly sees in this "the dawn of creation in miniature, with motifs in Haydn's symphonic art"—and yet, this symphony is one of his earliest.

The earliest symphonies have three, or sometimes five, movements. Later, Haydn settled upon four, not because his predecessors

A)
B)
C) VIOL. I
VIOL. II
D)
E)
tr
F)
G)
H)
B — — B —
I)

in Mannheim and Vienna had chosen that number but for another reason, which also operated in his quartets. The first movement is nearly always a vigorous, sustained allegro, the pattern of a piano sonata, after the manner of Haydn's teacher, C. P. E. Bach. First the main theme enters; a strongly contrasting motif meets it in the dominant; toward the end a third subject is introduced. Free transitional passages link the various motifs, and close this first part in the key of the dominant. The second part provides the working-out and development of the motifs, and terminates in a coda which once more recapitulates the principal subjects in suggestively condensed form.

The second movement of a Haydn symphony is always slow. He had the courage to try an *adagio* and, moreover, *adagio espressivo*. The slow movement, of course, had already been used in the operatic symphony, but there it was usually a *grave* which was introduced for purposes of effect; it was, so to speak, a portal whose slowly opening doors let in the *presto* for which the audience was waiting and which would soon carry the field by storm. With Haydn there is no ulterior purpose of providing contrast. His slow movements are absolutes. They are instrumental songs, pure effusions of the soul which explore a wide range of emotional experience; hope and renunciation, fulfillment and yearning, are placed side by side. Haydn's knowledge of the potentialities of minor keys grew as he composed more of these *adagios*.

The third movement Haydn usually arranged as a minuet, as Stamitz had done before him. The probable reasons for this are several: The public for which he wrote, the prince or, better, his noble guests, were probably not unqualified admirers of *adagio* movements. The *adagio* was unfortunately middle-class and pensive; it evoked the mood of someone sitting still, hand to brow, on a pavilion bench. The minuet, however, was the vehicle for courtly and complacent images of ladies and gentlemen moving in formal dance patterns. This is what Haydn wished the third movement to connote; the minuet turned its back upon thorny problems and presented a life which was established and light-hearted.

Some of Haydn's contemporaries were not at all in sympathy with this practice. "Minuets in a symphony," wrote the famous Leipzig organist and critic, Johann Adam Hiller, "affect us like rouge on the face of a man; they give the piece a dandified appearance and impair the masculine impression which the uninterrupted succession of three related serious movements always makes." To censure Haydn as a panderer to the style of gallantry was not at all fair. Had these serious listeners listened a little more closely, they would have discovered something strange about Haydn's minuets: That in these third movements fate—or, if we will, Haydn's own temperament—was playing him a trick. Close listening reveals that these minuets are not real minuets at all. Inescapably they suggest that the dancers are people for whom dancing is an unwonted art. It is, in fact, the *Third Estate* dancing, the class to which Haydn belonged; it is the common people trying to accommodate their clodhopping style to the delicate figures of the courtly minuet. Haydn was, to be sure, living like a courtier himself; he did not feel toward the minuet that special malice that his younger brother Mozart evinced toward the aristocratic dance in the second act of *Don Giovanni,* written on the eve of the French Revolution. Don Giovanni, representing manhood, Don Ottavio as flower of knighthood, Donna Anna as dignified woman, and Donna Elvira as grand lady, are dancing the noblest minuet ever conceived—when suddenly the two clowns, Leporello and Masetto, burst in and start stamping a clumsy *Ländler,* a kind of village waltz that was bound to put the aristocratic minuet to rout for good and all. Haydn was not capable of such mischief; yet Wagner, who generally showed no great understanding of Haydn's genius, clearly saw that Haydn's third movements were not minuets but "exuberant *Ländler.*" Their tone made the greatest impress upon Beethoven, who was amused by the secret discrepancy between the minuet form and the peasant dance in Haydn's music. And so, in his symphonies, Beethoven simply struck out the word "minuet" and entitled the movement *scherzo,*—"joke."

Haydn usually composed the fourth movement of his symphonies as a *presto* in rondo form. The mainspring and the meaning of these movements was *joie de vivre.* As if he had restrained himself in the previous movements, in the finale all the horses seemed to run away with him. (Yet this was only seeming; the *presto* movement is as carefully worked out as the *adagio.*) It was in these fourth movements that Haydn most frequently incorporated melodies he had picked up in taverns and on the street—it was not the use of them, but the transformation of these popular songs, which but for Haydn would have been forgotten long ago, that was the astonishing thing.

Just as some painters prefer particular colors, so some composers prefer particular keys. In the cases of certain painters, the rationale for their preference is quite clear. A whole series of definable reasons operates, from psycho-physiological compulsions and philosophical convictions down to plain laziness about cleaning the brush. With composers, the lasting preference for a key is harder to explain. Alfred Einstein attempted to explain Mozart's preferences; no explanation has been found as yet for Haydn's. The fact remains that more than one quarter of his symphonies are in the key of D-major. What can this mean? Is that key the "ultimate" to which the master always returned, after all digressions and modulations? Did it have for him the "harsh glare of reality" which has been ascribed to it? Did it denote for him, as it did for Richard Strauss, the having done with heaviness and doubt and the return to a "simple, manly certainty," as did the song of the painter Barak in *Frau ohne Schatten?* Perhaps. But possibly such a preference was based on considerations of technique also. Stringed instruments sound good in D, and, most significantly, the eighteenth-century trumpet was keyed in D; and that was an important factor for Haydn. Even while he developed the potentialities of the strings, he simultaneously extended the use of the horns. Although his symphonic ideas were strongly influenced by his "pianistic ear" and still more by the resources of the string quartet, the symphonies were nevertheless far from being conceived as chamber music; at every moment his symphonies remained "orchestral complete works."

For Haydn is the father of modern orchestration. His ear perceived greater distinctions, was capable of more differentiation, than that of any other composer before Mozart. The orchestration of the baroque age sought to achieve a stiff, terraced effect—which was consonant with its respect for "dignity" and social distinctions. Sharp, angular, and piercing tones that went ill together were actually sought for; otherwise, it was believed, "the architectonic structure could not be made sufficiently distinct." That "jump in music" of which Guido Adler has spoken, the revolution of style that began about 1750, was above all a change in the "ear"; it involved a different way of hearing. Music ceased to be judged by structure; instead, its emotional quality was prized, and the sensuous individuality of the instruments became the important feature. Instead of the stiff and unexpressive sound of baroque horns, the lyric tone of the strings was now preferred. According to the temper of the times, the strings were better fitted than the horns for the expression of personal feeling. (Later in the romantic era, this was to change again.) The similarity of the violin's sound to the vibrations of the human voice recommended it to Haydn. He made his instruments "sing" because he saw in them "enchanted" human beings; he conceived of them as individuals. He achieved an intimate relationship with each instrument, and was constantly concerned with each instrument's physiological and psychological expressiveness; and he taught composers, down to modern times, which ideas, for example, should be entrusted to which instruments.

In spite of the revaluations of musical style that were undertaken by the Romantics and by Wagner, we still profit today from Haydn's "ideal of saturation." This ideal consisted of allowing each separate instrument to show its individual hard tonal contour, but at the same time having it supported by the social community of the other instruments. Only an incredibly sensitive ear could replace the orchestral hierarchy of the baroque age by the *consonance* of classicism, and Haydn had such an ear. Where the baroque composers plumed themselves on their horn solos, Haydn recognized that giving great prominence to a single instrument was a violation of the essential idea of the symphony; he deliberately blurred the special tonal color of the horns by the use of accompanying strings. Yet he had nothing against the horns. Though he deprived them of their "full" voices, of their solitary glory, he assigned to them new tasks. It was he who first really "discovered" the romantic French horn. This horn, with its faculty for softening tones and drawing them out, became, as it were, the pedal of the orchestra, animating and saturating the whole. Until Haydn's time the violas were slavishly bound to the bass viols or the first violins, and served to bridge the differentiation between high and low pitch; Haydn liberated them.

Today all these things are taken for granted—but someone had to be born who for the first time would hear music as we do. There is a peculiar feature about this matter of hearing. Like every great innovator, like Handel, Beethoven, or Wagner, Haydn not only had a more delicate sense of hearing than his contemporaries, but also, when necessary, a coarser ear—that is to say, he bluntly opposed their so-called refinements and feeble idiosyncrasies with a healthy and ruthless "I don't understand that." Without this sort of not-understanding, no artistic progress is possible. The gallant style, for example, would not have the first violin and violoncello present octave passages; *that* "offended the ear." Haydn laughed at this, and wrote octave passages whenever he had the impulse. Twenty years later no one could recall that it had once been forbidden.

And for all his consciousness of his strength, Haydn possessed the humility of a man who knew how short is life and how long is art. "Am I to die now?" he lamented, when he was nearly eighty, to the pianist Kalkbrenner. "And I have just begun to understand the wind instruments." This recalls the parallel words of the great English master who in his eightieth year wanted "to begin really painting at last." It is also the feeling of a father who wants to do something for his children; all his life Haydn acted with paternal tenderness toward the instruments. When Anton Weidinger, a Viennese maker of instruments, invented the keyed trumpet, the sixty-five-year-old Haydn promptly sat down to provide the newborn instrument with a fitting *concerto.* He tried to be just to each one instrument in turn, to make none feel scorned, to provide for all. Often we imagine that Haydn loved the members of his orchestra (about whose selection and hiring he had much to say), so that he wished to do each of them a personal kindness. While this may seem to be putting too familiar an interpretation upon the matter, we must remember that the factors of kindly domesticity were more important in the life of Haydn than in that of any other musician.

Haydn's way of jesting exhibits, perhaps, in purest form the paternal meaning of his art. He liked to toss a theme among the instruments like a ball. The ball must never touch ground; the instruments would have their jest; and Master Haydn, most of all, would enjoy it.

Humor so predominates in Haydn's music that in spite of the noble gravity that distinguishes his symphonic productions, his contemporaries not only smiled but often laughed outright—laughed as the King of Spain had laughed over *Don Quixote,* as the eighteenth century laughed over Laurence Sterne and the nineteenth over Gottfried Keller. It was the sort of laughter only a great, profound, and yet comic creative artist can inspire. Haydn did not achieve his humorous effects by instrumental jests alone; he concealed a wealth of jokes within his melodic structure. It was as though he was hiding Easter eggs for children. Every listener becomes a child, finds something, and shouts "I have it!" A few of Haydn's most famous effects were produced by interpolating, in the middle of a serious passage, a bit which gives the impression of a slip of the pen. The listener hears it at once, and the incongruity produces an immediate, comical effect. Such practices were common in the comic opera. We recall, for example, the duet of Almaviva and Susanne, in *Figaro,* in which Susanne by mistake says "No!" when she ought to say "Yes." Haydn, thirty years before Mozart, introduced this same drollery in his first symphony; in a G-major andante he creates a surprising hiatus by the use of an A-major chord:

Karl Geiringer has pointed out a number of other such surprise effects. Haydn is no dramatist; his developments are epic in character; his "dramatic movements" are really the "abrupt transitions of a narrator." They are, in the words of Sir Donald Tovey, the greatest student of Haydn of our century, "the tersest thing in the fine arts: the movement of the short story." It is precisely because Haydn is a born narrator that he is aware of the perils and the possible boredom that lie in the use of the flowing epic line. He interrupts it in a hundred places by the element of surprise. There is, for example, the technique of the "mock recapitulation." The listener is led to believe that the music is returning to the keynote and the principal subject, but he soon finds that he is mistaken. The composer lures him almost all the way back, and then at the last moment carries him away again. With perfectly innocuous means Haydn often achieved his greatest effects. We know that his popularity in England was due largely to the sudden, wholly unexpected drumbeat in the *andante* of the *Surprise Sym-*

phony (No. 94). At the first performance, it is said, the audience started out of their seats. In reality, Haydn had used this device of a sudden drum-forte much earlier, in his sixtieth symphony. The technique of surprise effects can be found throughout his symphonies.

The spiritual content of his symphonies was, of course, different in his sixties from what it had been in his thirties. Between 1763 and 1793, tremendous historic events took place in Europe. Even a man who lived in isolation and absorbed completely in his art, could not help being moved by them. In his early symphonies Haydn took leave of the rococo temper, and asserted the strength and vigorous character of the middle class. In any case, Haydn's temperament, conditioned by his origins, had never been very close to the rococo, although he outwardly gave it its due. In the seventeen-seventies his art showed certain parallels to the "Storm and Stress" period of contemporary literature. Sighing, syncopations, lamentations, vows, tears, the restlessness of night, and a sense of momentous change, can be felt in his symphonies; he went in for "Wertherism" in a way which had no precedent in his early period. Most of the symphonies that he wrote between 1770 and 1780 present moods of melancholy succeeded by strong passion. The cheerful keys of his youth became clouded; he suddenly began to write symphonies in C-minor, E-minor, F-minor, F-sharp minor. He wrote a *Mourning Symphony* (No. 44) and asked that its E-minor *adagio* be played at his own funeral. Although he was in perfect health and had almost forty years to live, his music suggested the dark tones of a burial; it was full of pathos and heroics.

Was this solely due to the literary fashion of the day? Outwardly, Haydn had had no experiences that might have justified such a mood. But about that time, groups of players were invited to Esterhaz. It happens that their repertory is known to us. They performed *Julius von Tarent,* a Renaissance tragedy by Leisewitz, one of the dramatists of the German "Storm and Stress" school. Far more important, they also played Goethe's *Götz von Berlichingen,* the story of that stout-hearted man who would not stoop before injustice. And, above all, they presented *Hamlet, King Lear* and other plays of Shakespeare.

Haydn was poorly educated. It is not known that he read any books beyond the Bible, some volumes of musical theory, and a few Latin texts. But he had only to enter the world of the drama to be gripped by it. This naïve, wonderful child, who himself was so great an artist, identified himself completely with the plays he witnessed.

When *King Lear* was shown at Esterhaz, Haydn at once wrote an overture, and an intermezzo with many chromatic expressions which he entitled *Hatred for Ingratitude*. Lear's daughters had fascinated him, and, of course, he wrote a *Lear's Madness* and *The Storm on the Heath* also. Haydn, whom life had scarcely tried, who was the soul of tranquillity, was shaken to the core by these vicarious experiences; his emotion is reflected in his musical writings which have passages so subjective that they sometimes seem to anticipate Beethoven. But at this time Beethoven was still unborn, or only an infant.

In the seventeen-eighties the "Storm and Stress," which had so suddenly cropped up in Haydn's work, as suddenly disappeared. Haydn again resumed his peaceful way. Had the clarity of his younger brother Mozart released the elder master from confusion and turmoil? But what can we know of the tensions that existed within the heart of an artist who lived entirely within himself and was outwardly nothing but a quiet burgher and a smiling courtier?

And then Mozart died. Haydn entered the nineties completely alone, and became, with his London symphonies which were called "incomparable," the most famous composer in the world. But he had been famous earlier. In the eighties the "Spiritual Concerts" of Paris had ordered eleven symphonies from him; in the seventies he was very well known in Germany; and as early as the sixties his reputation had spread throughout Austria. This is surprising, for, in spite of his cautious manner, he was definitely an innovator, and the masses have seldom been so musical that they have welcomed innovators. There must have been private traits in his music, middle-class traits, which endeared him so much to people—people which, apparently, could not be reached by Mozart's immaculate canon of beauty or, later, by Beethoven's passionate pride.

Men cannot endure perfection; it does not console them. If Beethoven wrote music for Titans, then Mozart wrote for gods. "I can't stand Mozart's perfect cadenzas," a modern composer once exclaimed. Haydn's art did not disturb anyone by its superhuman features, as did Beethoven's, nor did it have the geometrical perfection, the Olympian serenity, and the ethereal lightness which seemingly bewildered the public in Mozart's music. Somehow Haydn represented more universal, if more average, feelings; though his art was profound and pure, it could, nevertheless, be lived with on familiar terms, and its creator was felt to be a fellow human being.

PRIVATE LIFE OF A GENIUS

WHAT was it like, the everyday life of this genius in Eisenstadt and Esterhaz, outside his brief duty of standing in blue frock-coat in the antechamber, to wait upon his prince, or conducting the band, of evenings?

When young Haydn came to Eisenstadt, it was a sleepy, small town containing not many more than five hundred houses. Each household knew its neighbor's business. The life of the townsfolk, the butchers, shoemakers, and grocers, flowed along at an even pace. Mornings and evenings one could hear the cows lowing, for a number of the people of rank conducted farming operations. The most prominent building of the town was the prince's castle. Its square towers, roofed with copper and tin, glittered brilliantly. Originally there had been a moat and a medieval drawbridge for defense against besiegers, but in the eighteenth century they were removed. Upon an artificially created height stood the famous Bergkirche where Haydn directed masses and where he lies buried.

Of Eisenstadt's five thousand inhabitants, one minority spoke Hungarian and called the town Kiss-Marton, which means "Little Martin." There was another minority who were the subject of much talk; they dwelt in the age-old Jewish quarter, and the patriarchal families were ranged in a hierarchy which was an imitation in miniature of Christian Eisenstadt. The Eisenstadt synagogue produced a number of famous rabbis and scholars who had dispersed all over Europe; among them were Samson Wertheimer and Meir ben Isaak.

When Joseph Haydn and his wife, Anna Aloysia, came to Eisenstadt in 1761, they lived, as did the other members of the prince's band, in the "music building," a stately edifice near the church. In this house were quartered all the men who, with the passage of years, were to become Haydn's friends: The drummer Adamus Sturm, the first violinist Tomasini, the oboists Braun and Kreibig, the tenors Diezl and Friberth, the gifted cellist Josef Weigl and his wife, Barbara

Scheffstoss, who was a singer; later these were joined by Anton and Michael Prinster, first-rate horn-players. Michael Prinster was among the longest-lived veterans of Haydn's band. As late as 1868 he used to bask in the sunlight in the courtyard of the "music building," his velvet cap tilted over his ear and his snuff-box in his hand, and talk about Haydn.

The closeness of the quarters and the thinness of the walls made life in the little artists' colony somewhat difficult. Children screamed, women quarreled, noises of housekeeping mingled with the *études* of the practicing musicians. Fiddling and tooting went on incessantly from morning to night. There was a special rehearsal hall at the kapellmeister's disposal. However, the main orchestral rehearsals or the opera rehearsals were held in the castle.

Obviously, Haydn did not have friends only in Eisenstadt. The prince's First Kapellmeister, the old invalid, Gregorius Werner, who also lived in the musicians' building looked askance at this vice-kapellmeister whose artistic stature was far above his. In his youth Werner had studied under Fux, the famous kapellmeister of Charles VI, and he had written highly esteemed church music as well as a musical joke called *The Vienna Peddler's Market* which was fresh, talented and witty. But in his old age he became conservative; he spoke derogatorily of Haydn, calling him "fashion plate" and "organ grinder." In 1766 the deaf and embittered man died. The inscription on his grave is a pungent example of eighteenth-century attitudes toward death, humor and music:

> Here lies a choir-master who served for many a year
> A noble, princely house; his tunes no more we'll hear.
> B-minor and the sharps always gave him fearful pain,
> He never knew how to resolve them, or where to begin again,
> Until he learned the art of waiting patiently,
> And then he waited all his life, nor better hoped to be.
> But to Thee, Almighty God,
> Pleadeth now this humble clod,
> That of the dissonances
> He wrote ere he went hence
> Thou wilt make consonances
> To bless his penitence.
> Since with his latest cadence he fell into the grave,
> For this good end canst Thou his former follies waive.

O Saviour, take him up into Thy heavenly choir
Which never eye shall see, nor human ear admire.
And when the trumpet blast
Calls all to Judgment Day,
Let him not be outcast;
Beside Thee let him stay.

When Gregorius Werner died, the Haydns did not move into his quarters but into a newly purchased house where the composer hoped to have more peace and quiet than had hitherto been granted to him. The house he purchased was No. 82 Klostergasse. In the Eisenstadt land records it is described as having two stories and being a comfortable dwelling with two large, stuccoed rooms. On the ground floor were porch, bedrooms, kitchen, vestibule, and shed; on the other side of its yard was a small barn with room for a cow and a calf. Also belonging to the house was a kitchen garden on the outskirts of the town, a few vineyards, several parcels of woods, and a pasture. All this was transferred on May 2, 1766, to Kapellmeister Joseph Haydn.

He had hoped for an idyllic life here, but, unfortunately, he found himself among malicious neighbors. The home of Magdalena Frumwald adjoined that of the Haydns; on the other side lived Theresa Späch. These two women, with Anna Aloysia, formed a trio whose furious quarrels shattered the quiet which Haydn needed for his work. One morning, at half-past five, Frau Frumwald, in order to annoy the Haydns, had a mason begin tearing down her chimney. The bricks rained furiously down on the Haydns' roof. On April 29, 1769, Kapellmeister Haydn lodged in the Eisenstadt court a complaint against Frau Frumwald. His petition demanded a legal decision on the question whether Frau Frumwald was justified in having her chimney torn down, and asked for a ruling on the ownership of the fire wall that had been erected between the two houses. The suit dragged out for four years, to the delight of the lawyers. We do not know the outcome. Two years later, however, the other neighbor, Frau Späch, brought suit against Haydn for having erected a roof which deprived her house of light.

Being wedged in between such neighbors could not be very pleasant for a creative artist. Haydn was glad to sell the house, and in 1778 he made it over to the bookkeeper Liechtscheidl for no more than two thousand gulden. It had cost him far more than that, for it had twice been burned down in the great fires that had devastated Eisenstadt.

Haydn had suffered a loss of almost one thousand two hundred gulden, and received no compensation. One hundred and four houses had burned down, and since the town was not very wealthy and had too many wounds to bind, Haydn received (as the town archives indicate) twenty-six and a half gulden in total compensation. The worst damage, however, was not that to the burned furniture, but the incalculable loss of many music manuscripts. Burgenland had not been devastated by the enemy; but the two terrible fires had caused Eisenstadt also to pay its toll to the times.

It is the common fate of a genius to suffer along with the world in which he lives. Haydn's spirit would have been unassailable had he had a loving wife to share his bed and board, but his marriage with Anna Aloysia deteriorated year after year. That Anna was shrewish, we know, and the more meekly Haydn bore himself the more violent she became. According to Haydn's pupil Neukomm, she was also extravagant. But, above all, she was jealous, and that at a time when she had as yet no reason to be. It is scarcely likely that in the first decade of his marriage, Haydn sought pleasures outside of the marital bond. He wished greatly for children. The fact that his wife bore him none did more to undermine the marriage than did Anna Aloysia's character. "She was incapable of bearing children," he later said to Griesinger, "and therefore I was less indifferent to the attractions of other females." Anna's extravagance was linked to her unusual bigotry, among other things; she constantly invited clerics to their table, and, behind Haydn's back, paid for countless masses. Because of these habits, for years he found it necessary to conceal his income from her. As she could not get enough money out of him to meet her demands, she insisted that he give her sacred compositions, which she then gave away to ecclesiastical institutions. On the other hand, Anna was more than indifferent to his music. It did not matter at all to her, Haydn complained, whether her husband was an artist or a cobbler. Was this malice, or merely stupidity, in her? Michael Prinster declares that this loving wife even used some of Haydn's scores for hair-curlers, and that others went into the oven as lining for her cake-tins. Whether or not this is true, it is characteristic of Haydn's Christian forbearance that in describing his spouse to others he usually used no stronger an expression than "frivolity." He was not always forbearing, however; we shall see that the intensity of his feelings could sometimes provoke a phrase like *bestia infernale*.

Unfortunately, he had no one with whom he could share his woe. His father he had lost in September, 1763. Shortly before death the wheelwright had come to the palace in Eisenstadt for a visit; he had admired his son in his blue velvet coat, and had actually heard him praised by His Highness the prince in person. Back at Rohrau and resuming his trade, he had suffered a fatal accident. A great heap of wood in the workshop collapsed and crushed the artisan's ribs. Mathias Haydn left behind him a horde of children. His son, the great composer, was to have none at all. Soon after his father's death, Haydn took the youngest of his orphaned brothers, Johann Evangelist, into the prince's musical establishment, in order to have the boy near him and under his guidance. His favorite brother, Michael, now cathedral kapellmeister at Salzburg, was far away, and Haydn felt very lonely.

Children, children . . . In winter, when he looked out of his window, Haydn saw them going to school. He smelled the roasted apples which they bit with small, white teeth. He heard their high, thin cries as they, dressed in warm jackets and fluffy fur caps, skated over the ice. He was enchanted with children as Brahms was later. And it is to this trait of his that we owe a splendid jest, the *Toy Symphony*.

At a carnival Haydn had met a group of children who were not content with the usual methods of producing noise, but had sought more complicated ways. They had gone up to a peddler who was selling noisemakers—a tin cuckoo, a night-owl, bugles, rattles, drums and cymbals—and, since they had no money, implored him to lend them some instruments, "just for a little while." Haydn, passing by, had a sudden inspiration; he would make an experiment. If children could play on the stage—he thought of Kurz-Bernardon and his troupe of child actors—why should they not form a band? He bought the toy instruments for them, and asked them to go on playing. Listening, he perceived that there were laws even for this infernal din. These toys were pitched differently from orthodox instruments. Haydn bought for himself another batch of noisemakers, bundled them up, and at home, began in all seriousness to compose a symphony for them. As cement for the whole he added a bass viol and two violins which were keyed in G and E, to play a cuckoo motif. Trumpets and drums sounded in G, and the quail called in F. He arranged that the last movement was to be played three times—as a *moderato*, *allegro* and *presto.* After he had arranged the instrumentation with enjoyment and acuteness, he called his orchestra to an important rehearsal on the following morning. We can imagine the musicians' amazement when their conductor handed out a dozen preposterous instruments! Was it not beneath their dignity to raise these things to their lips? The master pointed out to them that the music sounded good; he urged them to forget their "silly seriousness"; music could also be something amusing, he said.

We do not know whether the musicians were outfitted in children's clothes at the first performance; later this became customary. The work was performed everywhere for adults, as a "carnival jest." But it still sounds best when it is performed by a miniature orchestra of nine- and ten-year-old children.

Thus humor helped the master to shake off the sadness of his domestic life. Haydn broke through the barrier of his personal isolation and formed intimacies with a number of persons who, though they did not become his nearest and dearest, nevertheless were very close to him. The forty-year-old composer had no family, but he enjoyed the largest of families in the people of Eisenstadt. There his position was undoubtedly much like that of Wagner's Hans Sachs in old Nuremberg—and this at a time when he was in the prime of life and had not a single gray hair. He drank with the people in the "Angel" tavern, and watched the draymen and peasants who came in from the surrounding country. He listened intelligently when the talk turned to the harvests, the rise and fall of prices, the deaths of cattle, and marriages and births. The people liked him as one of their own, and when a friendly butcher requested some music for his daughter's wedding, Haydn served him as well as if the client were Prince Esterhazy himself. Such was the origin of the *Ox Minuet,* so called because the pay was in kind—or, rather, in kine. One fine moonlit night Haydn heard a lowing in front of his window. A noble ox, its horns adorned with green garlands and wearing a beribboned hat on its head, was led into his yard; this was the pay for his minuet.

Haydn sometimes composed clockwork flute pieces for his friend, Gassmann, the Vienna court kapellmeister. These are based on homely and provincial subject matter; among them are the *Kaffeeklatsch,* the *Quail Call,* and other imitations of nature.

The worries of people in a country town are always connected with the weather. Therefore, Haydn's music usually contains an initial glance at the weather. The symphonies reflect the season of their composition. Are they of harvest time? Then a number of symphonic measures will reflect the glowing weather of August and the vigorous light of September. October marks the grape harvest; in November outdoor work is over, and the spinning wheel begins its labors. In his old age Haydn was to celebrate pastoral life in Homeric fashion in *The Seasons*. At present, however, he was still young; every moment that was not spent in waiting on the prince, or scribbling a host of notes on paper with his goose-quill, was passed in the open air. As long as sixty years after Haydn's death, the Croats of the vicinity, Kuhač tells us, used to praise a robust man by saying of him: *To je lovac i ribar kao Haydn.* ("He is as good a hunter and fisherman as Haydn.") We can see Haydn, the huntsman, an hour before dawn, a frequenter of the dense, mist-blanketed thickets of reed from which the birds fly up with a rush of wings at the gun's first report. His music also knows the frost of the winter, so keen in this country; the snow-storms, which overnight bury whole villages so completely that only their chimneys can be seen, like isolated milestones. And Haydn, the man, knew the January sun, the wonderful noonday sun which transformed the whole landscape into a C-major white.

In the month of March we can see Haydn going out to the heath in the twilight mist to pay a visit to the gypsies' carts. He approaches, is known to them, and invited to share their savory stews cooked in battered pots. Ragged children flock around him; in return for a few coins these exotic, much-traveled people play their melancholy songs for him; he transcribes them, takes the notes home with him and incorporates the melodies into his own work—all this eighty years before Liszt!

Haydn's life was never dull, even when *le grand monde* was not present—in any case, it was never far off. Overnight the prince might order a magnificent festival to be prepared. Or Haydn and his musicians would be loaded into coaches and taken to Pressburg for two weeks to assist Prince Anton Grassalkovicz, whose theater gave such magnificent performances that they were talked of for years afterward.

Nicholas the Splendid conjured up the grandest of his festivals for the Empress Maria Theresa when she paid her first visit to Esterhaz on September 1, 1773. The great palace had been standing for many years, and now, at last, she came, accompanied by a large retinue, to honor her faithful paladin and "see with her own eyes all the marvels of which she had been told." In her entourage there were all of three archduchesses, with her son-in-law Albert of Sachsen-Teschen and her younger son Maximilian—an elect company, indeed!

Prince Nicholas had ridden out as far as Oedenburg to meet the empress. Thousands of country people in Magyar costumes lined the road that led from the town southwest to the shore of Neusiedler Lake. There stood the palace, waiting "to be laid at the monarch's feet." Maria Theresa admired the fairyland quality of the buildings, the beauty of the temples to Phoebus and Diana, the paintings and all the other art treasures. After dinner a two-act operetta by Haydn was given in the opera house: *L'Infedelta delusa,* in Italian. Whereupon Her Majesty declared, "If I wish to hear good opera in the future, I shall come to Esterhaz"—a piece of unabashed flattery which must have raised Haydn in the opinion of the prince. (The year before, in a letter to her daughter, Marie Beatrix, dated November 12, 1772, she had expressed a less friendly opinion of Haydn; "he has," she wrote, "isolated ideas, but can never get past the beginning.") The opera was followed by a *bal masque* that ranged through all the splendid salons of the palace. The monarch gave the prince her arm; the couple stood in the gallery of mirrors of the Chinese summerhouse and looked out upon the palace and gardens gleaming in a sea of light. Behind them stood the host of noble Hungarian cousins whom Nicholas had invited.

Haydn and the band, dressed in gala uniforms, had taken their places on a platform, and for the first time the strains of his Symphony No. 48 rang out, with their flourishing *allegro* of "oboi, corni, timpani": This was the *Maria Theresa Symphony.* Even after the empress had retired to her suite, the maskers wandered about the gardens in the warm September night. Without interruption, the festival went on into the morning and into the grand dinner at noon, for which Haydn's band again supplied music. At four o'clock the empress entered the prince's puppet theater to witness a puppet play with music by Haydn, *Philemon and Baucis.* It was a touching little sketch which made the listeners take out their handkerchiefs. They saw before them the frail, old couple out of Greek mythology, represented by exquisitely carved puppets which moved and gestured with wavering motions. The music has been lost; only the overture survives:

After supper the two-day festival reached its peak, in the long awaited "greatest fireworks of all times" in honor of the guest. A Parisian pyrotechnician had arranged it. He approached, and on bended knee asked the empress to start the fireworks personally. Promptly there began a long succession of figures, rockets, and fiery wheels that changed night into day. But even louder than the crackling and roar of the fireworks were the shouts of two thousand country people, who, dressed up with ribbons and carrying shepherds' crooks, and seeming half like a national ballet and half like a classical chorus, came crowding into the gardens. They cried, *Eljen a mo királynönk! Eljen Maria Theresia!* ("Long live our queen! Long live Maria Theresa!")

The prince had ordered his serfs to attend the festival—perhaps with the political intention of demonstrating to the monarch that his "subjects" were happy. In reality, they were not, for no serf had a happy lot in Hungary. Undoubtedly, the prince knew this and, moreover, knew pretty well that the empress knew it. A year before this time, Maria Theresa had written to Kaunitz, her chancellor, to inform him that one of the aims of her government was the abolition of serfdom, "for which alone the government is still worth living." It was a goal that she herself could never attain; her hands were tied in too many ways. But Prince Nicholas and the other Hungarian aristocrats knew well that her son and co-regent, Joseph II, seriously hoped to carry out this program. The young emperor was known to spend whole nights reading the theses of Rousseau who once had written: *Every man being born free and his own master, no one, under any pretext whatsoever, can make any man subject without his consent.* Was this not the end of the feudal social order? Nicholas probably breathed "a sigh of relief that Joseph, the 'peevish scholar,' had not accompanied his mother, and therefore could not disturb the joviality of the festival . . ."

At this festival Haydn was at last to be introduced to the empress —Haydn the man, since she had known the boy at Schoenbrunn and Vienna and as we have read, had intervened in his life. Haydn, we may assume, had drunk a bit too much Tokay; otherwise he would not have presumed to refer jestingly to the whipping that had been administered to him at Schoenbrunn and to his later expulsion from the Vienna choir-house. The empress was taken aback at first; she raised her brow, then she smiled; at last she gave Haydn a gold snuff-box set with diamonds, in somewhat belated recompense.

It was a curious scene, possible only in that rococo age, and specifically in the Austrian kind of rococo. For, even twenty years before the French Revolution, Austria was still a large-scale nursery. Maria Theresa's ideal of ruling a matriarchal state by gentleness and by the use of gifts which aided individuals to rise above the evils of the social order, colored every expression of the culture.

For *his* part, Haydn was no longer her "son." He had long been feeling himself the *father* of everyone around him. He fathered all the instrumentalists and singers under his direction. In the course of decades, hundreds of musicians were to study under him. Tomasini and others already had children of their own; a second and a third generation would enter Haydn's *kapelle*. The nickname "Papa" had become attached to him much earlier. It is known that this nickname —which strikes us as an epithet for a grandfatherly sort of man was applied by Haydn to himself when he was only thirty-five years old. Dignified old age had nothing to do with it; rather, it was used in imitation of the comedian, Kurz-Bernardon, who, when referring to himself before his troupe, used to employ the third person and say, instead of "I," "*der Herr Vatter*." Haydn took up the usage. "Papa thinks . . . papa wishes . . . ," he would say in speaking of himself. And his musicians addressed him as "good, dear, kind Papa!" Even his servant and copyist, Joseph Elssler, was on the same terms with him. And all of them had good reason to be, for Haydn looked after them as if they were actually his children; he settled their quarrels, tried to obtain wage increases for them and, though he was so little adept at writing, drew up petitions for them when they had angered the prince by lack of punctuality, overextension of leave, or similar faults, and might expect to have their wages docked, to be subjected to house arrest, or even to be dismissed.

Haydn's fatherly attitude, his kindness and great-heartedness, toward his musicians is, perhaps, best indicated by the circumstances surrounding his *Farewell Symphony* (No. 45). According to one of the prince's regulations, the musicians of the band were required to come to Esterhaz, for the summer season, without their families. Naturally, this caused emotional hardship, both to the men and to the children and the wives who were left behind at Eisenstadt. Excepted from this ruling were only two of the singers, the violinist Tomasini, and Kapellmeister Haydn himself—an exemption which did not altogether delight Haydn, since he had reasons for wishing that his dear spouse could be left behind.

The reason alleged for this measure was that the palace of Esterhaz, had no room for so numerous a company. We know, however, that the palace contained hundreds of guest rooms. But the prince's employees were not guests; that was all there was to it.

In 1772 the musical summer in Esterhaz lasted a long time; it seemed as if it would never end. The musicians became more and more unhappy; they brought their grievances to Papa Haydn. He shrugged; what could he do? In reality, he had already taken steps; secretly he had prepared a kind of trap for the prince. It was a new symphony which was to be performed one evening for the prince and his guests; it stood last on the program.

At first, there seemed to be nothing particularly remarkable about it, except that its key—F-sharp minor—was gentle, misty, and melancholy. In the first movement, *allegro assai,* nothing special occurred; in the *adagio* the muted violins played in a somewhat more melancholy mood than was usual with Haydn; the minuet and trio in F-sharp major spoke somewhat briefly of the joys of life. It was not until the *presto* that the audience was favored with the ebullient gladness of a Haydn finale. Then, after no more than a hundred measures, all the instruments suddenly stopped on the dominant of F-sharp. Quite unexpectedly, when four violins began playing a new theme, something altogether incredible occurred; the second horn-player and the first oboist stood up in the midst of the performance, packed up their instruments and left the platform. Eleven measures further on, the bassoonist, who had nothing to do up to then, raised his instrument to his lips, but only to sound briefly, in unison with the second violin, the beginning of the first theme; then he blew out the light over his stand, and also departed. After seven measures more, he was followed by the second horn player and the second oboist. Then the cello, which up to now had followed the bass viol, parted ways with it; at a modulation—unexpectedly C-sharp became the dominant—the bass viol also left the platform. The music became thinner and thinner; it began to wheeze. Haydn went on wielding his baton as if he had not noticed anything amiss. A few more *adagio* measures in A-major. But while they were being played, one after the other the cellist, the third and fourth violinists and the violist vanished from the scene.

The orchestra was almost dark by now; at one stand alone two candles still burned. Here sat Luigi Tomasini and a second violinist, who were to speak the last word. Softly, muffled by mutes, their violins weaved in and out in thirds and sixths and then died away in the faintest of breaths. When all the musicians had gone, like shadows along the wall, leaving behind them a depressing sense of autumnal solitude, Haydn himself, tiptoeing, tried to follow them. But the prince intercepted him. Gently he placed his hand on his kapellmeister's shoulder. "My dear Haydn, I understood. Very well, then, we shall pack up tomorrow."

The members of the orchestra were waiting anxiously in the anteroom, for their chief. Had his kindly trick succeeded? As soon as he appeared, his look reported the fortunate outcome; they embraced him heartily.

The incident has piqued men's imaginations. It wryly suggests how music alone can soothe the savage breast; it is also illustrative of the delightful frivolity of the rococo age. Rossini, who worshiped Haydn and rushed to the defense when Haydn's serious music was disparaged as trivially light-hearted ("Yes, indeed, his light-heartedness was his seriousness"), in 1830 conceived the notion of writing a brief *opera buffa* around the scene, of which Haydn was to be the hero. The character of the musicians in revolt against a bureaucratic order and desiring to return to their families; Haydn, a harassed husband who had, alas, his wife with him and was thinking only of the happiness of the others; the arrogant prince, conquered by music—it is unfortunate that Rossini never carried out his intention. In 1838 Felix Mendelssohn gave a performance of the symphony; a "curious, melancholy little piece," it was called in the program notes; and, faithful to the tradition, the musicians left one by one. Robert Schumann, who was not overfond of Haydn, wrote at the time that he was deeply moved as the musicians put out their lights and softly left the platform. "And no one laughed, for it was not at all funny." Latest of all, Serge Koussevitzky re-enacted the scene in Boston. Dressed in the blue-and-silver costumes of the eighteenth century, his musicians played by candlelight, and the conductor himself acted as Haydn.

THE STRING QUARTETS

Yes, Esterhazy loved Haydn—and he loved him so much that he continued to be very stingy about sharing the person of his kapellmeister with others. We can be sure that, during these thirty years, Haydn did not once receive permission to go abroad; he could not, without permission, even go to Vienna for a single day. When he visited Vienna it was within the prince's retinue, and his lord had to be informed of all his doings. But, instead of Haydn, his works went far afield. By some clause of which we have no record, Nicholas the Splendid had permanently abrogated the fourth paragraph of the contract which, we recall, denied the composer the right to copy his own works for other than the princely use. By the eighties, Haydn's works, for that reason, were printed now all over the world, in Vienna, Leipzig, Berlin, Paris, and even in London.

If Haydn had confined himself to the symphony form, he would not have become so well known. But since for the performance of a quatuor only a small apparatus was required, it were rather his string quartets (which were early, and not quite correctly, called "chamber editions of the symphonies") which, as Max Graf relates, "flew over the world like birds in spring time. Whenever four musicians tuned their stringed instruments and sat down to play chamber music, Haydn's quartets lay on their desks. Musicians and music lovers said to one another, 'You must play Haydn; you will enjoy it,' with the appreciative smile of a connoisseur recommending a wine of especially choice vintage."

From youth to extreme old age, Haydn worked at string quartets. This could not have been a matter of chance. There is a strange attraction about the number four. It satisfies the human sense of proportion. In music, one voice is a monologue; it can make music, but the music cannot be prolonged without becoming wearisome; it is musical solitude. A second voice signifies complement, harmony, and, if all goes well, "marriage," but more frequently it tends to indicate dissension, a splitting into two opposing parts; contention. For this reason the number three is better; it unifies the opposites, and, as in the idea of trinity, it forms a religious principle.

But, in the sense that it exceeds three, four satisfies the human sense of proportion. It is earthy and understandable. The number four stands squarely on four legs, as do the animals. A building stone has four surfaces; our houses have four walls. The ordinary man speaks of four winds and recognizes four quarters of the globe. Four ingrained in us by architecture and otherwise, seems to fill a deep psychological need in men. In evolving a chamber music for strings in which four voices participated instead of three, Haydn was consistent with the squareness, the basic earthiness of his character.

"The string quartet," Goethe once wrote to Zelter, "is the most comprehensible of all varieties of instrumental music. We hear four sensible persons conversing with one another, and we are led to believe that we may profit by their discourse and become acquainted with the peculiarities of their voices." How right he was! A full orchestra does not convey this feeling; in the orchestra the instruments speak up at the command of the conductor, but do not have "personal relations" among themselves. The sense of intimate participation, which quartet playing evokes in the listener, is based on the illusion of eavesdropping upon four voices which speak to one another as do characters upon a stage.

Quartet music became, quite naturally, the delight of the German bourgeoisie which saw, before its eyes, the instruments transformed into human beings, carrying along their own whims and temperaments. No concert hall, stage, or lofty salon was required. An ordinary, middle-class room sufficed: for expressing middle-class sentiment.

In his *Musical Encyclopedia* of 1837, Gustav Schilling observed that distinct elements of the comic often entered into the composing of quartets; when an emotion was expressed by the "wrong" instrument (for example, a declaration of love by the aged, ungallant cello), the emotion as such was parodied. This comment helps us to understand why Haydn, with his secret bent for parody, transcribed the humorous elements of his environment, the concord and the dissensions of his fellow men, in quartet form (*sub specie di quatuor*). Their strifes and their reconciliations formed the material for his "comic opera." Even in his extreme old age he was a lively observer of the human comedy, and surpassed himself, as he had been in his youth, in the freshness and acuteness of his observation. For proof of this, we need only to listen to the *Witches' Minuet* which he wrote in 1797 for Count Erdödy (Op. 76). In his quartets, more than in his other music, Haydn abjured routine solutions; each day unfolded new phases of himself. In the course of years, the writing of quartets became, as it were, the keeping of a kind of diary; into them Haydn put his moods and experiences of the moment. At the time he was writing *The Creation* he incorporated the famous passage, "Let there be light," into one of his quartets. His creative experience meant more to him than anything else, and he was therefore impelled to prepare the *Seven Last Words of our Saviour on the Cross* and the *Austrian Imperial Hymn* in quartet form soon after the composition of those choral works.

While he was young he had no real vision of the possibilities of the form which he had invented. He seemingly shows little knowledge of the "equal rights" of the four instruments. The first violin still defines the character of the entire work; the other three instruments are for the most part simple "pursuers" which contribute harmony but do not venture any views of their own. The reason for this must be sought in the influence of the "gallant style" upon Haydn. Homophony had just been discovered; people wanted to hear melodies which would be easily recognized. Was such hard-won happiness to be imperiled again by vesting the three subordinate voices with the same independence as was granted to the first violin? In his early quartets Haydn did simply not dare to do this; in time, however, his quartets became more and more "dialectic," like life itself. For when four persons begin to converse, either four gradations of opinion will arise or the conversation will be dull.

Several decades ago the English critic E. Heron-Allen passed a very harsh judgment upon these first twelve quartets. "They seem to us sadly feeble in the present day," he wrote; "there is not enough flesh to cover the skeleton, and the joints are terribly awkward; but there is the unmistakable infant quartet, and certainly not more clumsy and unpromising than the human infant." This verbal image is not a happy one, for the thing that we find so amazing in the infant is precisely that it possesses all the attributes of the adult, and possesses them in a more charming manner, with a divinely fresh sweetness. Brahms, although the beneficiary of the romanticists' developments in the realm of harmony, would not have conceded that Haydn's early quartets were awkward. On the contrary, he saw them as wonderfully well formed. Conjured up apparently out of nothing, they are biologically the early stages of Haydn's later magnificent quartets. As Sandberger observes, the strength and originality, the freedom and correctness with which he handled the instruments in these early quartets, are inexplicable and unparalleled.

"There were string quartets before Haydn, but nobody troubles to revive them," comments Sir Donald Tovey. Even in the early quartets he sees a "drive towards the quality by which Haydn's lifework was to effect a Copernican revolution in musical form." Tovey also thinks that the early quartets, from class motives, seem to call into question the imperturbable, aristocratic symmetry of older music. Before Haydn, nothing like his irregularity existed, nor is it to be found in any of his contemporaries. The only approach to it was a single "recipe" made fashionable all over Europe by some Italian composers. It consisted in making a four-bar or two-bar phrase repeat either itself or its latter half, and then, as it were, tie a knot by making a firmer cadence of the last echo. But this was only a cliché for producing irregular rhythm while shunning the responsibility of not reducing this irregularity to another kind of tedious regularity. Haydn was not content with a routinized originality; his work was a constant discovery.

At first he was undecided how many movements his quartets ought to have. Were the traditional five movements proper—*presto, minuet, adagio, minuet, allegro molto*—or should he launch a three-movement structure after the fashion of the "operatic symphony": *allegro, andante, allegro molto*? He quickly decided, however, that in a quartet it was best to keep to the number four; there were only four instruments, he would have four movements.

In the six quartets written in 1769 the four-movement structure has become a matter of course. We know that Haydn would have had no regrets about dropping the second minuet; he was not a "gallant" composer, and the writing of minuets was, for him, merely a concession to the courtly spirit of the times; it did not spring from the heart. He was slowly but surely edging the minuet out of the symphony; he certainly did not want it included in the form in which he spoke most intimately, the string quartet. And even though he retained the second movement of the quartet as a minuet, he did not make it a true, courtly minuet; it was closer to the peasant dance, and often was tinged with wistfulness and sadness. In 1769 Haydn's quartets became more and more "inward," more and more German. His *adagios* formulated the moods and passions of the Werther period two years before Goethe wrote *Werther*. Earlier than the literary artist, the musician sensed the sentimental tide coming in. The brightness of the "major" sky was darkened by "minor" clouds with syncopations; *fermatas* produce heartrendingly expressive pauses. All this, of course, would not have been possible without a newly developed love for polyphony. (Polyphony, it seems, sometimes fills out, in music, the rôle that is assigned to psychology in literature.) However, Haydn was a wise craftsman who did not shed a tool he had once found useful; even while he was magnifying the rôle of the other stringed instruments, he remained as faithful as he could to the old "primadonna," the first violin. He even invented more and more brilliant parts for the virtuoso of that instrument in the Esterhazy orchestra, Tomasini. The magnificent D-minor (Op. 9, No. 4), quartet with its tempestuous finale, showed what Haydn could do forty years before Beethoven:

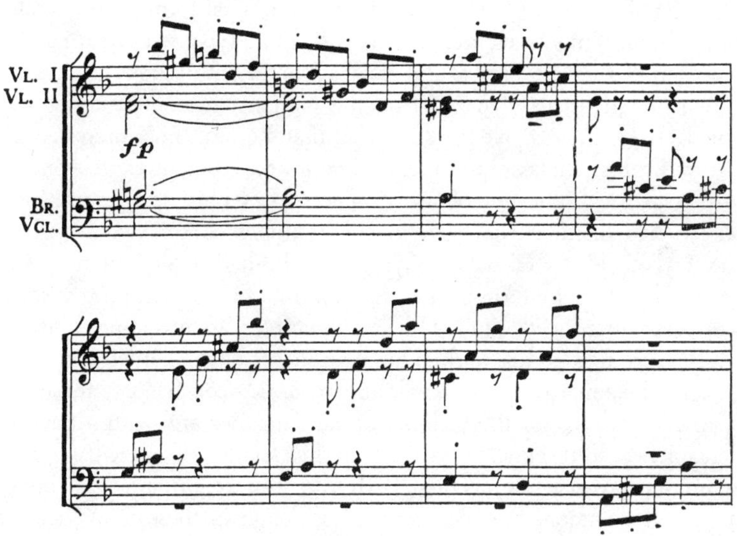

In 1772 we find Haydn again restlessly laboring to bring the form to perfection. He completed the *Sun Quartets* (Op. 20), so called not because there was any "program" connected with the sun, but because of the pretty symbol of the rising sun in an old edition. And yet the name does not lack a deeper aptness for it was only now that the sun was really rising to reveal the Haydn who took up the classical tradition with the strictest ethical logic, and who soon came to personify it.

Twenty years earlier, he had felt the fugue as something alien to himself. At that time everything within him urged him to sing in melody, to enjoy the simple pleasure of juxtaposition. Then came the pleasure of polyphony and psychology. Now for the first time he understood the wisdom implicit in the "bonds" with which Johann Sebastian Bach had fettered melody. He had been entirely wrong, as a young man, in thinking it "dry." When Haydn began to write in contrapuntal form he did not do so out of mathematical pedantry, any more than Bach had done; nor was Haydn prompted by any historical motives or a taste for archaizing. He had simply learned the compelling lesson that in order to do proper justice to emotion, the outburst of emotion must be concentrated. There was no better way to achieve concentration than in the contrapuntal form, and so we find that in the chief of the *Sun Quartets* Haydn uses the fugal form for the finale. These fugues, moreover, were of the true, older type, with *dux, comes,* inversion of themes, *strettos* and *ricercatas;* and with scholarly pleasure Haydn noted in his own hand on the margins what these terms signified. Nevertheless, we must repeat that he was not interested in exhibiting his scholarship but in finding a new mode of expression; he turned to the fugue out of artistic necessity. (This newly arisen necessity had manifested itself in his symphonies somewhat earlier; about 1765, in his *Christmas Symphony,* he had incorporated a Gregorian choral in the form of a *cantus firmus.*) This search for a vertical structure introduced, into Haydn's quartets, architectonic tensions which were new to his work. The instruments were charged with new powers of expression. The masculine voice of deep feeling, the cello, opposed the treble of the violins in a new manner and with a new independence. But Haydn's gift lay in his faculty of presenting new techniques even while keeping faith with his old principle of "building in all directions at once." And so, although in these *Sun Quartets* his main interest was in vertical structure of depth, he nevertheless sought new sources of melody. He found them in folk music, and used melody of unprecedented richness to point up his new vertical style.

And then, in 1772, the master stopped his writing of quartets; there began a pause that was to last for almost ten years. This is a remarkable gap in his work. Shall we assume that Haydn thought that he had really exhausted the physical and psychological possibilities of expression with four instruments? Or was he solely dropping one form in favor of the many other forms which tempted him? These may well have been contributory motives; but perhaps there was a more important reason for his neglecting for ten years the deliberation of chamber music. For at the same time he plunged into a period of extreme productivity; not only symphonies came from his pen, but an oratorio on a Biblical theme, *Tobias,* a highly colorful piece that would have reflected credit on the best Neapolitans of his time. Above all, he wrote six Italian operas. This last was, we feel, a departure for him and quite unlike his usual self. The deluge of operas could not be explained simply by the requirements of Haydn's position in the palace of Esterhazy. Some personal experience must have been behind it.

> "This something that I cannot name
> I feel within my bosom flame,"

Tamino sings in Mozart's *Magic Flute.*

> "Can this mystery be love?"

It was. Master Haydn was in love—for the first time in his life.

Book Three

NOONDAY GALLANTRIES

Haydn's works are an ideal language of truth, connected in all their parts by necessity, and full of life. They may perhaps become outmoded, but they will never be surpassed.

GOETHE

L'INVITAZIONE ALL' OPERA

"FIN des plaisirs, commencement des désagréments," wrote the great French musician Méhul, on the last page of one of his operas. He was undoubtedly right. When the pleasures of composition were over, the operatic composer could look forward only to the strife of presentation, to the struggles for the limelight.

The essence of opera is unrest. Wagner has given us a vivid description of the atmosphere in Paris in 1841, on the occasion of a first performance of an opera by Halévy: "Passion, jealousy, enthusiasm, curiosity, speculation, artistry and business—everyone is excited about it, glows, flickers, sparks, yawns, laughs, weeps, calculates, hopes and fears." The opera thrives upon excitement of this sort; far from being distressed by intrigue, malice, and envy, the singers seem rather to be inspired by them. They like the temperature in their inferno. And so also the great operatic composers—hadn't they also their share of the qualities of lion-tamers, mountebanks, and exorcisers of devils? We need only recall the manners of Handel and Wagner.

Not Haydn's! He, of course, seems out of place among such a crew. He is the "genius of tranquillity,"—it is really hard to imagine him as a composer of operas. The facts that he did not fail, that twelve of his operas all contain some good music and two or three are still performable, are due to the circumstance that he was spared the necessity of frittering away his energies in rivalries and intrigues. For Haydn was not writing for an open market; he composed his operas for the palace theaters in Eisenstadt and Esterhaz; his public consisted only of a few thousands who—though the personnel might change—nevertheless remained a comparatively small group.

But why, we may wonder, did he write operas at all? Prince Nicholas did not order twelve operas; he would certainly have been content with three or four. Moreover, the prince's household musicians had one of the best repertories of the time: From Pergolesi's *Serva Padrona* to Martin's *Cosa Rara*. It seems odd that Haydn should have entered a field incompatible with his especial genius. Did he wish to "prove" himself? It is well true that a great artist ought to be able to do everything in his sphere. We love the man who is not too specialized. But it is an altogether different matter when he can but does not *like* to digress from his principal field of activity. Haydn, however, greatly liked to write operas.

There was a good reason for this. The opera is an erotic art form; indeed, it is eroticism in art. Haydn, condemned to so unsuccessful a marriage, found, in his operas, consolation and fire. The composition of instrumental music did not altogether relieve the harshness of his lot, but the writing of operas and the producing of them brought him into contact with the feminine half of the world.

"The songstress," as Hofmannsthal puts it, speaking of the culture of old Venice, "is the Venus of the eighteenth century." It was the image of this Venus that filled the wish-dreams of all men. And, venerating this image in his great novel of musicians, Massimilla Doni, Balzac did away forever with the "asexual origins of the song." He shrugged at the man "who never looked a woman in the face either in the theater or on promenades." Neither the trill nor the coloratura of the eunuchs was any longer then the highest form of musical expression: "Only the perfect feminine voice accompanied by a violin. In it flows that current of the elements which reanimates all joys and carries man out of himself into the glorious light of the universe."

In any case, the palace theaters of Eisenstadt and Esterhaz did not engage eunuchs. Women sang and, as a singing teacher, Haydn dealt with real women. His second attempt at opera, *La Cantarina* ("The Songstress") was a story based on the lives of opera singers. Haydn's task was to compose an *opera buffa,* but in this case the libretto was one of especial interest to him. The story concerns a young singer, Gasparina, and Apollonia, her stage chaperone, who are conducting an intrigue which involves the rising diva with two lovers at once. One of them, Don Pelagio, appears to be on the point of throwing Gasparina over. Since she is financially dependent upon him, she aims at him the entire arsenal of feminine weapons—threats of suicide, fainting spells, all in song—desperate cavatinas which both lovers take seriously, while the public, by the character of the music, has been made aware of the travesty. Gasparina is, however, a good actress, and gains her point. Finally she receives expensive presents from both lovers.

Haydn wrote the music with remarkable ease. There were personal experiences back of this facility; he must have noticed similar occurrences among the young women of his cast. He was a man of sober character, and certainly no Lothario (he thought of himself as unattractive and ugly), but as singing teacher in the prince's entourage he held a degree of power. He did not, of his own accord, abuse this power; more than one young woman encouraged him to become something more than teacher.

There is every reason to believe that Haydn was a vocal teacher of the first rank. He had learned from Pórpora how an aria ought to be executed. In the original contract, Prince Paul Anton had included the clause that Haydn must see to it that the hired singers "did not forget what they had elsewhere acquired at great expense." Pórpora, who knew all that could be known by any of the masters of Naples and Venice, gave a very thorough course of vocal instruction and was very exacting with his pupils. Haydn had absorbed his teachings but not his method. He himself was a very patient teacher. He had, moreover, no objection to prolonging the hours of instruction. They gave him temporary freedom from his shrewish wife; they replenished his senses with the fragrance of femininity and gave him a glimpse of those romantic joys which had hitherto passed him by.

With such encouragement, he wrote, after *La Cantarina,* two good comic operas: In 1768 *The Apothecary* (*Lo Speciale*), and, nine years later, *The World of the Moon* (*Il Mondo della Luna*). Both librettos were by Carlo Goldoni, the greatest writer of comedy of the time, whose sophisticated dialogue was highly admired in the theater. Haydn, himself famous for the technique of dialogue in instrumental style, had now opportunity to apply to the opera this symphonic comic technique.

It is interesting to note that in these two erotic comedies the women are not the most important characters, but the cuckolded men. Both works concern fools of Molièrean statrue. In the one case the typical apothecary, Sempronio, wants to marry his ward Grilletta; it is a common situation in Italian operas. Instead of attending to his mortar and pestle, he heats his imagination with thoughts of travel, and he plans extensive itineraries. The true type of the half-educated man, he gloats upon the antiquities of which Italy holds so many:

Never in his life had Haydn seen the arena of Verona or the towers of Cremona. The sole *anzianità* that he had seen up to this time was the fragment of the triumphal arch in the marketplace of Petronell, between the village of Rohrau and Hainburg. But his lack of experience made for no deficiency in musical skill. When he desired to do so, he could write music as brilliantly Italian as that of any native of Italy.

A character similar to the foolish apothecary Sempronio appears in *The World of the Moon,* in which a humbug of an astronomer has the credulous Bonafede look through a specially prepared telescope, and shows him things until then unknown in the universe. The comic effects of this opera are conveyed much more vigorously by Haydn's music than by the text. Haydn could perpetrate more audacious jokes in music than the author could in dialogue. (In *The Apothecary,* for example, there is a conversation on the palliative effect of rhubarb, in a case of constipation, which Haydn illustrated by unmistakable sounds.) Bits such as these demonstrate what Haydn the symphonist meant when he confessed to a friend, "Sometimes one is seized by a wantonness of spirit that simply can't be controlled."

In his Turkish opera, *L'incontro improviso* ("The Unexpected Encounter"), written in 1775, we are plunged once again into a comic-strip world. We may well wonder why Haydn had to compose such an opera with its tocsins, tambourines and triangles and its shrill and often ear-splitting oriental rhythms. The problem points (not for the last time) to the dominant influence that politics has always exercised in the realm of music. In 1683 the Turks had almost overrun Vienna, and since that time the people of the German Empire trembled lest the invaders might try again. This widespread fear of the Turks was equalled only by the later fear of the French Revolutionists. Every Austrian artist of the eighteenth century was duty-bound to do his share to dissipate this dread of the "Eastern barbarians." What better means of dispelling anxiety was there than ridicule? In his operetta Haydn made Turkish customs and Mohammedan characters ludicrous, just as Mozart did six years later in his *Abduction from the Seraglio.*

Thereafter Haydn delved into a new vein. He gave up comic operas—or, when he wrote them, they were no longer quite so comic. The epoch of the *opera seria* began, and Luigia Polzelli entered his life.

LUIGIA POLZELLI

HER maiden name was Luigia Moreschi, and she came from Naples, the cradle of opera. Mention of the very name of the city implied song. When Luigia was married to Antonio Polzelli, a violinist, she was sixteen; when she came to Eisenstadt she was nineteen. In March, 1779, Haydn saw her for the first time. He was then forty-seven. He fell in love like a stone plummeting into a well.

For almost twenty years a "married bachelor," he had not been faithful to his shrewish wife, but, in a spiritual sense, he had not been unfaithful to her. His occasional infidelities had been adventures of the body. In an era that doted fatuously on the theme of love, Haydn had remained indifferent. But now his great love had come—overnight, it seemed, although in reality its onset was not so sudden—though the man Haydn had not suspected what was to come, the artist had already felt it. In his own operas he had heaped up logs and brushwood, and now the flames were mounting high to celebrate Luigia's triumphal entry.

She conformed fairly well to our mental picture of a young Neapolitan girl: small, not impressive, but charming; with a delicate figure and deep black eyes that were sharp as briar thorns; chestnut hair, dark eyebrows, and a soft peachbloom complexion. Her voice range was *mezzo soprano;* her singing was held to be neither especially good nor bad. In any case, when Musical Director Joseph Haydn, who was so powerful at court, took a liking to her, Luigia instantly sensed what importance this might have for her future. She could well afford to be Haydn's protégée, and she accepted his suit.

We do not know whether or not she really loved Haydn. We know only that she did not get on well with her husband, the violinist. Antonio Polzelli was even older than Haydn, and she may well have wondered why it should always be her unhappy fate to have attracted aging men.

At the moment, however, she had more material concerns. Neither her own performances on the stage nor her husband's musical ability had especially impressed the prince. The couple cost him nearly a thousand gulden a year, and Nicholas apparently thought he would rather spend so large a sum on artists whom he would like better. A year and a half after the Polzellis were taken into the Esterhazy service, Prince Nicholas rudely declared their contract void. (This was in December, 1780.) It was an uncomfortable situation. Luigia was young, pretty, and energetic; she might well have returned to Italy and found work there. But it was more difficult for her husband. He was an invalid, and brief engagements requiring him to travel from town to town might have taxed his health fatally. However, the decisive factor that kept the Polzellis at Eisenstadt was Haydn's love for her.

As soon as Haydn heard of the dismissal, he sought an interview with his master. The prince must have been astonished to find his ordinarily taciturn kapellmeister becoming suddenly so eloquent. Perhaps Haydn solemnly vowed that in the singer Luigia Polzelli were the potentialities of a great star. Perhaps he hinted at the quantity of operas he hoped to write for the house of Esterhazy, and insisted that he needed this very singer to stimulate his talents. In any case, the prince gave in. Certainly, Haydn deserved a favor. Why should the prince not meet him halfway? Perhaps, also, Haydn met the prince halfway. The contract with the couple was renewed for a period of ten (!) years, and it is not at all impossible that Haydn agreed to share the financial burden. It is worth noting that the violinist's name disappeared, soon after 1780, from the active list of the orchestra; he was retired on account of illness; but he continued to receive his salary. It seems quite probable that Haydn sacrificed some of his own income.

The assumption is borne out by our knowledge that Luigia had the provincial Italian girl's instinct for amassing ducats. Haydn was well paid, and was accustomed to keeping close accounts of his expenditures. He could not have failed to notice how Luigia exploited his generosity, but he probably shut his eyes and accepted Luigia's love without troubling himself about her avarice.

There was another reason for Haydn's forbearance. He perceived with considerable sympathy that Luigia acted as she did largely for the sake of her son, Pietro. She was an extremely good mother, and Haydn, who had been denied the bliss of children from his own marriage, envied her the son. In letters he called the boy his "Pietruccio"; he felt a paternal love for him, was proud of him, and helped the growing lad, wherever he could. Later, when Luigia went to spend a season in Italy, Haydn suggested that Pietro be sent to him. "I will dress your son well and do everything for him; I do not want you to have any expenses; I will provide him with everything he needs. My Pietruccio will always be with me. But I hope that he has always been an obedient son to his dear mother; when he has not been I do not like him, and you must write me the truth. I do not want an ungrateful boy; no, if he were, I would desert him on the spot." Half in jest, half in earnest, Haydn added a stern postcript: *"Un baccio al tuo figlio, se tu sei contenta di lei, se no, venti cinque sul cullo.* ("A kiss for your son if you are content with him; if not, twenty-five on his behind.") Pietro Polzelli died of consumption in 1796, when only nineteen, and was deeply mourned by Haydn.

Haydn's letters to Luigia were written in Italian. She knew no German, or, at most, but a few words; and as for Haydn, we know that he was uncomfortable and unskillful in written German. Only when he spoke German in his own Lower Austrian dialect did he sound like himself. There is a heartiness, a strength and a free-flowing ease in these Italian letters; they are not wooden and uncertain as are most of the letters that Haydn composed in German. They do not compare in spiritedness and grace with the letters of Mozart, who, as a master of three languages, could append to a sentence in French another sentence in Italian and a third in the Salzburg dialect, and make fun of all three languages at once. Haydn was not blessed with *esprit,* but he had a warm heart. For this reason they were beautiful letters that this aging man wrote to his lovely mistress who was thirty years younger than he. He had long dreamed of marrying her—and she would not have refused if she had been free. When at last old Polzelli died, Haydn apparently had to wait only for the death of his own wife. With a frankness and hardness that are truly astonishing, he wrote to Luigia at the time of her husband's death: "Dear Polzelli, perhaps the time will come for which we have so often wished, when four eyes shall be closed. Two have already been closed; the other two—well, the other two as God wills!"

She was, indeed, much younger than he, but why, after all, should he not marry her? When, on April 22, 1783, Luigia was confined for the second time, scarcely anyone who knew them doubted that Haydn was the father of her child—and Anna Aloysia Haydn must also have known it well. The child was named Aloys Anton

Nikolaus, and Haydn cared for him as if he were certainly his own son. A letter to him from Haydn bears the salutation, "My dear son."

Joseph Haydn's relationship with Luigia Polzelli lasted, with many variations of ardor, for a full twenty-one years. Sometimes it was clouded by Haydn's consciousness that he was becoming old (in his art he never aged); then he would try to inure himself to the thought that Luigia, obeying the law of nature, might prefer a younger man. He would ask only that she tell him beforehand, "so that I shall know by name the one who will be so fortunate as to possess you." After her husband's death she would be free; why, he thought meekly, should she, who was so much younger, wait for him to be free? At another time he would cry out his repudiation of the possibility of their ever parting. *"O cara Polzelli, tu mi stai sempre nel cor, mai, mai mi scorderò di te.* ("You dwell forever in my heart—never, never shall I part with you.")

But in the end, although he might have married her after the death of his wife, in 1800, Haydn did not espouse her. Perhaps, after twenty-one years, there no longer seemed any reason for marriage, since Luigia's charms had already been sufficiently enjoyed. Perhaps—and this seems highly likely—Haydn in his old age found bachelor life after the death of his wife more attractive than any new marriage could possibly be. His trip to London in 1791 was to blame for this; it was the first time he had been separated for any lengthy period from Luigia. The change had a remarkably rejuvenating effect upon him; it showed him what an unfettered man who also happened to be famous could indulge in when in foreign lands. At sixty he could engage in small gallantries and adventures that did not affect the soul. Above all, however, it was his decisive renunciation of opera, in the most important decade of his creative life, which finally turned him away from Luigia Polzelli.

RENUNCIATION OF THE OPERA

DURING the peak of his love for Luigia Polzelli Haydn wrote many operas. We might assume, from what we knew of his temperament, that he would compose comic operas, but, instead, he devoted himself earnestly to the *opera seria.*

In the opera, *La Vera Constanza* ("True Constancy") which was performed in the spring of 1779 in Esterhaz, no part is as yet ascribed to Luigia. This opera is remarkable not only for its excellent music but also for its unusual libretto, which has social implications reminiscent of Beaumarchais and Daponte—that is to say, of *Figaro.* The libretto deals with a group of nobles who do their best to break up the love affair between a daughter of the people, a fisher girl, and a count. The aristocrats are defeated, and "Rosina, *pescatrice virtuosa e di spirito* (a virtuous and intelligent fisher girl) and Masino, *capo dei pescatori, fratello di Rosina*" (chief of the fishermen, Rosina's brother) emerge victoriously. The opera closely resembles one that was produced fifty years later, that by Auber entitled *The Mute of Portici,* which also dealt with fishermen and in which Haydn's Masino is called Masaniello. However Haydn's opera is forgotten, while Auber's is world famous. This work of Haydn was not especially successful. The initial performance was to have been given in the Court Theater in Vienna, but it was banished from this theater by a series of intrigues with which Haydn was unable to cope. Nevertheless, the opera shows Haydn's true mettle. With great skill, he altered burlesque interludes with serious ones. He met fully the traditional test, "the finale alone proves the operatic composer," having fashioned a seven-part finale, running through a succession of keys, varying in tempo and meter; to cap the climax he added still another nine-part finale of remarkable grace. With his instinct for the stage, he arranged it so that the actors are required not to stand around stiffly waiting for their parts in the chorus, but to enter and exit as they sing.

Haydn's next opera was written expressly for Luigia Polzelli's voice. It was the *Isola Disabitata* ("The Deserted Island.")

The book was by Metastasio. The libretto must have awakened strong emotion in Haydn, recalling to him the time when he, a young lout, had met the powerful court poet on the staircase of St. Michael's House. Metastasio had given him the first entry into the world of courtly art. And now this poet was his collaborator, this "very nice old man" who, amazingly, was still alive—"Maria Theresa's caged songbird," he liked to call himself sardonically. Born in 1698, he did not die until 1782, and thus lived to see his *Deserted Island* put to music by that "peasant lout," Joseph Haydn.

The great solitudes have attracted the imagination of every great musician. The plight of the dying hero in the last act of Wagner's *Tristan* is the more poignant for its setting on the wild Irish coast; Dvořák's *New World Symphony* evokes the boundless solitudes of the American prairies. Haydn's next opera provided ample pretext for Haydn, the great composer of symphonies, to write several graphic overtures. He did, in fact, write one which, in its aristocratic sadness and lofty loneliness, is worthy of the great Gluck. But later, in the opera itself, Haydn violated his inclination toward epic writing. He contrarily felt a special need for expressing everything in dramatic and vocal mediums. The heroines of the opera are two sisters (the rôle of the elder was sung by the famous prima donna Ripamonti, that of the younger by Luigia Polzelli), who have been kidnapped by pirates. Their abandonment on a Crusoe's island and their discovery by the elder sister's husband is the theme of the libretto, which is developed with considerable psychological interest. It is, however, not a dramatic theme, and Haydn unfortunately divided Metastasio's text, which had been continuous, into two acts, without consulting the author. He thought to create suspense, but the "improvement" did away with what suspense there was, and, in spite of the lovely, lyrical music, the opera is boring. Nevertheless, Haydn fought for this opera as he had done for no other. He sent it to Paris, to Modena, and to Madrid, and wrote to the publisher Artaria that "no such work has ever been heard in Paris, and perhaps not in Vienna either"—a remarkable pronouncement for a man of his modesty.

Whether or not he wished it, as a composer of serious operas Haydn had entered into rivalry with Gluck, the universally recognized master of the heroic opera. The rivalry, however, was not competition; in the *Isola Disabitata* Haydn bows to Gluck's leadership and fully accepts Gluck's principles, Gluck's musical landscape, his characteristic melodic line, his psychological phrasing and the measured, nobly simple style of singing—in short, Gluck's famous "inwardness." But since Haydn had his own special sort of inwardness, these mannerisms were rather damaging for him. It was neither the originality of C. P. E. Bach in his youth, nor that of Handel in his old age, which could jeopardize Haydn's originality. It was Gluck, and only Gluck, who, during the best years of his manhood, reduced Haydn to a state of faithful imitation. Haydn not only took over problems of form which, originally, never had been his own problems. The example of Gluck even compelled him to traverse, uselessly, the same path over which the other man had gone from Neapolitan opera to the verge of "music-drama." For example Gluck could say of himself, "Before I begin my work, I try to forget that I am a musician." In his struggle to create a dramatic work of art, he almost anticipated Wagner. But what affinity had Haydn for such a development?

Nevertheless, we see Haydn persuading himself, that the cause was indeed his own, that the opera was as much his life mission as the symphony or the quartet. Throughout the middle period of his life he dragged along the burden of operatic responsibility, and he wrote not only for his prince or his little mistress. He was moved by sincere artistic convictions when, in 1782, he tried his hand on a heroic drama, *Orlando Paladino,* and in 1784 chose to put to music Torquato Tasso's *Armida*—glittering, chivalric subjects perfectly suited to Gluck. But such heroic subjects lay outside Haydn's sphere.

Gluck strove to portray the hero in art, and ended, as had Sophocles and Shakespeare, by making the hero incarnate in humanity. Both the theme and the resolution, however, were foreign to Haydn's sensibility,—were, in fact, beyond his grasp. Haydn was imbued with the humanitarianism of the eighteenth century. He was, to boot, a good Catholic, and never doubted the possibility of happy solutions for the problems of life. Both as a rationalist and a Christian he was unreceptive to "tragedy." Without a leaning toward tragic solutions, the writing of the heroic opera is scarcely possible. Even where Gluck was forced to compromise with debased contemporary taste and to supply a "happy ending" to his tragedies (as in the last act of *Orpheus*) he believed in the lofty ideal of a "tragic necessity," a heroic ideal, which

Haydn did never share. (Even in *The Creation,* as we shall see, there are no heroic features. God, the Creator, is a workman.)

It is again characteristic of Haydn that the best music in *Orlando Paladino* is assigned not to the actual hero and his adventures, but to the boaster Pasquale, the stock dramatic figure of a vainglorious soldier, who converts heroism into absurdity. Haydn did not plan it thus; his pen ran away with him. It was only by rigid self-control that he kept himself from being a parodist. He had felt much more in his element when in 1775 he composed his semi-parodistic Turkish opera *L'incontro improviso.*

Armida, however, did not get out of hand. Modern students of Haydn take the master's operatic writing far more seriously than did the older school of critics. Geiringer, for example, recently stated that "*Armida* possesses a greatness of expression and considerable dramatic force." But even this school of thought admits that in this very opera "the artist was forced to abandon the naturalness, simplicity, and humor which are the most irresistible aspects of his genius." In this work Haydn gives one the impression of a man who is standing on stilts. Affectation of this sort is not unusual; there are whole pages in Wagner and his successors where similar pretense can be observed. But in Haydn, with his genius for naturalness, forced nobility is distinctly out of place.

"The peculiar dramatic force of Haydn's mature symphonic style . . . was, indeed, hopelessly paralyzed when he wrote for the stage." This was Tovey's final judgment on the Haydn operas. Tovey, admiring as he did the directness and sure grasp of material in Haydn's epic works, wondered why he wasted his energies on the field of opera, whose tedious formalities and slow pace were entirely counter to Haydn's temperament. Tovey observes that in the time it takes Gluck's Admetos to force his wife to confess that she has sacrificed herself for him, Haydn could have roused the listener with three vigorous finales. Tovey overlooks the fact that Haydn had to reach eventually a point at which instrumental music would satisfy him no more than it did Beethoven in his *Ninth Symphony.* Haydn, too, was seeking ways of bringing back the human voice. As Paul Henry Lang observes that even if Haydn's operatic endeavors were a mistake, "many of Haydn's operas contain remarkable sections which served Haydn as excellent preparation for his *later choral works.*"

Even there, however, the profit was not large. Haydn could have more logically laid the groundwork for *The Creation* and, above all, for *The Seasons,* by studying the German *Lied.* But his absorption in operas, and the association with Luigia Polzelli which led him to write arias, alienated him from the latter. Oscar Bie, who has excellently described German song as the "tuneful, cordial, domestic *Lied,*" distinguishes between *Lied* composers and aria composers. Haydn was by nature one of the former, far more so than most of his contemporaries; and yet he, incomparable discoverer of the richness of popular music, put himself into the straitjacket of aria composition. In 1781 and 1784, when Haydn's first collections of *Lieder* were published, they turned out to be far removed from the popular, music-hall *Lied.* The *opera seria* exerted a baneful influence over Haydn's simplest songs. Fortunately, however, the *opera buffa* was also in his mind, as in the amusing *Praise of Laziness,* one of Haydn's best vocal pieces. The feebleness of the texts which Haydn selected, or accepted without protest from his literary mentor, Court Councilor Greiner, is another indication of how much out of touch with the German spirit Haydn had become at this time. To think that he never did set to music a line of Goethe!

And yet, during all the time in which Haydn was devoting himself exclusively to Italian modes and was laboring with the problems of the opera, he must have sensed that his struggle was in vain; his self-scrutiny went too deep for him to have failed to understand this. And indeed, ultimately he acted upon his inner knowledge. Yet he continued to hope, and apparently he did not consciously perceive his mistake, for in later years he grumbled to an intimate friend: "Instead of writing so many quartets and symphonies, I should have composed more songs; then I should have become one of the foremost operatic composers." At another time, in his old age, he sighed: "With my grounding in song and instrumental music, what an opera composer I should have become if I had only had the good fortune to go to Italy!" He was utterly mistaken, of course. He carried Italy within himself; the best of the Italian composers could have taught him nothing. His operatic writing failed because he was never born to be a dramatist; opera did not answer his inner needs as did the epic forms of expression—the symphony, the quartet, and the oratorio.

We know to the minute the occasion upon which he decided to give up opera. Gluck had just died, at the age of seventy-three, in Vienna. Coincident with his passing, a new master of the opera had emerged. The time was December, 1787; a short time previously Mozart had achieved a great success in Prague with his *Don Juan*. Mozart was then contending with the difficulties of an unstable life and lack of employment. Prominent persons in the musical circles of Prague had written to Haydn to ask whether he could supply them with an *opera buffa*. In a spasm of intellectual love (a feeling which affects us as outweighing in importance his long-standing relationship with Luigia Polzelli), and out of an impulse of artistic responsibility, Haydn wrote his reply. There is no parallel to it in the lives of creative artists.

The answer begins with a tentative acceptance: "I am highly honored. Why not? Since you ask me, I shall be glad to comply." But then the letter becomes more hesitant, more thoughtful; Haydn goes on to say that the plan probably would not succeed, because he has become so accustomed to conditions at Esterhaz, to especial singers and an especial public. He would have to consider carefully whether or not he ought to accept the commission. And then, suddenly, we find that he has considered, and the blunt truth comes out: Why should they ask *him* for an opera *so long as Mozart is alive!* Such a great master can occupy the field alone.

"Ah, if only I could persuade every friend of music, but especially the great ones, to understand and to feel Mozart's inimitable works as deeply as I do and to study them with as great feeling and musical understanding as I give to them. If I could, how the cities would compete to possess such peerlessness within their walls. Prague would do well to keep a firm grip upon this wonderful man—but also to reward him with treasures. For unless they are rewarded, the life of great geniuses is sorrowful and, alas, affords little encouragement to posterity to strive more nobly; for that reason so many promising spirits succumb . . . It angers me that this unique man Mozart has not yet been engaged by some imperial or royal court. Forgive me, honored sirs, for digressing, but I like the man too well . . ."

FRIEND MOZART

LET us, uncovered, bow our heads when we speak of the friendship between Haydn and Mozart, for this is a sacred theme. Only the friendship between Goethe and Schiller bears comparison with it.

What ties were there between the two men? In external appearance they made an odd pair. To anyone who saw them walking together, about 1786, bound for the Vienna Freemasons' lodge, "Toward True Concord," they presented a curious appearance. Haydn was not tall, but Mozart was considerably smaller. Haydn behaved with great decorum and dignity, and was always carefully dressed; he was, after all, only a visitor to the city, having come to Vienna in his master's entourage to spend a brief few weeks there. But the volatile Mozart looked different on different occasions. According to the testimony of the actor Backhaus, he sometimes looked like a poor apprentice and sometimes like a dashing cavalier, taking an almost dandyish delight in lace, charms and watch-chains. At times he might be depressed and taciturn, but usually he was lively and happy-go-lucky. He could not keep his hands still, and played piano on everything in sight; he could not pass by a window-seat without drumming his fingers on it; at table, he played with the salt and pepper shakers as if he wanted to beat time with them. Haydn would probably have been soundly thrashed by his father had he showed signs of developing such bad table manners.

In spite of the nervous excitation produced in him by his work, little Mozart managed to stay rotund. He was plump and round as a mouse, and the nervousness of a rodent showed in his gray face, in his sniffing, rather large nose, in his eyes which, curiously enough, seemed dull—Ludwig Tieck, the German romantic writer, went so far as to call them "imbecilic"—when there was nothing to cause them to sparkle. When, however, a musical idea occurred to him, his eyes glowed and remained glowing for hours at a time, only to go out again at last and become dull and cold as dead ash.

Haydn's, on the other hand, was no such split personality; he was at harmony with himself, and his calm eyes were more those of a painter than of a musician. His rather long, kindly face was heavy around the jowls. One could see, by the very look of him, not only that he meant well by everybody, but that he was destined to remain long upon this earth.

Mozart's kindly spirit was also evident, but his sharpness in noting human weaknesses frequently provoked him into making malicious remarks. (His was an Austrian kind of malice, the well known reverse side of Austrian charm.) Haydn's wit never took an offensive turn, and he reserved his satiric vein for music. Mozart, with theatrical talent, liked to gesture and parody. When Mozart made faces in front of friends or quaveringly mocked a diva in some opera: *"O Dio! Questa pena! O principe—O sorte—io tremo—io manco—io moro—o dolce morte!"* Haydn was amazed. He could never do anything quite so funny.

It was reserved for posterity to link the names of Haydn and Mozart; to their contemporaries their gifts seemed as diverse as their persons. Both their contemporaries and posterity were partly right. The biologic, cellular similarity of their musical inspirations is frequently stunning. Two modern French writers, Bourguès and Denéréaz, have pointed out in *La Musique et la Vie Intérieure* that both in Haydn's and in Mozart's first piano sonatas the same germinal idea appears:

It is a triviality, but characteristically developed. "Haydn, the more concentrated composer, attacks the F with utter ruthlessness. Then, as if this brusque procedure had exhausted his energies, Haydn closes the rhythmic phrase by a descending movement which is still striking in its affecting conciseness. With Mozart, however, this same phrase rebounds elastically, as if it were choosing to toy with what it has already achieved . . . The rhythmical accent is more powerful in Haydn; it is heavier than Mozart's, but also less persistent and has a shorter breath . . . This power of the rhythmical accent in turn gives to Haydn's phrase the characteristic note of good humor."

This is quite correct. But the closest reading still fails to explain the relation between the musical brothers, Haydn and Mozart. The kinship of their works remains something mysterious. Their intentions frequently overlap. It is not true that Haydn inveterately wrote more ponderously than Mozart; often he composed phrases of a quivering, "rebounding" elasticity; and, vice versa, Mozart's writing was often more Haydnesque than Haydn's itself.

There was, however, one marked difference between the two. Mozart had been a child prodigy—something not unusual among Mediterranean peoples, but extremely rare among Germans. His precocity determined the course of his whole life; it condemned him to the overheated existence of a hothouse plant. On the other hand, with Haydn slow growth was the rule; he was a flower with a hard chalice, like those flowers of the Alpine regions whose petals cling tenaciously to the sturdy stem and do not drop until late in the autumn.

When they met, Mozart was twenty-nine, and Haydn almost twice that age. In spite of the great difference in years, the older man and the younger one had behind them the same musical experiences and, strangely enough, both possessed the same tastes. But, indeed, we should not wonder at this; their instinct for true quality drew them to the same music; they both understood instantly what was good art and what was bad. The precocious Mozart and the slowly maturing Haydn also understood each other's work. In spite of the modesty that distinguished both of them, they knew that, except for Gluck, they were the only two musicians of their time who counted. This united them inwardly, though outward destiny tended to separate them. Mozart's fame was a boy's fame, the fame of a piano virtuoso, and by 1786 there was the threat that it would fade away entirely. (Three years later the unfortunate composer had to cancel an amateur concert in Vienna because only one subscriber came forth.) On the other hand, Haydn's fame was steadily growing; he was thoroughly established, and consequently, in the beginning of this strange relationship, the older man necessarily appeared in the guise of benefactor.

The friendship began one February evening in 1785 at a private musicale at the home of one of Haydn's friends. Some quartets of Mozart had been played for the first time, and after the performance Haydn rose up and said solemnly to Leopold Mozart, the father: "I, as an honest man, tell you before God that your son is the greatest composer I know in person or by name." This sincere and forceful praise from a man at the height of his own fame was reported at once to Mozart. In reply, he sent his next six quartets to Haydn, with a dedicatory letter written in Italian, the mother-tongue of music: *"Un padre, avendo risolto di mandare i sui figli nel gran mondo, stimo doverli affidare all protezione e condotta d'un uomo celebre.* ("A father who has resolved to send his sons into the great world naturally wishes to confide them to the protection and guidance of a celebrated man.") Naturally, for these were six sons in whom the father placed great hopes. *Essi sono, è vero, il frutto d'una lunga e laboriosa fatica.* ("They are, in truth, the fruit of long and laborious toil.") "Let us hope," Mozart continues, *"che non ti sembreranno dei tutto indegni del tuo favore* ("that they are not altogether unworthy of your favor.")

"Padre, guida, ed amico!" Father, guide and friend! There was no flattery in this letter; every word was written sincerely. "That was in the line of duty," Mozart said later, "for I learned from Haydn how to write quartets. No one else," he said, "can do everything, jest and shock, create laughter and profound emotion, as Haydn can, and no one can do everything as well as Haydn can." Niemetschek later recalled that when Mozart spoke of Haydn he sounded not like the almighty Mozart, "but like an enthusiastic pupil." Mozart would tolerate no adverse criticism of Haydn; he became very angry when anyone dared to say in his presence a word against the older master. "So you don't like Haydn's quartets?" he said irately to Kozeluch. "I tell you this, sir: If the two of us were melted into one, we would still be a long way from amounting to a Haydn." When Kozeluch pointed to a page of music and objected, "I would not have written it that way," Mozart burst out: "Neither would I. Do you know why? Because neither you nor I would have been so inspired."

Mozart's dedication of his quartets to Haydn had been preceded by a long, long study of Haydn's quartets. The older master had not written any quartets for nine years; between the *Sun Quartets* (Op. 20) of 1772 and the six quartets (Op. 33) dedicated to Grand Duke Paul and hence called the *Russian Quartets,* he had done nothing in the form. These last quartets were, as Haydn emphasized, composed "in an entirely new and special manner." In them he abandoned the contrapuntal style as suddenly as, ten years earlier, he had taken it up. He bade farewell to scholarship—for by this time learning had been imbued with the richest sort of life. Everything now gave the appearance of ease although it was written with great profundity. "These quartets," writes Alfred Einstein, "in their combination of originality and spirit are a great achievement of human invention, quite apart from their historical significance. 'Learning' is replaced by the principle of obbligato voice-leading, and one ventures to say that were it not for these quartets such an ideal instance of obbligato writing as the first movement of Beethoven's *Eroica* would not have been possible."

Mozart was tremendously impressed by these *Russian Quartets*. Had he been younger, at the time, he might have assumed an attitude of slavish submission like that of Haydn's to the operatic style of Gluck! But, in 1785, Mozart had already found himself; scarcely any work of his shows more distinct individuality than the group of six quartets dedicated to Haydn. What separates them sharply from the quartets of the older master is that they are "music made of music" or "filtered art," as Einstein puts it. Haydn, on the other hand, never ceased to depend upon his ear, upon his perception of the external world. He was a lover of nature, and his ear was a virtual trap for nature's voices. Mozart could never have written anything like the *Bird Quartet* (Op. 33, No. 3), which seems to have been composed at an open window, and is absolutely inimitable. But Mozart was already greater than Haydn in the delineation of inner tension. He commanded chromatic methods that surpassed Haydn's diatonic clarity.

We do not know how many hours Mozart spent in the study of Haydn's works. But as a creative artist—and this is additional proof of the accuracy of his instincts—Mozart took from Haydn only what he could certainly make use of; all the rest he wisely set aside. Mozart, as a man, might well have shared the pleasure with which Haydn eavesdropped on peasant festivities, but such experiences did not appeal to him as an artist. He was an "indoor composer" who sought different effects, a different sort of perfection. No trace of a world outside that of the human heart intrudes, for example, upon that first monstrous scene of *Don Juan* when the stabbed father writhes, the daughter shrieks for help, the seducer derides them, and Leporello wishes he could depart from the scene. (Incidentally it may be said that the scene is founded on four voices which constitutes a quartet.) But there is no longer anything of Haydn in this quartet; it is the work of the greatest theatrical writer of music and the most musical writer for the theater.

Amazingly enough, Haydn understood Mozart's theatrical genius. He appreciated the many dimensions into which Mozart's stage music was cast. He comprehended the high seriousness of the plots—in great comedy there is always high seriousness. Haydn understood that Mozart's jests touched upon eternal truths. He sensed how Mozart, though fashioning conflicts between voices and characters, kept the work as a whole always upon the plane of beauty. To the latter element, as we have seen, Haydn was not receptive by nature. Mozart's exaltation of beauty, his tireless drive to achieve beauty, that "beauty which verges upon death," remind us of Schiller; whereas Haydn, as did Goethe, tended to look upon beauty as adventitious and to exalt the typical.

Against the background of the prevailing opinion of the times, Haydn's appreciation of Mozart stands out as conspicuous praise. The supreme "authority" of the time, the Emperor Joseph II, granted that Mozart had instrumental gifts, but considered him only a mediocre operatic writer.

Haydn waged a sturdy battle on behalf of Mozart's operas. Had he been sufficiently well educated to undertake disputes in matters aesthetic, it might have gone harder with him, but his simple, healthy instinct guarded him against delivering mistaken judgments. As is well known, poor Mozart was attacked furiously for the "immorality" of his subjects. Haydn, with his blunt common sense, did not understand what the argument was all about. "I can't settle that," he said on one occasion, "but I know this, that Mozart is today the greatest living composer." At the dress rehearsal of *Cosi Fan Tutte,* Haydn, who had come from Esterhaz for a brief stay in Vienna, spent the entire evening with Mozart and was intoxicated by the music. (Indeed, how could anyone help it?)

Puritanical Beethoven was indignant over Mozart's *Don Juan* and *Cosi Fan Tutte,* and perhaps even over *Figaro.* He considered the choice of such themes a degradation of music. How differently Haydn viewed the matter, although he, no more than the composer of *Fidelio,* would have been incapable of writing a scene or a line of *Don Juan!* Before Goethe, E. T. A. Hoffmann or Kierkegaard (writers like these he would in any case scarcely have understood), Haydn sensed the true principle that lay behind *Don Juan;* he understood the synthesis of the "daemonic" and the "humorous." And, in fact, after *Don Juan* the cleavage between serious and comic opera ceased to exist. In 1829, almost forty years after Mozart's death, Goethe grieved that Mozart had not lived to set his *Faust* to music; Mozart alone could have done it, Goethe said.

The relationship between Haydn and Mozart lasted from 1785 to 1790; only five years of association were granted to them. They were like two companions of the road, each taking his turn at leading. Haydn recognized sooner than Mozart the perils of the homophonic style and the one-sidedness of straight narration. The epical works of his middle years are singular precisely in their reversal of his youthful ideals. Counterpoint is admitted where he felt it to be necessary—and prolonged only to the point of aural toleration. The contemporary musician Ernst Ludwig Gerber wrote in 1792 in his encyclopedia: "Haydn commands every harmonic refinement, even if it comes from the Gothic period of the gray contrapuntists. But as soon as he prepares it for our ear it assumes a pleasing character in place of its former stiffness. He possesses the great art of making his music oftentimes seem familiar. Thus, despite all the contrapuntal refinements that may be found therein, he becomes popular and pleasing to every amateur." Mozart, who died in 1791, might well have sighed on reading a similar eulogy—not from envy, but solely because it came much harder to him than to the drier Haydn to retrace his steps to Johann Sebastian Bach, while retaining a "pleasant" and even "familiar" character. The Italian in Mozart recoiled from the Gothic grayness. And yet he had to experience the fugue—else he would not have been our Mozart.

Haydn, however, could not imagine that anything presented difficulties to Mozart. He overlooked the line in that dedicatory letter of 1785 which spoke of *"lunga e laboriosa fatica."* He was continually in awe of Mozart's "divine facility," of the graciousness and inspiration that were apparent in all his works. "Believe me, I am nothing compared to Mozart!" he told the English critic Burney after his friend's death.

During Mozart's life Haydn took the rôle of the benefactor in their friendship. But after the younger man's death toward the close of 1791, old Haydn assumed the rôle of the departed Mozart's disciple. As we shall see, it was Mozart's genius that was to inspire the London symphonies of Haydn.

A NEW BOURGEOISIE

Toward the end of the eighties, Haydn's visits to Vienna in Prince Nicholas's entourage were growing less and less frequent; the stays in Esterhaz longer and longer. And Vienna now struck him as lovelier, livelier, and more desirable than ever. A new bourgeois spirit was sweeping through it; many of the outmoded forms of life had been whisked away. Maria Theresa had died; since 1780 her son, the bourgeois emperor, had been reigning alone. Joseph II, the liberator of the serfs, was at odds with the land-owning nobility and even more so with the land-owning church.

Another sort of bourgeoisie was rising, a bourgeoisie of trade and industry. Allied to it by ties of friendship and kinship was a class of new, individualistic intellectuals, university professors, and high officials in the government. Haydn was attracting a new type of patron. There was, for example, Josef von Sonnenfels, whom in his youthful days he had heard much maligned, for Sonnenfels had been the victorious antagonist of Kurz-Bernardon and of the Viennese popular theater. Sonnenfels was an enthusiast who had the utmost regard for Haydn's art, and who was in turn respected by Haydn. The man's career had been an astonishing one: Baptized grandson of a rabbi, newspaper publisher, leading aesthetician, arbiter of good taste, Imperial Theater censor, later university professor of law and economics, reformer of the police and of Austrian criminal law. Sonnenfels had succeeded in having abolished judicial torture. He was a humanitarian of rare caliber, such as only the brief period of Joseph's reign in Austria could have produced.

Another of Haydn's new patrons was the Grand Master of the Freemasons' lodge, Ignaz von Born, a mineralogist who plumbed the secrets of the earth. He was the model for Mozart's Sarastro, the high priest in the *Magic Flute;* Mozart also celebrated him in his cantata, *Joy of Masonry:*

See, how to the probing scientist's eye
Nature gradually reveals her face,
how she fills him with lofty wisdom,
fills the mind and fills the heart with virtue,
That is pleasure for the Mason to behold,
that is true, ardent Mason's joy.

There were also the writers Michael Denis, Alxinger, Blumauer, Schikaneder; the amateur musician Bernhard von Kees; Court Councilor Greiner who, as we have noted, often helped Haydn in selecting texts for songs; and Gottfried van Swieten, the savant, son of the famous physician of the same name, who was later to write the text for *The Creation* and *The Seasons*. There were also the wholesale merchants, Puchberg and Tost, both well known in musical history; one of them lent money to Mozart, to the other Haydn dedicated his most mature quartets, the *Tost Quartets* (Op. 54).

All these men were Freemasons. Georg Friedrich Nicolai of Berlin, himself an enthusiastic Mason, took a census of world Freemasons in 1782, and arrived at the estimate of between five and ten million. This was, undoubtedly, a gross exaggeration; nevertheless, the order was by this time more of a "church" than a lodge. It need not surprise us that Mozart became a member. He must have been heartily in accord with a group whose preaching was for fraternity and equality of all men and against "superstition." The Masonic ritual, with its curious mingling of rationalism and mysticism, evidently appealed to Mozart, and he conferred true immortality upon it in his *Magic Flute*. In addition, we must remember that Mozart was an extremely lonely person. The haste, inconstancy, and vicissitudes that often imperilled the harmony of his life could, Mozart thought, best be combated by his entering a group of "brethren." There he would have a bond not only with the most influential, but with the best men of his age.

It is not so easy to understand Haydn's entrance into the Masonic order. He was not a literary person, as were most of the Freemasons, and in his earlier days philosophical idealism had been entirely foreign to him. He did, of course, share Mozart's hunger for "society," for in spite of the burdensome social duties that were imposed upon him in Esterhaz, Haydn very often felt a sense of loneliness there. But this longing lacked the undertone of nervousness that we find in Mozart. Biographers and musicologists have, therefore, generally assumed that Haydn's infrequent visits to the Vienna lodge, "Toward True Concord," constituted little more than an act of courtesy, that he went there for friendly gatherings and did not feel any profounder obligations.

It would, however, be wrong to take the view that Haydn entered the Masons solely out of social considerations; such insincerity was foreign to his character. The letter he wrote on February 2, 1785, to Count Anton Apponyi, Imperial Chamberlain and a high-ranking Mason, is proof to the contrary. "I can scarcely wait to enjoy the inexpressible good fortune of being one in a circle of such worthy men," he wrote, and added that he looked forward anxiously to his acceptance into the order. Haydn could not have written in this manner had he hoped merely for social advantages from joining the Masons.

The official address at his initiation was delivered by Josef von Holzmeister (1751-1817), a councilor in the Ministry of War, who stressed, in significant fashion, the meaning of Haydn's adherence to the Masonic order. Holzmeister declared that Haydn was the inventor of a new order of things in the orchestra. (Today we would say, unhesitatingly, "the inventor of orchestral democracy.") He had established new principles governing the duties and the rights of the various instruments. "If every instrument did not consider the rights and properties of the other instrument, in addition to its own rights, if it did not often considerably diminish its own volume in order not to do damage to the utterances of its companions, the end—which is beauty—would not be attained. Instead of melting, moving music, an intolerable hodge-podge of ill-united sounds would be produced." Such words must have been very pleasing to Haydn, for they showed an understanding of his musical purposes. Nevertheless, he, unlike Mozart, did not write music for the use of the lodge. The probable reason for this was, simply, that never in his life had Haydn been one to take the initiative. If the lodge had "ordered" music from him, he would have written it; that it failed to do so was its mistake.

Haydn had in reality a deeper tie with the lodge than had many of its other members. This tie was the "workman cult" of the Freemasons. Haydn's ancestors, for many generations, had been hardworking artisans. Now he lived in a princely household where any kind of physical labor was contemptuously looked down upon as the obligation of a lower social class. But in the ideology of the Freemasons he could find, for the first time, a view that was congenial to his inherited class-consciousness. The Masons placed a lofty symbolic value upon manual labor. To this day, when Masons assemble anywhere in the world, they wear the workman's apron. Since Adamson's *Constitution of Freemasonry* had been published in London in 1723, the members of the "third estate"—merchants, business men, even artisans—had flocked to the Masonic lodges and had subscribed to the Masons' watchword: "Diligence confers more holiness than prayer." Austrian Freemasonry never went quite as far as the Bavarian order of Illuminati, who bluntly declared: "Prayer is laziness and religion is fraud." But such campaigns as Joseph II conducted against the excessive number of Catholic church holidays were in consonance with Masonic ideas of industry. Sonnenfels, who was one of the most influential of the Masons, emphasized in his writings that the "bourgeois artisans" constituted the most important segment of the population. This was flattering to Haydn's pride of craft, and was probably the chief reason for his warmth toward Freemasonry.

Haydn may also have been enticed by the fantastic assertions that were made concerning the historical origins of the order. According to Adamson's wild mythology, Freemasonry was a gift that God gave the First Man, who passed on to his sons the knowledge of masonry and of geometry. God himself was the first "overseer and foreman." According to Adamson, Solomon was the grand master of a lodge in Jerusalem, and Solomon's friend King Hiram "the grand master of a lodge in Tyre." It was from Tyre that Solomon had drawn the workmen for the building of his temple, and all these workmen, Adamson alleged, had been raised as Freemasons. One of the rules of the lodge required that rough, unhewn stone be present at every meeting; it played an important part in the ritual. For, Haydn was taught, "the human heart is the rough stone which must be hewn to its destined form and incorporated artfully into the Temple of Solomon, the noble temple of humanitarianism."

This ethical system, dressed out in the symbols of craftsmanship, awoke echoes in Haydn. But whether or not the Masons were merchants, poets, or professors playing at being artisans, they were a bourgeois group, and therein lay their magical attraction for Haydn. Though many of these men had been admitted to the nobility, they belonged to the most recent patent nobility, not to the old military or landed aristocracy. All that Haydn had previously known of Vienna was the petty-bourgeois existence of his childhood and youth; later he had experienced the patronage of the great nobles who permitted him to eat at their tables, but never abridged the distance that separated a born count from an employee. Now for the first time Haydn was, so to speak, among men of a class he could accept for his own. He spent what free time he had in Vienna visiting the home of Peter Leopold von Genzinger, university professor and Mason. However, this man's Freemasonry was not his principal feature.

MARIANNA SABINA AND THE PIANO

GENZINGER whom Maria Theresa had ennobled for his services during an epidemic, was a doctor who specialized in the treatment of women's diseases; if only for that reason, he was the center of a social circle. The household's chief ornament was his wife, Marianna Sabina. She was a young woman of thirty, the mother of six children, and the person who drew the aging Master Haydn to Vienna—whether or not he admitted this to himself. In letters full of old-fashioned phrases of respect, he informed her of his affection; but sometimes he forgot to hold the soft pedal down—and then, in the unguarded moment, a loud outcry of passion might be heard, whereupon the alarmed composer would hastily silence such impropriety. What did he want? He wanted nothing at all, for he was a man of honor. Once, when a letter was lost—perhaps stolen by some enthusiast—he reassured Marianna Sabina: "Your grace may be quite calm in mind, for my friendship and esteem, tender as these are, will never be compromising."

This relationship began in June, 1789, when the lady, then unknown to him, wrote a letter to Esterhaz. Enclosed with her letter was a piano arrangement she had made of a Haydn *andante* (we do not know precisely whether it was the *andante* of a string quartet or of a symphony). She asked the master for his opinion of it, and Haydn found the arrangement an excellent piece of work. Letters on musical subjects soon became letters of friendship. How, indeed, could Haydn help falling in love with Frau von Genzinger? She was the first real lady with whom he had ever associated closely. His Anna Aloysia was lower middle-class and a bigot; his Luigia Polzelli a singer, a demimondaine who would, after all, sell herself, and who, strangely enough, developed with the passage of years traits similar to Anna Aloysia's. Both women had an altogether excessive interest in money. The noblewoman Marianna—a daughter of Court Councilor von Kayser—asked no more of Haydn than common artistic experience through the medium of the piano. The sort of thing that other artists received quite naturally in their youth, the stimulation and friendship of a salon lady, Haydn received for the first time at the age of fifty-seven. This was all the more reason for him to cherish it.

There is no doubt that Marianna Sabina considered him a great composer for the piano. Had she thought differently, she would have been in disagreement with the overwhelming majority of her contemporaries. No sonatas known were more expressive than Haydn's piano sonata No. 20 (E-minor) of 1771, or No. 32 in B-minor of 1776. Today we hold another view concerning them, though we may not go so far as Alfredo Casella, who wrote in 1940: "Haydn was a mediocre composer for the piano." But we cannot forget that Beethoven, Schubert, Schumann, and Chopin have lived since Haydn's day —all of them composers of stirring, subjective music for the piano. Haydn's métier had been objective writing; when he composed subjectively because of his overwhelming inner feelings, as in his relation with Marianna Sabina, it was almost against his will.

In any case, the piano had for decades tempted him with its possibilities, as did every other instrument. The piano had then, as it has today, two natures—"characteristics" would be too weak a word here. In the first place, it was just another in the family of instruments, one of many capable of playing in the orchestra and accompanying other voices. In this aspect it fell far short of more noble instruments. Although it surpassed certain of the wind instruments, such as the trumpet, in mellifluousness, when compared to a violin or to any "singing" instrument the piano was "hoarse"; its tone was tinny and hard. Even in concertos written solely in honor of the piano itself, it often sounded like an intruder; its voice would not blend with the others; the attempt to accord equal rights to piano and orchestra necessarily led, as Huneker has put it, to a "cacophonic result." The sound of the piano seemed to come from another realm, and an uglier one. It had grave technical deficiencies, such as its being incapable of a *portamento*. To produce an ampler sound upon the piano, the foot had to be employed, when it should have been the natural task of the hand. Where delicate emotion was invoked, the piano turned out uninspired *arpeggios*.

And yet the piano had its second nature: If one had only a piano at one's disposal and put other instruments out of one's mind, what marvels of music could be made to emerge! A homophonic figure on the piano might have an incomparably unique, emphatic, and persuasive power. And with what other instrument could such vigorous harmonic effects be achieved? A third or a fourth on the piano was inimitable. After a quarter hour of playing the piano, its sound becomes so absolute, its solitary dominion so thoroughly established that a flute would sound nasal and cold and the violin squeaking. There is no longer any desire to hear other voices; the piano produces the illusion of a complete orchestra. This instrument, which has no kinship with any other, is somehow, incomprehensibly, capable of substituting for them all.

Haydn knew of the two natures of the piano as well as did the great masters who succeeded him. He lived in a transitional and revolutionary age, when a hundred attempts were being made to improve the acoustics of the old harpsichord. Music lovers wanted to infuse it with soul, at a time when it was still soulless. Oscar Bie had described these endeavors to breathe inner life into a mechanism:

> "Now the string choruses were tuned in octaves, now pedals were added for low notes, now the soundboards were strengthened, now the lower strings were made of copper and the higher of steel. Leather plectrums appear everywhere, in order to make the tone softer and less metallic. The forte and piano stops were combined, ever more artistically, into as many as two hundred and fifty permutations, so that an endless number of shades was possible.
>
> "The solution of the problem was the modern hammer-clavier or pianoforte, in which the strings are no longer plucked but struck with hammers, so that every nuance of touch depends on the fingers."

Although Haydn was aware of this evolution, the master of quartet style at first contributed little to the "liberation" of the piano. For a long time he abstained from putting the piano to emotional uses in the chamber music written for it. His piano sonatas were often filled with rather empty jollity or an undemanding sobriety. Some of them even recall the tinkling chilliness of the sonatas of Muzio Clementi. But the Roman musician was a virtuoso, and Haydn was not.

We are somewhat taken aback by the fact how long Haydn seemed unconscious that the piano, more than any other instrument, required subjective expression; and yet he had frequently heard Mozart improvising. A time was soon to come (though Haydn would not live to see it) when the piano would begin to drive out even the quartet. In the nineteenth century the piano became the "altar of the soul," and no respectable middle-class home was complete without it. The imposing furniture of the nineteenth-century bourgeoisie came not only from the shops of cabinetmakers, but from piano makers like Pleyel, Erard, Duysen, Bluethner, Bechstein, Boesendorfer, and Steinway.

A development of this sort could not be foreseen in the eighteenth century. Haydn, however, caught some glimpses of the era of romantic self-expression. There is a remarkable passage in a letter of his dated February 9, 1790, and addressed to Marianna Sabina von Genzinger, in which he suddenly speaks of his familiar piano as a "subject" which has a will of its own. He calls it "perverse and disobedient and irritating rather than soothing." If this had not been said in jest it would have been a Beethoven-like comment.

A profound personal experience, that of undeclared and never requited love, had first to intervene before Haydn succeeded in creating anything unusual in piano music. In the E-flat major sonata, No. 49, which he dedicated to Frau von Genzinger, he suddenly rose to the heights of genius. Hermann Abert has called this sonata, with its deeply dyed *adagio* the greatest of Haydn's compositions for the piano.

Besides the *adagio* are the thematically rich first movement, the sovereign development with its return to the recapitulation, the bold and independent coda, truly admirable; the vigorous, masculine and majestic finale—all these are a far flight from Haydn's routine sonatas. This lately acquired mastery remained with him in his further productions for the piano. Sonatas 50 through 52 actually seem to foreshadow a Schubertian future (recently Kathryn Dale has pointed out how many rhythmic, harmonic, and melodic devices Schubert derived from Haydn), or some of Beethoven's marvels. In the E-major *adagio* of the E-flat major sonata there are foreshadowings of the kind of ornament that Chopin employed so skillfully. Such is the timelessness of the great composers. Insofar as they are true masters of their art, they are akin. "Progress" in art is an ambiguous term; for in each advance there are prefigurements of everything that is to come, and it remains only for the later composers to make explicit what is already implicit.

As Haydn's love for Luigia Polzelli had given him insight into the operatic aria (of which he was a fluent master although he failed in the opera as a whole), so his love for Marianna liberated Haydn as a composer for the piano. It was a respectful and spiritual love, in contrast to the distinctly earthy love that still bound him to Luigia. Nevertheless, it was love. He was eager to present her with a piano, one better than her own and "more suitable to a female mode of playing." But how could he dare to give *her* a present? Nevertheless, Haydn diplomatically contrived to have Nicholas the Splendid present a piano to the wife of his deserving physician. The piano was sent from the Schantz piano factory. Undoubtedly, Marianna was aware that the instrument was in reality Haydn's gift. He thought of her day and night; he wished he might remain permanently in Vienna, and was unhappy because he could not. But there was no element of the *pathétique* in this unhappiness; he promptly diluted it with humor. His letters to Frau von Genzinger are redolent with the magical compound of earnestness and jest which is Haydn's unique tone. These letters were written in a hand wholly unaccustomed to German correspondence. When Haydn had occasion to use a word thrice, he wrote it differently each time, and always spelled it wrong. Yet these unbelievably misspelled letters make us feel very close to his world, to that "bachelor" world of his that yearns for good food as well as for love, for the life of the salon and for "culture."

Esterhaz, February 9, 1790

Much esteemed and kindest Frau v. Genzinger:

Wel, hear I sit in my wildernes; forsaken, like some poor orfan, almost withoud human society; melancholy, dwelling on the memory of passed glorious days. Yes, past, alas! And who can tell when these happy hours may return? Thise sharming meedings? where the whole circle have but one hart and one soul—all those delightfull musical evnings, which can only be rememored, not described. Where all those insbired moments? All gone—and gone for long.

You must not be surbrised, dear lady, that I have delayed writing to expres my graditude. I found evrything at home in confusion; for three days I did not know wheather I was Kapellmeister or Kapellservant; nothing could console me; my apartments were all in confushon; my bianoforte, which I formerly loved so dearly, was perverse and disobedient, and rather irritaded then soothed me. I slept very little, and even my dreams persequted me, for while asleep I was under the pleasant delushon that I was listening to the opera of LE NOZZE di FIGARO, when the plustering north wind woke me and almost blew my nighthcap off my head.

I lost 20 pounds weight in three days, for the effects of my good fare at Vienna disabpeared on the jurney. Alas! Alas! thought I to meself, when forced to eat at the restauranteur's instead of cabital beef, a slice of a cow 50 years old; instead of a ragout with little balls of force meat, an old sheep with yellow carots; instead of a Bohemian feasant, a tough grill; and instad of good and juicy oranges, Hungarian salad; instad of pastry, dry apple-fridders, and hazel-nuts, &c. Alas! alas! thought I again to myself, wood that I now had many a morsel that I despised in Vienna! Here in Esterhaz no one asks me: Wood you like some chocolat, with milk or widdout? Will you take some coffee, with or widdout cream? What can I offer you, my good Haydn? Will you have vanilla ice or strowbery? If only I had a piese of good Parmesan chiese, partichlarly in Lent, to enable me to swallow more easely the black dumplings and puffs! I gave our porter this very day a commission to send me a couple of pounds.

Forgive me, dear lady, for taking up your time in this very first ledder with so wretched a scrawel and such stupid nonsence; you must forgive a man sboiled by the Viennese. Now, however, I begin to accustom myself by degrees to gountry life, and yesterday I studied for the first time, and somewhat in the Haydn style too.

Such a letter must have delighted the Genzinger family; it still has power to delight us today. With the passage of time Haydn's cries of distress from his desert became increasingly sincere, increasingly desperate. "Oh, if only I might spend but a quarter of an hour with you, gracious lady, in order to pore out my troubles and savor your grasious consolation," he writes. But then he consoles himself—as usual: "Well, in God's name, this time will also pass and that other time come agen when I shall have the priceless bleashure of sitting at the piano besite your grace, hearing Mozart's masterworks played and kissing your hands for their gifft of so many beautiful things." Again and again he speaks of Mozart—and, indeed, he was never to cease to speak of him.

"I AM SALOMON OF LONDON"

THE biographers of Nicholas Esterhazy tell of the depression that the prince fell into in his old age. He stopped inviting guests, saw no one, and forbade Haydn the journeys to Vienna he longed for. At the age of seventy-six the great Hungarian landowner was a misanthrope. Political developments were among the causes of this hatred of humanity.

The old empress, who had been very attached to him, was dead. Nicholas and his brother had served her handsomely once upon a time, at the Diet of Pressburg (though that was now half a century ago) and later during the Seven Years' War. In those bygone days Maria Theresa once had fled before the Prussians to her "faithful Hungarian subjects"; in the presence of all the fur-coated magnates, she had broken into helpless weeping in order to move their chivalrous hearts. She had brought with her the little Joseph, then a six-months-old infant, and had carried him on her arm. The infant, "more like a squirrel than a human being," to quote a contemporary, had looked around wide-eyed. And this had been the same Joseph who later, as emperor and king, planned the most disastrous laws against the same gentry of Hungary.

Certainly, Nicholas remained the commander of the nobles' guard, and knight of the highest Hapsburg order, the Golden Fleece. But these titles were now empty; his services were forgotten. The coldness that Emperor Joseph—himself no longer a young man—manifested toward him had nothing to do with personal dislike or hatred; it was simply due to the fact that domestic tension within the realm had increased with the years. On the one side stood Joseph, liberator of the serfs, anxious to complete his work of reform; on the other side stood this patriarchal lord of over one hundred thousand souls, leader of a powerful caste who were fighting for their privileges.

In addition, the hostility between Austria and Hungary, which had been latent, was now flaring up again. Here the emperor was the attacker; he wished to found a united state and to discard the Hungarian constitution, which seemed to him outmoded and theatrical. He hated Hungariar nationalism and he hated the Hungarian language, as well; he wished to replace it by German. As Otto Zarek, in his *History of Hungary,* asserts, what Joseph hated most in the Hungarian body politic was the hangovers of the Middle Ages, the remnants of the feudal era.

The abolition of serfdom struck a mortal blow at the wealth of the Esterhazys and the other landed aristocrats. The liberated peasants poured into the towns and became factory workers. If they remained on the land, they would no longer perform any of their accustomed services unless they were paid. This was a revolution of magnitude, and no wonder Prince Nicholas considered this idealistic emperor a poor thinker and arm-chair philosopher who knew nothing about the people, and was ruining himself and others with the dangerous concessions he made to the common folk. The year was 1789. In France the throne had been shaken; the dragon of revolution was eyeing the royal couple. The Queen of France was the Emperor's sister—but still Vienna refused to learn its lesson. The emperor was absorbed in working out new laws which would render impossible any defense of the throne or of property. Was this not "revolution from above"? Nicholas Esterhazy gave up trying to advise a man who would not listen. Sulkily, he retired to the country and held his tongue; he became chary of permitting members of his own retinue to visit the sinful Babylon of Vienna. Thus, he forbade Haydn furloughs in Vienna, although he did not do so outright; he sought and found tactful pretexts. "It can scarcely be believed," Haydn wrote to Marianna Sabina von Genzinger, "and yet this refusal is put in the subtlest manner, in such a way that I simply cannot broach my request."

Perhaps these actions of the prince were the whims of a very old man who wanted to sit in his armchair and have no more to do with the world. But then he was stricken with his severest blow. On February 25, 1790, after fifty-three years of married life, his wife, Princess Maria Elisabeth, died suddenly. Nicholas could put up with diminution of prestige and wealth, but he could not get over the death of his wife. Haydn, who had just written in an almost impressionistic style to Marianna to describe his own irritation, was greatly shocked and depressed. As he put it, he was "exerting all his energy to shake the prince out of his sadness." He had the rather unhappy idea of giving chamber-music concerts and an operatic performance on the first three evenings after the princess's funeral. The result was inevitable. "The unfortunate prince, upon hearing the first of my favorite *adagios,* was plunged into so profound a melancholy that I had all I could do to lift him out of it again by playing other pieces."

However, the emperor had died in Vienna at the age of fifty, on almost the same day as Princess Esterhazy. A tragic life was brought to a close; for Joseph II was a just and noble person who put himself at odds with his world less by his liberalism than by the tempo with which he inaugurated his reforms. A few days before his death the emperor, menaced by internal and external enemies, had revoked most of his reforms "in order to save the monarchy." Now Nicholas could breathe more easily, for the Hungarians would be able to get along with the emperor's successor, Leopold II, who was known as a moderate. But these political matters no longer concerned Nicholas. For months at a time he sat by the fireplace, gazing into the flames and recalling his beloved wife. He survived her by only half a year, dying on September 28, 1790.

The impossible had happened: after thirty years Haydn was free. He wept sincerely for the prince who, surrounded by incense and pomp, was stretched upon his bed of state, in face once more as handsome as he had been in his youth. Here lay the man to whom Haydn owed most in the world. Twenty-five years before, he had dedicated a cantata, the *Esterhazy Cantata,* to this prince; in it he had prayed that the treasures of sea and of land, pearls and gold, might be put at the disposal of his magnificent patron. The words had been baroque enough, in all conscience, and at the time Haydn had known little of gold and pearls. But since then he had become better acquainted with wealth.

And now Nicholas the Splendid was dead. At first, Haydn did not grasp the full meaning of it; for days he went about in a dreamlike state. Was his contract with the house of Esterhazy ended? Fortunately for Haydn, Prince Anton, the successor, proved that he was a great and noble lord, even if he was unmusical. He made it clear that he had no interest in the continuance of a court orchestra, an opera house in Esterhaz, or any of the other cultural traditions which caused unnecessary outlay of money. But he would not think of cutting off the world-famous Haydn without recompense. The kapellmeister was pensioned off, but continued to receive his full annual salary of 1,400 gulden, a very large allowance which protected him against want for the rest of his life. In return he was required only to continue to term himself "Kapellmeister to Prince Esterhazy."

Then he was really free! He grew dazed at the prospect and at the sudden rush of events. He hastened off to Vienna, leaving even his furniture behind, in order to consult with friends. The Prince of Oetingen-Wallerstein, a rich nobleman of Württemberg, had been trying to acquire his services since the previous summer. In addition, he now received an offer from Prince Anton Grassalkovicz, one of the most powerful of the Hungarian landowners, who had always envied and attempted to match the ways of the great Esterhazys. His taste, however, was a good deal poorer. When the empress visited one of Grassalkovicz's palaces, the host had presented for her entertainment a combat of bears and wild boars costumed as domestic servants and chambermaids, whereupon the outraged Maria Theresa had left the scene.

Haydn was showered with offers from all sides. The most important of these was one from the reigning king of Naples, Ferdinand IV, in Vienna for the double wedding of his daughters to two Austrian archdukes, one of them later the Emperor Francis. Haydn had written music on order from this king. Ferdinand's favorite instrument was the *precieuse* "wheel lyre," the *lira organizzata,* an instrument that today is as obsolete as the barytone or clockwork flute. Haydn, who could do anything in music and who never declined a commission, at once supplied the king with five *lira organizzata* concertos, as well as a number of nocturnes that delighted Ferdinand. All the more reason for the king to press Haydn, now that he was free, to return to Naples with him. Haydn was strongly inclined to go; he had felt old and discontented for a few years, and the mere thought of Italy's sun rejuvenated him.

He was on the point of signing the contract when a stranger called upon him. Rushing impetuously into Haydn's room, the visitor cried out: "I am Salomon of London, and I've come to take you there. Tomorrow we shall draw up an agreement."

During the remaining nineteen years of his life, Haydn often recounted this scene, with lively enjoyment. Consequently, we know a good deal about the herald of destiny—even to his personal appearance.

"Salomon of London" was Johann Peter Salomon, born at Bonn

on the Rhine as a subject of the Elector of Cologne, and probably of Jewish descent. His father had been a friend of Beethoven's father; they had lived in the same house and filled it with music. Johann Peter became a talented violinist and later served as concert master for Frederick the Great's brother Henry, who had an orchestra in Rheinsberg. Here he early took up Haydn's music, which was not too easy in his Prussian environment, for the Prussians at that time considered Haydn unlearned and jocosely Austrian in disposition. Johann Peter Salomon went to London for the first time in 1781 and established his permanent residence there, first as a celebrated virtuoso and occasional composer and later branching out into the promotion of concerts. He promoted many subscription concerts. He was the impresario for the blind pianist, Maria Theresa Paradis; he played a violin duet with the child prodigy William Crotch. In 1790 Salomon visited the continent for the purpose of engaging Italian singers for the London season. On his homeward journey he read in the Cologne newspapers of the death of Prince Esterhazy. He promptly reversed his route, and drove straight to Vienna. In previous years he had frequently written to Haydn to suggest that the composer come to London, and had never received a satisfactory reply. Now, however, the situation had completely changed.

Haydn listened attentively as this foreign entrepreneur talked. He heard Salomon praise London's musical life, of which Haydn knew virtually nothing. He did know, however, that as a child prodigy Mozart had earned laurels in London, that virtuosos were even more highly esteemed there than they were in Italy, that all circles of London society felt a great need for music, that competition there was sharper than anywhere else in the musical world, but also that, strangely enough, not a single English composer had as yet established himself in London. Since the death of Handel, the English played exclusively Italian and German music. These facts gave Haydn much to think about; he asked a number of questions and received heart-warming and enthusiastic answers from Salomon. Without intending flattery, Salomon gave Haydn a factual account of the fame he had won in England. Haydn could verify this; for years he had had dealings with a London publisher, Forster, who had often sent him handsome royalties in British guineas. Haydn quartets and symphonies were frequently printed in London.

Nevertheless, it was hard for the composer who had lived a secluded life for thirty years to think of traveling to London. He asked time to consider, but Salomon only pressed him the harder. In an authoritative manner that scarcely brooked objections, the Londoner outlined his plans, and at the same time placed a contract on the table. He would agree to pay five hundred pounds sterling for six new symphonies (including publication rights); three hundred pounds for an opera which was to be performed by the London manager, Sir John Gallini; two hundred pounds for twenty new smaller compositions which Haydn himself would conduct at concerts; and, in addition, two hundred pounds sterling for a benefit concert. That was a total of twelve hundred pounds. As an advance guarantee, Salomon would deposit five thousand gulden with a Viennese banker. These were certainly wonderful terms, and Haydn accepted them. He had five hundred gulden for travel money, and borrowed an additional four hundred and fifty from Prince Anton Esterhazy. Securities which he did not want to cash for this purpose he gave into the care of Marianna Sabina von Genzinger; to his own wife, he gave, we may be sure, just enough money to run the household.

At this point Salomon began to worry that Haydn might call it all off at the last moment. During the weeks that intervened before the trip, Salomon followed the master about Vienna like a shadow. He did not let him out of his sight, and, perhaps out of superstition, wrote no word to the London newspapers of the great blessing that was about to befall the British capital. Not until December 29, 1790, when Haydn was already en route, did the first announcement appear in London: "Haydn, whose name is a tower of strength and to whom the amateurs of instrumental music look up as the God of the science," Haydn was coming; Haydn was en route; Haydn was soon to land in England.

Salomon was concerned about Haydn's health, but he need not have been. Never had this man of almost sixty been sounder in body than now, when ambition and creative eagerness were carrying him to his greatest adventure.

Book Four
THE GLORIOUS AFTERNOON

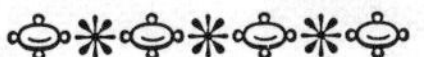

When wise Copernicus the orbs arranged,
The system of Astronomy was changed . . .
Haydn! Great Sovereign of the tuneful art!
Thy works alone supply an ample chart
Of all the mountains, seas, and fertile plains,
Within the compass of its wide domains!

CHARLES BURNEY:
Verses on the arrival of Haydn in England, 1791

THE STUNNED TRAVELER

It was hard for Haydn to say goodbye to Mozart. But it was the younger master who wept.

"Ah, do not go, Papa! You are not suited for the great world, and you command so few languages."

Haydn looked at him in astonishment. "But the language I speak is understood the world over!"

Mozart shook his head. He foresaw evil. It was twenty-eight years since he himself had visited London, as a weakly, seven-year-old child. But he, at any rate, had been protected by his father. Nevertheless, he had fallen ill from overstrain and anxiety when he was to perform at court. Afterwards, however, the "invincible Wolfgang," as his father Leopold called him, had recovered and had "conquered London," as the phrase goes. In reality, he had conquered nothing at all; and now, at the age of thirty-five, the great composer seemed old and oppressed by many premonitions.

On the last day the two friends spent together, December 14, Mozart murmured again and again: "This is the last time we shall see each other." Luigia Polzelli had the same conviction; "Haydn will die," she wrote. And later, as if the whole affair were an intrigue in some Italian opera, she declared, "An enemy has followed Haydn to London in order to ruin him there."

Meanwhile, on December 15, 1790, Haydn set off, quite calm and at peace with himself. Three days later he and Salomon arrived in Munich, where he made the acquaintance of Cannabich, the distinguished conductor, and transmitted Mozart's regards. Their second stop was at Bonn, Salomon's birthplace. There the Elector received the travelers with exceptional courtesy. This Electoral prince was an old acquaintance of Haydn's, no other than Archduke Maximilian, brother of the emperor who had recently died. To the master's surprise, the court orchestra performed one of his own works.

This Hapsburg—now Archbishop of Cologne—was, according to

one of Mozart's malicious remarks, "the grower of a goiter and blessed with stupidity." Nevertheless, it was this same Prince of the Church who discovered young Beethoven and appointed him, at the age of eighteen, to the post of vice cathedral kapellmeister. Who can say whether or not—as Haydn sat in the dim light of the auditorium at Bonn, listening to his own music—two dark, burning eyes were not at that very moment fixing the image of this famous guest? Beethoven knew Salomon well, since their fathers had been friends, but at this time he would not have ventured to request to be introduced to Haydn. A year and a half were to pass before the two men met.

After a dinner given by the Archbishop for the travelers, Haydn and Salomon left Bonn. Irregular sleep and bouncing about in a carriage made the master lose weight (a fact which he duly reported to Marianna Sabina von Genzinger), but did not affect his courage or his high spirits. On the day before the New Year he reached Calais and saw the sea for the first time. He stared in astonishment at "that huge monster with his boisterous waves rushing on"; but at last he smiled as he recalled the clown Kruz-Bernardon, who forty years ago had commanded him to compose music for the sea. Then he set foot on shipboard for the first time; the weather at the beginning of the New Year was excellent. They arrived at Dover, and at once set out for London.

"The first thing that struck Haydn about London was that it lacked a St. Stephen's tower," a member of the Prinster family later recounted. The tower of St. Stephen's in Vienna was like a shepherd who gathered around him even the most remote of the city's herd of houses. In London there was no such architectural and spiritual center. In 1666 the Great Fire had destroyed 13,200 houses and some ninety churches, but London had risen out of the ruins mightier than ever and thrust out westward beyond the old boundaries. Since the beginning of the eighteenth century the city had been *caput mundi*, the capital of the world. From it all quarters of the globe were governed. Great Britain owned India and Canada; it hardly mattered that she had lost thirteen colonies in America. The average Londoner scarcely knew where these new United States were situated; so great was Britain's wealth, so various the cargoes brought from all parts of the world to her ports, that she might have lost far more without noticing it.

It was a splendid city toward which our stunned traveler was being driven. The weather was foggy and damp, but not cold. The buildings looked substantial, as befitted a tenacious, strong-armed race of men. The Thames wound a serpentine course through the center of London—or rather, through the many Londons.

Salomon sat in the carriage beside Haydn. Hand on the composer's arm, he pointed out to his subdued, silent friend some of the buildings. St. Paul's, the work of Sir Christopher Wren, had been standing now for a hundred years, the Bank of England had occupied for sixty years its place on Threadneedle Street, which was so narrow that it well suited its name. But the joke meant little to Haydn; little was conveyed to him by all the names of the vast structures that blocked the horizon, such as the Palace of St. James, Kensington Palace, Whitehall, Westminster Abbey, Somerset House, and Marlborough House. They were but names to which scraps of history adhered; some of them occurred in the Shakespeare plays that Haydn had seen at Esterhaz; but he would never feel at home in this city.

On shipboard Haydn had suffered a slight attack of seasickness. He had, as he reported to Marianna Sabina, fought it down much more easily than had most of the other passengers. But now, when he arrived in London, he began to suffer from headaches. Travel was such an unaccustomed experience. Perhaps, too, his headaches could be ascribed to his astonishment at the sight of London's frightening vastness. A whole nation seemed to be inhabiting this place.

Because of his headaches, Haydn kept his eyes closed as much as he could, and thus it happened that he made his first acquaintance with London through his sense of hearing. The noise was terrifying; it was like the roaring of surf in a storm, and indeed the competition was stormy among the hardworking breadwinners who tried to outshout one another. The variegated activities of the city, the feverish life of the Stock Exchange and the thunder of burgeoning industries, filled the streets with a din that horrified Haydn—there was not a note of it that was intelligible to him.

But the components of the din were, after all, human voices. Rising above the general level of the noise were the cries of the food peddlers. Honey, vinegar, and oysters, delicacies such as gingerbread, apples, and other fruits, were carried from door to door. Girls with baskets on their heads sold shrimps; others with panniers on their arms vended lavender, vegetables, and tarts. They all cried their wares at the tops of their voices. There were the itinerant carpenter, the knife and scissors grinder, the huckster of female finery, the almanac seller; there were the chair mender and the old-clothes man; the seller of baskets walked about with her wares piled high on her head; there were the tinker, the china mender, the peddler of kitchen utensils. Adding to the commotion was the hurly-burly of continual fights, when the roars of the mob urged on the combatants; there were the cracking of whips by the coachmen, the shouting of shrews conducting their arguments from windows and porches, the snarling hubbub of stray dogs engaged in fights, and the roaring songs of roisterers reeling to and from the taverns. It was too much, too much for a stranger! Days passed before Haydn was reassured about this infernal racket that pressed in upon him from all sides.

He spent his first night in London with one of his publishers, John Bland. The latter was a great admirer of the master, and had once paid a visit to Esterhaz in order to meet Haydn. He happened to enter the room while Haydn was shaving. The razor was dull, and the composer exclaimed irritably, "I'd give my best quartet for a decent razor!" Without a word, Bland ran out of the room, went to his luggage, and returned with his own razor. Haydn was punctilious about promises; on the following day he presented the Briton with his famous *Razor Quartet*.

Bland and his Jewish wife put Haydn up this first night. The latter provided him with his first English pea soup, which he found excellent. The following day he moved into Salomon's house, 18 Great Pulteney Street, where the Italian cook provided him with meals which suited him better than the heavy English cuisine; it took time for him to accustom himself to the English cuisine. Nevertheless, he dined out six times in the first week (so he wrote to Marianna Sabina). The Austrian and the Neapolitan Ambassadors responded with invitations to his courtesy calls; and London, "this mighty and vast town with its various beauties and marvels," began to impress him as more amiable.

It is almost certain that Haydn's appearance and personality at first disappointed London society. A man of his fame should not have been so modest and timid. Handel had habituated people to a proud and arrogant manner; they felt that such an attitude was characteristic of genius. By this standard, the unassuming Haydn was found sadly wanting.

Salomon had handled the external arrangements very effectively.

The barn from which a genius sprang:
HAYDN'S BIRTHPLACE IN ROHRAU

The Bettmann Archive

"Anyone can see by the look of me that I mean well by everybody":
HAYDN IN THE MIDDLE OF HIS LIFE

Nicholas the Splendid

A great magnate and protector of the arts

Mozart the Friend

"Posterity will not have another such talent in a hundred years"

Young Beethoven the Pupil

"Do you think I am easier to be played on than a pipe?"

The press was excellently prepared for Haydn's coming. However, the manager had his hands full arranging the programs and supporting artists for the subscription concerts. It was therefore meet that someone else took the socially awkward Haydn in hand. This person was a countryman of his, the young Austrian composer Adalbert Gyrowetz, who had been living in London for two years. He was an adroit and very popular man who, among other advantages, had the friendship of the Prince of Wales, subsequently George IV. It was his task to convince society that certain peculiarities of the master were a part of Haydn's nature and must be loved as his music was loved. For the master was prone to sit silent during great dinners, and scarcely to reply even when addressed in German. Once, at a banquet given for him by the singer Mara-Schmehling, he hid his face in his hands when his health was proposed; the "three cheers" and the resulting din were too much for him, and he seemed confused for some time afterward.

Haydn, Gyrowetz explained, was one of those naïve geniuses who might be bodily present in society, but whose souls and minds were far away; they were "transported"; they lived in another world. Gyrowetz was Haydn's constant escort at gatherings. He would coax Haydn to sit down at the piano; and when he did, and began singing German folk songs, contact with "society" was swiftly established.

Alone with this helpful companion, Haydn was not at all shy. With passionate curiosity he questioned his young colleague, not only about musical matters, but about almost everything that concerned the civil affairs of London and the English. His interest in people was all-embracing; it extended from the Prince of Wales down to the coachman in the street. Was it true that the citizens of London had enjoyed street illumination at night since 1416, although Joseph von Sonnenfels had only recently put through such a reform in Vienna? What had the building of St. Paul's cost, and was it true that a coal tax had been levied to raise the money? What did people here think about the French Revolution? Were they afraid of the infection's spreading?

Gyrowetz furnished him with rules of conduct for life in London where (as he later explained in his autobiography) "everything was different from the rest of Europe: a different air, a different architecture, different regulations, different customs . . . and quite different people." They were indeed different people. The thing that must first have struck a visitor from Middle or Eastern Europe was the extraordinary lack of respect shown by the lower classes toward the upper classes. (Even fifty years later Edgar Allan Poe wondered at the *satire,* "abounding in England.") Yet it was not the same as it was in France, where hatred divided the classes.

At the time when Haydn visited England, there was a great vogue for the satirical engravings of William Hogarth, the best illustrator of the manners of the times. His caricatures evoked fascination and horror. They depicted people who behaved like animals, and animals who behaved like people. No traits, no types were spared; the portrait gallery included the habitual drunkards, either the tavern sots who sat all day over porter and ale, or the more desperate slaves of gin; there were usurers, misers, prostitutes, the brutal-minded onlookers at a cock-fight; the apothecaries and physicians who acted as "procurers for death." In all of them human vileness was exposed, as it was to be found in royal chambers, lawyers' offices, taverns, cook shops, *maisons de rendezvous,* poorhouses, pawnshops, barber shops and refuse heaps.

What, in these circumstances, happened to music in England? A people whose greatest amusement was derived from social caricature might be expected not to care much for the most abstract and introspective of arts. But the best of theories fails to account for popular aptitudes. Not Paris, not Berlin, but London was the most important center of music in the northwestern part of Europe. There were complicated reasons for this.

England had always had its foes of instrumental music, who maintained that fiddling and tooting were not worthy of serious-minded men. (With singing, however, it was another case.) Moreover, the Puritan revolution was at bottom hostile to music; and what counted most was the fact that the nation's creative forces were, for centuries, diverted by religious and political struggles. The people, nevertheless, were very hungry for music, although it appeared for quite a time that they would have to listen to foreign music only. But then, in the autumn of 1710, George Frederick Handel came to the British Isles, an Anglicized German who was born in Halle. Within a dozen years the immigrant became more Anglo-Saxon than the natives. Whatever elements of German, Italian, and French music Handel incorporated into his compositions, they were nevertheless British to the bone.

Handel's creed was set forth in the opera and the oratorio. For three quarters of a century the forms he established exercised a despotism that Guido Adler rightly compares to the terroristic despotism of Wagner. Musical progress took place within the limits of Handelian structure. The numerous musical societies that sprang up in London—the St. Cecilia Society, the Academy of Ancient Music, the Anacreontic Society—and so on, appeared to have, as their sole reason for being, the performance of works by Handel, the absolute monarch.

Yet the principle of free competition, so dear to the English nation and reflected so variously in English economy and philosophy, was to have its play also in the realm of music. The defeat of Spain had made the British nation the richest on earth, and with wealth came the desire to purchase. Thus, London bought the services of the virtuosos of the entire Continent; and this broke the absolute dominion of Handel. The singers and instrumentalists from abroad brought with them the artistic styles of their native lands. The consequence was, that nowhere else outside of Italy was there so much singing in Italian as in London, and the Austrian, Polish, Czech, and Hungarian violinists and piano virtuosos whom Haydn met in England, such as Felix Yaniewicz, Clement, Giornovichj-Jarnowick, Dussek, Young, Hummel and Raimondi, brought the chamber-music art of central Europe to the London musical marketplace. It is in terms of supply and demand that we must think of Salomon's engagement of Haydn. (This does not apply to Salomon personally, who revered Haydn and had a good basis for doing so, being himself a talented musician.) The English public, however, looked upon Haydn as another of its "imports"; he was not, to them, so much a creative master as a sort of composing virtuoso. He was extraordinary in that he represented the greatest international value upon the musical 'Change.

Haydn was to encounter in London competition of the fiercest sort. At first he suspected nothing; he was still ignorant of the English language; but he soon realized that even for the most famous visitor to London the path was not going to be made easy. His friend Salomon had a difficult time concealing from Haydn the talk going about London society concerning the master's advanced age. (He was sixty years old.) A number of statements were inserted into the daily press, to combat the premature criticism of Haydn on this score. Salomon insisted that Haydn's music would prove his youthfulness of spirit.

The competitive struggle went on twelve hours a day. Haydn found himself involved in animosities such as he had never dreamed of. As we know, his music was in especially high esteem in Italy (ten years earlier the Academy of Modena had appointed him an honorary member), and he often thought of himself—though incorrectly—as in the Italian tradition.

Haydn had brought with him to London a composition, in the Italian style, of which he was particularly fond, the solo cantata *Arianna a Naxos*. This was based on the famous myth of Ariadne, the girl who was deserted by Theseus; the theme had been a favorite with composers. It is an important lesser work of the master's in which Italian *bellezza* is combined with the power and psychological verity of Gluck. Even before Salomon inaugurated his series of concerts, this work was performed at a semi-public concert given by a ladies' club that wished to honor Haydn. The composer accompanied on the piano, and played better than was usual with him. The chromatic passage in which the heartsick Ariadne climbs up the promontory to discover her lover's treachery excited the admiration of all:

The vocal part was not sung by a woman, as might have been expected, but by the Italian tenor Gasparo Pacchierotti. So magnificent was this singer's voice reputed to be that there was a story current of a Roman orchestra's having forgotten to accompany him when he lifted his voice. "What's the trouble with you?" the singer had demanded, testily, whereupon the conductor had bowed and said, "Forgive us, signor, we are weeping."

Pacchierotti sang Haydn's *Ariadne* to such effect that the London *Morning Chronicle* wrote: "Haydn's cantata will accordingly be the musical desideratum for the winter . . . The modulation is so deep and scientific, so varied and agitating, that the audience was thrown into ecstasies. Every fiber was touched by the captivating energies of the passion, and Pacchierotti never . . . was more successful." Nevertheless, there were Italian musicians in London who were infuriated with Haydn for having ventured to use what they considered one of their own subjects. *Porcheria Tedesca!* ("German swinishness!") was the mildest comment they made about it.

Competition was tough in London.

THE OPEN MARKET

EIGHT weeks after his arrival in London, Haydn was no longer a dumbfounded traveler; he had settled down, and knew how to conduct himself. His self-confidence rose materially when Salomon's rivals, the gentlemen who ran the "professional concerts," attempted to win him over. At first they showed him exceptional courtesy; later they were to offer him money to desert Salomon; this Haydn, of course, refused to do. But even before Salomon could begin his concerts, the Professional Players, conducted by Cramer of Mannheim, performed some of Haydn's works—a symphony and a quartet, among others. The concert took place on February 7, 1791. The composer received a free ticket; he sat in the hall and applauded diplomatically.

A few weeks before this concert, a social event of the highest importance had taken place. On the queen's birthday, January 18, the Palace of St. James was thrown open for a ball attended by the court and prominent members of society. Among those present were the Dukes of York, Clarence, and Gloucester, and the Prince of Wales. The uniform of the future George IV was ornamented with diamonds valued at eighty thousand pounds. At the beginning of the ball he asked his private secretary, John Doyle, what the crowd gathered in front of the palace had thought of his dress. "Oh," the secretary replied, evasively, "I think they were all sincerely delighted."

"Did they say anything in particular?"

"I heard one fellow say: 'Look at those fancy frills the prince is wearing on his shoulders—diamond epaulets; did you ever see the like of it?' 'Fancy enough,' another replied, 'so fancy that we'll soon be bearing the burden of them on our own shoulders.' "

The prince was taken aback for a moment, then he said: "Doyle, you made that up. Oh, well, come to the buffet and let's drink to your health."

At that moment Haydn, who had been invited, entered in the company of his friend Salomon and of Sir John Gallini, who was paying for the Italian opera which was to open shortly. Haydn was two steps ahead of his companions. The prince, who did not know Haydn but had probably been prepared for his coming by Gyrowetz (who was one of the prince's favorites), caught sight of the composer and bowed first to him!

This extraordinary act of courtesy created a tremendous stir. The Prince of Wales occupied himself principally with incurring debts and leading a rake's life that often bordered on outright depravity. But by avocation he was an accomplished cellist; the story was told of him that at the age of three he had attempted to crawl into a cello, "to see whether there's a flute inside." Such blends of vice and talent no longer exist; nowadays our elegant gentlemen would be profoundly bored should their radios give them modern music instead of racing results. But in those days it was one of the requirements of a nobleman to possess real mastery of some musical instrument; all the European courts had their aristocratic dilettantes. Thus, if we examine the matter closely, it was not the Prince of Wales who bowed to Haydn, but the prince as a cellist.

Nevertheless, the act itself instantly altered Haydn's position. He was no longer an outsider, no longer considered partly a master composer and partly an odd, "bohemian" character, who had been summoned to London as had been so many other musical virtuosos; he was now an accepted member of London society and one who enjoyed the respect of the court.

In a letter to Frau von Genzinger, Haydn referred to the prince as "the handsomest man on earth" (though he also begged her to say nothing of the prince's debts). We may well wonder how he communicated with his hosts on this and similar occasions. Few persons at court or in society understood his dialectal Austrian German though a considerable number could converse with him in Italian, and German was spoken at court. That Haydn did not speak yet a word of English, was rather fortunate for him; for the host of impressions would probably have overwhelmed him had he understood English. He did, however, make the attempt to learn the language; when the weather became warmer he "went out into the open air with a grammar," as he reported, with shy self-consciousness, to Marianna Sabina. He could not have made much progress, for the following summer, at the farewell dinner that was given him before his departure from England, Salomon had to be invited, "partly as the intimate friend of Mr. Haydn, partly as an interpreter, Dr. Haydn having not made sufficient progress in the English language," as the annals of the Musical Graduates Society record.

Poor Salomon had his troubles in the early days of Haydn's stay. On January 15, 1791, the press had published the first detailed announcement of his twelve subscription concerts. Tickets were five guineas, and the advance sale was excellent. Haydn, the star of the occasion, had to deliver a newly composed piece of music for each evening and was to direct the performance himself from the piano. He was available, of course, but Salomon needed another star who was not: Davide, the great tenor, whose participation was an essential part of the plans. Davide was at this time forty-one years old and at the height of his career. He had a contract for a season's appearance in Gallini's Italian opera company. Unfortunately, the opera was postponed, and in consequence Salomon had also to postpone his own concerts—postpone them twice. The "Professional Concerts" profited by this; their directors spread the rumor that Salomon's undertaking would not get started that season.

Behind the continual postponements of Davide's debut at the King's Theater lay the rampant spirit of musical rivalry. It had reached a pitch of fantastic ferocity, and had even penetrated to the royal family. George III and his son were waging a feud in artistic matters. The king was supporting the Pantheon Opera Company; the Prince of Wales favored Sir John Gallini's, which was to open first. In a pique, the king had stated that two theaters for the performance of Italian opera were too much for the city of London. Half the court endeavored to change his mind about this, but the king refused to revoke the royal veto. Finally, the Prince of Wales advised the despairing Gallini to pay no attention to the king and to go ahead with his rehearsals. This was done; the company began rehearsing Paisiello's opera *Il Pirro,* which was to be the opening work of the season. Davide was in his best voice; the dress rehearsal was set for March 8. The house was full of invited guests; thousands stood outside; and even the stage was so overcrowded with visitors that the dancer Vestris could scarcely perform without bumping into them. But still the king's permission for the official opening of the theater was not forthcoming.

Salomon correctly calculated that this permission would never be granted, because the king was the stronger of the two parties. He therefore took precautions to make sure that Haydn's prospects would not be damaged any further. He was a personal friend of Gallini's, and contrived to convince Sir John that he must interpret Davide's contract so that the singer's appearance in the dress rehearsal for *Pirro* could be considered a "public appearance." In order to please Salomon, Gallini agreed, and it became possible to hold the first Haydn concert on March 11.

The rehearsals had not been easy. Salomon's orchestra consisted of sixteen violins, four violas, three cellos, four bass viols; horns and percussion made up another fourteen musicians. The nervous tension at the rehearsals arose not from doubts of Davide's ability to be present, but from Haydn's inability to express himself in English. His D-major Symphony, No. 93, which was to be played for the first time at this concert, begins with a short adagio

the melody of which is introduced by three identical notes that—although a fortissimo is indicated—must be played very softly. The rehearsal began, but instead of the notes' being played "melancholically" they were thundered out "cholerically." Haydn interrupted—very calmly at first—and Salomon translated his criticism. The notes were repeated, but no more softly. Haydn protested again. An embarrassed silence ensued, during which a German cellist murmured somewhat loudly to his neighbor: "You know, this is going to turn out fine. The first notes don't suit him; what's it going to be like later on?" Haydn, tears of agitation in his eyes, turned around and said: "Gentlemen, forgive me for not speaking English. I will demonstrate what I mean on the instrument itself." He snatched up a violin and played the three notes himself—very loud, but soft at once. The hearts of the musicians were won, and the rehearsal continued satisfactorily.

The concert was a great triumph, Haydn's first personal triumph in the "open market." For thirty years he had been far away whenever his music was played in public; the only applause he had heard was that of the Esterhazys' guests. The *adagio* of the symphony had to be repeated on public request—something unheard of in London. Haydn wrote proudly to Luigia Polzelli: *Nel primo concerto del Signor Salomone io ho fatto un furore con una nuova Sinfonia, loro hanno fatto* *replicare l'adagio.** Curiously enough, the symphony appeared on the program not as a symphony but as a "new grand overture." This was, undoubtedly, done on Salomon's advice, and we may deduce from this fact that London, in spite of its vigorous musical life, was in this respect half a century behind the times. Master Haydn had long ago made the symphony and the overture take different ways, but in London the old-fashioned French nomenclature was still in use.

Haydn's caution was indicated by his insistence that the D-major Symphony be placed at the beginning of the second part of the program. He was so afraid of the noise made by late-comers that he made this a rule for the entire series.

The financial success of this first concert was so great that it underwrote Salomon's entire group of concerts. "Haydn's newest overture (!) was declared by all connoisseurs to be a wonderful work," the *Morning Chronicle* wrote. "Let us hope that the foremost musical genius of our time will now see fit to establish residence permanently in England."

The second Salomon concert was given on Friday of the following week. The Prince of Wales arrived in time to take pleasure in Haydn's triumph; it was he who gave the signal for the beginning of the applause. At Haydn's request, the concert was begun with a Mozart symphony; of Haydn's own compositions there were a string quartet and the D-major Symphony, No. 93, which the London audience apparently wished to hear again and again. The following Friday the third concert took place; it included the first performance of the C-minor Symphony, No. 95 and a new Haydn cantata which had been composed for the soprano Storace. In April there were four more concerts and also four in May, each of which was sold out, and on June 13 the twelfth and last of the season's concerts was given. But before that, on May 16, Haydn had given an unscheduled benefit concert in which his own compositions formed the major part of the program. He had composed a new aria, with oboe and bassoon accompaniment, for the tenor Davide, and by general request the great Pacchierotti sang *Arianna a Naxos*. The profit from the concert was very satisfactory indeed—three hundred and fifty pounds sterling.

The exactness of these dates is noteworthy. We know far more about the year and a half which the master spent in London than we

* In Mr. Salomon's first concert I created a stir with a new symphony; they had to repeat the *adagio*.

do about his thirty long years in Eisenstadt and Esterhaz; the earlier period is often so undocumented that some of the works written during it have not as yet been dated satisfactorily. But there is nothing strange about this—London was an open stage, where outstanding personalities were observed very closely indeed. The newspapers kept very close accounts of Haydn's activities. A second and a very rich source for the biographer is the accounts of contemporaries. A third is the large number of detailed letters that Haydn wrote to Frau von Genzinger; it was due to her charm that the taciturn man who suffered greatly because of his lack of education became an eager and a voluminous correspondent. A fourth and most remarkable source, however, is the series of diaries that the master kept while he was in London.

At home the idea of keeping a diary would never have occurred to him. A journal presupposes an interest in one's own person which the modest composer lacked. He felt toward himself a classic impersonality. These diaries that he kept in London are especially interesting because they served as a kind of self-defense against the turmoil of events and experiences; against the strange land, the strange people, and the many demands that were made upon Haydn. In this sense they are notebooks rather than diaries. It is quite possible that Gyrowetz advised the master to keep them, but they are entirely Haydn's in form and spirit.

These diaries have been preserved, for the most part. There are three volumes; the fourth has been lost, possibly burned by a servant girl in Vienna. The first two deal with Haydn's first visit to London; the third, which dates from his second stay in England (1794-1795), is by far the most interesting of the three. When this third diary was published by I. E. Engl in 1909, the editor said, in his preface: "Any change in Haydn's punctuation and orthography has been avoided as a distinct injustice to the author." Unfortunately, Theodor von Karajan, who first published Haydn's letters to Frau von Genzinger, in 1861, did not act with so much insight; he translated the letters into High German. In so doing he not only robbed them of their peculiar charm, but rendered inexplicable the tragi-comical incidents that occurred, because Haydn often could not make his meaning clear in a letter, even to his best friends. Thus, he once asked Frau von Genzinger to send a copy, needed in London, of a symphony; he had to wait a whole year for it because she could not make out what he was asking for.

The London diaries comment shrewdly upon Haydn's experiences with concerts and concert artists. Occasionally he made use of these notebooks of his to take private pokes at his opponents. There was, for example, the well known Italian violinist Giardini, who remarked haughtily, shortly after Haydn's arrival in London, "I have no interest in meeting that German dog." The insult went the rounds of London society, of course; but apparently Haydn did nothing about it publicly. In his diary, however, he wrote bluntly about a certain concert: "Giardini played like a pig."

The diaries also contain Hogarthian anecdotes about celebrations such as the noisy and very liquid banquet that the people of London gave for their new Lord Mayor on November 5, 1791. Haydn also set down *bon mots* he had heard; he took naïve and distinctly undignified pleasure in risqué stories and phrases. He noted, for example, some popular verses on David and Solomon which he must have particularly enjoyed because his manager's name was Salomon and his singer's was Davide.

> A pair of great sinners were Solomon and Davy,
> Had beautiful wifes and manny progeny,
> But Age sapped heir strength, who all passion calms;
> Hen the one wrote songs and the other wrote psalms.

"Mr. Lord Avingdon sat it to music, but did a wretched job," Haydn noted. "I did it somewhut better."

During both of his stays in England, Haydn was attracted by statistics—any sort of statistics. He noted the circumference of the Isle of Wight, the number of towers in the city of Peking, and the age of the Chinese emperor—his interest in these latter facts having been aroused by a projected trade treaty between England and China. The might of England as a world power excited Haydn's imagination; he seized the opportunity to inspect warships, and noted carefully that every ship of the line "must have 3 decks and at leasd 64 cannon; a cutter on the other hand possesses at mosd 16 cannon." Perhaps he hoped that such figures would impress his Viennese friends; after all, no warships sailed upon the Neusiedlersee, and the "Kingdom of Esterhazy" had no navy.

Frequently he noted down Latin phrases and added his own meticulous translations. Above the curtain in the Haymarket Theater, for example, was the inscription: SPECTAS ET TU SPECTABERE ("You see and you yourself are seen"); Haydn copied it and commented briefly upon it. Another Latin phrase noted by him pertained to his own art: *Curas cithara tollit* ("The zither drives away care"). He also copied, from a Latin author, *Mulcet ut magus* ("He soothes like a magician"), a phrase that bears a suggestive similarity to the inscription that was placed upon Haydn's own gravestone: *Mulcendi pectora primus.*

Finally, the diaries contained English verses; Haydn, although unable to understand ordinary English, was very fond of English poetry, and perhaps noted down the words with the intention of later setting them to music. These verses were always written out quite correctly. Occasionally, however, Haydn transcribed in English some remark he had heard, and then, as the British music critic Marion Scott has put it, "Haydn's spelling is sheer delight. One entry, '6 Schiots, 12 deto' beat even H. E. Krebiehl, the musicologist, when he tried to interpret it. May I humbly submit that Haydn perhaps bought 18 shirts." (But Marion Scott may be guessing wrong, too.)

Haydn was most telling in these diaries, in spite of his preposterous German spelling, when he commented upon manners and morals or recounted a dramatic anecdote. Here he brought to bear the same sharpness and descriptive talent that distinguished him as a musician. A good example of his talent for concise and pointed description is the following entry: "Milord Chatham, Minister of War, was so drunk for thrie days that he coud not sign his name, with the rezult that his subawdinate, Lord Howe, togedder with the entire Fleet could not sale from London."

OXFORD DOCTOR

"The admirable, the matchless Haydn." These were the words employed by the four-volume *General History of Music* at the beginning of its article on the new arrival. The last volume, which discussed contemporary music, had just appeared in 1789. The author of this book was the most important person Haydn met in London.

In those days the English were not yet great travelers, but Dr. Charles Burney had repeatedly made tours of the Continent to gather source material for his book. In 1770 he had been in France and Italy; on another trip, in 1772, he went to Holland and Germany.

Dr. Burney had paid visits to Austria also. The domestic architecture of that country convinced him that Austria was a middle land between Germany and Italy in a spiritual as well as a geographical sense. In Vienna the houses struck him as poverty-stricken, gray and black, as if there were no light in the sky; there was a smoky German provinciality about them. But the top stories were Italian, of milk-white marble, and bathed in sunlight, so that they seemed to be half palaces, half hovels. The "poor quality of goods" struck the Englishman as a characteristic feature of Vienna; such furniture and cloth would not be tolerated in London, he noted. But he was pleased with the Viennese "fondness of the theater." Among the few German words that Burney understood, *Gott* was one; and he found the repeated swearing and cursing in Lessing's *Emilia Galotti*—*"Bei Gott!"* and *"Gott verdamm' ihn!"*—shocking and tasteless.

One of Burney's reasons for visiting Vienna was the hope of meeting Joseph Haydn. But the latter was in Esterhaz at the time, and Burney's reverence for the master was not strong enough to make him risk a journey to Hungary, a land probably inhabited by savages. He therefore had to be content with Gluck, and did not consider that he had struck a bad bargain. "Gluck," Burney noted with awe, "is as formidable a character as our Handel used to be—a very dragon of whom all are in fear."

The result was that Burney did not make the acquaintance of Haydn until the composer's visit to London, a full nineteen years later. The influential Oxford doctor was now organist of the Chelsea Church, where Haydn called upon him. They could converse easily in Italian only; but Haydn was slowly beginning to learn English, and so was able to spell out with difficulty what the infallible pope of music had said about him in his *History*. Burney did not object to Haydn's "bold modulation, rests, pauses, and unexpected flights, freaks, whims, and even buffoonery"; on the contrary, he enjoyed them. "Haydn's oratorio, *Il Ritorno di Tobia,* composed in 1775, has been annually performed at Vienna ever since, and is as high in favor there as Handel's *Messiah* in England." For a Handel worshiper like Burney, this was a stunning comparison. Of the *Seven Last Words of Our Saviour on the Cross,* Burney wrote: "These strains are so truly impassioned and full of heartfelt grief and dignified sorrow, that though the movements are all slow, the subjects, keys, and effects are so new and so different, that a real lover of music will find no lassitude or wish for lighter strains to stimulate attention." He indicated his preference for Haydn's *adagios* rather than his faster *tempi:* "His *adagios* have a more pathetic effect on my feelings than the finest opera air united with the most exquisite poetry. From his productions I have received more pleasure later in my life when tired than from most other music."

However, Doctor Burney's great influence upon Haydn's life was indirect. He took the composer to the grand Handel festival, held in the last week in May in Westminster Abbey. It was a tremendous experience for Haydn, for the master had probably never heard a note of Handel's in his whole life. Although Haydn had spent years studying North German music, and considered himself a humble disciple of Carl Philipp Emanuel Bach, he had altogether missed contact with Handel, who had moved out of the North German group and become an Englishman long before Haydn had a chance to gain acquaintance with his music.

The vast nave of the abbey had been turned into a concert hall and was filled with waving gold and silver banners. "The band was a thousand strong," William Gardiner reported, "ably conducted by Joah Bates upon the organ. The orchestra was so steep that it was dangerous to come down, and some accidents occurred, one being of a ludicrous nature. A person falling upon a double bass, as it lay on its side, immediately disappeared; nothing was seen of him but his legs protruding out of the instrument. For some time no one could assist him for laughing." After recounting this Hogarthian incident, Gardiner continued, on a more sober note: "Haydn was present at this performance, and with the aid of a telescope (!) which had been placed on a stand near the kettledrums I saw the composer near the king's box. The performance attracted persons from all parts of Europe, and the demand for tickets was so great that, in some instances, a single one was sold for twenty pounds."

George III sat surrounded by his dukes. He wore civilian dress, with no decoration but the small medallion of the Handel Festival, whose patron he was. Honoring of Handel was a legacy that had been imposed upon him, for in his childhood the great composer had stooped down to him and declared: "You are a dear child, are you not? *You will protect my music when I am dead!*" The boy had promised, and the man had kept his word; all his life the king gave his royal patronage to Handel's music.

The festival lasted four days. On the last day, June 1, when the celestial thunder of the choruses rang out, flooding the cathedral with the music of *The Messiah,* the audience rose as one man. The king in his box gave the signal; for a passage like "For the Lord God Omnipotent" none ought to sit. The emotions aroused by this demonstration were too much for Master Haydn; he covered his face with his hands and wept aloud. "He is the master of us all," he repeated in a shaking voice.

Had this incident occurred twenty years earlier, Handel might have been as much a danger to Haydn's musical independence as Gluck had been. But by this time Haydn was too sure of himself to succumb; he could incorporate Handel's magnificence into his own work, as he did in *The Creation,* but he could no longer become a slavish imitator.

"Conceive the highest you can of his abilities, and they are much beyond anything you can conceive," Dr. Arbuthnot had said of Handel fifty years earlier. Haydn might well have had the same feeling; but he could not identify himself completely with Handel's music. It did not speak his language. The difference was a religious one; Haydn was a Catholic and Handel was not. The eighteenth century was not so "enlightened" as to make this immaterial. Handel's church music differed principally in the choral treatment, from the music to which Haydn was accustomed. Handel's was thoroughly Protestant. Catholicism does not accept the existence of an *anima communis,* a "soul of the congregation"; the Protestant church, however, follows the Old Testament belief that God spoke to the "people." The people is the unit, not the individual. For this reason, the choruses of Bach and Handel are unlike those inspired by the Church of Rome. Among the Protestants the people confront God; they sing and strive with Him; they take an active part, split into sections, contest with one another in semi-choruses, and at last join in submission to God. This was the reason for the indescribable power of Handel's vast choruses which, as it was said, "have to carry the sword of God between their teeth."

Haydn was greatly moved by all this, but he was also disturbed. Yet how wonderful it might be, he thought, if that mass of singers consisted of children, whom he loved so dearly and who would sing, not like the sword, but like the palm branch! He was, in fact, stirred to the depths when he heard four thousand orphan children sing at the Charity School's anniversary in St. Paul's Cathedral. Once more the king was present. With bowed head George III, at this time already verging on insanity, listened to the sweet voices of the innocents. "I have seen a hundred grand sights in the world," Thackeray wrote later; "popes' chapels with their processions of long-tailed cardinals and quavering choirs of fat *soprani*—but I think in all Christendom there is no such sight as Charity Children's Day. *Cantant non Angli, sed angeli.*" With flushed cheeks and clear, strong voices, the thousands of children sang the hymn written by Handel's disciple, the organist John Jones:

Haydn, the former choir-boy of St. Stephen's, copied the music as he heard it. "All my life I have never been so strongly moved by any music as by these innocent and reverent notes," he wrote in his diary.

Burney, in his huge scholar's wig, set himself up as Haydn's mentor and guided him through London. The historian of music had an extremely pleasant surprise in store for Haydn: The composer's appointment as an honorary doctor of Oxford University. Every few years the university conferred an honorary degree in music upon someone it considered worthy of this dignity. The custom was frowned upon by some; sixty years earlier it had met with vehement protest. A university, it was asserted, had other business "than to be prostituted to a company of squeezing, bawling, outlandish singsters." But by Haydn's day, solemn Oxford had grown more modern and friendlier toward the art of music.

The artists who participated in the ceremony at Oxford were drawn from all the various factions in English musical life. Members of the Italian opera company orchestra sat beside members of the "Professional Concerts" company, members of Salomon's orchestra beside the best singers of the Royal Choir of Windsor. Haydn enjoyed the ivy-clad tranquillity of the little town; he was glad to be out of London. But he dreaded being called upon to speak in English before hundreds of persons. Fortunately, he was spared this trial. Vice Chancellor Growe, speaking in Latin, conferred the degree upon him. Master Haydn bowed silently when the black silk gown was placed over his shoulders and the square, tasseled cap was set upon his head. This ceremony took place in the morning. By the time he entered the concert hall, in the evening, to hear the performance of his *Oxford Symphony*, conducted by Cramer, he had completely recovered from his embarrassment and was in excessively high spirits. With a broad smile on his face, he took his seat in the flower-wreathed chair.

When, after a few bars of slow introduction, the first subject appeared in the violins, supported by the remaining strings and, at the close of the exposition, the second subject followed, the maestro closed his eyes. Then he opened them again, savoring the second movement, with its long, flowing melody given by the violins

After the minuet and trio, the finale crept in, in a truly Haydnesque manner, "in the beginning like a kitten, but soon developing tiger muscles"

Haydn was so amused by the acrobatics of the music he had written, by the informal fugues and unexpected changes of key, that for a while he could not help chuckling.

"He seemed to be in excellent humor," a newspaper reported. "Grateful for the applause he received, he seized hold of and displayed the gown he wore as a mark of the honor that had in the morning been conferred on him. He exclaimed the three simple words, 'I thank you.' Then he became silent; the emphasis, with which he thus expressed his feelings, met with an unanimous and loud clapping." From then on, so long as he remained in England, Haydn apparently manifested a typically German respect for the doctoral degree, and always signed himself Dr. Haydn. In his diary, however, he noted with his usual, careful thriftiness: "For the bell-ringing at Oxford on accowt of the doktor's degree I had to pay 1½ guineas and for the gown ½ guinea; the trip cost 6 guineas."

The academic honor was welcome balm for the disappointment that Haydn had suffered with his Italian opera, written on contract for Gallini, *L'Anima del Filosofo*. He had spent months of work on it. Since the king stubbornly adhered to his stand that there was too much singing in Italian in London, and refused to permit the new company to perform, the whole project came to nothing. Nevertheless,

Gallini paid the composer 300 pounds, for it was not, after all, Haydn's fault that his work was not performed. The tale is told that rehearsals had already begun, but that after fifty bars the doors were flung open and a royal constable entered with a written order forbidding any further rehearsing, under penalty of imprisonment—concerts and dances might be held in the theater, but no operatic performances. Thus, fate would have it that even in London Haydn had no luck with his operas. We have little reason to regret the fate of *L'Anima del Filosofo,* an opera on Orpheus *after* Gluck. Haydn was certainly not the man to rescue Eurydice from Hades. His rôle was that of a symphonist, and, as Burney pointed out, "the master of the *cantata,* which means of narrative chamber music."

Haydn spent August and part of September on the country estate of the banker Brassey, where he enjoyed himself greatly among the lovely ponds and espaliered trees. Everything was done to make his stay as pleasant as possible and to help him to recover from the excitements of London. As he wrote to Vienna, he was reminded of the atmosphere in Professor Genzinger's home. But Brassey had his idiosyncrasies. Once, when Haydn was telling him how poor he had been in his youth and how this poverty had stimulated his ambition, his host reacted in an astonishing, a Hogarthian manner. "Let me have pistols!" the rich man suddenly bellowed. "I shall shoot myself on the spot! I have never been poor, know nothing but swilling and gorging, nothing but superfluity—and I am sick to death of it!" With great difficulty, the alarmed composer calmed him.

As soon as the pleasant summer ended, however, trouble began again. Throughout his London stay, Haydn had given no thought to his Esterhazy master. But now there came a letter from Prince Anton firmly requesting Haydn to return. Emperor Leopold II was expected to visit Eisenstadt shortly; it was essential that Haydn speedily compose an opera for the occasion. It is highly questionable that the successor to Prince Nicholas had any legal right to force Haydn to return. The band had been dissolved, and Haydn was now kapellmeister to the prince in name only. But he was still receiving a salary which might be stopped, and this prospect caused him several sleepless nights. He wrote despondently to Frau von Genzinger: "I now expect my dismissal, but hope that God will be so gracious to me that I may redeem this loss by my diligence." His fears proved to be unjustified. When he wrote, loyally, to the prince that he was bound by contract to remain with Salomon for another season, Esterhazy decided that he could do without the opera and did not stop Haydn's pension.

There were other matters to depress Haydn, however. Salomon's enemies were preparing a coup which was in fact directed against Haydn. As star of the "Professional Concerts" for the coming season they hired Ignace Pleyel of Strassburg. Haydn was well acquainted with this elegant Alsatian and citizen of France, for Pleyel had been his pupil in Eisenstadt for a time. And Haydn was more deeply offended by the fact that this man was called in to compete with him than he would have been by any other choice. The slur was all too clearly intended: the pupil would surely outdo the aging master. There was in the project a lack of respect which made it seem most cutting to Haydn, who set such store by deference. Whenever he thought of the impending season he began to hate this London music market and its vicious struggles. This feeling was expressed in the letter he sent to Marianna Sabina on October 13, 1791:

"My dear lady, I shall argue mildly with yor belief that I prefer the sity of London to Vienna. I do not hate London, but I shoud be incaipable of spending all my days heare even if I knew I wood earn millions. Oh, how often doo I long to spend a quarter hour wid Your Grace at the piano and then to have some good German soup. But we cannot have evryting in dis world . . . In any case, I hop to se Your Grace within six months. I shall have much to tell."

At this time the master overestimated Pleyel's power. Haydn went about a good deal in society, sometimes to private dinners, sometimes to public banquets. Everywhere he encountered persons who, out of malice or stupidity, spoke blandly to him about Pleyel and asked his opinion of the man. The newspapers had begun to carry exciting items about the rivalry, as if it were an impending boxing match. All this made Haydn very nervous. Had he been better acquainted with Burney's book he would not have been so concerned. For (Volume IV, page 591) Burney had written: "Pleyel—whether this ingenious and engaging composer does not draw faster from the fountain of his invention than it will long bear, and whether his imitation of Haydn, and too constant use of semitones, and coquetry in *ralentandos* and pauses will not be soon construed into affectation, I know not; but it has already been remarked by critical observers that his fancy, though at first so fertile, is not so inexhaustible, but that he frequently repeats himself and does not sufficiently disdain the mixture of common passages with his own elegant ideas."

Posterity has confirmed the verdict delivered by Burney in 1789; however, a composer whom the high priest of musical criticism had treated so severely could not have constituted a danger to Haydn, no matter how extravagant the newspaper publicity. Haydn's fame was too firmly established; he had many occasions to be mildly amazed by his elevation in the musical world. When he was invited to spend a few days with the Duke of York, who had just married the seventeen-year-old daughter of the King of Prussia, he was astonished by the skill with which "the Printz of Wallys" (this was what he always called the heir to the throne) played one of his pieces on the cello. The Prince of Wales also ordered a painter, John Hoppner, to paint Haydn's portrait. Haydn was flattered, as he well might have been, for it was a flattering work of art. (This masterpiece of character painting hangs to this day in Buckingham Palace; it shows Haydn, radiant with lively good nature, in a red coat, his right hand holding a quill pen.)

Haydn found cause for astonishment in almost everything. He asked the young Duchess of York why, when he sat at the piano, she always "hummed along." She replied: "I've heard all your compositions in Berlin." Haydn was gratified as well as surprised, for he had always thought that musical Berlin was cool to his work. Evidently, he had been mistaken.

He was mistaken about Pleyel, as well. The thirty-four-year-old composer's visit turned out very differently from what everyone had expected. He arrived one evening, shortly before Christmas, with a briefcase full of new compositions, and hastened at once to see Haydn. With the greeting, "My dear Papa!" the young Alsatian testified anew to his respect for his old teacher; and from then on, the two saw each other daily. They appeared together in public; they went to the theater arm in arm, and provided a salutary lesson for London gossips. When Haydn was troubled with rheumatism, Pleyel sat with him and adjusted his pillows. Each of them regularly attended the other's concerts. Master and pupil "refused to be incited against one another," the *Morning Chronicle* remarked.

The New Year came around. A fateful year was ending, and 1792, one of the most memorable in the history of the world, was beginning. It was to be a year of war. England was not yet taking part in the war, but Prussia and Austria were girding themselves to fight France and fend off revolution from their own lands. The smell of gunpowder was in the air.

Pleyel and Haydn sat together over punch. They had declined numerous invitations to noisy parties, for they wished to greet the new year silently. They did not talk about politics, or about their careers and the concerts they had still to give. They sat silent, mournful, moist-eyed, thinking about the news they had just heard.

For on December 5 Mozart had died.

THE LONDON WORKS

When the news reached London, Haydn at first refused to believe it. False rumors of the deaths of prominent men were common; such a rumor of his own death had gone the rounds in 1774, but after such falsities one went on living with a renewed consciousness of being alive. How could Mozart have died at thirty-five? There was little reassurance in the thought of his short span of life; Haydn could not have been entirely unaware of the frivolity of his friend's life, burning the candle at both ends, pursuing pleasure by day and working over his music all night long. Added to this was Mozart's utter incompetence in matters of money. "I have three gulden in my pocket," he said to his wife, at the last; and that was, in fact, his entire fortune. Haydn both knew and did not know about this, for men of their sort did not talk of profane necessities. Mozart, who borrowed money from so many friends, would never have thought to trouble Haydn for it.

There is even less reason to believe that they had ever talked of death. Haydn's image of Mozart was of a tremendously vital person, a genius whose future would be even greater than his present. He did not suspect that this same Mozart could write, in letters to others: "Since death (to be precise about it) is the true, final goal of our lives, I have endeavored for the past few years to make myself so well acquainted with this faithful and best friend of men that the thought of him not only holds no terrors for me any more, but affords indeed consolation and tranquillity . . . I never go to bed without thinking that perhaps (young as I am) I shall no longer be on the following day, and yet none of those who know me will be able to say that I have been sad or irritable in company." *That* he certainly was not, and his demeanor deceived Haydn as it deceived so many others.

Our medical knowledge of the actual cause of Mozart's death is comparatively recent. In 1905 a French magazine printed the opinion of Dr. Barraud, a physician who had made a close study of the recorded symptoms: "Mozart's death can be ascribed to overwork, constant excessive fatigue, and material wretchedness. At the age of thirty-five all his life-forces were exhausted. The condition that finally killed him consisted of swift emaciation, choking fits, faints, and swelling of the bones. All these are symptoms of nephritis. Mozart very probably died of albuminoid degeneration, but he was treated as though he had a case of meningitis."

Of this, of course, Haydn could know nothing; the fact of death was sufficient for him. For a few days he doubted the report; then a letter convinced him that Mozart was really dead, and he broke down completely.

He wrote a distraught, stammering letter to Marianna Sabina von Genzinger which culminated in the sincere and forceful exclamation: "Posterity will not have another such talent in an hundred years."

By early January Haydn had sufficiently recovered his composure to think of Mozart's family. He wrote to a mutual friend, the Viennese Freemason Puchberg: "For a gonsiderable time I was uttely distrawt at Mozart's death and coud not believe that Prevision [meaning Providence] wood so soon call such an inimitable man into the odder world. Above all, I regrett that Mozart before his death did not have the chanse to convince the English, who are still ignorant, of the truth of what I daily preach to them [meaning Mozart's great talent]. Will you, my dear freind Puchberg, have the gindness to send me a list of dose works of Mozart's that are still unknone here. I shall make every effort to promote dem for the benefit of his widow. I wrote to the poor woman myself three weeks ago, telling her that wen her dear son reaches the proper aje, I will devote all my strenth to teaching him combosition without fee, in order to somewhat fill the blace of his father."

To fill the place of the father—such was, indeed, the natural wish of "Papa" Haydn. It was fortunate for Haydn that he was not in Vienna at the moment and did not have to witness the misery that had befallen Mozart's family. His own share in the tragedy of Mozart's death was spiritual; with the death of Mozart the sense of an invisible communion increased. Haydn felt as though strengthened and befriended by some supernatural agency. Traces of this effect can be discovered in his works of 1791; in the following year, which began for Haydn with the news of Mozart's death, it is far more evident.

It is not necessary to interpret this influence in any mystical sense;

what happened was no more mysterious than spiritual changes always are. After the old master had for so long been the giver, the relationship between the two composers changed with a suddenness that, indeed, was Mozartian in character. As we know, nine years earlier, Mozart had suddenly become a disciple of Haydn; now Haydn became a disciple of Mozart. Now the latter was paying posthumously his debt of gratitude, by adding his genius to the genius of the older master.

"On Monday Mozart composes like Haydn and on Tuesday Haydn composes like Mozart." This was a favorite Viennese joke in the middle of the nineteenth century. In reality, Mozart had struggled to free himself from the influence of Haydn's music. With mercurial swiftness, he ran through and beyond Haydn's tonal discoveries. Then he turned, smiling, and looked around at his more deliberate friend.

Haydn had often served Mozart as a model since that October 31, 1783, when the young man had written to his father, Leopold, from Linz that, for an impending concert, he would have to write a new symphony "at breakneck speed." This, really, was not possible without some slight borrowing from Haydn. So he set down his *adagio* in the six-quarter time and in the same mood as the *adagio* of Haydn's *Maria Theresa Symphony* of 1772. Contrarily, when the Londoner Haydn began to write in the Mozartian manner, it was less from necessity to work "at breakneck speed" than from the deep conviction that posterity would "not have another such talent in an hundred years." The first six London symphonies (we might say seven, since Haydn had already finished the *Oxford Symphony* when he came to London) show to varying degrees an abundance of Mozartian features. In the brilliant finale of this *Oxford Symphony* the main subject, in its meteoric flight, continually sheds part of its substance and gives birth to new subsidiary themes. The finales of the next symphonies, Nos. 93 to 95, are even more a legacy of Mozart. They are a departure from Haydn's usual custom of bringing the audience to their feet and ushering them out of the hall with a lively *presto*. The Mozartian *rondo* form was calculated to keep the audience in their places to the last moment.

Number 94 is Haydn's most famous symphony—or, at any rate his best known. It is the *Surprise*, which the Germans call "The Symphony with the Drum-beat." Its *andante* is, as we have already noted, a German folk song. But what mysterious loveliness Haydn introduced into this comparatively insignificant air! It may be considered as Haydn's personal motif; it is naïve, but there is a nobility in its simplicity; it is both touching and majestic. Solemnity often embarrassed Haydn, however, and, characteristically, he did not permit this mood to persist; after a pianissimo he suddenly introduced the drum-beat, accompanied by a *fortissimo tutti,* the kind of "surprise" that Mozart would have loved. Gyrowetz, whose memoirs supply intimate insights into Haydn's mode of work, later stated that the drum-beat had been introduced deliberately, with the intention of "arousing the women," who might otherwise have fallen asleep. There is no proof to the contrary; Haydn, who rather prided himself on his knowledge of the softer sex, might really have had such a thought. But in any case, in the variations of the movement he omitted the drum-beat, at the bidding of his musical sensitivity. The symphony deserves its fame for other reasons, not the least of which is the manner in which Haydn makes the melody of the *coda* tumble down a slope of romantic harmonies—a device that would have evoked Mozart's strong admiration. For Mozart himself was the only other composer who was master of this particular art, which Haydn developed to a peak three years later, in his *Military Symphony*.

To Symphony No. 96, in D-major, was given the strange title, *The Miracle.* According to August Reissmann, a Berlin biographer of Haydn, at the first performance many members of the audience left their seats to look at Haydn at close range as he sat at the piano. Suddenly one of the huge candelabra of the hall crashed to the floor. Before any panic could ensue, loud cries of, "A miracle, a miracle!" rang out. Not a single person had been injured, although a few moments before all the seats under the candelabrum had been occupied. We do not know whether or not this story is true; if true, it affords another instance of the proverbial good luck that followed in the wake of Haydn's music—the luck that was later to save Napoleon's life and to which Haydn himself alluded shortly before his death. It was during the bombardment of Vienna, when he called out to frightened persons in his house: "Don't be frightened; nothing can happen where Haydn is."

The next symphony, No. 97, in C-major, is extremely Austrian in tone. In point of fact, it was Schubert who elaborated a really Austrian music—"mourning wreathed in vine leaves." In Schubert the sadness is not found in the melodies; it is rather produced by the sudden change in illumination, the darkening of the harmony (which is often accomplished in a single measure). Haydn had only inklings of this essentially modern quality of Schubert. In the C-major symphony, however, he introduced toward the end a wholly unexpected tragic passage. Was he now beginning to think, after all, about death? He scarcely mulled over the prospect of his own death. But now Mozart had died! His last London symphony of 1792, No. 98, in B-flat-major, showed how deeply he had been afflicted, and that his sorrow was even more profound than, perhaps, he himself knew. London was noisy and diverting; the scramble for recognition and appreciation had not abated; but when Haydn sat down to write Symphony No. 98 he forgot the wearing competition, and lost himself in the memory of his beloved younger brother. As Tovey puts it, he wrote the *adagio cantabile* of the second movement as a requiem for Mozart. The joyfulness that, nevertheless, breaks through in the final movements gives one the feeling that Mozart's spirit was near by, persuading Haydn not to give way entirely to grief.

The quantity of sheer labor that went into these London symphonies of Haydn was tremendous; he exclaimed, with a sigh, that never in his life had he worked so hard. The number of pages in the symphonies was 124; in addition, there were 110 pages of the *L'Anima del Filosofo,* 48 pages of quartet music, 46 pages of piano music, 12 pages of minuets, and two marches comprising ten pages. Besides all this, there were flute compositions, then the complete *Storm Chorus,* "Hark! The wild uproar of the winds"; the Oxford canon on the words, "Thy voice, O Harmony, is divine"; a number of arias for Italian singers with whom he had become friendly; and several occasional pieces written to meet debts of gratitude, on which Haydn nevertheless lavished the full measure of his talent. (Exactly this he always had done. When a German spinster in Coburg had asked him to make immortal some of her poodle's exploits he had complied and had sent her his "Poodle Romance." And when the pet dog of the singer Rauzzini had died Haydn had written for the inconsolable dog lover his famous "Dog Canon" over the words "Turk was a faithful dog and not a man.")

In a similar spirit of kindness Haydn acted now toward a London music publisher, William Napier, who had recently gone into bankruptcy and was threatened with incarceration in the debtors' prison in Fleet Street. Haydn who had begun to study Scottish and Welsh folk songs shortly after his arrival in England wrote arrangements of these songs for Napier's benefit, and they sold so well that the publisher could make a fortune with them. A second collection which Napier offered at a subscription price compensated Haydn handsomely. It would be reasonable if Haydn had worked up thirty or fifty of these songs. A hundred would have seemed a great many, for writing them would have meant that he spent all his leisure time in a field that (unlike Schubert's) could never be his principal scene of activity. But the fact is that Haydn wrote (as his catalog of 1805 proves) three hundred and sixty-five songs! The fertility of nature was embodied in a mortal man; it is inconceivable that he was able to write so many, even though he composed the greater part of these songs not in England, but later on in Vienna, while in the spell of nostalgia that overcame him when he thought of England. He wrote songs for three publishers, William Napier, William Whyte, and George Thomson of Edinburgh. The eloquent pride in Scotland cherished by Thomson led Haydn to a study of the native folk art.

According to the original agreement, Haydn was to supply violin, cello and piano accompaniments to the melodies and texts supplied him by the publishers. But he soon threw off these restrictions; he arranged the melodies himself and wrote his own preludes and postludes. Thus, these foreign songs ultimately became his own spiritual property. Haydn certainly considered them so; one day he wrote to George Thomson the amazing sentence (in his customary Italian): *Mi vanto di questo lavoro, e per ciò mi vivere in Scozia molti anni doppo la mia morte* ("I am proud of this work, and flatter myself that through it I shall live in Scotland for many years after my death"). That is a matter for the Scots to decide—and there have been Scots who have compared Haydn with Burns.

What is most amazing about this enterprise is Haydn's courage in composing songs in a language which he did not speak, which he could hardly understand when spoken, and which he could not read without assistance. In London, however, he did have assistance—and once more it was a woman who provided much of the stimulus. She was Mrs. Anne Hunter, the wife of a famous surgeon. We do not know definitely whether Haydn was in love with her; probably he was, for in his avuncular, gallant bachelor's manner he was a little in love with almost every woman he met.

THE LONDON LADIES

THE lady's husband, John Hunter, was exactly the same age as Haydn, and a man of great fame. An indefatigable researcher in the field of zoological anatomy (if we credit Herman Melville, even in the anatomy of whales), he stunned all his visitors by the enormous size of his collection of bones. At the time of Haydn's arrival, John Hunter was Surgeon General of the British Army with his office in Leicester Square. This man, who "had raised surgery out of the art and mystery of barbers to the rank of a scientific profession," evidently had the most amiable intentions toward Haydn, though his actions may have seemed somewhat brusque. Even after a year in England, Haydn's ability to understand English was very limited. Consequently, he probably listened rather abstractedly when the famous surgeon broached the subject of Haydn's nasal polyp, remarking that it "distorted his face and frightened away the ladies." (Concerning the latter statement, Haydn had reason to differ with Hunter.) One day the composer received a note asking him to come at once to Leicester Square; the matter was urgent. "So I went," Haydn later told one of his biographers. "After a brief exchange of greetings, two powerful fellows stepped into the room, seized me from behind and wanted to tie me to a chair. I shouted, screamed, pounded and kicked with my feet until I was able to free myself and make it clear to Mr. Hunter, who already had his instruments in his hands and was concealing them behind his back, that I absolutely refused to permit him to operate on me. He was amazed at my stubbornness and, it seemed to me, he pitied me for denying myself the pleasure of experiencing his skilful surgery. Did I wish, he asked me with faint reproach, to take my foe [*i.e.*, the disfigurement] to the grave with me? I declared that such was my intention and hurried out of the house."

The scene might be the subject for one of Hogarth's engravings. The physical struggle between the musician and the male nurses over a nasal polyp—such a spectacle could take place only in London!

Haydn recovered from his alarm, and visited Leicester Square more and more frequently, to pay court, in his old-fashioned manner, to Mrs. Anne Hunter. As long as he lived in London he adhered to the principle of the Frenchwoman who had told her son: "For your social career, I bequeath to you but one counsel: 'Be in love with all women.' " He was repaid sometimes in a touching way. "I dinned at the home of a Mr. Shaw" he wrote in his diary. "And as I was bawing to everyone, I notised that all the ladies wore arownd there necks a pearl-golored band imbraidered with the name of Haydn." Master Haydn was sincerely convinced that every London woman who invited him to tea was actually "the most beautiful woman on earth." One time it was young Mrs. Shaw, another time the singer Elizabeth Billington. Mrs. Bland was the only woman he found really unattractive. Haydn had never visited Paris; he knew only the unassuming women of Austria and Italian women of precocious but short-lived beauty. What probably most impressed him about the women of England was their delicate coloring, an effect of the climate. Their complexions were fair, their eyes blue, their hair blonde—a triad of qualities that existed among the Germans, but in cruder form. It seemed as if the dampness of the atmosphere kept their skin smooth and silken for a long time, and the art of using cosmetics was far more highly developed in England than it was on the Continent.

The London woman did not age; Haydn became aware of this when a lady of almost sixty fell in love with him. She was a wealthy Londoner, the widow of a German pianist named Schroeter. Her husband had died three years earlier. Soon after Haydn arrived in London, she went to him with the request that he give her piano lessons. Haydn was no piano teacher; he had had far more experience in teaching singing; but since he often played the harpsichord at concerts, the notion soon spread that he gave piano instruction. This misunderstanding benefited his pocketbook and led, at least in one case, to a very amusing instance of snobbery. A lady of the very highest society boasted to her friends that she was Haydn's pupil. Several times a week she sent her carriage to bring the master to her home. There he waited in a room that did not even contain a piano. At last the highborn woman appeared, chatted with him for fifteen minutes, and then sent him away. He received so much compensation for these visits that for some time he was quite content to go on giving such "lessons."

Mrs. Schroeter, however, was a real music lover who took her lessons very seriously. Her husband had often played Haydn's music for her; it was a short step from love of the music to love of the composer. Haydn made copies of letters he received from her, and took the copies with him to Vienna, along with his English diaries; probably he was requested to return the originals before he left London. The letters were written in English, which was easier for Mrs. Schroeter; but their conversations were apparently conducted in German.

We know neither the lady's first name nor her maiden name. All we know about her is that her beautiful home near Buckingham Palace, at 6 James Street, became a homelike asylum for the aging Haydn, a refuge where he could feel at ease and where he was definitely pampered. He later declared to Dies, the painter, that he would have married the rich and beautiful Mrs. Schroeter if he had been free. Probably memory was deceiving him, for so long as he remained in London he showed no sign of real passion for her. He let himself be loved, which in his case may have been the pleasanter rôle.

The course of the affair can be readily traced in her letters. At first it was only their mutual interest in the piano that led the two together. But soon tenderer emotions awoke in the woman: "No language can express half the love and affection I feel for you; you are dearer to me every day of my life." It was hard for her to be separated from him for even a few days. "Oh, how earnestly I wish to see you! I hope you will come to me to-morrow." She was concerned about his health, for she saw what others seldom realized—that this stay in London, with its burden of work and public appearances, was a strain on a man of his years.

"My dear," she wrote on April 19, 1792, "I was extremely sorry to hear this morning that you was indisposed. I am told you was five hours at your studio yesterday; indeed, my dear Love: I am afraid it will hurt you. Why should you, who have already produced so many wonderful and charming compositions, still fatigue yourself with such close application? I almost tremble for your health. Let me prevail on you, my much loved Haydn, not to keep to your studio so long at one time. My dear Love, if you could know how very precious your welfare is to me, I flatter myself that you would endeavour to preserve it, for my sake as well as your own. Pray inform me how you do and how you have slept." This warm interest was welcome to Haydn. Fame in the huge and strange city was not sufficient nourishment for the heart. Mrs. Schroeter was of a far loftier type of woman than Luigia Polzelli,

The Bettmann Archive

A performance of Haydn's "Creation" saved his life from a bomb attempt in the Rue Nicaise:
NAPOLEON BONAPARTE,
THE FIRST CONSUL, IN 1800

The Patroness of Haydn's old age:
PRINCESS MARIE-HERMENEGILDIS ESTERHAZY

The Bettmann Archive

"Am I to die now? And I have just begun to understand the wind instruments":
HAYDN IN HIS EIGHTIETH DECADE

The Bettmann Archive

THE HAYDN LEGEND:
The "Creation" was not composed during a sea storm—but the 19th century would have it so.

in social position and on a cultural level. She was the sister-in-law of the famous German actress Corona Schroeter, Goethe's friend. She more closely approximated Marianna Sabina von Genzinger than she did Luigia Polzelli.

Mrs. Schroeter was deeply saddened by the prospect of Haydn's leaving England soon. After the last of Salomon's concerts on June 6, 1792, she wrote, that very night: "I cannot close my eyes to sleep until I have returned you ten thousand thanks for the inexpressible delight I have received from your ever enchanting compositions and your incomparably charming performance of them. Be assured, my dear Haydn: That among all your numerous admirers no one has listened with more profound attention, and no one can have such high veneration for your most brilliant talents, as I have. Indeed, my dear Love, no tongue can express the gratitude I feel for the infinite pleasure your music has given me: accept then my repeated thanks for it; and let me also assure you, with heartfelt affection, that I shall ever consider the happiness of your acquaintance as one of the chief blessings of my life, and it is the sincere wish of my heart to preserve, to cultivate and to merit it more and more."

An elegiac note underlies these sincere and wholly feminine words; the writer of them must have known that they would be her farewell to Haydn, for he was on the point of departure. Before long she would be no more than a pleasant memory to him. Interestingly enough, Haydn did not see Mrs. Schroeter again during his second stay in London, in 1795; but later, in Vienna, he dedicated three trios for piano, violin and cello to her; and thus the name of his London friend has been preserved in his works.

GLIMPSE OF THE COSMOS

Shortly before his departure from London, Haydn made a visit he never was to forget. Armed with a letter of recommendation from Burney, he visited the man who was "closer to the heavens than any other Englishman of his time"—to paraphrase a saying of King George III. This man was William Herschel, the astronomer. On June 15, in the afternoon, he received Haydn at his tower at Slough, near Windsor, where stood the great telescope that he himself had built. Earlier that same day, Haydn had attended a horse race in Ascot. From long residence in Hungary he knew enough about horses to recognize that the English were expert horsemen. He later wrote enthusiastically about "these horses, light with very slender legs, the manes plaited into braids, the hoofs very neat." He admired the jockeys, "as lean as greyhounds, and clad in silks each of different color, pink, green, blue, red—dashing with ever increasing speed between many thousand spectators." But his enthusiasm over the horse race was soon forgotten in the presence of the great astronomer.

William Herschel, only six years younger than Haydn, was born on the Continent as the son of a poverty-stricken German musician. Early he emigrated to London where he gave music lessons. He was especially interested in the mathematical theory of music. From this realm of thought he was led to the study of astronomy. The stars, too, moved in calculable orbits; if anyone should violate the laws of numbers, there would follow chaos, disharmony and destruction. The wonders revealed by the telescope made him long for the possession of so glorious an instrument, but telescopes were far too expensive to buy. "Therefore I began in my leisure hours to build telescopes of my own, at first of two feet and finally of twenty feet in length." In order to solve the mystery of Saturn's rings, he invented a system of mirrors which he incorporated into his telescope. Never quite satisfied with his mirrors, he himself polished four hundred, many of tremendous size.

Haydn, who had had such a struggle in his youth to acquire the tools of his trade, could not fail to be moved by the similarity of Herschel's experience. The latter had, without assistance, done in astronomy what Haydn had accomplished in music. But what touched Haydn most was the fact that Herschel's astronomical researches were an avocation; he earned his living by music and since he was a member of an orchestra, his time was constantly taken up by rehearsals and evening performances. "Often," he told Haydn, "I stole away from the concert hall or theater to glance up at the starry sky, but I always returned in time to take my place in the orchestra."

Not until Herschel had discovered the planet Uranus, in 1781, did King George III take steps to free him from his wearing daily occupation. From then on, with an annual stipend, he was able to live for his researches. The long winter nights, with darkness falling at six o'clock, gave the astronomer a chance to work for extended, uninterrupted periods. "Would you believe me," he said almost casually to Haydn, "that in a strip of space fifteen degrees long and two degrees wide there were 50,000 fixed stars and 466 nebulae?"

The vastness of space was staggering to the imagination, and Haydn was awe-stricken as he stood in the semi-darkness of the observatory with this man who was on a familiar footing with the stars. Food and wine were brought. The woman who served them in silence was the astronomer's sister, Caroline Herschel, who worked as his secretary. Haydn recovered somewhat from his amazement, but when his host led him up to the platform to show him the sky through the telescope, Haydn at first flatly refused to look. Later he did look, but very briefly. At his first glimpse of the cosmos through this monster forty-inch telescope, his perception of space was so shocked that he became cold. Trembling, he turned up his collar, although it was a June night. More than twenty minutes elapsed before he could utter a word. Then he murmured, "So high . . . so far . . ."

The transition was made, though with difficulty, from the infinitude of space to the finiteness of art. The host handed Haydn a poem that he had written, probably the only one he had ever written. It was entitled *Address to the Star,* and had been published four years before in the newspaper, *The Star and Evening Advertiser*. It expressed the sincerity of a Pythagorean spirit who understood the harmony of numbers in music and in the universe.

What Star art thou, about to gleam
In Novelty's bright hemisphere?
How shall we note thine orient beam
Among the millions wand'ring there?

Art thou some rude, chaotic world
Of atoms, in confusion thrown,
By fortune's hand at random hurl'd,
To find a tract in rolling on?

Or shall some Genius wheel thee round
Thine orbit, circumscrib'd, and fair,
With ever-beaming crescent crown'd,
The glory of the evening air?

A planet wilt thou roll sublime,
Spreading like Mercury thy rays?
Or Chronicle the lapse of time,
Wrapt in a Comet's threat'ning blaze?

Whate'er thy phasis and thy force,
Hope not to find a sky serene;
Tempests may dim thy radiant course,
Or orbs opposing intervene.

Yet fall not, like rash Phaeton,
Sinking among the waves of Po;
But like his father constant run,
And light the grateful world below.

Haydn's English was undoubtedly too poor for him to judge the poem as such or to understand the meaning of every line, but he was nevertheless profoundly moved by the loftiness of the sentiment, especially when Herschel informed him that it was a custom among the Greeks to transpose their dead heroes to the heavens. Was it, then, possible that a star represented the soul of a hero? The most Greek, the most harmonious of musicians, Mozart, had just left this earth forever. Such verses, Haydn may have thought, ought to be dedicated to a spirit such as Mozart, not merely to a "new star."

That night, Sir Donald Tovey believes, the germ of *The Creation* sprang to life within Haydn.

A PUPIL NAMED BEETHOVEN

When Haydn, on his way home, reached the Rhine in July a great political event was to take place in Germany. Emperor Leopold II, who had reigned only two years after his brother Joseph, suddenly had died and now his nephew Archduke Francis, had to succeed him on the throne.

All the German princes and the great barons of the Holy Empire were gathered at Frankfurt to witness the coronation—among them also Prince Anton Esterhazy. Since the Elector of Bonn, Maximilian Francis of Hapsburg, an uncle of the new emperor, had already left the city for the festivities at Frankfurt, there was all the more reason for Haydn not to linger on. But the Electoral Prince's orchestra insisted on Haydn's attending a breakfast which was to take place outside the city, in the charming countryside around Godesberg where elevated gardens gave a lovely view of the Rhine. That afternoon an event of great significance in the history of music occurred, an event which had far-reaching consequences.

A young man of twenty-three, whom Haydn might have glimpsed when he first passed through Bonn a year and a half earlier, went up to the master. He was Ludwig van Beethoven, a black-haired musician with sallow, almost Spanish, complexion, and a pair of compelling eyes whose look of burning earnestness was in sharp contrast to the cheerful, easy-minded glance of the other musicians. Beethoven was at that time second kapellmeister and choral director at the court of Bonn.

After the banquet, young Beethoven succeeded in drawing the master into an adjoining room, where he played on the piano, for Haydn and a few others, his *Cantata in Mourning for the Death of Emperor Joseph II*. This was certainly outdated, since Joseph's successor, Leopold II, had also died. But the young composer's choice of this particular piece was a demonstration of his seriousness about himself. He had written it two years earlier, but he was convinced that he had not done any better work since, and he naturally wanted Haydn to hear his best.

A requiem for the Emperor Joseph was not a theme which Haydn found overly sympathetic. He had never been on very good terms with the late monarch, and he had heard that the emperor was wont to criticize his music unfavorably. Although Haydn, together with Mozart, represented the apex of the Age of Enlightenment in music, Joseph, "the Emperor of the Enlightenment," was said to feel that Haydn was not serious enough, and to dismiss his work quite casually. Once he had complained to Dittersdorf that Haydn's chamber music were "too trifling," that Haydn in his operas "annoyed the singers by drowning them out by orchestral accompaniment," and that in the whole, Haydn's music could be compared "to a pretty snuff-box of foreign manufacture." Perhaps Dittersdorf invented this story, or distorted the emperor's remarks—with that secret malice that old friends often exhibit. At any rate, Haydn had heard about it and had been deeply wounded.

Haydn did not know of the curious bond between Beethoven and the late Emperor Joseph. Five years earlier, the Elector had sent the young Rhenish musician to Vienna on a musical tour. There Beethoven had met Mozart who, however, paid little attention to him. The prince had also probably given him a letter to the emperor, but the seventeen-year-old lad had no thought of using it. Instead, he had looked at the emperor from afar with shy idolatry. Emperor Joseph II embodied for the young Beethoven all that a sincere and thoughtful man might expect of a ruler. Although Beethoven himself lived at an ecclesiastical court (which, however, was in many ways linked with the Enlightenment), Joseph's struggle with the papacy, his abolition of serfdom, and the issuance of the Edict of Tolerance, inspired his imagination; he felt that the emperor had performed Herculean labors, and Beethoven was convinced that no greater man had ever lived. Beethoven's tribute to Joseph the Liberator was the cantata he now played for Haydn.

It was a very curious piece of music, and yet Haydn was profoundly moved, from the very first notes. Here were eleven *largo* measures of strange music in E-flat major, music which seemed to be floating in empty space,

in a vast area depopulated by a great disaster of unknown nature. Then there is a moan in the eleventh measure, carried by soprano, alto, tenor, and bass. In muted tones, a word is murmured: *"Death!"* The next measure is orchestral alone, *mezzo forte*. Then again the four voices sigh: *"Death!"* and hollow sounding and accompanied by a weeping clarinet, come the words: " 'Death!' moans the desolate night, the desolate night!" It was all novel and full of intense pathos such as could be found in poetry perhaps, in the works of Klopstock and Schiller only. Although Beethoven, at the piano, could only indicate the orchestration, Haydn grasped the originality of the work. This unknown youth, with his then unknown cantata, aroused in him the same feeling that Brahms experienced eighty years afterward when he exclaimed: "All of it is Beethoven through and through; if there were no name on the title page the composer would unfailingly be guessed."

As the *cantata* went on, however, Master Haydn began to smile. After all, a genius does not emerge out of the blue; when young Beethoven played the following pleasant harmony of words and music (which he would later adopt and adapt, almost without alterations for his *Fidelio*): "Then the human race rose, rose up to the light, then the earth turned more joyously around the sun, and with radiance divine the sun warmed the earth," Haydn recognized that the young man had carefully and successfully studied Haydn's own oratorio, *Il Ritorno di Tobia.* Nevertheless, the surprising thing for Haydn was not how much of his own music was incorporated into this cantata, but, rather, how much of the young man's composition was absolutely new; the style, in essence, had no precedent.

When he finished playing the last chords of the funeral cantata, Beethoven swung around in his seat. It was at this time that he probably informed the older master of his intention to make a second journey to Vienna, in order to study under Haydn. Flattered, Haydn promised to speak with the prince about the matter. He did so in the next few days. We may assume that Haydn, in Frankfurt, told Maximilian Francis that he thought highly of Beethoven. The prince must have been impressed, for he gave his consent. Since Beethoven was very poor, a financial agreement was reached between the prince and Haydn, and Beethoven's journey was planned for the fall.

As it turned out, it took place even sooner, and was of more far-reaching significance than either man expected; it resulted in a total change in the course of Beethoven's life. The conferences of the princes at Frankfurt and the accession of Francis I to the German throne were to lead to a vast European calamity. Intervention in France by a coalition of German princes became a reality. Intending to crush the Revolution, an Austro-Prussian army under Ferdinand of Brunswick invaded Lorraine. In Paris, Danton issued the call to arms; and for the first time in history the *Marseillaise* was sung in challenge to a foreign foe.

The initiation of this war had some curious aspects. Maria Theresa's daughter, Queen Marie Antoinette, consort of Louis XVI, had for years been living in great peril; in reality she was held as the "prisoner of the people." Her brothers had not raised a finger to aid her. Neither of the emperors Joseph or Leopold nor the Elector, Maximilian Francis had dared to intervene in behalf of their sister; peace with the French had seemed a more important end to them. But now, at the most unsuitable moment and when it was already far too late, Marie Antoinette's nephew, Francis I, marched an army into France to rescue her. The reaction to this move was terrible. The Duke of Brunswick was routed from French ground; the French, hot for revenge, appeared on the Rhine; Marie Antoinette and Louis were beheaded. The spark of war had been loosed in Central Europe and was to go on setting fires for the next twenty years.

Among the earliest persons to be affected were the members of the court in Cologne and Bonn. Maximilian Francis had to flee, and young Beethoven precipitately set off for Vienna, never again to return home.

When he presented himself to Haydn for the promised lessons, he found a different personality from the one he had met in Godesberg and who had since occupied his thoughts. This was not surprising; Haydn had undergone intense intellectual and spiritual changes. His experiences in London were only now beginning to be absorbed, and he had begun to wonder whether he had not been altogether wrong to leave London. In consequence, he was often distracted.

Suddenly he found that he no longer liked the provinciality of life in the Austrian capital. (Yet how recently, in Eisenstadt and Esterhaz, he had longed to be living in Vienna!) Now he missed the constant tension, the competition, the newspaper publicity, the honors London had piled on him. Utter strangers had gone up to him at concerts, stared at him as if he were some marvelous beast, exclaimed, "You are a great man!" and departed. Although he himself could not speak English, he experienced a feeling of let-down because, naturally, everyone spoke German to him in Vienna. He began longing for England, and was fond of talking about how much bigger and better everything was in the island kingdom. During his stay in London he had acquired not only a great deal of money, but also such practical necessities as stockings, handkerchiefs, and shirts, the excellent quality of which delighted him. Now these things were wearing out, and in Central Europe they could not be replaced. Austria, in particular, was far behind England in industrial development; even the townsfolk were semi-agrarian, and there was not sufficient wealth for lavish expenditure on art. Fabulously rich landowners like the Esterhazys were, after all, rare. Previously no such observation would have occurred to Haydn, but after eighteen months in England his insight into social phenomena was considerably keener.

As far as externalities went, his life was pleasant enough. He now owned a home in Vienna. While he was still in London his wife Anna Aloysia had written to ask whether she might buy a small one-story house, with a garden, on the west side of Vienna, in the suburb of Gumpendorf. It would be good for her to have a home "for her widowhood," she had written. Haydn was highly annoyed with both the tone of the letter and her request for two thousand gulden. Why should this woman assume that she would outlive him? He did not send the money, but as soon as he returned to Vienna he went to inspect the house. It was No. 19 Steingasse; the street is now called Haydngasse. "I liked its quiet, solitary situation," Haydn informed his biographer. "I bought it and during my second journey to London I had a story added to it. My wife died eight years afterward, and now it serves me in my widower's state."

Upon his return Haydn did not find Luigia Polzelli, for she was at the time singing in Bologna. Throughout his stay in England he had never ceased to write to his former mistress. He had even visited her unhappily married sister, Christine Negri, who lived in London, in order "to talk with her about my Luigia." He acted prudently, however, in complaining frequently to her of how hard it was for him to make ends meet among the English. Had Luigia suspected what sums he was making, she would have "bled" him more than she did. Her husband had just died and she was financially more dependent upon Haydn than ever before.

The passionate tone of Haydn's London letters to Luigia was genuine, but, nevertheless, superficial. The impression these letters give is of a temporary ardor felt mostly during the writing and forgotten, perhaps, a day later. Haydn readily became strongly attached to persons, and it was not like him to break with one with whom he shared many pleasant memories. However, with his increasing age, Haydn's relationship to women—for all its outward show of naïveté—tended toward a surreptitious Don Juanness. This can be ascribed partly to the operatic conventions in which he had been steeped; partly, too, perhaps, to the acquisition of fame and money; for he had learned only too well how these unlocked the hearts of women. In any case, he no longer took women so seriously as he had in his days of youthful shyness, although he knew that they "could still warm his old age like sunshine." To stretch a figure of speech, it may be said that he now seemed to be applying his technique of symphonic composition to his relations with women—for a few measures a certain instrument held the ear, then the master turned away from it and passed the melody to another.

Beethoven, however, could not be treated as a woman—the "father of orchestration" was deluded if he thought he could satisfy the young man with a few cursory attentions. To such treatment Beethoven might well respond as did Hamlet: "Do you think I am easier to be played on than a pipe?"

Beethoven wanted the *whole* Haydn; he did not desire occasional signs of interest. In 1788, Gluck and Carl Philipp Emanuel Bach had died, and Mozart had followed them in 1791. Since then Haydn had been left as the sole prince of European music. Beethoven well knew this; he knew it better than did the Austrian aristocrat in Bonn, Count Waldstein, who had written into Beethoven's album, on the young man's departure to Vienna, a rather deprecating remark about Haydn: "Mozart's genius lingers, to bewail and grieve the death of its master. It sought refuge in Haydn, but found no place there. It now seeks other refuge. If you are diligent, you will surely receive the spirit of Mozart from the hand of Haydn."

Quite contrarily, as a composer young Beethoven felt closer to Haydn's art than to Mozart's. In spite of due admiration, the rather regular beauty and geometrical purity of Mozart did not exert so great an appeal upon a composer conscious of his own strength as did the joyous crudity in the work of the older man. Even in the matter of sentimentality, there were a number of points of contact between the youthful Beethoven and Haydn. Shortly before he left Bonn, for example, Beethoven had composed an *Elegy on the Death of a Poodle* that was quite in the Haydn manner.

Nevertheless, serious differences of opinion in musical matters at once came to the fore when the two met in Vienna. The outward reason was that Haydn did not take his instructorship seriously. He had promised to teach the young man strict counterpoint but he let weeks pass without correcting his pupil's notebooks. Beethoven prepared two hundred and forty-five exercises for him, and, incredibly, Haydn overlooked most of the violations of the rules. Was distraction the only reason for this? We think that the source of the difficulty lay deeper. As Botstiber correctly observed, in 1927:

> Seldom have the tendencies that Nietzsche called Apollonian and Dionysian and that others term classical and romantic been expressed in as pure a form as they were by these two men. Beethoven stood for an *individualism* that shut itself off, physically and socially, from its environment and created wholly new artistic values in opposition to that environment. Opposed to this was Haydn's *universalism* which

> adroitly adapted itself to conditions, people and art-forms. Nevertheless, the meeting of the two was a gain for themselves and for art. Beethoven's early works sometimes sound like imitations of Haydn's music; but of far greater importance is the fact that, later on, Haydn's work became the basis for Beethoven's vocal music. But for the example of Haydn's *Creation* there might have been neither the *Missa Solemnis* nor the *Ode to Joy* in the Ninth. .

A relationship between two persons of such diverse temperaments might have been expected to end in an open quarrel, but Haydn was enough of a diplomat to avoid this. "The jovial old master did his best," writes Emil Ludwig, in describing this relationship, "to tame the demoniacal youth, as Socrates had tamed Alcibiades, though Haydn was by no means in love with his pupil. At the height of his mellow wisdom, which streamed forth in ever purer harmonies, Haydn was not to be won over by the swarthy and rebellious youngster who reminded him in no way of his own youth. Only his perfect equanimity made it possible for him to put up with the young man, let alone give him recognition. It is partly to Haydn's credit that they never had an open break in the sixteen years they both moved in Viennese society."

These lessons which were not lessons, nevertheless lasted for a full year. Beethoven came regularly, and teacher and pupil apparently went for outings in the country around Vienna, for Beethoven's diary contains notes such as: "Twelve kreuzer for chocolate for Haydn and me. Six kreuzer for coffee for Haydn and me." At first thought, it seems odd that Beethoven should have paid for Haydn, who was so much wealthier than he. But we must not leap to conclusions and label Haydn a "stingy peasant" who managed not to throw away a penny. Beethoven insisted upon the privilege of "taking out" his teacher. The emperor's uncle had promised to pay for Beethoven's studies, but since the French had reached the Rhine he had been unable to keep his promise. This must have meant that Haydn was not paid, which fact made Beethoven sensitive about playing the host on the outings.

Although Beethoven realized fully that he was learning nothing from Haydn, he continued to appear for his lessons—which throws considerable light on *his* diplomacy. The later Beethoven would probably have thrown the uncorrected notebooks into his teacher's face. But in his youth he was more tactful, and, instead, sought a way to deceive Haydn and receive instruction elsewhere without offending his teacher. Through a priest he made the acquaintance of the composer of *The Village Barber,* Johann Baptist Schenk, a kindly old pedant who enjoyed a considerable reputation as a teacher of counterpoint. He undertook to teach Beethoven without charge. Every day Beethoven brought to him the lessons that he had prepared for Haydn, with all the mistakes that Haydn had left unmarked. Schenk corrected these lessons, and Beethoven then copied the work over in his own handwriting, so that Haydn should not notice the deception. Beethoven and Schenk exchanged solemn promises to keep this honorable subterfuge a secret between themselves. It was, in fact, hidden until several years later when Gelimek, the priest who had introduced Beethoven and Schenk to each other, talked about it in society. In this manner the story came to Haydn's ears. Haydn was embarrassed, but he smiled about it.

He had, after all, no reason to be angry, for the fault was his alone. There have been a good many attempts to explain Haydn's curious behavior toward Beethoven. The most untenable of all farfetched explanations is that the old man was jealous of young Beethoven and therefore deliberately led him astray in musical matters. This would not only have been dishonorable, but a violation of professional ethics. Not the slightest proof has been advanced to support the idea that Haydn was *afraid* of Beethoven. Among his close friends Haydn always spoke in a somewhat humorous vein, of Beethoven's personality. He made fun of the young man's self-assurance, and good-humoredly dubbed him "the Grand Mogul." Professor Fischenich, who was profoundly convinced of Beethoven's genius, wrote in 1793 to Charlotte von Schiller: "Haydn has written to someone here in Bonn to say that he has abandoned grand opera to Beethoven and will soon have to give up composing altogether." Professor Fischenich was naïve to swallow any such statement of Haydn's, for it was meant ironically. Not even the emergence of Mozart, whom Haydn had considered a divine composer, had induced Haydn to "give up composing altogether." Why should Beethoven have had any such effect upon him? He appreciated Beethoven's gifts, but there was a good admixture of humor in this appreciation. When Master Haydn had feared the arrival in London of his own disciple, Pleyel, he had not at all been in a joking mood, for Pleyel had been brashly called in to compete with him. But there was no need for him to fear Beethoven, for no one expected any rivalry between the two.

The reason for his being so bad a teacher for Beethoven is found in the fact that his mind was elsewhere. At this particular time he would have been a bad teacher for any pupil, for he was preparing for a second trip to London in the spring of 1793. Everyone in Vienna, including Beethoven, knew this. When Beethoven was polite to Haydn, he did so not merely because Viennese society would never have forgiven him had he behaved otherwise. There was another reason for his self-control and good temper: Beethoven seriously hoped that Haydn would take him along to England, as his secretary!

He misjudged altogether Haydn's instinct. If anyone were to accompany him to London, it would not be a famulus, and certainly not a creative artist; at most, Haydn wanted with him a servant like young Johann Elssler, who would attend to his physical wellbeing just as Johann's father, Joseph, had done for many years. Social intercourse between Haydn and Beethoven was possible only in Vienna, where the numerous points of friction were cushioned by the environment; but in London the natural antipathies between the two men would have culminated in an explosion which would have been dangerous to Haydn's health. For deep within Beethoven's psyche lurked a feeling of suspicion toward the rest of the world. He scented conspiracies where none existed. Beethoven would dutifully dedicate his piano sonata Op. 2 to Haydn—but almost in the same breath he wrathfully forbade anyone to call him Haydn's pupil. Once he snapped angrily: "I have learned nothing from Haydn!" But he could have meant only that he had learned nothing from Haydn's formal instruction.

Even earlier than this, when Beethoven had given, in Prince Lichnowsky's salon, a performance of his first piano sonata, Haydn had given friendly, if moderate, praise to the first two movements. "But the third," he said, "you ought not to publish in *that* form." Beethoven was immediately offended; he suspected jealousy, which was completely foreign to Haydn. The latter was implying that the third movement was too difficult to find immediate acceptance with the public, but Beethoven would never believe that this had been Haydn's thought. He threw a furious look at the older man and refused for a long time to be placated.

Those were the days when Beethoven began striding through the salons of Vienna with the short, smart step of a conqueror, keeping his hands clasped behind his back as an artillery captain named Bonaparte had done.

THE LONDON RECAPITULATION

For all Haydn's eagerness, he might never have departed for London had not a sudden blow shaken his whole life in Vienna. On January 26, 1793, only six months after his return to the city, Marianna Sabina von Genzinger died at the age of thirty-eight. She was only three years older than Mozart had been at his death. We do not know the cause of her death. The busy "doctor to ladies," Peter Leopold von Genzinger, Rector of the University of Vienna, was unable to save his wife. Marianna Sabina's death was a terrible shock to Haydn. Not only had he lost the one friend who was close to him as an artist and as a man; he now also began to feel what it meant to outlive those younger than he.

In his sorrow he took refuge in work. The rumor appearing in the newspapers that he was working on a sequel to Mozart's *Magic Flute,* was, of course, sheer fabrication and nonsense. In his orchestral works, however, his spiritual community with Mozart became more evident than ever before.

It was not until the summer of 1793 that Salomon sent the new contract, which once again required Haydn to write six symphonies for London performance. This time Haydn was wiser; he wrote the greater part of them in Vienna, for he now knew how wearing the strenuous life in London could be. He tried also to spare his strength for the impending voyage to England, and went less into society. His principal companion was young Pietro Polzelli, Luigia's son; the mother was again staying in Italy. Anna Aloysia Haydn had earlier taken her own nephew, Ladislaus Biedermann, into her house, in the hope that Haydn would come to love him. Now she even permitted the son of the woman she hated to live in the Haydn household—an indication not only of young Pietro's usefulness, but also of a softening of Frau Haydn's character.

The date of Haydn's departure was set for January, 1794. A few weeks earlier, an honor was conferred upon the master which moved him deeply because it brought him back to the beginning of his life, to the threshold of childhood. A descendant of that Count Harrach who had employed his father invited him to the unveiling of a memorial—to Haydn himself—in Rohrau. There the most famous of the living composers could read the inscription in his honor: "To the memory of Joseph Haydn, the immortal master of the art of music, to whom heart and ear in rivalry pay homage, dedicated by Count Karl Leonhard von Harrach in the year of our Lord 1793." And then, in the neighborhood, the guest would find the geese waddling along as always with outstretched necks, the flock driven by barefoot children with sticks. Just such a child he himself had been . . . Afterwards, he was seen to go into the village and kneel down in prayer before a thatch-roofed cottage, the house in which he had been born so many years ago.

To "return" is one of the deepest and most mysterious longings of the human heart. "Return," however, means a return to a place. No one can return to a time. It is only in the realm of music that one can return to a time. In music, as Guenther Anders puts it, the recapitulation of a theme expresses the dialectical fact that music is capable of simultaneously proceeding forward and returning. Every *da capo* and every variation represents an attempt to fix forever what ultimately cannot be fixed. Every recapitulation expresses the ardent wish to overcome time by means of music.

Several semi-conscious motivations were behind Haydn's second visit to England. Was it fame? Yes. Money? That, too. There was no doubt, after the sad example of Mozart, that even an artist needed a fortune. But the third motive was most important; it was the impulse toward recapitulation. One had to be faithful to a theme. Life demanded that the theme be restated.

The London recapitulation began with a few comic measures. First of all, it was on this journey that Haydn and Elssler were taken for a pair of potters. Secondly, in the hotel in Wiesbaden, one evening, Haydn heard the CC-EE-GG-E, FF-DD-BB-C from his *Surprise Symphony* being played in some distant room. He tracked down the sound, and found a group of Prussian officers gathered around the piano. He introduced himself, but none of them would believe that this old man could be the composer of so vigorous and childlike a melody. In order to prove his identity, Haydn at last produced a letter from King Frederick William II and showed a diamond ring that had accompanied the letter. This convinced the Prussian gentlemen, and they ordered champagne in his honor.

In the next few "measures" of the recapitulation, the principal subject of his first visit to England recurred in its full glory. He enjoyed a marvelous reception in London; Salomon greeted him with open arms—and once again his first concert had to be postponed and postponed. He was surrounded by his old friends: the Czech Dussek, the singer Mara, Mrs. John Hunter—but not all of his friends were still alive. On October 16, 1793, John Hunter, the famous surgeon, had died, leaving his wife and two children. Haydn faithfully provided them with consolation—we can imagine the manner of it. The experience was beneficial to his art. He had already written *Six English Canzonets,* in 1792. Now, under the influence of Anne Hunter, he wrote six more. These were not folk songs, but art songs. Some of them were of an extraordinary range of emotion; such was *The Rover,* built up on a diminished seventh and, in its ghostliness, more akin to Weber's *Freischuetz* than to anything else in Haydn. Then there was *The Sailor's Song,* exemplifying Haydn's ability to identify himself with maritime life. And there was, above all, the best song Haydn ever wrote, *Despair.* The bold, independent piano prelude

clearly indicated the line that Schubert was to resume twenty years later. These English canzonets are, in a sense, the "missing link" between Haydn's insignificant rococo songs and the later vocal marvels of *The Creation* and *The Seasons*.

The London recapitulation was developed faithfully. There were the same jokes with the orchestra over Haydn's ignorance of English, also practical jokes which he suffered without a murmur, and he gave the usual expensive private lessons to members of the nobility and of high society.

Yes, everything seemed to be the same as it had been, even to the thunderous applause at concerts and the demand for encores of the slow movements of the symphonies. But, of course, nothing was actually the same. The composer's sensitive ear and alert mind noted the differences. The world was two years older; the French Revolution had not yet been checked and had become a maelstrom drawing everything to itself. The world could not remain unchanged, and there was intense tension in the air and widespread anxiety, even in England which was so haughtily and safely girdled by water.

The oddest events took place. Haydn who kept a diary again, noted: "During the month, on Sept. 7, 1794, there was an attemt to assassinade the king. the principal murderers were very young, one was a watchmaker, the odder a chemist. they made a kind of blow pipe from which they were going to shoot a little boisoned arrow to kill the king in the theater. their plan was to start a quarrel just belaw the king's box, during which one wood raise their canes in the air, threatening to beat each odder, while the arch-griminal would then undertake to shoot his arrow at the king: two more have been disgovered. One of them is a book deeler. the watchmaker's name is la Maitre, probably a Frenshman, the chemist is called Higgins. the book dealer calls himself John Smith, the fourth Upton. The watchmaker inverted [i.e., invented] the weapon!"

This was no repetition of the Hogarthian scenes Haydn had so often witnessed in London; rather, it was an instance of the political chaos which was overwhelming the whole world. That a Frenchman was involved seemed inevitable: Were not the Jacobins everywhere? Regicide had become an article of export which those bloodthirsty French were trying to distribute throughout the world. Unlike his pupil Beethoven, Haydn was old and conservative; he hated the Revolution with all his heart.

As if they already had not foes enough, on February 1, 1793, the

French had declared war on England. At this time, the war was little more than a series of naval skirmishes. But what would happen if Austria and Prussia were unable to tame the Parisian dragon? Then England would have to raise a land army and fight on the Continent. Few prospects could be more unwelcome to the British. The strength of the French was fearful to behold. Although the Revolution was consuming itself, and although former friends were daily sending one another to the guillotine, the monster of the Terror constantly grew new heads. England and London were swarming with refugees who told bloodcurdling tales. What would come next? Everyone felt a keen sense of insecurity, and this also affected art and its practitioners.

Never before had Haydn's works had so melancholy and serious a tone. His last six English symphonies had been written beforehand in Vienna, but they had been composed, it seemed, with a premonition of the gloomy future. A delicate and transparent sadness seemed to have been breathed into their often evanescently swift rhythms. The mood was one of parting—parting from a century of security. Certainly, there was no feeling of bidding farewell to life; Haydn's strength was unimpaired. Even now he invented jokes of orchestration such as the extremely original one in No. 102 in B-flat major where he delivers such a poke in the ribs to one of his prima donnas—a first violin—that it actually begins to stammer. The instrument tries to repeat the principal subject, but does not get beyond the first few stammering notes. Haydn had already played jokes upon all the other instruments; this latest jibe had been due for at least half a century. But, in general, the element of parody was much rarer in his last six symphonies than it had been in his previous works. Instead of jesting, he wrote with a deep seriousness which, however, was not so much in the subjects as in the orchestration and, above all, in a novel kind of harmony. The harmony was that of the romantic period which Haydn was adumbrating in these symphonies.

Romantic harmony owed its origins—at least partly—to a feeling of general insecurity. To the eighteenth century, such a feeling was quite foreign. The eighteenth was a secure century. Its mood of certitude sprang from many sources—from the belief in reason, in humanity and progress, a faith such as was exemplified in Joseph II; from its conception of a positive Christianity as expressed by Johann Sebastian Bach, and from its belief in the goodness of God which was exemplified in the work of the German poet Gellert. Haydn's harmonies, too, had always expressed pious affirmation; never had they been negative, never doubtful. Now all this was changed. In his old age Haydn was to return, in the oratorios *The Creation* and *The Seasons,* to affirmation; but now he wrote the remarkable group of "transitional symphonies," Nos. 99 to 104. These, it should be noted, were his last symphonies. Their subjects are, to be sure, not tinged with morbidness; in them we may still find the vigor and vitality so typical of Haydn; but the melancholy iridescence of the harmonies belies the message of the thematic material, and it is this dichotomy that makes these works so incredibly modern.

"Incredibly modern" is the correct phrase. For example, when you play a recording of the slow movement of Symphony No. 103, you can bewilder inexperienced listeners by asking: "Was this written by Brahms or by Mahler, or is it an unfamiliar work by Mendelssohn?" For this synthesis of German folk song and march, which stamps along with exaggerated clumsiness, is permeated by such strange harmonies and such novel instrumentation that it sounds like the work of a late-romantic or neo-romantic composer. The whole movement is obscured by the shyness and bashfulness with which modern composers approach well beloved folk tunes (the so-called *Brahms effect*). Indeed, nobody will suspect that the composer was a son of the eighteenth century—until a schoolmasterly gesture, overmuch faithfulness to a theme, or some other slightly pedestrian trait, betrays the truth—that this astonishing masterpiece was really written by Joseph Haydn, the father of all modernists.

It is indeed astonishing, and no one manifested more astonishment than—Richard Wagner. When he was writing his *Siegfried,* in 1869, the complications of his life had reached a crisis. Cosima von Buelow was with him; the two were living in Switzerland and waiting with great anxiety to find out whether Cosima's husband, Hans von Buelow, would give her a divorce. The difficulties of art and life almost exhausted their strength. "Guess how we have spent the last few evenings?" Cosima wrote at the time to a distant friend. "We have been playing Haydn's symphonies four-hands and, just imagine, with extraordinary eagerness! We chose the English symphonies which Haydn wrote after Mozart's death; their musical structure is wonderfully careful and delicate."

"Wonderfully careful and delicate!" What had become of the lackey who never knew a moment's discontent—the man whose memory Wagner had slandered? Now, in his state of inner tension, such innovations as the romantic horn finale resolved by the trumpets—that almost embarrassing outpouring of the wind instruments in Haydn's *Symphony with the Drum Roll*—inevitably awoke Wagner's sympathies. And Haydn must be considered the inventor of those breathless pianissimos and hushed silences of which Wagner was later to become the master. The dynamic contradictions—"contradictions" is far too weak a word, for "soft" and "loud" constitute different worlds—are nowhere present with such intensity (in any music before Beethoven's and Wagner's) as in Haydn's London symphonies. There is, for example, the apparently simple but in reality marvelously inspired passage in the *vivace* of *The Clock* (No. 101) where two subjects race along beside one another in double counterpoint for forty pianissimo measures, until they are joyfully greeted by the splendor of the full orchestra.

The piano could not fully render the marvelous tonal coloration and *chiaroscuro,* the restiveness of the orchestra. Nevertheless, it satisfied Cosima and Wagner. Clearly, these two could not spend hours with any idly diverting music when their future destinies were at stake; only the greatest art could have met their need. Haydn was, to be sure, a *mulcendi pectora primus,* but Richard Wagner and Cosima did not play his earlier symphonies, with their affirmative tone; they chose instead the works where profound unrest underlies apparent calm.

One of the most remarkable features of these symphonies is Haydn's mastery of the percussion instruments. No. 103, for example, begins with that singularly bold and unheralded initial drum roll to which it owes its name. This drum roll is followed by a mysterious passage of the bassoons, cellos, and contrabasses, in unison. Then comes a series of full rests that have a quality of "singing silence" and are no less mysterious than, say, the full rest at the beginning of Wagner's overture to the *Flying Dutchman.* "The contemporaries of Beethoven," writes Sir Donald Tovey (he may be thinking, rather, of the romantic worshipers of Beethoven such as Robert Schumann or Hector Berlioz), "must have forgotten the darkness of Haydn's introductory theme

if they thought Beethoven's genius more eccentric than that shown in this opening." This opening might be called, if one wished to give it a name, "the hand of fate rests on the beam of the scales." The mood was appropriate to the times, for the destinies of men were no longer decided in men's hearts and in the realm of private life; they were now entrusted to politics, to armies. The "Age of the Drum" had dawned.

It is generally recognized that the drum is not a crude, but an extremely sensitive, nervous instrument. There is nothing more spectral than the low drum beats in Haydn's *Missa in Tempore Belli,* the so-called drum mass which he wrote in 1797 when the French armies were moving on Steiermark. The essence of drumming is that it expresses both courage and fear—the courage of those whose drums are sounding and the fear of the enemy who is threatened by them. To this ambiguity, which was well known to primitive peoples, is due the overtone of fatefulness in all percussive music.

Haydn reached the apex of novel orchestration in the symphony that bears the significant No. 100, the *Military Symphony*. It is characterized, to some extent, by "Turkish ornamentation" (although Haydn does not go in for the *alla Turca* melismas of Mozart's well known *Turkish March*). The big drum is played with both a big stick and a little stick at once, the big stick marking the accents while the little one keeps up a trotting rhythm. The cymbals clash in time with the big stick, while the triangle rings an alarm, or else trots along with the little stick. Curiously enough, the *Military Symphony* does not contain a march such as Beethoven wrote into the final movement of his *Seventh Symphony*. The gap between Haydn's *Military Symphony* and Beethoven's "forced marches" was bridged by the music of the French Revolution, the *élan terrible* of such composers as Gossec, Méhul, and Catel, in whose methods and inspiration Beethoven believed. By contrast, Haydn's *Military Symphony* is not a stirring and compelling call to action; it is rather frail, and often there broods over it a phantasmal calmness. Its tone is iridescent. Haydn's work has no similarity to the famous, radiantly sunny military march of Franz Schubert. Only in Schubert's trio, where a moment of sadness slips in, do we find a reminiscence of the older master's melancholy.

The allegro begins with a theme so typical of Haydn that, as Tovey puts it, "we are apt to forget that in the whole range of classical music no other symphonic first theme has ever been scored in that way." The military mood is conveyed not by the rhythm, but by the instrumentation; the unaccompanied theme is introduced by a flute and two oboes. Even in the merriest sections of the *allegro* the good cheer is not quite genuine; there is an unreal, a surrealistic feeling about it, as if the composer actually intended something altogether different from gladness. In the *allegretto,* the triangle, cymbals, kettledrum and alto clarinet are added, but as yet no march emerges. The melody of the principal subject has, rather, a narrative quality.

The theme is an old acquaintance; Haydn had often toyed with it, and had used it many years earlier in a lute concerto. *"La gentille et jeune Lisette"*—it is the sort of ballad that soldiers like to sing. This *allegretto* is indeed "blithe," as soldiers are reputed to be. But gradually the blitheness is dispelled—not so much by means of variations as by means of the harmony and orchestration; the melody becomes increasingly grave, more and more hesitant. An acrid, autumnal fragrance blows over the musical landscape. A moment before all was rich and summery; now, almost without transition, the romantic ballad world collapses; a seven-bar trumpet signal begins. (Ten years later Beethoven was to recall this trumpet blast, in his *Leonore Overture.*) The trumpets sound nakedly, without accompaniment; they are followed by a roll of the kettledrums that rises from *pianissimo* to *fortissimo.* (To this day nothing simpler or more effective has been discovered.) The real stroke of genius is to be found in the finale: the entire orchestra precipitately joins in the fortissimo, and thus anticipates (twenty-five years before Weber) the principal effect of the *Freischuetz* overture. In his earlier days, Haydn would then have returned cheerfully to the affirmative opening bars of his ballad. But the older

Haydn knew that the past was irrevocable, that it was time to bid farewell to the pleasant eighteenth century. Like a weary stagehand regretfully carrying off the sets, he therefore wrote

The discreet, melancholy acquiescence of these measures is unsurpassable. The old play was done with; a new drama was to take the stage, a grand spectacle directed by one Napoleon Bonaparte.

The first performance of the *Military Symphony* took place May 4, 1795. Salomon conducted, as usual, and Haydn accompanied on the piano. In his diary he noted quite materialistically: "The entire audienze was exdremely pleasured and so was I. I took in 4,000 gulden this evening. this is the kind of thing that can only be done in England." (He could not know then that the first performance of *The Creation* in Vienna would net him the vast sum of 9,000 gulden.)

Among the select audience at this benefit concert of Haydn's was the heir to the British crown. The constantly misspelled "Printz of Wallys" became even more strongly attached to Haydn than he had been three years earlier. For a time the prince saw the composer almost daily. Theirs was a strange companionship, and it was, no doubt, fortunate for Haydn that he was a practised courtier. The two men were so different by nature that anyone less experienced than Haydn might well have committed some grave *faux pas*.

HOME CALLS AGAIN

INCREDIBLE as it sounds, England's Prince of Wales owed Haydn money!

The man who later became George IV spent a hundred thousand pounds sterling a year on clothes but forgot that musicians needed to earn their livelihood and did not bother to pay Haydn. How then was Haydn to collect his salary for the twenty-six concerts given in Carlton House, the prince's home? The heir to the throne, if not drunk, was far too nice to be reminded of such minor things, so Haydn later sent his bill, which amounted to three hundred guineas from Vienna and was paid promptly.

Haydn had grown to like the royal wastrel and never forgot that during his first stay in London he had had the enormous luck of being courted by the cello-playing prince. Now, in the midst of the English recapitulation he tried again to "preserve a theme."

Speaking of debts: according to the statement of the British Parliament, the total debts of the heir apparent amounted to no less than 642,890 pounds. The manner in which the prince liquidated his debts proved to be more scandalous than the debts themselves. His only course was to disregard his secret marriage to a woman of not equal birth and make an official marriage with some wealthy princess. As the popular rhyme put it (Haydn could hear the jingle on every street corner):

"The King he said unto his son, you know you're deep in debt, Sir,
So you must have a wife, 'tis vain to pounce and fret, Sir.
I'll have you send to Germany to fetch a pretty cousin . . ."

The unfortunate cousin was Caroline of Brunswick. Without suspecting anything of conditions at the English court, the "bride" came to London and was married to the Prince of Wales on Wednesday, April 8, 1795. Three native composers contested for the honor of supplying music for the ceremony in the Palace of St. James. Haydn, who previously had hoped to conduct the ceremony himself, counseled them wisely, and although all three were at first angered by his advice, it was finally followed. At the wedding itself the only music played were organ pieces by Handel. Caroline gave her "yes" in a firm, clear voice, but the prince spoke so low that the Archbishop of Canterbury could not hear him. He looked inquiringly at the prince—and at that point the heavens intervened. A cloudburst began. Amid fearful flashes of lightning and crashes of thunder, the ceremony ended. The roar of the thunder competed with Handel's chords. In the general chill of spirits occasioned by this ill omen, the newlyweds departed for their official residence.

Two days later, on April 10, the princess gave her first reception, at which Haydn was the guest of honor. Salomon, too, was present. "An old symphony of mine was played," Haydn noted in his diary, "and I aggompanied on the piano; afderwards their was a quartet; then I had to sing German and Englich(!) songs. the princess sang with me; then she played a goncerto on the pianoforte fairly good." At this time peace still prevailed in Carlton House; the warfare between husband and wife did not begin until later, after Haydn's departure from England. The prince began to make a habit of inviting, to his home, bands of drunken friends whose filthy boots ruined the carpets and the furniture. The poor princess declared that it was worse than living in a tavern; and twenty-five years later, when her husband was crowned king, the humiliated wife was compelled to realize that not even this tavern belonged to her.

During his first visit to England, Haydn had not met the prince's father, the "master of the world." George III was a man of unimpressive appearance, tenacious will, and middle-class habits who "ruled England as if the country were his household, with the proverbial stinginess of a German potentate." He outlived the revolt of the American colonies as well as the French Revolution and the Napoleonic Empire. However, it was only his body that remained alive; toward the end of his life his mind was shattered, and blindness was visited upon him. It is moving to read that this pitiful wreck of a human being went on, to the end of his life, listening to Handel's music. The old man rejoiced and wept with a deeply personal feeling when Handel's blind Samson killed the Philistines.

Haydn had often been told that the king was not interested in contemporary music. "I will have no innovation in my time," he had once declared sternly. It was therefore not strange that Haydn had not yet been presented to him (besides the fact that George III, generally, shunned the entourage of his son to which, although inofficially, Haydn belonged). But in this respect the London recapitulation added a motif to the subjects of the first visit. At a concert given by the Duke of York, the king went up to Haydn somewhat shyly, and said to him in German: "Dr. Haydn, you have written a good deal."

"Yes, sire," Haydn replied modestly, but with that wit and facility that he so often possessed in courtly affairs, "and, I think, a great deal more than is good."

"Oh, no; the world contradicts that," the king replied, pleasantly. He then asked Haydn whether or not it was true that he sang quite well.

"God forbid!" Haydn replied. "My voice is no bigger than this—" and he raised the tip of his little finger. The king liked the gesture, and he liked the man. He introduced Haydn to the queen, who was also a German, formerly Charlotte of Mecklenburg-Strelitz. The queen invited him to several soirées at Buckingham Palace, and also had him visit her privately. One day she asked him why he did not remain permanently in England. "I should give you a suite in Windsor Castle for the summer, and then—" she smiled at the king—"we shall make music *tête à tête*."

"I am not jealous of Haydn," replied George III, whose dislike of Italian teachers of music was well known. "He is a good, honest German."

"To preserve that repute is my greatest pride, sire," Haydn said, swiftly.

The next time Haydn came, the king asked whether he had decided to remain. Haydn was evasive. Perhaps His Majesty did not know that he was married. "That does not matter," King George replied. "We can simply send for your wife."

"She will not even cross the Danube; how could one persuade her to cross the sea?" Haydn countered, with finality.

Certainly, Haydn did not refuse to stay in England out of consideration for his wife; there seemed to be every reason for his remaining. Of money and honors he could acquire more in England than anywhere else in the world. He would move in circles where, in the royal family, the ordinary language was German, or, in the world of musicians, Italian. His decision against settling down in England was due partly to the "impulse toward recapitulation," which he now felt more strongly than ever. There was still an unfinished theme in his life, and he had to return to it. This time the theme was Eisenstadt. After a four-year reign Prince Anton had suddenly died, and his successor was Nicholas, named after his grandfather. The young man, moreover, had inherited the temper of his grandfather, Nicholas the Splendid, and requested Haydn once more to take up residence in Eisenstadt; this second Nicholas intended to rebuild the Esterhazy orchestra.

At the prospect of once more having his own orchestra, Haydn felt immensely stimulated, and forty years younger. The old theme was returning once more. He accepted the offer; he was to spend the remainder of his life (a good many years) in Vienna and at Eisenstadt. While he was still in London, his thoughts turned away from the city.

His refusal to stay in England was another indication of the sureness of his instincts. For in spite of the king's cordiality, he would never have made Haydn his court composer. Haydn was, after all, a Catholic, and Catholicism was one of the things the king really hated. The "Defender of the Faith" was a bitter enemy of "popery"; he did not permit any Catholics to enter his army, and would never have conferred an official post upon a non-Protestant musician—if only for the sake of Handel's memory. As for Haydn, his Catholicism was more deeply ingrained than he himself realized. After spending an entire day among the ruins of Waverley Abbey, with his companion, Sir Charles Rich, he wrote an entry in his diary which spontaneously expressed his deep identification with Catholicism. "Whenever I look upon this bautiful wasteland, my heart is obbressed by the thought that all this onse stood under the protektion of my holy religion." As an Austrian and a Catholic, he could not have been satisfied to make his permanent home in a non-Catholic country.

This, however, did not prevent him, as a thoroughgoing cosmopolitan, from enjoying all that England had to offer. As he had done three years earlier, he traveled a great deal. His friend Burney took him to see Bath. What apparently most interested him there, aside from the music and a Mrs. Brown,—who, he noted casually, was "a very beautiful woman"—was the stone with which the buildings had been constructed. Haydn remained an artisan's son; he made a point of examining the unusual stone very carefully. "It is guarried in the nayboring hills and it is so sofd that it can be easely cut into all shapes, and is very white. the longer the stone is out of the earth, the harder it becomes." Here was a parable for his own art. In his youth, Haydn was soft and pliable, and followed many models. Later his understanding of his own unique qualities became harder and more definite.

Since he was interested in money, no wonder that his diary has a long note on his visit to the Bank of England; its arrangements are punctiliously described. "In order to see the main safe-deposet boxes, it is necessary to be guided by three of the directers, each of whom has a speshial key." He was impressed by the secret vaults "which wood certainly be very useful in case of a rebellyon." He mentioned with awe the amount of money stored in these vaults. For the moment he seemed to feel himself a native Englishman. He had the same feeling when he went to Portsmouth and inspected a French warship, the *St. Just* of eighty guns, which the British had captured; and he seems to have shared the emotions of Julius Caesar who, on beholding the Isle of Wight, declared, "This is the realm of the gods."

Haydn permitted himself a long "coda" to the English movement; in the finale he once again recapitulated all his favorite themes. His encounter with William Herschel was also repeated, though in the form of a variation; in a library, not in an observatory, he glimpsed the immensity of the cosmos. Depressed by the sight of so many books, he sighed, and said, "What should I compose? One subject is just as worthwhile as another, but none of them is eternal." A friend of his, Barthelémon the violinist, took a Bible from the nearest shelf. He opened to the first chapter of Genesis and said, "There, take that; begin at the beginning." Once more the master felt the cold of space all around him, as he had when he looked timidly through Herschel's great telescope. *Could he write music for eternity?*

At last, satiated but content, he bade farewell to the English, and returned to the Continent. The uncertainties of war prevailed there now, but it was his home, and when his time came to die he wanted to be buried at home. For the present he had no thought of dying; he was happy and full of plans, and his pockets were well filled. He had earned twelve hundred English pounds, on this journey. He had left Vienna accompanied by Elssler, his faithful servant, only, but when they returned, there were three instead of two. A messenger from the realm of beasts cowered on Elssler's shoulder. It was a wonderful green parrot, with a spot of red on his breast and a yellow tail, a present from Haydn's English friends. "Come, Papa Haydn!" the bird cried.

Book Five

THE PURPLE EVENING

For fifty years, playing and listening to Haydn's works has repeatedly produced in me one general sensation. I have felt an involuntary urge to do something good and pleasing to God. This feeling arose pure and independent of reflection and passion. . . . When Haydn is, sometimes, reproached for a lack of passion in his music, I have only to say that passion in music, as in all arts, is easier than people think. . . . It does not bear the marks of originality; it is a product of the moment, and in the opinion of the ancients it hides the purity of nature and impairs the beautiful.

GOETHE

HARDSHIPS OF WAR AND THE IMPERIAL ANTHEM

When he reached home, Haydn was grossly disappointed.

As far as external activities were concerned, there was more than enough for him to do. A new *kapelle* had been established, and there was a spirit of general confidence in the new prince, Nicholas II—the fourth Prince Esterhazy whom the gray-haired master now served. It was said that Nicholas was "not stingy"; he strove to emulate his grandfather and merit the epithet of "splendid." But this second Nicholas had one flaw which was unusual in an Esterhazy: he was fundamentally unmusical. Not wishing to admit this, he frequently passed hasty and foolish judgments upon music. The more insecure he felt about his own taste, the more definite he was in making assertions that inevitably offended the musicians. No one realized that the prince's deprecatory remarks were purely mechanical fault-finding, and that he felt obliged to censure in order to give himself the air of an expert. He feared that praise would betray him as a dilettante.

Haydn, of course, was not to be disturbed. When most of his biographers state how much, in his last fourteen years, he "suffered" under the yoke of that prince, we have reasons to doubt it. His innate self-assurance restored the balance. Once, at a rehearsal, when Nicholas made some remarks that were especially malapropos, Haydn exclaimed: "Your Highness, this is a matter for *me* to decide." Whereupon his Highness was struck speechless, and left the room.

Proud Beethoven, on the contrary, was not so lucky in his dealings with Prince Esterhazy. When, in the later years, old Haydn lay ill and, unable to leave Vienna, could not undertake to provide the customary mass the name day of Nicholas' wife, the assignment was given to Beethoven. In accepting the commission, Beethoven wrote to the prince a letter which remains a remarkable document, because it shows how highly the man, who had already composed the *Eroica* and *Fidelio,* still respected Haydn. "May I add," Beethoven wrote, on August 9, 1807, "that I shall send you this mass with a great deal of trepidation, since you, prince, are accustomed to hearing the masterpieces of the inimitable Haydn." After the performance of the mass, which Beethoven had made a special journey to Eisenstadt to attend, Nicholas II received the composer with the typical condescension of the Austrian nobleman (he had to carp about something). "But, my dear Beethoven," he said in the nasal tone of the aristocrat, "what in the world have you pulled off this time?" Whereupon Beethoven, in a ferocious rage, turned on his heel, and left the palace forever.

Therein is shown the difference between the characters of the two composers. Haydn did not turn on his heel, but made the prince himself walk out. For the sake of his art, this patient but tenacious man was able to turn everything to the best possible account. The prince's lack of feeling for music proved highly advantageous to Haydn in some respects, for he was required to provide much less music—less and less as time passed. In the end, the services demanded of him amounted to no more than writing a mass once a year. Since he needed no more than three months to work on a mass, he was left with nine full months in which he could compose what he pleased. It is to this happy chance that we owe Haydn's chief works, *The Creation* and *The Seasons,* which were not written on order for Nicholas, but composed by Haydn as "free enterprises." And yet, although he worked far less for the second Nicholas than he had for the prince's predecessors, he was clever enough to get more money out of Nicholas than he had ever received before. His already considerable salary was increased by a third.

A woman had her hand in the game. Marie Hermenegildis, Prince Esterhazy's wife, shielded Haydn in his relations with the prince. As Haydn grew older, he was increasingly fortunate in enjoying the favor of noblewomen. For a full fourteen years, until he died, Princess Esterhazy was his guardian angel. At the death of Johann Evangelist, Haydn's younger brother who had been a member of the Esterhazy orchestra, the princess traveled in person all the way from Eisenstadt to Vienna to break the news gently to Haydn. It is to her that we are indebted for Haydn's six great masses, which were all written for her name day, September 8. (To some extent Haydn was impelled to competition, carried on in a fraternal spirit, with Michael Haydn, who was now, in Salzburg, a highly esteemed composer of church music.)

The first of these masses was the so-called *Pauken Messe* ("Drum Mass"), which received its first performance in Eisenstadt on September 13, 1796. Haydn wrote it in a time of widespread anxiety. The war which the Emperor Francis II was waging against the French had begun to take a turn for the worse. While the Emperor's brother, Archduke Karl, was engaged in the North against Moreau and Jourdan, General Napoleon Bonaparte, then twenty-seven, swept with incredible speed across the North Italian plain and threatened Mantua, then a well-fortified Austrian stronghold. He took the city after a short siege and rushed victoriously on through Tyrol and Carinthia into the heart of Styria. On April 10, 1797, the French moved into Graz.

Indescribable panic gripped Vienna. Half a century earlier, when the house of Hapsburg had lost its wars with Frederick of Prussia, the people of Vienna had still gone on dancing and making merry. Those dynastic wars were not taken seriously—for all that a great deal of blood was shed in them, and for all the people's loyalty to Maria Theresa. The battles were far away from Vienna, and the Prussians did not try to come closer. Moreover, they were human beings. But now the case was different—these Frenchmen seemed to combine the traits of devils and tigers. Here an entire nation was on the march, shattering the old order in the name of a new idea. Where the French came, there remained, literally, no stone unturned; they inverted the order of society, the lowest became highest, dynastic kings lost their crowns . . .

In the autumn of 1796 the Austrian court impressed on the populace the fact that this war was no longer restricted to the soldiers; that it was a war of whole nations in which everyone—man, woman, and child—had to do his utmost. A pamphlet entitled *The Perils of the Times* was published. It contained dire threats: "Whoever shall be charged with speaking of peace (!) so long as the enemy remains within our boundaries, whoever criticizes any measure decreed by the authorities, will be publicly tried and, if found guilty, will be treated as an enemy of our country and—whoever he may be—*turned over to the vengeance of the populace.*"

Thus "traitors" and "sympathizers with the cause of the Revolution" were being threatened with lynch law—an indication of the extent to which the emperor's government had lost its head and given way to hysteria. On the other hand, a host of enthusiastic, courageous young volunteers joined the colors—the recruiting campaigns were great successes—in order to fight the terrible Bonaparte. In those momentous days Haydn created a work of religious art that was wholly novel in character, for its temper was obviously topical. His *Drum Mass* followed the ancient liturgy, as do all Masses, for no deviations from or innovations in the text are permitted. But the instrumentation betrayed the anxiety of the times; it was impregnated with an uncanny nervousness.

We will recall that in London Haydn discovered a new instrument, "the human heart thudding with anxiety," which he presented in the guise of drums playing *pianissimo*. He now used this instrument in his mass; in the midst of the most sacred of music he introduced the wholly earthly anxiety of the living creature on the point of perishing. Legation Councilor Griesinger, who during Haydn's latter years obtained much authentic biographical information from the master himself, wrote, in this connection: "In 1796, when the French were in Styria, Haydn composed a mass to which he gave the title, *Missa in Tempore Belli*. In this mass the words *Agnus dei, qui tollis peccata mundi* are rendered in unusual fashion with drum accompaniment, *as if the enemy might already be heard* in the distance. For the following words, *Dona nobis pacem*, Haydn abruptly had all the voices and instruments movingly chime in."

It was, in fact, the English Haydn, the Haydn of the Salomon symphonies, who was once more coming to the fore. He did not hesitate for a moment in introducing the thitherto forbidden drum into ecclesiastical music. After the quiet, deeply emotional melody of the *Agnus dei*, carried by the choir and the strings, a number of drum measures were introduced into the score:

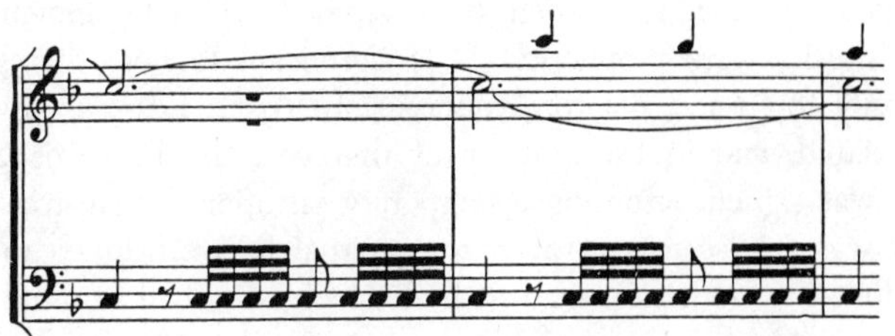

The muted rhythm with which the drum accompanies the uneasy syncopes of the first violin and the long-drawn-out plaint of the oboe (later this rhythm is taken up by the other wind instruments, the bassoon, the clarinet, and the French horn) is overpowering in its effect. No doubt about it—this is the beating of the human heart. But it is also (Griesinger is quite correct) the pounding of the French drums, the faint thunder of the French armies rolling down the Alpine slopes. The astonishing fact is that the rhythm and the manner are really those of *French* drums. In 1796 Haydn could scarcely have been familiar with the anapestic rhythm so characteristic of French drummers

Haydn was acquainted with only the somewhat clumsy English signals he had heard in London when he strolled through Leicester Square. These have a dactylic base

Nevertheless, Haydn made the heart of Austria throb to the beat of French drums and to the *élan terrible* of the revolutionary spirit—proof that he had the gift not only of portraying reality, but of *inventing* it if necessary.

This bold experiment involved Haydn in serious difficulties with the guardians of "pure" ecclesiastical music. (We shall return to this matter.) For the present, however, his prayer was heard. The words

Dona nobis pacem, for which he composed especially moving and sincere music, were prophetic. (It is significant to note that Haydn asked only for peace, not for "victory.") In April, 1797, an armistice was declared, and in the autumn of that year the Peace of Campo Formio was signed, affording a temporary salvation for Austria. However, it was a false peace; the fierce internal fires continued to burn. These fires the German poet, Friedrich Hoelderlin, had in mind when in his ode, "On the Peace of Campo Formio," he spoke of Napoleon Bonaparte as "the inexorable, terrible son of Nature, the ancient Spirit of Unrest":

He stirs
Like fire flaring in the core of the earth,
That shakes the ancient cities like ripe fruit trees,
That rends the mountains
And consumes the oaks and the very rocks.

One other time Haydn also drew his inspiration from the events of the day and created undying music out of the passing show. Before the armistice in April, 1797, he wrote *The Imperial Anthem.* In England he had been struck by the tremendous power of *God Save the King* to rally the hearts of the British. The populace of London was not noted for respecting persons or institutions, but whenever the anthem written by Henry Carey rang out, the critics of the House of Hanover fell silent. At that time national anthems were not a matter of course. It was a novel experience for people to feel in such music the kind of inner force which only religious hymns conveyed. In those times of stress Haydn felt the impulse to write such a "consolatory hymn" for the German nation, pressed so hard by the threats of the ever-spreading French Revolution. Through the mediation of his friend, Baron Gottfried van Swieten, he sought aid from the Ministry of the Interior. Count Saurau, the Minister of the Interior, appointed a "poet," Leopold Haschka, an unpleasant fellow who sometimes served as a police spy, to compose the text. (A volume of Odes, written by Haschka, was later termed a "Gorgonic grimace" by Goethe.) No one suspected that the uninspired text that Haschka produced would become the basis for an immortal anthem. For Haydn's anthem is still heard, although its immediate inspiration, the Emperor Francis, has fallen into the oblivion which he well deserves:

("God preserve Emperor Francis, our good Emperor! Long live Emperor Francis in Fortune's brightest gleam! Wherever he goes the laurel springs to form a crown of glory for him. God preserve the emperor!")

It was to this man, whose political misfortunes were apparently to be without end, that Haydn dedicated the popular anthem in which every measure breathes a spirit of *pious security*. The contrast is most moving. Haydn liked certain bourgeois traits—or shall we, rather, say petty bourgeois traits?—that the emperor evinced in his private life. Some biographers of Haydn believe that the composer was also influenced by the fact that this emperor was the first of the Hapsburgs to appreciate his music. Maria Theresa had enjoyed Haydn's music only to the extent that it was, more or less, Italianate, and Joseph II sometimes seemed so embarrassed by Haydn's "instrumental noises" and "frivolities," that he did not act when his majordomo, Kilian Strack, banned Haydn from the Emperor's domestic concerts. But the Emperor Francis himself played Haydn's quartets—played them, it was said, with a great deal of enthusiasm. However, whatever Haydn's motives may have been, no emperor ever received a more royal gift.

The tripartite structure of this anthem, through which the tranquil melody flows as through the aisles of a church, is of an astonishing peacefulness. Haydn designed an imperial palace without a single niche for a statue of Mars. There is nothing military about the music. In other anthems—for example, Rouget de l'Isle's *Marseillaise*—the marching beat of the melody is heard in the very first measures. One can see the soldiers' knees swinging higher and higher with each fourth, fifth, and octave. And in *God Save the King* there is the asthmatic, restive lingering on a staccato note repeated four times. In comparison to these, Haydn's *hymn,* with its falling rhythms, seems utterly passionless. In the same moment in which he pays tribute to the highest power on earth, he expresses this power as a friendly and gracious one, endowing it, at the same time, with an air of condescending majesty. As the folds of the emperor's ermine robe flow down from his shoulders, so this melody glides downward—a melody of incomparable calmness and dignity.

We have precise record of the natal day of the anthem. It was also the emperor's birthday, February 12, 1797. To raise the depressed spirits of the people of Vienna, the Court Theater put on an evening performance of a favorite comic opera, a work by Dittersdorf, the friend of Haydn's younger days. The name of the opera was *Doctor and Apothecary*. It had sprightly music and an amusing text, dealing with a dispute between the two professions. Various amours were woven into the plot, and a termagant of a mother-in-law went about boxing everyone's ears and "stealing the show." The Viennese derived a certain amount of amusement out of a song that described what a bourgeois bride needed for her trousseau

Now everything the bride wears
Must be as new as new.
Her petticoats must come in pairs
And she be dressed as she were two.

When the word *two* was significantly accorded two full measures (the bride also had to have six bed jackets and nightcaps) the theatergoers roared with laughter. In these hard times the solid citizens of the middle class could not afford to outfit their brides in such fashion. (However, the day after the performance a rich Englishman created a stir in Vienna, when he provided twenty-four bridal couples with a trousseau and a wedding banquet.)

Before the operetta began, leaflets bearing the text of Haydn's anthem were distributed among the audience. The anthem was to be sung as soon as the emperor entered his box. But Francis (and this was one of his winning traits) disliked being acclaimed in public. Therefore he deliberately came late. But this did not help matters; the director of the Court Theater simply postponed the singing of the imperial anthem until the first intermission. After the music had been played once by the orchestra, the entire audience suddenly rose and sang the words to the monarch, who stood listening with deep emotion and embarrassment. Enthusiasm broke all bounds, and it was a long while before the company could continue the operetta.

Later, the Germans took the anthem away from the Austrians and applied the words of Hoffmann von Fallersleben to it. Thus, it became *Deutschland, Deutschland über alles*. The Austrians, however, refused to be deprived of it and continued to sing their "God preserve the emperor" through the First World War and the days of the Republic, each time changing the text, of course. But there is nothing remarkable about this. Great Music is destined for great things.

What is remarkable is that the song has an extensive prehistory. In the eighteenth century the matter of intellectual property was not treated so strictly as it is today. But in the case of the Haydn anthem we are dealing not with borrowing, but with entire appropriation. Franz Kuhač, the Croat nationalist, demonstrated in 1868 that the first measures (and thus the germinal cell of the melody) came from a Croat folk song

However, W. H. Hadow, the English musicologist who was usually only too happy to support Kuhač's assertions, had to admit the weakness of the ending of the fourth measure of the Croat folk song. "It frequently happens," Hadow wrote, "that a Croatian or Serbian tune will begin with a fine phrase, and then fall to an anti-climax—either losing sight of its tonality, or wavering in its rhythm, or ending with a weak and commonplace cadence." Now, the second strain of the folk tune was too short to fit the second line of Haschka's poem, so Haydn extended its cadence and wrote

This may be no more than a slight emendation, but if it be true that the unimportant pastoral Croat song was the germ of the national anthem, it was this very slight emendation that immeasurably ennobled the melody.

Remarkably enough, not only the Croat peasants knew Haydn's melody before it was born: Georg Teleman (1676-1738), the great master of the North German baroque style, also had known it, at least its first measures. But even more remarkable is the fact that also the song's final section, with its characteristic "condescension"—the gracious, descending rhythm—has its antecedents. The Berlin scholar, Wilhelm Tappert, has listed no less than eleven earlier forms of this part. Curiously enough, Haydn was well versed in two of them—one written by Mozart (in his violin *Sonata in F-major*), the other written by himself in the *Seven Words:*

Tappert was so astonished by this and similar discoveries that in 1868 he developed the novel theory of "wandering melody." Could not, he asked, Darwin's principle—that all animal and plant forms derive from a few organisms which in the course of time naturally became diversified—also be applied in the realm of music? In music there are so many apparent "plagiarisms"—which are, in fact, not plagiarisms at all, but rather transmutations in the evolutionary sense. (One of the most modern musicologists, Ernst Kurth, similarly speaks of melody as a "biological being" which possesses a life of its own.) According to Tappert, every melody, "no matter how complex or cultivated, has a simple basis." It is this simple basis that moves the hearts of the people; it is this that carries a song from concert hall to home, to factory, that travels down all highways and crosses all borders. The anonymous melody is picked up by the ear of one musician after another, is absorbed and changed by his artistic genius, although its skeletal structure remains unchanged. Herder once made similar observations about words, not music. It is a dubious theory, but it would certainly have pleased Haydn, who considered music something quite other than merely the product of one man's personality.

In regard to personality, we may well wonder whether Haydn was aware of the musical significance of his anthem. Certainly he was fond of it. Otherwise he would not have incorporated the famous melody in his *Emperor Quartet* (Op. 76, No. 3) where we find it again, *poco adagio cantabile,* in the form of a theme and variations. The last of these variations, with its tune floating slowly upward and then gently descending, is a magical passage of almost indescribable beauty:

But, in another sense, Haydn apparently was not so conscious of his anthem's unique worth. For when the emperor sent him a gold portrait box in return for the work, Haydn wrote an almost servile letter. He addressed it to the Minister of the Interior, Count Saurau, writing:

"Your Excellency: In all my life I have not experimented [i.e., "experienced"] such surbrise and so much greciousness, esbecialy for the picture of our good monark, and gonsidering my own small talents. I thank yor excellensy from the Heart and am respectfully at the Service of Your Excelancy in all things. Before eleven o'glock I will bring the gopy of the song. I am in deepest reverence your most humble and obediant servent, Joseph Haydn."

Note that this letter was written not to the emperor himself but merely to a minister. Beethoven's pride would never have let him compose such a letter, but Haydn's nature was such that the excess of humility apparent in the letter did not degrade him. By the time the anthem was written, in February, 1797, he already had matters of concern other than the "good monarch." Among them was the remarkable Baron van Swieten who was becoming increasingly important in Haydn's life.

VAN SWIETEN AND THE DUEL WITH HANDEL

THE Court Librarian, Gottfried van Swieten, who was destined to write the text to Haydn's chief work, *The Creation,* was the son of Maria Theresa's famous personal physician, Guerardus van Swieten. In 1745, at the age of eleven, he had accompanied his parents to Vienna, where the empress's favor and a careful education had prepared him for a diplomatic career. He, then, was sent as ambassador to the most important political centers of Europe—above all to Berlin, where, five years after the Peace of Hubertusburg, he represented Austria at the court of Frederick the Great. The reports the young diplomat wrote revealed the author as a good psychologist, a talented narrator, and an intelligent arranger of material, with some "sense of orchestration," too.

The old king himself was a political musician of parts. Since he was very well aware that van Swieten had other interests besides diplomacy, their conversations tended more and more to turn to matters of art. The gouty king seldom played his flute any more, but he retained his fondness for music. One day Frederick performed for the Austrian ambassador a fugue "by a certain Bach," and thus first introduced the Viennese gentleman to the great North German school of Protestant music. Van Swieten, although a Catholic, was of Dutch origin, and therefore not unreceptive to such Low German cultural influences. When he quit the diplomatic service the following year, 1776, in order to become court librarian, he brought back to Vienna an extensive musical library consisting chiefly of the works of Bach and Handel.

Vienna, of course, would not take to "learned music"—as the Viennese deemed Bach's counterpoint. For almost a quarter of a century, van Swieten exerted a great deal of patience, pedantry, and schoolmasterly anger in trying to persuade the aristocracy of Vienna to listen to contrapuntal music, but without success.

I cannot to love compel thee
But shall not grant thee liberty

as it is put in *The Magic Flute*. These verses suited the case exactly. The stern Herr van Swieten would not let the easygoing Viennese go their way in peace; he would not let them stay home when he sponsored performances of Handel's oratorios, in his home or at the court library. When a nobleman once asked how long the performance would last, he wrote, angrily, "Bring our nightcap along." Malicious gossips in Vienna even asserted that he sometimes locked the doors from outside, during his concerts. "He sat always in the first row," John N. Burk wrote in his biography of Beethoven, "and at any sign of whispering during the performance he rose slowly, stood in all the ponderous authority of his wig and double chin, gazed long and pointedly at the disturbers and slowly sat down again"—a schoolmasterly gesture, not to be loved by anyone. However, his labors were not intellectual alone; he also raised money from the aristocrats, the Dietrichsteins, Lobkowitzes, Schwarzenbergs, Lichnowskys, Apponyis, and Batthyányis, to meet the fees of the singers and the orchestra (for the performances were not public). For a time he engaged as musical director Wolfgang Amadeus Mozart who, out of respect for van Swieten, submissively studied Bach's polyphonic style. Poor Mozart was even compelled to arrange Handel's oratorios, *The Messiah* and *Alexander's Feast,* for which task he was basically and radically unsuited. (Romain Rolland has given us a very fine account of this.) But it was impossible to say "no" to a man like Gottfried van Swieten. It was he who acquainted young Beethoven, just come to Vienna, with Homer and Shakespeare; and it was out of more than mere politeness that Beethoven dedicated his first symphony to him. Van Swieten exhibited a naïve vanity in demanding such honors, but in this he was not different from other men of his era.

The question, who should provide a man like Haydn with texts for vocal compositions, was a more difficult problem for him than it was for many other composers. His lack of education, which struck even such friends as Griesinger as distressing, made it necessary for him to obtain "instruction and protection" from someone who was superior to him as a scholar and humanist—though not as an artist. This man turned out to be van Swieten, although his protection was somewhat tyrannical, as it could not help being with an egotist like him, whose holding of multitudinous offices was virtually an invitation to megalomania. Van Swieten was, for example, president of the "official censorship commission" which decided the fate of every book in Austria. (He did not abuse his office, however; in fact, he saved many Austrian writers from starvation by providing them with government sinecures.)

Van Swieten, of course, was a lover of books. Now, Haydn had brought, from his second journey to England, a small book that he had taken out of Salomon's hand. "This here," the old friend and manager had said, "is something Handel was asked to compose music for, but he was unwilling to do it." It was, in the form of dialogues, somewhat like the Biblical story of the Creation and had been written by a man named Lindley in lofty, poeticized language which apparently derived largely from Milton's *Paradise Lost.*

Haydn was frequently timid when confronted by works of literature, especially those written in foreign languages. He took no pride in this timidity; but instinctively he feared anything that went beyond his own special field, the creation of pure music. This work, however, excited his interest. If Salomon's information was correct, it had been written especially for the almost legendary Handel, who had been dead these forty years. That fact aroused Haydn's mettle; it heightened in him the fever of rivalry which is to be found in all great men.

During Haydn's stay in London, Charles Burney had repeatedly told him the story of Handel's life. His account had been so vivid that Haydn was aware, at every moment, of the great differences between himself and Handel. They were differences of physique, of temperament, of artistic aims, and of philosophy. Handel was "the lion of Judah in the realm of music." A huge man, with large hands and feet, but with crooked legs he would come lumbering up like a big bear, head lowered as if sniffing along a trail. But when he shook off his bemusement and raised his head, he revealed a countenance of true majesty.

Nature exerted no dominion over him. He composed day or night. During the few hours in which he was not either sleeping or composing he abandoned himself to utter gluttony. He would enter a London restaurant and order three dinners; and when the waiter asked whether he wished to wait for the rest of the company, he would reply sharply: "I am the company!" At rehearsals he would rail at the musicians in four languages. The poor fellows trembled before his thunderous voice; they did not feel that their lives were safe with him. During one rehearsal in London, when Madame Cuzzoni, the Italian prima donna, refused to sing an aria as Handel wished it, he seized her around the waist and dragged her to the open window, saying: *Oh, Madame, je sais bien que vous êtes une véritable diablesse; mais je vous ferais savoir, moi, que je suis Beelzebub en person, le chef des diables.** In spite of these humorous words, he would probably have thrown her out had she not promised obedience.

His music was, like the man himself, cyclopean. Its fundamental element was wrath. All of Handel's people rage tempestuously through his operas and oratorios; they are ready to singe the world with the heat of their ire, or to consume themselves. The choice of his subjects flowed from this trait, for such a degree of burning passion can be found only in certain characters in Aeschylus, Shakespeare, and the Old Testament. Hercules, Alexander, Samson, Belsazar, Tamerlane were Handel's heroes: he would seldom touch on lesser ones.

But, as with most choleric individuals, Handel's own forcefulness was a torment to him. This was one of the features of Handel that most affected Haydn. No other composer's music projected such yearning and worship of tranquillity and peace of mind; no other composer had written so many *largos* and *larghettos.* Handel yearned for calm—*la calma del alma, la calma del cor.* Most of his characters share this longing with him. The tremendous appeal of Handel's music is due precisely to its wide range over the whole gamut of human emotion, and to the tension between wrath and tranquillity. No insomniac can listen without tears to the unearthly plaint of Semele, "O sleep, why dost thou leave me?" Handel's secret is comprehended in that aria—dissonance that becomes consonance, torment that becomes peace. Haydn was himself spared such tensions—it was not necessary for him to gain peace by means of war—which was all the more reason why Handel's art moved him so deeply.

Although he listened devoutly to Handel's music, he had probably noted, even while still in London, that it was a prey to the worm of time. Haydn had lived through the most flourishing epoch of rococo art and through the softening influences of the French style, and he could not help knowing that the more relaxed temper of the time was already tiring of the baroque elements in Handel's music. A

* "Oh, madam, I know very well that you are a real she-devil; but I will have you understand that I—yes, I myself—am Beelzebub in person, the chief of all the devils!"

good many of Handel's arias must have sounded to him like the outcries of a Fury struggling in a straitjacket. Undoubtedly, he felt that the progress of melody in Handel was marred by violent and inappropriate use of *colorature*. The Italians used it to express charm; Handel employed it to make the passions, evinced in his arias of vengeance and wrath, seem even more gruesome. Men of the rococo age found this practice repulsive. They began compromising, cutting, changing the dynamics of the music, "toning down" this dreadful giant. Even Beethoven's admiration for Handel was, perhaps, not strictly musical; it was the respect of one titan for another. However, when Handel's name was spoken in his presence, Beethoven is said to have bent the knee. He considered Handel the greatest composer of all time.

Haydn had been of the same opinion when he went to the concert in Westminster Abbey. He revered Handel's music, although there was so much that was alien to Haydn's spirit, in the man himself as well as in Handel's acts of violence. Haydn respected him also for his death; his pathetic end endeared Handel to him as the tempestuous life had not. What a fate had been his—the giant became blind! As an eyeless Samson, Handel, a failing old man, was led to the church organ by a boy. No candles were burning above the keys, for the organist could no longer read the music. When he played to the text

> Blackest night! No day, no light,
> My face is veiled by darkest night!

a shudder ran through the audience. Soon the old man stopped playing. For a long time he sat before the instrument; he was quarreling now with God, now with himself. But God—every child in England knew this legend—took pity on his servant. He called the Angel of Death on Good Friday and bade him bring "that man Handel" before His face at once. But the Angel of Death replied: "Let him die rather on Saturday, so that he will be closer to the Day of Resurrection." And thus it was that Handel closed his eyes on Saturday, the day before the Easter Sunday of 1759. Haydn, the composer of *The Seven Last Words of Our Saviour on the Cross,* always spoke with deep emotion of this Easter legend.

Such, then, was the man whose heritage Haydn was to take up. The small book that he had taken back to Vienna with him lay untouched for months. He deliberately avoided looking at it. The alternation of attraction and repulsion which is so familiar in the history of great art began. One day, however, Haydn gave the book to van Swieten, and asked him what he thought of it. That was a fateful moment in the history of music.

What did the Court Librarian answer? Haydn already owed the baron a considerable spiritual debt; for it had been van Swieten who had enabled him to change *The Seven Last Words of Our Saviour on the Cross,* originally composed as a purely orchestral work, into a *cantata.* This had been done after his first return from London. He had asked van Swieten to expand the originally not sung, but only spoken text—and just this was an extraordinarily difficult task because it would have been tasteless to augment the brief Biblical sentences by sentimental padding. But, as ever in such kind of work, the Court Librarian succeeded.

When van Swieten now held in his hands Lindley's text and was asked by Haydn whether he would make a German version he at once recognized the difficulties. He knew that artistic taste had changed in fifty years and that the times were hostile to pathos; in the Age of Enlightenment a fulsome baroque oratorio was scarcely possible. With great cleverness, van Swieten tacked around these problems. Though he was himself a worshiper of Handel, he adapted the text to suit Haydn's special bent. Moreover, he did more than provide a good text; he gave intellectual guidance to the composer, in the most diplomatic manner possible. When the Leipzig *Allgemeine Musikalische Zeitung* asked van Swieten what his share in the arrangement of the English text had been, he modestly replied that he had "on the whole faithfully followed the main outlines of the original, but deviated in details whenever it seemed to him necessary for the course of the music and the requirements of musical expression." This is understatement; manuscripts have been discovered, in the Eisenstadt archives, which show that in addition to composing the German text van Swieten supplied the composer with detailed instructions on points he should regard. For example—after the tenor aria, "Now vanish before the holy beams the gloomy shades of night," van Swieten wrote: "In the composition of the chorus the darkness remains to make the instant transition to light very strongly felt. The words 'Let there be light!' must be spoken only *once.*" We may imagine what would have happened if Haydn had had an Italian instead of a Dutchman as collaborator on *The Creation!* Then the words, "Let there be light!" would have been repeated four times—on the principle that repetition makes for forcefulness.

Similar instructions are to be found on every page of the manuscript, and Haydn disregarded not a single one, not even the instruction that "the movement of the fish must be swift." We do not agree with Pohl in his regret "that Haydn was under the thumb of so self-important a person who thought as highly of his poetical gifts as he did of his social importance." Without such a collaborator, Haydn would not have written the immortal music; with van Swieten's support, Haydn had the courage to risk a duel with Handel's formidable shade.

"ACHIEVED IS THE GLORIOUS WORK . . ."

THE Biblical account of the creation says that God completed his work in six days. When Haydn began composing *The Creation,* he came to one significant conclusion: If he wished to narrate, in two or three hours of music, the work of the Lord, he would have to employ the artistic device of *condensation.* This sounds simple enough, but to Haydn it was quite new.

All his life he had had "time" for his composing, or, rather, *space* —he had had more than enough space. He had been able to utilize every inspiration at his leisure, to think up variation upon variation, to omit no subsidiary aspect of a theme. He dwelt contentedly in a realm of absolute music in which he was undisputed master. There was no outward pressure upon him, no requirement of the stage, no haste to finish as with Mozart, no "abruptness from within" as with Beethoven. Except for his experience with the *Seven Words,* he was now, at the age of sixty-five, confronted for the first time with the necessity for brevity in treatment of a theme. When he sat down to work on *The Creation,* Haydn could not pursue the immanent laws of the music; he had to submit to his "subject."

It was a vast subject—God's creation of the world. He had worked at His creation like an artisan, doing one task after the other, completing infinite details, countless individual forms sharply distinguished from one another. Haydn had to imitate this; in consequence, his forms, though sharply distinguishable, must be small—or, in a musical term, brief. He would have to write brief orchestral movements, vocal solos, mass choruses. But in spite of this necessary brevity, all must sound mighty, noble, filled with inimitable dignity and magnificence. The difficulties were all too obvious.

Why had Handel forborne to compose the story of the Creation? Flexibility, swift changes in point of view, and the sudden breaks in continuity imposed upon the composer by the material, were they perhaps not suited to Handel? When he had directed the course of his instruments toward a given object, he no more liked to stop precipitately and shift his ground than did Wagner, later. But no, this could not have been the reason. For in *Israel in Egypt,* Handel provided a direct model for the kind of thing that Haydn did in *The Creation:* the sketching in of brief scenes. In his description of the Egyptian plagues, Handel had even simulated the jumping of frogs and the clicking sound of locusts' wings being rubbed together. Handel's reason for abandoning the project of a *Creation* was altogether different; we shall examine it later.

Haydn's chief difficulty was, then, the question of conciseness. Some of the condensations are true miracles. Every Creation must, of course, begin with "chaos." It would not have seemed excessive had Haydn accorded a few hundred measures to the "waste and void." But he did not have the time. Fifty measures would seem a more reasonable homage to nothingness—but Haydn did even better; in only twenty measures he portrayed the void that existed before God intervened. Twenty measures—but those twenty revolutionized the music of the time and created a new form of musical expression.

"The crown upon a royal head," Goethe's intimate friend Zelter called these opening bars of *The Creation.* They do not begin with a dissonance, for then there would no longer be room for mounting intensity, and Haydn was too clever for such an error. Instead, they begin *forte,* with a single awe-inspiring hollow octave which is neither chaos nor cosmos, but the universe itself which can be filled with either formlessness or form. It is in the second measure that we hear true formlessness, the slithering and crowding of matter that floods through the void

Thomas Hardy remarks, in *Two on a Tower,* that in contemplating the facts of astronomy we soon reach a point where solemnity ends and horror begins. This mood is illustrated here by Haydn—without, of course, the slightest trace of atonality. Haydn, like Herschel, seems to be proceeding to explore the musical universe with a telescope of greater and greater power. While Herschel arrived at conclusions as to the motion of the solar system, Haydn established his musical cosmos in and around C-minor—with ambiguities and bold strokes which indicate that he is fully aware of the paradox inherent "in any thinkable notion of chaos." Tovey is right in pointing this out, for before we can imagine the state of chaos we must ourselves have lived in a state of order. Haydn did live thus, and therefore the ghastliness of space is redeemed by the interweaving of a subtle solemnity.

But there is still no light—or, in acoustic terms, there is not yet any harmony. The musical portrait of the void still prevails. A mournful motif in descending semi-tones appears; but when the void has been plumbed, the soul rises again in semi-tones. Glad certitude overpowers the listener: The knowledge that the Almighty will act. D-flat major, the key of the "miracle of life" approaches, proclaims that God will create. Soon we shall be fully in C-major. Let there be light!

"Not I, but a Power above, created that," Haydn later exclaimed, weeping. But he himself had struggled to wrest the masterpiece from that Power above. His sketch-books for *The Creation* are preserved in the libraries of Vienna and Berlin. Haydn, who for half a century had composed directly and without hesitation, never troubling to sketch the outlines of his work, now took to writing down inspirations —altering, hesitating, cutting, improving, compressing.

The sketches show that originally he assigned the chaos music to the first violins, the French horn, and the clarinet. These instruments complement one another very well, but they can be heard too distinctly. It suddenly occurred to him that the primeval vagueness of the uncreated world could not be reproduced by such instrumental colors. The tone of the clarinet is smooth, sweetishly full, nasal, "slightly intoxicated." He therefore replaced the clarinet and the clear, decisive horn by bassoon and viola, thus achieving the dim, oppressive feeling he desired.

He had similar difficulties with many other passages in *The Creation,* but the music does not show it; the ultimate effect is one of wonderful ease. Yet even the choice of forms was complex; new ones had to be found, every few minutes, to describe the course of the Creation. There is a magnificent wealth of forms in this music. One moment a German Lied—or, rather the beginning of one, rises sweetly over the scene; then in the orchestra a charming violin solo begins (which the nineteenth century would have turned into a full concerto); then come fragments of an operatic aria with *coloratura* which is followed by an unaccompanied recitative. It is a source of unending amazement to observe the swiftness and adroitness with which Haydn introduces a tiny symphonic movement or constructs a little chorale, and abandons these as soon as the needs of the subject require it. The music sounds as fresh as if the ink were still damp upon the paper; there is a wonderful, youthful strength about the work that is incredible of a man of sixty-five.

The most astonishing feature of it, however, is Haydn's sense of drama, for *The Creation* is a dramatic work, full of action and suspense. Although the three archangels, Raphael, Uriel, and Gabriel, narrate everything that happens, the work is, nevertheless, not epic. The audience participates; matter exhibits a will of its own, and chaos does not surrender at once; the primeval night stirs restlessly and attempts to surge back once more, before it yields. "Affrighted fly hell's spirits black in throngs." But then everything bends to the hand of God. The majestic purifiers of Creation, the winds, appear *fortissimo* and, like servants with their brooms, sweep up the clouds "like chaff." Then follow the lightning, the rolling thunder, a mist in the flute that becomes rain; then "the dreary, wasteful hail" beats down in *pizzicato* figures interrupted by eight-note rests. Finally, mysterious and quiet, falls the snow, so familiar to Haydn from his native Burgenland.

The music rises to dramatic peaks where the grand choruses display their might. These choruses confirm the individual works of the Creation, less by enumeration than by illustration of their grandeur. And when the final chorus of the first part proclaims: "The Heavens are telling the Glory of God," we see whence Beethoven derived the power for his *chorale,* "The Heavens Praise the Fame of the Eternal."

Radiant in the sun, and clad in greens, blues, silvers, purples, and golds, the world stands resplendent, so that the angels of heaven cannot tire of looking upon its mountains, meadows, brooks, rivers, and seas. But it is still uninhabited. The second part depicts the creation of the beasts. These musical pictures have been the delight of millions of listeners, and have confounded many critics. They have been called, variously, sketches by a well known imitator of animal sounds, or likened to "cabinet pictures such as are painted on small boxes," and "typical eighteenth-century pastoral scenes such as decorated folding screens." These "precious" comparisons are inadequate. The music sings of animal life in its essence; the primordial experience with animal creation is reproduced in music for the first time. In these pages Haydn abandoned the commonplace pastoral tone as well as the naturalistic mode. His method is rather that of the expressionist who invents individual motifs for every creature: "Cheerful roaring stands the tawny lion"—"The nimble stag bears up his branching head"—"Up heaved from the deep th'immense Leviathan"—The eagle soaring higher and higher into the sky, writing with mighty plumes. And then the turtle-dove! Here Haydn completely transcends "musical imitations." Never did doves coo like this in nature:

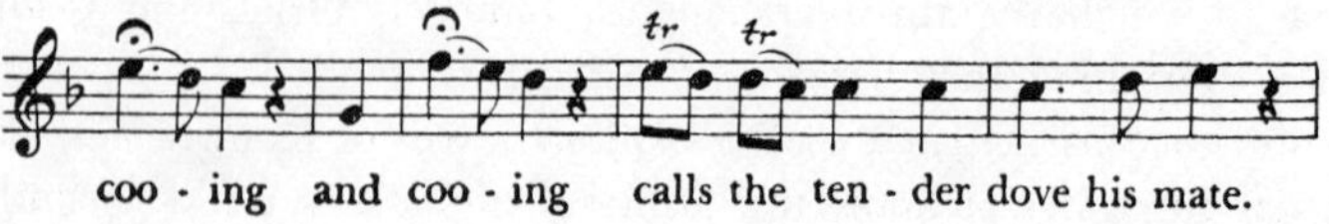

But such is the stylizing power of great art, that after hearing this music we expect doves to sing in such manner. It is also noteworthy that the appeal to both eye and ear in this music is the same. The glimmering colors of the birds swooping through the air, or the fish swimming in endless schools through the vast ocean, could have been portrayed by Haydn quite simply by the use of older customary "Italian" devices. But here again he achieved a miracle of condensation. He also needed only eleven measures to describe the shimmering, swarming humming hordes of insects and the myriads of creeping worms, although they come in "unnumbered as the sands"; and yet there is a freshness about the music, as if men were seeing these creatures for the first time.

Then, as the crown of Creation, God created man "in His own image." Patterned after such a model, man has no call to show humility. This concept, however, cannot be ascribed to Haydn, for it is foreign to his nature; van Swieten must have insisted upon it. It is seemly for man to be grateful, but his chief characteristic is pride. Except for Mozart's *Magic Flute,* the eighteenth century's pride in the human estate is nowhere expressed more forcefully than here:

In native worth and honor clad,
With beauty, courage, strength adorn'd,
Erect, with front serene, he stands
A man! The lord and king of nature all.

His large and arched brow sublime
Of wisdom deep declares the seat
And in his eyes with brightness shines
The soul, the breath and image of his God.

Then God saw everything that He had made, and He saw that it was good. Jubilantly, the heavenly choir closed the sixth day of the Creation: "Achieved is the glorious work!"

In recent times the third part of *The Creation,* the life of Adam and Eve in Paradise, has been held in very low esteem; its omission has been recommended and even practiced. Yet the traditional division of the oratorio into three parts, established by Handel, had its rationale. A drama requires a third act. It has been argued, foolishly, that "Adam and Eve" is an idyll without relevance to the story of the Creation.

Aside from the fact that deleting this section means losing some of the most beautiful music ever written, the idyll is basic to Haydn's fundamental concept. To Haydn, connubial love was the true crown of creation. The deep feeling which he infused into the relationship of Adam and Eve was evident to the hearers at the first performance. A letter of Princess Eleonore Liechtenstein informs us that when Adam and Eve turned their heads toward each other and sang "Graceful consort!" the entire audience began to weep. There is an element of personal sorrow in this. Haydn, unhappily married, was writing for those to whom marriage meant the highest form of happiness.

Is "Adam and Eve" an idyll? Unquestionably, the dramatic tension is past, and in its stead is the unbroken tranquillity of Paradise. Three flutes, two horns, and the *pizzicati* of strings enter with a theme that is the morning breeze itself translated into harmonies. Such musical rendering of mood later made Grieg famous; the "Morning" section of the *Peer Gynt* suite is in the direct Haydn tradition. Haydn also foreshadowed the prelude to *Lohengrin* when he had his *largo* begin in limpid E-major colors:

In the second part of *The Creation* the angels marvel over the created world; in the third part the first men express their awe. And we, too, are filled with awe when the "father of orchestration," to express his reverence for the mystery of fertility, has the tympani perform a sixteen-bar *pianissimo;* or when, for the words, "The heavens and earth thy power adore," he has the strings play tremolo for forty-eight measures. Often as God is praised in the work, He is praised in ever-new forms whose variety is consonant with the manifold aspects of divinity. The laudation is limitless, as is the act of Creation. For "the bright sun that cheers the world, the eye and the soul of all," rises afresh each day. The moon never desists from her circling, and the mighty elements "are making their ceaseless change." All of them sing the praises of God. Then, in a great thanksgiving, they join in the finale for an *andante* in E-major, built majestically upon a Handelian double fugue. A bass solo, descending very low, accompanied by woodwinds and strings, opposes the torrent of the chorus and seems about to cry "Amen!" But the end is not yet; on an A-minor chord the harmony explodes with magnificent effect and turns toward G-major before the whole work sinks into the final peace, the "Amen!" in B-flat major.

The first public performance of *The Creation* took place on April 30, 1798, in the palace of Prince von Schwarzenberg. The preliminary publicity, which had been conducted by Baron van Swieten, one of the chief promoters of the affair, had kept the Viennese waiting eagerly for weeks. On the night of this great cultural occasion, thousands for whom there was no room besieged the entrances to the prince's palace. An unparalleled police force—fifty men on horses and on foot—were needed to keep the traffic open. The grain and vegetable venders of the New Market suffered considerable damage because of the crowd, and the prince later was required to pay.

Haydn himself conducted. At first the applause was muted, apparently from a sense of religious awe, but then it reached thunderous heights. All the newspaper notices, including those of the foreign correspondents, were rapturous with enthusiasm. But not only the "high-brows" cried "hosannah"; the common people instantly felt the appeal of the work. A widely read popular journal of the time, *Eipeldauer's Letters,* which was written in Viennese dialect, said of the first performance: "When the music began, there was instantly such a silence that you could have heard a little mouse run; and had people not clapped their hands, you would have thought that no one at all was in the theater. But, my dear, I shall never hear such beautiful music again in my life. I should not have been sorry if I had been forced to sit three hours more, even if the stench and the Turkish bath had been still worse. I should never have believed that the human bellows, the gut of sheep, and the skin of calves, could produce such miracles. The music alone expressed thunder and lightning, and you could hear the shower of rain and the new water, and the birds really sang and the lion roared, and you could really hear how the worms creep in the earth. In short, I never left a theater so delighted, and I dreamed the whole night of the creation of the world."

Even amid such unreserved admiration we find some traces of the persistent conviction that Haydn was chiefly an imitator of animal voices. This imputation, however, never harmed his reputation with the singers or the public. On the contrary, for more than a hundred years such "concessions" to popular taste have resulted in *The Creation's* playing to full houses. In *The Creation* Haydn offers something to every listener, as Shakespeare captivates the groundlings by humor and the "high-brows" by philosophy and drama. Zelter speaks of a performance in Berlin in 1830, conducted by Gasparo Spontini, which all the conductors within reach attended, although the work had been frequently performed in the German capital. Later, Verdi began his career as a conductor with *The Creation*. But once again some æstheticians pounced upon the music for its comic effects. At the head of these critics was Schiller, who was repelled by the abundance of realistic detail in *The Creation*. "It is a characterless hodge-podge," he wrote. "Haydn is a skillful (!) artist who, however, lacks inspiration (!)." Schiller was unable to appreciate the noble simplicity of this oratorio. He could not understand how Haydn could presume in his music to express undiminished joy over each separate act of God's creation, to be as glad for the lion as for the finch. Schiller's aristocratic æsthetics could not put up with such "low" indiscriminateness. David Friedrich Strauss explains this: "But when afterwards first the doves cooed, then the nightingale fluted, then the lithe tiger sprang, and the stag raised his mighty antlers—all these miniature portraits of Noah's ark were too much for Schiller's sober temper, although we other children rejoiced in them." Beethoven, who was the great master of "chaos" music, spoke deprecatingly of Haydn's "animal" music. Schiller and Beethoven were men of tragedy. If the tiger had torn the stag to pieces, if they had smelled blood, they would have felt that the work was more true to nature. They were, unfortunately, not faithful readers of their Bibles—for over the animals in Paradise the peace of God reigned.

Despite these and similar deprecations, Haydn's *Creation* was immediately recognized throughout the German-speaking world. It was championed by not only Wieland but by Goethe as well. But not even the approval of these men could stem the rumors that the Church was offended by certain parts of the great work.

A FLOCK OF MISUNDERSTANDINGS

EVEN before the completion of *The Creation,* certain persons wondered about Haydn's attitude toward himself and The Almighty. Although a pious man and although he told his friend Griesinger that he was never so devout as during the composition of *The Creation* ("Every day I fell down on my knees and prayed God to lend me strength to carry out this work successfully") gossip had it that the chief aim of Haydn's piety seemed to be the welfare of his own music. The devoutness of Palestrina and Bach, his detractors said, was very different from that of Haydn's naïve and somewhat egotistic religiosity. Haydn considered the Lord as his friend, a being who was glad to help such a good fellow compose by smoothing life's path for him. Truly, there was nothing of the dark, painful knowledge of God's wrath in Haydn's religious feeling, no glance in the direction of the terrors of hell. Haydn even omitted the Fall of Man from his Paradise because he did not like to see his God irate!

Haydn's true religion was, however, not only a matter of temperament but also one of social class. The artisans whose son he was and the peasants with whom he had associated were, indeed, devoted to their Christian faith and the calendar of the saints guided their actions throughout the year. On the other hand, such people could not permit religion to weigh too hard upon them. Religious brooding, torment, anxiety—all feelings that would get in the way of their appointed labors—are not possible for artisans. They were, consequently, foreign to Haydn who, for all his tremendous social rise, never quite abandoned the emotional attitude of his forebears.

In the third place, Haydn's somewhat worldly piety was conditioned by the age in which he lived. In this respect he was a true child of the eighteenth century. And it was just that eighteenth century against which a new kind of Christianity began to storm. More and more Haydn and Mozart were criticized now for the "superficiality" of their religious works. The Gothic temper and the lean austerity of the Middle Ages had just been rediscovered by the early Romanticists. They saw in Haydn a man who, like a peasant, would go to the church in shirt sleeves; and Thibaut, a well known Heidelberg jurist, who in 1819 wrote a book on *The Purity of Music,* went so far as to hint that Mozart had written his masses with only mercenary motives.

The truth was that Haydn and Mozart did not write their church music for the gloom of a medieval Gothic cathedral. They composed instead for the sun-drenched rococo churches of their own time, with their riot of inside color. All the churches of Austria and Southern Germany glittered in white, blue and gold. Painted wooden angels with puffed cheeks and windswept garments were stationed near the choir, and often The Holy Trinity was surrounded by hosts of laughing saints, to help the churchgoers forget the sobrieties of their daily lives. Sunday signified to them a union of solemnity and gaiety. Even fairs, with carousels, were held close to the church.

It eventually took the French Revolution to wipe out the lightheartedness from Town and Country. The Parisian political terror threatened Christianity, as it had never been menaced by heresy. In order to combat its enemy, Catholicism had to rediscover its true principles, and to cast off its false friends. The revived religion particularly demanded of the Austrians a "purification from worldliness and sin; sincere, unconditional obedience and submission to dogma even in the realm of the fine arts."

Haydn was no ally in these endeavors. The reformers resented the fact that in the tonal and instrumental structure of his music he recognized no fundamental dichotomy between ecclesiastical and secular ends. Very old grievances now were aired against him. Cited was the case of his *St. Cecilia's Mass* (1780), where, after the *Resurrexit,* he had stormed the heavens in a jubilant fugue, in which trumpets and the quavering violins continually gleamed. There was, further, the *Mariazeller Mass* (1782), where Haydn used for the *Benedictus* an aria borrowed from his own comic opera *Il Mondo della Luna.* Such practices irritated his contemporaries and while Haydn knew it, he could not help doing it. Once, when he was writing a serious canon on the *Ten Commandments*—a very academic canon, in strictest form—his wanton spirits got the better of him. For the music to the commandment, "Thou shalt not steal," he used a very well known melody composed by someone else. People were horrified by his inserting a joke into so deadly serious a matter as the Decalogue, the basis of all morality. But Haydn went even further than this; some of his excursions into jest seem incomprehensible even today—and not only to the fanatics among us. In his own age he once wrote a jolly canon that expressed fairly well the feeling Haydn, the "married bachelor," felt toward all women: "God in your heart, a good woman in your arms—the one confers bliss, the other warms." Such robust vitality is reminiscent of Luther or Goethe. The song was certainly not objectionable, but it was also not Catholic.

Who can describe the feelings of Haydn's contemporaries when they found that the composer, unabashed, had incorporated the melody of this canon into a holy mass, composed to celebrate the canonization of the Capuchin monk Bernhard of Offida? With a wonderful accompaniment of violins, violas, B-flat clarinets and cello the alto voice sang, *pianissimo:*

It is scarcely necessary to say that Haydn intended nothing sacrilegious when he used the melody of his old bachelor joke in expressing the holiest of facts, that "Christ was made flesh by the Holy Ghost in Mary, the Virgin Mary." He was here simply the victim of a slip which resulted (and this had happened before) from his fallacious view of melody. It was an Italian foible in this otherwise truly German master that he considered that any melody would serve for any given situation, if varied with sufficient instrumental artistry. He went almost as far as Rossini, who used in his *Semiramis* overture the well known Swiss song, "Freut euch des Lebens" (Rejoice in life) as the basis of a funeral march, simply because nothing else occurred to him at the moment.

Considering the storm now blowing against Haydn, one would think that he would have been more cautious. He was unquestionably one of the greatest modern composers of church music, what with the Nelson Mass (1798), the Theresa Mass (1799), the Creation Mass (1801) and the Harmony Mass (1802), and yet the Archbishop of Vienna, Sigismund von Hohenwarth, took sides with Haydn's adversaries. But Haydn seemingly overlooked the danger involved in the Archbishop's gesture.

However, when the use of trumpets and drums at the eucharist was banned and every trace of comic opera and "shameless rhythms of the dance hall" was prohibited in church music, Haydn of course obeyed and made many changes in his masses. But he was stubborn and did not always comply. Even Empress Marie Thérèse (not to be confused with the Emperor's grandmother, the famous Maria Theresa) had to threaten him and refused a performance of a certain mass until the master changed a passage which was believed provocative.

The story, told by Haydn to his biographers Albert Dies and Griesinger, is this: Suddenly, as he was setting the words *Agnus Dei, qui tollis peccata mundi* (Lamb of God, who taketh upon himself the sins of this world) he was seized by an "uncontrollable gladness." How strange, the Empress must have thought. How could anyone be seized by "uncontrollable gladness" at a moment of profound contrition? The Lamb of God suffers martyrdom—and the composer rejoices!

The Empress took him to task for this. "Well," he explained, not without some slight boldness, "we weak mortals sin mostly only against the commandments of chastity and moderation, don't we?" These, he continued with a note of peasant cunning, were not such deadly sins. And then he went on to say that in composing he had thought more of *tollis* than of *peccata,* more of the becoming rid of the sins than of the sins themselves. When the Empress, apparently not satisfied, shook her head, he finished his plea, most innocent and naïve, with the assertion that the certainty of God's grace had made him so happy that he wrote a joyful melody to accompany the sober words. With this he spoke the truth, and the Empress could not help smiling. For the melody he had used happened to be the same as the one he employed in *The Creation,* part III, when Adam sings to Eve "The dew dropping morn, oh how she quickens all!"

The Empress was now more or less silenced. She was a singer herself who, with her "pleasant, but weak voice," (as we learn from Griesinger's correspondence with Haydn's publisher, Breitkopf) used to sing the soprano parts of *The Creation* in the privacy of her family circle. After all, she knew her Haydn, the same Haydn who once said at a similar occasion: "Since God has given me a cheerful heart, He will forgive me for serving Him cheerfully."

This, perhaps, was the same remark that led to an especially charming incident in Goethe's spiritual life. Once, when Goethe lay in bed, ill and depressed, his friend Zelter attempted to revive his lagging spirits by recounting what Haydn had said to him: "Whenever I think of the dear Lord I have to laugh; my heart jumps for joy in my breast." Hearing this, Goethe wept—and recovered at once.

THE MASONIC LEGACY

Goethe's friend, Karl Friedrich Zelter (1758-1832), the true founder of Berlin's musical life and creator of the *Liedertafel,* was a somewhat pedestrian fellow, but of sterling character. He was a great admirer of Haydn and resembled the composer in a number of respects—he came from the same social class, had once been a master stone-mason, and had worked his way upward by overcoming great difficulties. Historians have suspected that it was his influence which kept Goethe away from Beethoven for so many years. At any rate, Haydn was well treated by Zelter. The latter appreciated Haydn's solidity, and energetically promoted his standing as a composer for the German family circle. And it was Zelter whose zealous efforts made *The Creation* the most frequently performed choral work in Prussia for more than one hundred years.

Another factor in the success of *The Creation* in Northern Germany was the strong affinity of its Old Testament material to the spiritual bases of Berlin's Jewish community. At that time the Jews were becoming the firmest supporters of the city's musical life, as they were to remain until the onset of the Hitler plague. Haydn's reputation among the members of Berlin's Jewish colony is best indicated by a letter written by Felix Mendelssohn's father, the banker. He speaks of the new developments in orchestral style, and continues: "Wealth is a fault only when we do not know how to use it. How, then, is the wealth of the orchestra to be applied? . . . An object must be found for music which by its fervor, its universal sufficiency and perspicuity, *may take the place of the pious emotions of former days.* It seems to me that from this point of view also, both of Haydn's oratorios are very remarkable phenomena . . . They have happily substituted the old positive and almost metaphysical religious impulses with those which Nature, as a visible emanation of the Godhead, in her universality and her thousandfold individualities, instills in every susceptible heart." In other words, *The Creation* and *The Seasons* provided for the contemporaries of Mendelssohn's father, the newly emancipated Jews, the intellectual tools needed by them for welding the Old Testament to the achievements of the Enlightenment, and this was of the greatest importance to them. The Jews of Berlin, Frankfurt, and Hamburg worshiped Haydn as they did no other living composer. When, in 1807, the painter Isidor Neugass painted Haydn, he represented the old master, somewhat resembling a rabbi, opening a scroll on which are the words of *The Creation:*

"Now vanish before Thy holy beams
The spirits of the Ancient Night . . ."

Generally, the Germans loved above all the optimism, the childlike gladness and worldliness which were displayed in Haydn's work. It was the same secularism that had aroused such grave concern in the composer's native land. Austrian objections to *The Creation* were based on even more serious charges than the "carelessness" and the "slips" with which a small but influential circle reproached Haydn's masses. Catholics sometimes considered *The Creation* an almost propagandistic work which tended to lead the listeners away from the Church. In reality, Haydn's oratorio was undenominational and could be enjoyed alike by all whose moral code was based on the Bible—Catholics, Protestants, and Jews. But this very attribute scarcely recommended the work to Viennese Catholics. Twenty years earlier, Migazzi, the Archbishop of Vienna, an opponent of the reforming spirit of Emperor Joseph II and the actual initiator of the Catholic Resistance in Vienna, had inveighed against the use, by the Austrian laity, of the German Bible in Martin Luther's translation. If read at all, the Bible was to be read in Latin and not in German. Later, this same objection was applied to *The Creation,* in which the Biblical text was expounded in a form understandable by all. Moreover, there were many passages in van Swieten's text which were considered in Vienna to be outright offensive. Viennese Catholics resented above all van Swieten's attributing to the Creator the character of a "workman."

"Workman" sounds rather Masonic; perhaps it was meant to. But what matter? The implications of Haydn's oratorio were certainly not novel. The teachings were no different from those of Sir Thomas More, three centuries earlier, in his *Utopia:* "Like unto an earthly artisan, the Creator exposes his world machine to the sight of man, because man is the sole being which can comprehend the wonderful immensity of it. God looks down with love upon whosoever admires this great *clockwork* and seeks to discover its ways and its laws; he gazes pityingly upon that man who responds like an unreasoning beast to this admirable spectacle." Also the other fathers of the Enlightenment, Boyle, Hume, Berkeley, and Leibniz looked upon the world as a marvelous piece of machinery similar to those made by human hands. Hereby we can understand why Handel had had to abandon the idea of composing *The Creation* after Lindley's text was presented to him. To his mind, God could only be a *hero,* not a God of Enlightenment or a working mechanic. In Haydn's *Creation,* God appears, as Eugen Diesel has pointed out, as the Greek "Tekton," the carpenter who made the world; or, in the Old Testament spirit, as an engineer. Werner Sombart, some years ago, has emphasized the artisan character of the Creator as He is portrayed in van Swieten's and Haydn's version of the Old Testament cosmology: "In the beginning God *created* the heavens and the earth. And the earth was without form and void . . . And God said, *Let there be light,* and there *was* light. (The implication is almost that of a dynamo being set up.) And God *made* the firmament (as a stucco worker and artist might adorn a church spire). He made the stars also. In Haydn's text the sun is actually a giant, proud and glad to run his course; in this case God may be likened to the builder of a racing car or of an ocean liner who looks with satisfaction upon his completed work. In the end, God also created man as an admiring audience and as His technical successor or apprentice."

So immoderate a doctrine leads one far from Christianity. In the Christian cosmology, the creation of the world proceeded not from the hands of God but, according to the gospel of St. John, from the word. It was therefore easy for pious contemporaries, and for later critics as well, to find in Haydn's oratorio very offensive traces of "materialistic deism on the English mold." Ecclesiastical authority was particularly sensitive to infractions of this sort. We must remember that the clergy in Austria had just completed a successful, but hard-fought battle against another heresy which, it was alleged, also came from England. This struggle had been waged against the order of Freemasons.

Emperor Joseph II, the anti-clerical ruler who had wished to prevent Rome from collecting tithes from his Austrian subjects was not a Freemason but was on very friendly terms with the Grand Master of Vienna, Ignaz von Born. Wherever Joseph did not care to engage in open political and cultural struggles with Rome he enlisted the services of the "unofficial" order of Freemasons, which enjoyed tremendous popularity among the intelligentsia. Joseph's government ordained that the Masons be given full protection; it even made the order exempt from police interference, and promised "never to interfere with the inner life of the lodges and to refrain from any obtrusive inquiries and inquisitions."

There can be no doubt that when, some years after the emperor's death, Haydn composed *The Creation,* he was aware of the Masonic implications in van Swieten's text. But at the same time it would be underrating his naïveté to imagine that he realized how sharply Masonic symbolism diverged from that of the Catholic Church. He probably was not even aware that the former Grand Master, Ignaz von Born, had written a *Natural History of Monasticism* which aped Voltaire in attacking Rome and the papacy. We can scarcely blame Haydn for his ignorance of Masonic assaults on the Church, for during the seventeen eighties, in Vienna—and in spite of papal disapproval—hundreds of Catholic priests were very close to, if not members of, the Masonic order. One of these priests, Karl Joseph Michaeler, custodian of the Vienna University library, went so far as to reply to the Pope, in a pamphlet demonstrating that a man could be both a Freemason and a good Catholic.

However, for all the protestations of Austrian Freemasons that they had no share in the French Revolution's bloody persecution of priests, Rome continued to frown upon the order. After the death of Joseph II the state, too, turned against the Freemasons, and by the time *The Creation* was first performed Masonic lodges in Austria had been banned for more than five years. Francis II hated the order; he thought it pernicious to the welfare of the state, if only for the reason that it had its secret statutes. All historians agree that the order, nevertheless, survived. A kind of "crypto-Freemasonry" continued to exist in Austria, with all the more ease because the imperial prohibition did not extend to Germany. It is, however, equally certain that the loyal subject of his emperor, Haydn, was not a member of any secret lodge.

When *The Creation* was first performed in 1798, cultured Viennese immediately recognized the allusions in which the oratorio abounds. In a letter, Princess Eleonore, wife of Prince Schwarzenberg, in whose palace the oratorio was performed, referred to the "deeds of the mighty workman"; thus, she spoke of God in the very terms which the ecclesiastical circles condemned. It was clear to everyone that van Swieten's adaptation of the English original often went further than was necessary. Haydn, in his innocence, composed a passage whose implications would never have escaped Beethoven's acutely critical mind. The passage was:

Mit Staunen sieht das Wunderwerk
der frohen Himmelsbuerger Schar.

The English had read innocuously:

The Marv'lous work behold amaz'd
The glorious hierarchy of Heaven.

But Haydn's libretto speaks in revolutionary, French-tainted terms; the compromising word *citoyen* is let slip. "Himmelsbuerger" is equivalent to "citizens of Heaven"—it is used as though the angels were members of a heavenly bourgeoisie whose agreement and applause God had taken into consideration when He was busy creating the world.

It is easy to understand that the Church wished to stop such blasphemies. It was all the more anxious to do so because the whispers circulating around the court that the text of *The Creation* was "Masonic" would inevitably reach the ear of the emperor, who had shown an almost morbid fear of such "secret societies" as the Masons. The Viennese police whom the Emperor Joseph had instructed "on no account to interfere in the inner life of the lodges" had girded themselves for the fray under Francis; as a result of their investigations they had issued a memorandum on the "conspiratorial organization of the Freemasons." Mozart's *Magic Flute* had been banned; it could not be given in the court theater because the timid emperor saw in it a glorification of revolution. Tamino, the prince who stood for man striving toward the light, was generally considered by the public to represent the late Emperor Joseph, and Pamina, kidnaped and later freed, was supposed to be the Austrian people. These identifications were sufficient to cause the banning of the *Magic Flute*. The ban, however, never went beyond this especial work, and neither Mozart nor his other religious and secular compositions were called into question. This is another indication of the tolerant manner in which the censorship of the time operated, in spite of all timidity and pettiness. Haydn, too, whose Austrian *Imperial Anthem* (*Gott erhalte Franz den Kaiser*) had endeared him to everyone, was not harried as man and artist, even though his most splendid work, *The Creation,* had been placed under a mild ban. Performance of the work in Catholic churches had been forbidden.

Thus, the oratorio was exiled to secular concert halls, and this exclusion deeply offended Haydn. Plan, a small town in Bohemia, had defied the ban of the Prague consistory and had given a performance of the oratorio in the local church. On the following Sunday a priest, who had probably never before heard Haydn's name, spoke in his sermon against the performance in Christian churches of oratorios by "heathens." (Haydn in German means "of the heath," but it also sounds like *Heiden*—heathen.) The affair aroused considerable excitement and might well have cost the school principal, Ockl—who had organized the performance—his post. In a strong letter filled with righteous indignation, Haydn assured the principal of his protection and denounced those who were slandering his oratorio. Half of Europe had saluted his composition as an unexcelled achievement, he declared with a pride unusual on his part. "God's Creation has always been looked upon as the noblest and most awe-inspiring work that man can behold. To provide that great act with a suitable musical accompaniment could certainly have no effect other than to intensify the feelings of awe in the hearts of men and to increase man's sensitivity to the goodness and omnipotence of the Creator. How can the instilling of such holy sentiments be disrespectful to the Church?" He was convinced, Haydn concluded, that after hearing his oratorio men's hearts would be far more deeply moved than *after certain sermons,* and that no church could ever be desecrated by a performance of his *Creation.* If the unfair attacks on his composition did not cease, he declared, he would appeal to Emperor Francis and his consort, who "have listened to this oratorio with the sincerest emotion and who are wholly convinced of the worth of this sacred work."

The wording of the letter betrays the fact that it was probably not written by Haydn alone. As in the cases of most such "official" letters, we can deduce van Swieten's participation. But the indignation is Haydn's own. The great composer of the *Seven Words,* who never began a work without writing *Laus Deo* on the first page or concluding it without *Soli Deo Gloria* on the last page, was infuriated at the charge that he had desecrated the Church. It was due to his own firm stand

and to the powerful protection he enjoyed at court that the stir the zealots had raised against *The Creation* died down.

In the meantime, something had happened that confirmed in an unexpected manner Haydn's proud assertion that his oratorio enjoyed European fame. Great music is destined for great things, and this time Haydn's music intervened in world history. An event took place in Paris that considerably influenced the political developments of the next few decades. What happened was essentially a misunderstanding, for *The Creation* was no more an expression of the conservative temper than it was of revolutionary or anti-Catholic tendencies. But that is no matter. The composer had sent his work out into the world, and now it proceeded on its own course.

⟡✻⟡✻⟡✻⟡

NAPOLEON AND *THE CREATION*

CHRISTMAS EVE in Paris began with a misty twilight.

The year was 1800, and this was the first Christmas after the turn of the century. The eighteenth, the humanitarian, century had departed in convulsions. Dreadful blood-lettings had weakened the body of France and of Europe. Now, however, peace seemed restored—at least, for the time being. It was little more than a year since the notorious Bonaparte had returned from Egypt and had set up that dictatorship which was called the Consulate. The troubled world began to hope that this meant peace. Since Marengo and the negotiations which had followed upon this French victory, Paris no longer resounded with the tramp of marching troops and the exercising of regiments. Instead, officials in gold-embroidered uniforms sat over law books, and the First Consul, in his green waistcoat, worked on the foundations of his "new order." The aims of the new state were to be peace and bourgeois diligence, industry, the welfare of all the citizenry; no longer class rule, no longer Jacobin terror, but freedom of the press, promotion of the fine arts; a powerful army (of course), but, above all, peace in Europe.

Would religion, too, have a place? For the present it seemed that the new French state under Bonaparte was still hostile to religion. Religion meant Rome and the Pope; it meant a spiritual dictatorship allied with the Bourbon dynasty. Rome had not yet forgotten that Paris had beheaded pious Louis XVI and had stained the altars with blood. Of course, Napoleon thought, he would some day have to strike up a reconciliation with the Pope—Pius, the seventh of that name. After all, no matter what else the Pope stood for, he was a man of order, and there was a title that Bonaparte coveted.

And now it was Christmas eve. Eighteen hundred years earlier, the Christian God was born and lay in the manger at Bethlehem, worshiped by shepherds and breathed upon by oxen and asses. Incomprehensible miracle!

The French government, which, after all, no longer consisted of revolutionists, pagans, and pure rationalists, had some reason to join in the celebration of this event—or so we should think. A few years later—and it would have seemed proper for the members of the government to attend the midnight mass in ancient Notre Dame and participate when the archbishop administered the holy sacrament to the kneeling worshipers. But at this time that would be impossible. No archbishop resided in France; the country had only recently become the land of Voltaire and of the Enlightenment, a land in which each could seek salvation after his fashion. Politics was a game of give-and-take, and the Pope had not yet thoroughly triumphed. It would not have been the right thing for French officialdom to do—flock to the cathedrals.

In any case, Bonaparte had not the slightest desire to attend a mass in Notre Dame, although Josephine, his deeply religious wife, might well have liked him to do so. Instead, however, of staying home and eating fish in his family circle, Bonaparte chose a middle course. He went to a place where the cultivated, if not the devout, citizens of Paris were foregathering. There, in the *Theâtre des Arts,* he was sure to meet the flower of the Parisian *intelligentsia,* the *élite* among the devotees of art. For the first Paris performance of Haydn's *Creation* was being given.

Ignace Pleyel and Luigi Cherubini, great admirers of Haydn, had overcome many difficulties in order to stage the performance. *Monsieur* Haydn was, to be sure, not unknown to the French. Some twenty years earlier, the *Concerts Spirituels* had given performances of his music, including a number of his symphonies. Among them *La Reine de France, La Poule* (the chicken) and, foremost, *L'Ours,* the Bear Symphony, in whose last movement a clumsy animal seemed imprisoned, dancing to the tune of a Croatian bagpipe. The educated classes idolized him—but they alone. The "man in the street" preferred the *chansons* that dealt with Louison or Marion.

For a time there had been talk that Haydn himself would come to Paris to conduct the performance of *The Creation*. Then word had arrived that he was ill—and people wondered whether his illness was political. It was too soon after Marengo for a good Austrian to come to the capital of the victorious enemy. Well, the French could hardly blame him for that, and victors could afford to be tolerant. Daniel Steibelt, who was to conduct the work, was a competent musician. Those who had seen the piano arrangement in Steibelt's possession insisted that there was no music like it. A noble *oeuvre* and yet naïve, fiery and nevertheless radiantly gay, as Protestant church music never was. "Only a Catholic could write a work like that," Bonaparte had been told. On the other hand, the really fervid Catholics were by no means delighted. The work was tainted by Freemasonry. Its deeply religious feeling was undeniable—but *The Creation* made no reference to the sin of Adam and Eve, or to the birth and Passion of the Saviour. Its protagonist was God the Father, who as yet had no idea that He would ever have a Son. It told the story of a cosmic artisan who created the world out of chaos and placed man on earth as His representative and the image of Himself. Not a word of the evil the first man brought into the world, or of Golgotha or of salvation. In fact, the world of the creation was so beautiful that it needed no redemption.

That is what Napoleon knew of *The Creation* as he prepared to attend its first Paris performance. It was probably no accident that the work was being performed on Christmas eve, and, moreover, in the state theater. Cherubini and Pleyel, who were responsible for the performance, certainly did not intend to antagonize ecclesiastical circles. But the fact that the French government, including the First Consul himself, turned out *en masse* at the *Theâtre des Arts* that night was unquestionably not a matter of chance.

Of what was the French dictator thinking as he rode to the opera house? Probably he was expecting to be dreadfully bored. He was just as musical as are most Italians. Music, he used to tell anyone who would listen, was the handmaid of *bellezza.* For this reason, there was only one real kind of music—Italian music with its pure, cloudless forms, its *limpidezza* or transparency.

And therefore Napoleon felt certain that he was going to be bored to death this very evening. No matter what they said about Haydn's magnificent, Haydn's paradisiacal music, the man was after all nothing but a cloudy, ponderous German. Otherwise Cherubini, the undisputed leader of French music, would not care for him. The First Consul despised French music because the French were, more and more, turning away from the Italian school. "However, we are not devoting ourselves exclusively to German music," he had been assured. The French school of music had taken a middle position and was developing after its own fashion. Yes, Napoleon thought, unfortunately it was doing just that. It was too functional, too noisy; it seemed all the time to be brooding restively over plans; it was full of a pride of power, of pathos and theatricality; it was too cold and too experimental.

"No matter what the occasion, sir," Napoleon snapped at Cherubini one day, "your music rattles away too loudly."

"Je comprends," the composer shrewdly replied, *"vous préférez une musique qui ne vous empêche pas de songer aux affaires de l'Etat."* ("I understand; you prefer a type of music that doesn't hinder you from thinking about the affairs of state.")

The text of *The Creation* had been translated into French, the dictator knew. That would certainly not improve it. The things these German composers did with the human voice were intolerable to his Latin ear. Why the devil was there always so much bad weather in German music, so much sultriness and dreary dampness? It was enough to spoil the whole next day for a man. Any normal man whistled while bathing or shaving, but could anyone whistle a German melody?

But, at any rate, Haydn would seem to have been a reliable friend of France, for otherwise how could his work be performed in Paris and, furthermore, honored by the attendance of the French government? If he had not been friendly to France, would Fouché, minister of police, have allowed a performance of *The Creation*?

In fact, neither Fouché nor Bonaparte knew all there was to know about Haydn. The composer was so thoroughly pro-English that he had spent whole days at Eisenstadt castle in the company of Lord Nelson, the world famous victor of Abukir. Haydn had written a cantata called *Lines from the Battle on the Nile,* in which he celebrated the achievements of Lord Nelson. The two men had exchanged presents, the composer giving the admiral his pen. The Englishman's mistress, Lady Hamilton, had exerted herself to be as charming as possible to the old composer.

All this was not known in Paris. Nor was it known that after Nelson smashed the French fleet at Abukir and ruined Napoleon's reputation—temporarily, to be sure—Haydn went wild with rejoicing. He had promptly—and this was only two years earlier—written a *Nelson Mass.* If Bonaparte had heard how the Austrian composer had sounded the trumpets and drums for the *Benedictus qui venit in nomine Dei* ("Blessed is he who cometh in the name of the Lord")—and that in a composition for the church!—he would not have honored with his presence this performance of the *Création du Monde.* If Bonaparte had known how much Fouché did *not* know, he would not have gone to the opera house in so serene a mood.

They were now passing through a narrow street, the Rue Nicaise. The First Consul sat alone in the foremost carriage. Behind him came his wife, his retinue, in gala dress, the ministers of the government. There, stupidly blocking the road, was a fully laden cart. Neither horse nor driver was in sight. Bonaparte's own coachman had to jump down from his box and, with the help of some passers-by, push the cart out of the way; he worked swiftly, and in a moment was back on his box. The coachman was an ambitious man, for all that he occasionally drank a drop too much. He knew that Napoleon liked to be punctual. "I'll have to make up for lost time," he thought, and whipped up his horses. Then came a frightful clap as of thunder, and a quick succession of peals. A hail of lead fragments swept the street. The cart had exploded—or rather, the bomb that was concealed inside. The sky above the street was red with fire, the street itself filled with screams of the wounded and dying. The First Consul's horses reared straight up for a moment, their forefeet high in the air; then they raced away. They were uninjured; Bonaparte was likewise uninjured. Three streets farther on, the skilled driver regained control of his team. No more than ten minutes late, the entire party arrived at the *Theâtre des Arts*—the dictator, his weeping wife, and the entire retinue pale with fright.

"Combien des morts? ("How many are dead?") Napoleon asked out of the corner of his mouth as he ascended the stairs.

One of the ministers replied that there had probably been twenty fatalities. "That means two hundred wounded," Napoleon murmured, mechanically. The street was a narrow one, and had not been crowded. Nevertheless, even some persons inside the houses must have been injured. It had been an explosion of tremendous violence, and the First Consul knew a good deal about the effects of gunpowder.

His face was chalk white as he entered his box. "Some scoundrels tried to blow me up. What's being played? Well, get started. Let me have the libretto."

The music began. The theater darkened. Violins and celli portrayed chaos. Napoleon did not hear. His ears were still filled with the roar of the explosion. His thoughts raced in circles. Who could they be, those scoundrels? He imagined he knew. He wanted to bring France peace, happiness, civil prosperity. Who was against those things? Undoubtedly, the remnant of the terrorists, those cursed Jacobins who hated him. They did not stop at assassination! Well, he would repay them all, every one of them who had planned or abetted this attempt!

His ear was deaf. Once he made an effort to listen to the orchestra, but the music did not penetrate his consciousness. The chorus sang, "Let there be light, and there was light!" He did not hear, nor did he feel the shudder of awe that passed through the audience. His mind was on the scoundrels again. Who were their accomplices? If within twelve hours Fouché failed to . . . He would make Fouché responsible. He would . . . He would . . . Suddenly Bonaparte's sense of hearing reawoke, and for the first time he became aware of the oratorio's message to him. The chorus was singing of the Evil One's band, of the hosts of darkness retreating before the Word of the Lord. And the music of the chorus rang within his own soul:

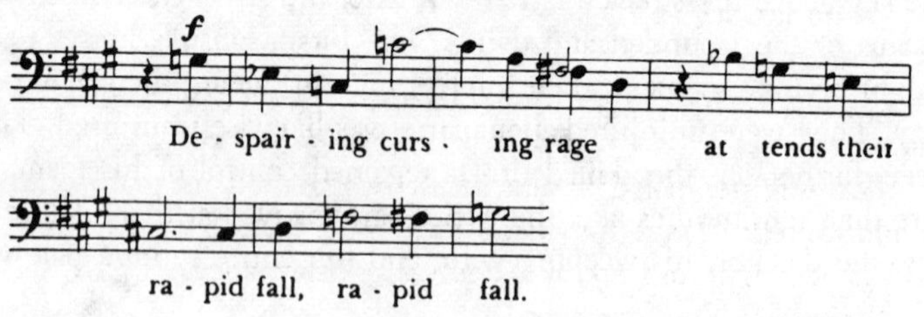

"Despairing, cursing rage attends their rapid fall." His spirits rose. Was this not meant for him? Wonderfully, the singing went on:

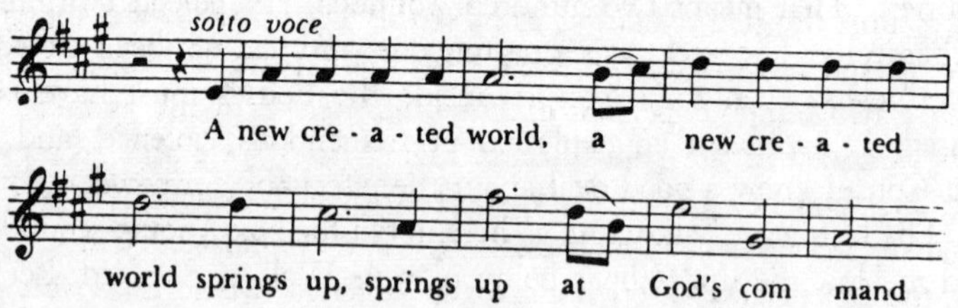

"Und eine Neue Ordnung erblueht durch Gottes Wort!" (This was what Haydn originally had in mind when he wrote his music. The English version: "A new-created world springs up at God's command," although it is absolutely correct, misses the significant meaning of the "New Order.") A "New Order"—was not that what Napoleon was

giving the French? The new order was the watchword of which he daily spoke. This man Haydn must be a genius. And had not Haydn's *Creation* saved his life? The driver had hurried in order to be on time.

Previously, Napoleon had always wanted music to distract him. Now, perhaps for the first time, he was hearing music that helped him to compose himself, to gather his forces. This music confirmed his destiny!

On the following day he could still remember exactly how the song of the avenging order had sounded: "Affrighted fly hell's spirits black in throngs; down they sink in the deep abyss to endless night." That next day was devoted to clearing away the chaos, the débris of revolution. Napoleon was the master of the world; he was at work; he felt akin to the creator of the cosmos of whom Haydn's music had sung. First of all, his anger turned against his incompetent minister of police, Fouché.

"Who was it?"

"I don't know."

"You're shielding your former friends. Weren't you yourself a Jacobin once?"

The minister paled at the insult—which had its grain of truth. He murmured: "I am convinced they must have been royalists. Enemies of the right and not of the left. English money . . ."

"Prove it!" Napoleon raged.

Fouché required several days before he was able to prove that a certain Georges Cadoudal, a royalist, was guilty of the attempted assassination. Meanwhile Napoleon's rage turned against the helpless left, against the few remaining men of the Terror who were known to have spoken against him in Paris cafés. Bonaparte would have liked to have two hundred persons executed at once—as many as there had been wounded in the Rue Nicaise. His advisers were able to prevent that; but Fouché's police made short work of a number of persons. Some suspect anarchists such as Topino and Arena were sent to Guyana, the fever-ridden French colony in America, where they were certain to die soon. Freedom of assembly and, above all, freedom of the press were abolished. Forty-eight hours after the bombing in the Rue Nicaise, sixty-three out of seventy newspapers were banned. After all, one newspaper sufficed to publish news and official bulletins. It was neither necessary nor wise to have a host of newspapers commenting on political affairs.

Everyone was terrified by the First Consul's outbursts of rage, and mystified, as well. Were they genuine? He dismissed the director of the state opera company, upon learning that the unhappy man had given a banquet that night, after the performance of *The Creation,* and, moreover, in the rooms of the *Theâtre des Arts.* Monsieur Devismes, the director, might have pleaded that toasts had been proposed to celebrate Bonaparte's escape from death. But the First Consul was in no mood to listen to such pleas. He dismissed Devismes "for breach of the regulations governing illumination." Paris was bewildered.

Among the many groups that congratulated the First Consul on the following day was a delegation from the Paris Conservatory of Music. "Where is your Monsieur Cherubini?" the dictator demanded violently. *"Je ne vois pas Monsieur Cherubini!"*

What was the meaning of this outburst? No one understood what was going on in Napoleon's mind. A moment later Cherubini himself stepped forward, *"croisant froidement et calmement,"* as our sources put it, *"son regard avec le regard de Bonaparte."* This scene suddenly illuminates the whole matter for us; we realize that the irritated superman was convinced that the French musicians would have rejoiced over his death. How he hated them, all these professors and composers of the "Conservatoire"! Had not all of them worked, without conscience, for the Jacobins, only a few years earlier, and glorified the Reign of Terror in their compositions? Had they not written mass hymns for the Revolution which the myriad voices of the people roared out under the open sky? A few of them had even humbled themselves so far as to write cantatas of rejoicing over the execution of Louis XVI! Gossec . . . Méhul . . . Cherubini. . . . It was Cherubini whom he hated above all. When Cherubini had been requested to compose a march glorifying Napoleon's victory in Italy, he had preferred instead to write a cantata dedicated to Napoleon's rival Hoche, the fallen general of the Army of the Rhine.

The dictator glanced around, but today he saw before him only the most submissive expressions. Therefore, instead of ranting at Cherubini, he briefly mentioned the performance of *The Creation:*

"The triumph of order was a mighty one."

It was a highly equivocal remark. A few moments later Napoleon left the audience hall.

The painful interview was over. The musicians wiped their

brows. "Gentlemen," said Cherubini (or perhaps it was Rey, the *chef d'orchestre*), "it is now time, I should think, to write to Haydn." Perhaps he intended to add, "who is now so intimately linked with modern history." But it was unnecessary to say this, for everyone felt it. Someone asked whether a medal ought not be struck in memory of the previous day's events. Would Napoleon approve?

"A medal for Bonaparte?"

"No, a medal for Haydn."

Suddenly it seemed to all of them that both possibilities amounted to the same thing. The medal was designed by Gatteaux. The musicians drew up a letter to Haydn:

"Les artistes français réunis au Théâtre des Arts pour exécuter l'immortel ouvrage de la 'Création du Monde,' composé par le célèbre Haydn, pénétrés d'une juste admiration, le supplient de recevoir ici l'hommage du respect, de l'enthusiasme, qu'il leur a inspiré et la médaille qu'ils ont frappé de son honneur." ("The French artists assembled in the *Théâtre des Arts* to perform the immortal *Creation* wish to convey their greetings to the famous Haydn. Animated by sincere admiration, they herewith ask him to accept this token of their respect and enthusiasm, and the medal which they have struck in his honor.")

This was a magniloquent eulogy indeed, both classic and Napoleonic in its temper. It is hard to say whether these French musicians were addressing Haydn or the Sun God when they added: "The moving conception of *The Creation* surpasses—if that is possible—everything that this ingenious composer has hitherto offered to an amazed Europe. In imitating the splendor of the sun in this work, the composer has provided us with a self portrait (!) and imposed upon us the duty of testifying that his name will be glorious as long as that star whose rays he has borrowed (*aussi longtemps que l'astre dont il semble avoir emprunté les rayons*)."

Conductor Rey was first to sign the letter. The musicians had reckoned on thirty signatures; suddenly they found they had a hundred and forty, because everyone in Paris who had anything to do with art insisted on appending his name. The Gatteaux medal, which was shown to Napoleon, had a head of Haydn on the obverse side, and a lute, with a crown of stars above it, on the reverse side. Since in this year of 1801 peace had finally been ratified, there was once again an Austrian ambassador in Paris, Baron von Cobenzl. The ambassador personally sent the medal to Vienna.

Suddenly, the official interest in Haydn's music reached unexpected heights. Haydn's work had been known in France only to an élite of *avant-gardists;* now Haydn became overnight the favorite composer of a host of people who, like Napoleon, were not partial to "German heaviness." Of every hundred persons in Paris, at least seventy had hitherto believed that music was equivalent to *bel canto,* and the Germans had suffered accordingly. They continued to suffer even after Haydn's rise to popularity. Mozart, for example, was, alas, a "Proteus"; the epithet was meant in its unflattering sense, and even ten years later Beethoven struck the French as "bizarre and baroque as a crocodile."

But Haydn, the "glorifier of order," was an exception. Whether rightly or wrongly, the French suddenly discovered that he was good and French in spirit; that, in fact, he closely approximated the Italian canon of beauty—the balance of form and ideas in his work, the well designed proportions, the adjustment of the dynamics, the singing qualities of his melodies. The understanding that the French refused to give to Mozart and long withheld from Beethoven was lavished upon Haydn. A torrent of favors and honors flowed toward Vienna for nine full years, until Haydn died. The company of the *Concerts de la Loge Olympique* erected a bust of Haydn and crowned it with laurel. Ignace Pleyel printed a pocket edition of Haydn's quartets; it was sold out immediately. Other admirers sent money to the composer, and the Demoiselles Erard shipped a concert grand from their factory all the way to Eisenstadt. A renewed series of warm invitations were sent to the master, pressing him to visit Paris, to live in France. On the first anniversary of the explosion in the Rue Nicaise, on Christmas day, 1801, a new medal of Haydn was struck (this one designed by Dumarest) on which the composer's head appeared with the symbol of the French Republic. With the approval of the First Consul, the *Institut de France* unanimously made Haydn a foreign member, thus paying him the highest intellectual honor at the disposal of the French state. This title had certain civil connotations, as was the case in ancient Rome when foreign kings were appointed "friends of the Roman people." Haydn was now officially, in Vienna, a kind of ambassador of the French spirit. Some strange events before his death and at his funeral (at which we shall later have occasion to marvel) are explained by this fact.

We may now well wonder how the composer, who was one of

the most un-French men on earth, reacted to all this inappropriate homage. Most of the misunderstandings in the life of a great artist are neither pleasant nor productive. This, however, was a very pleasant mistake, and one that was advantageous to his creative life. In all probability, Haydn was greatly pleased. Nevertheless, during this period of his life he was inclined to be irritable and even tearful. After enduring the tremendous strain of composing *The Seasons* he felt sickly and old. At first he took no notice at all of Napoleon's escape from death and of the Paris *première* of *The Creation.* That same Christmas day he conducted, in a church in Vienna, the moving and wonderful *The Seven Words of the Saviour.* What did he care about the life of a dictator or about bombs that exploded in Paris streets at the behest of Jacobins or British secret agents?

But when the letter written by Rey and Cherubini arrived, and with it the Gatteaux medal, Haydn wept with emotion. He wrote a humble letter of thanks, saying that the gentlemen in Paris had "in a single day rewarded the labors of sixty years, crowned my gray hairs, and strewn with flowers the brink of my grave." These are remarkable words for a man whose personality was generally far too dry for him to fall in with the usual sentimentality of the age.

What had happened to Haydn? He was really ill, and he wept a good deal. He felt himself close to death.

THE SEASONS I

HAYDN had never been really ill. An orderly regimen of work, abstinence from all excess, and the sturdy heritage of his ancestors preserved his health until he was almost seventy. Shortly before his first trip to London he apologized to the Prince of Oetingen-Wallerstein because eye trouble had prevented him from delivering some promised music; in England he had rheumatism; but it was not until 1801 that he had a first severe case of grippe, which kept him in bed for months. Constant headaches afflicted him. (Probably his illness was not so much grippe as the symptom of overwork.) At the same time his appearance changed; overnight he became an old man. He himself blamed *The Seasons,* on which he worked for two full years (1799-1801) until his strength was utterly exhausted. "*The Seasons,*" he declared to friends, "has broken my back."

The work was, in truth, enormous; the score, which was published by Breitkopf and Haertel, in 1802, contained 497 pages. Such extensiveness was, at bottom, not necessary; from their work on *The Creation* both the composer and the author of the text knew the effectiveness of compression.

But the size of the work is not the sole explanation for Haydn's physical collapse; the difficulty was, rather, that Haydn did not believe in the work; it was not at all congenial to him. Thus, he had to force himself to compose, and then he had to force himself to forget that he was forcing himself. In this he succeeded, for the music betrays only Haydn's famous "effortlessness." But he paid a high price for this—lasting physical decrepitude. In the eight years of life that remained to him Haydn never fully recovered his health.

The chief inspiration for *The Seasons* came from Baron van Swieten. The tremendous success of *The Creation* had given van Swieten no rest. But he could not very well duplicate *The Creation*. Therefore he had to write something that, if similar in tendency, was nevertheless wholly different in tenor. *The Creation,* we will recall, had aroused theological recriminations in influential circles. But why was it necessary for Haydn's music to give rise to disputes? It had within it the power to make men happier—and why should not that power be effective? Van Swieten was a musician himself, and he knew his Haydn. Suavely, the baron followed up the "heavenly oratorio" with an "earthly" one. No one could be offended by the theme of *The Seasons*.

Thus, he alone was responsible for the choice of the material. Haydn, with his modesty in the intellectual sphere, was undoubtedly overjoyed by the prospect of once more composing an English epic. But gradually his joy turned. The author of the epic was James Thomson (1700-1748) whose *Seasons*, first published in 1726, was both very English and very moral, a work of the Age of Reason. It described in a most objective manner the attractions and the terrors of the seasons. In his classical unemotionality Thomson showed himself a disciple of Virgil. The poet acquaints us with the influence of Nature on country life, and at the same time discusses the "moral reflections that Nature arouses in the countryman." If only Thomson's language were toned down, nothing could be more suitable to Haydn's musical needs.

His friend van Swieten had chosen for him a truly Haydnesque task, though the baron did not take so much as thirty lines literally from Thomson. All the philosophical observations, the scientific comment, and all the foreign vistas of England and Scotland were deleted. Haydn's native Rohrau and the hills around Eisenstadt, provide the landscape for *The Seasons*. Very rarely are there details with which Haydn was unfamiliar—as, for example, the torrent which "in its precipitous fall stiff, dumb and frozen from the cliff depends." (With one exception—on his boyhood journey to Mariazell—Haydn had never seen the Alps.) Van Swieten almost always chose words and pictures with which Haydn could feel at home. Normally, the composer would have been grateful for this. We may therefore well wonder at his dislike for this text, which was virtually made to order for him. Was this merely the crotchet of an old man, or were there deeper reasons for it?

In 1800, the year in which Haydn labored most earnestly on *The Seasons*, two absolutely different approaches to Nature were available to the artist: The idealistic and the realistic approaches. The first, which today we find wholly strange, was strikingly formulated by Schiller in 1795: "Pleasure in Nature . . . has less an æsthetic than a moral basis; for it is transmitted through the medium of an *idea*, not immediately engendered by observation. Moreover, it is not at all governed by the beauty of the form. What is there so pleasing in themselves about an unpretentious flower, a spring, a moss-covered rock, the twittering of birds or the humming of bees? *What claim upon our love do these things make?* Not these objects, but the idea represented by them, is what we love. We love in them . . . their quiet power to affect us, their existing according to their own laws, the inner necessity and eternal unity with themselves. They are what we were; they are what *we shall become again.* Once we were part of Nature like them, and our culture must lead us back to Nature."

In diametrical opposition to Schiller, who was rather embarrassed by Nature and who accorded to it a grudging tolerance only as long as it expressed an idea, we have the naïve approach of the great Dutch painters, those tremendous realists whose heritage, in musical form, descended to Haydn. In his middle period, Haydn had sufficient confidence in his realism to attempt anything. Now that he need no longer tread daintily in rococo, buckle shoes in the resplendent courts of Eisenstadt and Esterhaz, Haydn strode roughshod over the taste of the time. He composed the most daring canons based on scenes of rural life—canons which, his biographers declare, "cannot be printed." However, we disagree. Historians have no business being prudes. In 1765, Haydn composed for a friend the remarkable *Capriccio on Castrating a Boar.* It exists only in manuscript, but was photographed by Anton van Hoboken for his Viennese archives. The text, in the Austrian dialect, runs:

Eahna achte müassen s'sein
Wenn s'an Saubärn wollen schneidn
Zwoa voran, zwoa hintn,
Zwoa schneidn, zwoa bindn
Eahna achte müassen s'sein
Wenn s' an Saubärn wolln schneidn.

("There must be eight men to help castrate a boar. Two must stand in front, two behind, two must cut and two must bind. There must be eight men to help castrate a boar.")

This is the "Rabelaisian touch" which Bourguès and Dénéréaz, in their book *La Musique et la Vie Intérieure,* ascribe to Haydn's genius. The standards and the predilections of the rococo age often overshadowed the Rabelaisian quality, but Haydn himself had never lost it and van Swieten was well acquainted with it.

We must admire van Swieten's skill in finding, when writing the text for *The Seasons,* the precise middle course between Schiller's idealism and the realism of the early Haydn. ("Every modern librettist could learn from him," Max Friedlaender, the musicologist, remarked.) Since Thomson's poem was epical in nature, van Swieten introduced into it a sham element of drama. In the foreground he placed three characters: The peasant Lucas (tenor), the tenant's daughter Hanne (soprano), and the tenant Simon (bass). A similar device was used in the *terzetto* of *The Creation,* where the archangels Uriel, Gabriel, and Rafael sing and act in a pseudo-dramatic fashion. The choruses in *The Seasons* are treated even more artistically and with more personal reference to Haydn than are those of *The Creation.* The semichorus and the chorus of country folk sound even more typically Haydnesque than the paeans of the angels in *The Creation.* The technique of alternation is more highly developed in the latter work. Van Swieten, in breaking up the text into solos, duets, trios, recitatives, and arias, created virtually a theatrical work. When the score was published, contemporaries noticed that the word "oratorio" had been omitted from the title page. *Orare* signifies "to pray," and there was only a casual prayer in *The Seasons.*

Yes, the text was excellent. And yet the seventy-year-old Haydn sighed over it and complained of his lack of sympathy for the text. This is a psychological puzzle—but puzzles are made to be solved.

Van Swieten's original manuscript was lost for many years. When it was finally uncovered in Berlin, early in the present century, by Max Friedlaender, he was astonished to find that the text was accompanied by numerous "instructions written in a tone of command." These instructions directed Haydn *how to compose!* We know that in writing *The Creation* van Swieten had not been content merely to produce an excellent text, but had also exercised a decisive influence upon Haydn's method of composing. With *The Seasons,* however, he went much further. In many places he dictated the kind of instrumentation and suggested appropriate themes. He would request, for example, that at such-and-such a place Haydn should write "fugally" or that somewhere else he must bring in a "countersubject," or elsewhere introduce a recitative *secco* or *accompagnato.* "In the additional instrumental accompaniment I should like to hear the purling of the brook and the hum of flying insects," the baron requested for one particular passage. He virtually took the pen from Haydn's hand when, in the introduction to "Summer," he called for the "wailing cry of owls." Haydn obeyed, however, by making the violins, and later the clarinets, literally sigh. For the thunderstorm, van Swieten, who well knew the London symphonies, demanded a succession of "muted drum rolls." For the aria which Hanne sings during the thunderstorm, he asked that "she be accompanied by short *staccato* or *pizzicato* notes, after the manner of a recitative, in order to reserve the stringed instruments for the lightning." At this point Haydn rebelled. Faithful to the technique he had developed almost half a century before in *Le Matin, Le Midi,* and *Le Soir,* he expressed lightning not by the strings, but by zigzag passages in the flutes.

This was the way in which van Swieten went on, right down to the 497th page of the work. Even where the baron's instructions were in themselves excellent—which they were, for the most part—the tone of his prescriptions and proscriptions was too much even for Haydn. A rift threatened between these two men, the one so amenable and the other so haughty. We must remember how unpopular van Swieten was. Although this Dutchman had been living in Vienna for more than sixty years, he had never learned to react with the characteristically easy humor of the Viennese. He remained the eternal schoolmaster.

Now, however, the two seemed to be on the point of breaking. Since Haydn saw no way of putting van Swieten in his place on personal grounds, he lashed out against the text of *The Seasons,* and, infallibly, condemned all the wrong passages. The author had, quite justly for a work dealing with rural life, requested a number of voices of birds and beasts. Inexplicably, Haydn suddenly declared himself against such "animal sounds"; effects of that sort were beneath him, he declared; he may have added that he was composing for men and not for animals. How strange this seemed! Had he finally taken to heart Schiller's stern criticism? Had he been won over to the side of the few persons who had disparaged the "portraits of creatures" in *The Creation?* But after all, *The Seasons* was not an oratorio in that sense, and birds and beasts were certainly important features of rural life. However, Haydn stubbornly insisted, "I won't compose any croaking frogs; that sort of thing is vulgar, Frenchified trash." Why Frenchified? The amazed baron demanded an explanation, for he did not realize that

Haydn's animosity was directed against him rather than against the text of the oratorio. "That's the kind of thing Grétry has done," Haydn grumbled. Van Swieten might have replied that Grétry was a great composer who never dishonored his art. (This same Grétry, by the way, had declared as early as 1786 that any symphony of Haydn surpassed any French opera.) Instead, the baron went silently to his shelf of scores, opened *Israel in Egypt,* and showed Haydn how Handel had done the music for the plague of frogs that descended upon the land of the Pharaoh:

"They jump," Haydn may have replied, "but they don't croak." This was quite true. But, then, he must have quite forgotten that in 1789 he himself had composed a quartet for Frederick William II of Prussia (Op. 50, No. 6) in which gay croaking sounds weie produced by playing the same notes alternately on two adjoining strings. For this reason, everyone called the quartet "The Frog."

From the issue of the frogs the quarrel seems to have proceeded to the other depiction of birds and beasts in *The Seasons.* Haydn's anger mounted. Had he not, for decades, been plagued by the charge that he was an imitator of animal sounds? In England, actually a brochure had been written against him in which the style of fine—that is, Italian!—music was contrasted with his own cruder, German compositions. In this publication German music was symbolized by oxen and other beasts. Now Haydn was sick of it all. If he had been permitted, the pettish old man would probably have eliminated even his glorious cock-crow from the score of *The Seasons:*

But van Swieten prevented him such action. The baron was Haydn's social superior, besides being deeply learned in the history of music. He reassured Haydn by pointing out how often the crow of the cock had been used in serious music.

These disputes over the realistic features of *The Seasons* were serious enough, but an even worse conflict arose over the idealistic aspects. Haydn firmly refused to compose at all the "Praise of Industry":

So nature ever kind repays
The toil of industry.
By hope of gain inciting it
She ready help bestows
And all her power exerts.
From industry springs every good:
The hut that shelters us,
The wool that covers us,
The wholesome hearty food
Is all its grant, is all its gift.
From thee, O industry, springs every good!
Thou makest all virtues grow
And wildness rude is tam'd by thee!

Haydn attempted to convince the baron that these lines were falsely sentimental. He himself had grown up in the country, and he knew that Nature was *not* "ever kind," and that, unfortunately, she did not always reward the "toil of industry." Moreover, no peasant loved work. The city man, van Swieten, was silly enough to believe that any peasant chorus would sing an exalted praise of industry as the spring of all virtues. But Haydn was evidently incapable of explaining the matter coherently to the baron. Instead of making his point, he merely kept on muttering, "All my life I have been industrious, but it has never occurred to me to compose a 'praise of industry.'" This was the literal truth; he had, in fact, set to music a charming poem of Lessing entitled *In Praise of Laziness*. But, in a higher sense, his own lifework was even more the product of industry than of the gift of genius. After all, he was no Mozart, and the touch of philistinism implicit in his "praise of industry"—even *this*—would inevitably be truly Haydnesque. Van Swieten exerted all his influence over him, and the old Haydn reluctantly sat down to compose the "Praise of Industry."

Haydn aired his irritation by speaking to others against the baron; van Swieten heard about this, and became furious. Their relations were soon at the breaking point and it was now 1801, high time that *The Seasons* was finished. Haydn struggled through to the end—and the tremendous success of the work soon proved that van Swieten had been right on every point. It was, precisely, the significant mixture of realistic and moralistic features that listeners liked in Haydn's music.

Nevertheless, when we examine the quarrel between the two, from our vantage point in time and in the light of our knowledge of the development of music, we perceive that ultimately Haydn was right. A master cannot be hedged in by his own style, or limited by his own mannerisms. The genius must be free, and van Swieten sinned against this precept. "You are Haydn," he declared, in effect, "and now you must write like Haydn." Such constraint proved to be insupportable. Perhaps Haydn no longer wished to be himself; perhaps he was looking for something different, something new—like the octogenarian Verdi who in his *Falstaff* and *Otello* created tonal combinations that he had never used formerly.

James Gibbons Huneker, that great American æsthetician (1860-1921) championed this explanation of Haydn's dissatisfaction with *The Seasons*. He asserted that Haydn, the classic creator of idylls, instinctively sensed that romanticism was just around the corner. In the poems of Thomson and van Swieten, Nature was described objectively. To the romantic, however, Nature was but a part of the "infinite," and infinity could be expressed only in terms of extreme subjectivity. Only the intuitive powers of the individual could grasp Nature. Those great individualists, Goethe and Beethoven, were aware of this, and Schubert, above all.

"Perhaps," Huneker remarked, shortly before his death, to a friend in Paris, "perhaps Haydn wanted to compose like Schubert—and van Swieten stopped him from doing so."

"In 1801?" the friend laughed. "At that time Schubert was only four years old."

"What does that matter?" Huneker snapped. "Haydn may have been a pre-Schubertian Schubert."

THE SEASONS II

WHAT would Schubert have done if he had been required to compose four such cantatas as *Spring, Summer, Autumn,* and *Winter*—and why could not Haydn do the same? This question leads us to the immense difference between the musical ideal of classicism and that of romanticism.

There is no doubt that Schubert, had he composed *The Seasons,* would have centered the work around an individualistic "wanderer," a man devoted to wandering for its own sake, a man trying to escape from himself. *Wanderlust* and *Wanderer's Grief, Wandererfantasie, Wanderers Sturmlied*—such designations, such sentiments, did not exist in pre-Schubertian days.

The focus of a Schubertian song cycle, such as *Die Schoene Muellerin* or *Winterreise,* was always the stranger, the romantic stranger. Byron and Schubert, the wealthy and well born lord and the poor little Austrian schoolteacher, had little to do with each other, of course. But when Byron roved through Italy, Switzerland, and Greece, and when Schubert left his narrow quarters in Vienna to drift about the rural environs of the city, they felt the same profound sadness over being strangers—unbeloved, misunderstood. They were aliens everywhere.

In his wanderings, Schubert might encounter friends. Of course, they would not be sturdy peasants, but strangers also, misfits and outcasts such as the organ grinder (*Der Leiermann*), an old, old man with a discordant hand organ. Life, like the organ, is discordant; but Schubert could blend the discords of both into an immortal song, a heartrending, forever unsurpassable *Lied.* Or he might speculate about the mail coach sounding its horn on the high road. (*"Von der Strasse her ein Posthorn klingt"*) and his heart would leap to the joyful melody (*"Was hat es, dass es so hoch aufspringt, mein Herz?"*). But a few measures further on, he would be struck by the dreadful certainty that there was no happy message for him (*"Die Post bringt keinen Brief fuer mich"*).

Such highly personal emotions were foreign to Haydn. For him the countryside was home; rural life was his proper realm. He could glance at the nut tree and estimate the size of the year's crop. The cows, the wells, the haystacks, were all familiar to him. He could read the thoughts and the feelings behind the unexpressive features of the peasants. The rippling vineyards, the dread of hail, the ravages of aphids, all the joys and sorrows that constitute the symphony of the year, were what interested Haydn, were what he put into his classic idyll.

He knew that country life was a serious undertaking. The peasants labor in their fields; they do not drift about aimlessly. It was not only the work pattern that interested Haydn. He felt, moreover, that all the beauty of the bucolic scene had economic significance. This consideration, which is so carefully stressed in *The Seasons,* aroused Goethe's ire against van Swieten; on February 27, 1811, he commented, in a letter to Knebel: "If only the entire text [of *The Seasons*] were not so dreadfully absurd!" Goethe objected to what he considered excess of "practicality" as well as excess in description. (We may recall that Beethoven, in his motto for the *Pastoral Symphony,* plainly stated: "More expression of feeling than painting." He did not wish to delineate.)

However, *The Seasons* does more than sketch Nature; it "reveals" Nature, makes discoveries about it. The work even shows spiritual kinship with the writings of Goethe and Humboldt on natural history. For *The Seasons* is replete with wholly novel observations. Goethe, in his capacity of natural scientist, once consulted his musical adviser, Zelter, on the problem of "the raising of voices when the barometer climbs, and their lowering when the barometer is falling." It might be possible, the two men decided, "to determine future weather by the behavior of "voices in singing." Schumann, Berlioz, and the other romanticists would have laughed at such an approach to music as hopelessly philistine, but Haydn would have approved of it. All his life he had faithfully recorded in his music the vicissitudes of the weather.

He brought this practice to its height in *The Seasons.* In *The Creation* God is the protagonist; in *The Seasons* it is the year—the year in its most literal sense. The four seasons govern all the actions and thoughts of men. The manner in which Haydn develops this theme, with such ponderous, undeviating power still makes a tremendous, coherent impression upon the listener.

First comes spring; in a few orchestral measures the earth seems to liberate itself from winter. But then the weather changes suddenly; stormy winter returns, and with such violence that all hope for the coming of spring seems lost. Yet, after all, spring has slipped in. "Come, gentle spring," is sung, but the song is no longer needed. The plowman goes forth into the fields; he is escorted, remarkable to relate, by a motive from one of Haydn's English symphonies:

This is nothing less than the *andante* from the *Surprise Symphony,* No. 94. (Was Haydn right, after all, in holding that a melody can be used in any context?)

In the ensuing arias the noises of the countryside are heard. "What Haydn's musical ear catches is the precise difference between the bleat of a lambkin and that of a sheep, and the glitter of sunlight upon the wings of a bee," is Tovey's comment. Then summer begins.

Summer, the most concentrated section of the over-lengthy work, is an epic account of *heat,* which, silent and enervating, creeps up on all living things and works its will on them. And this heat comes from the sun. Thus Master Haydn must perforce portray the solar orb as a Moloch, a glowing furnace, the cosmic source of all heat.

Jens Baggesen, the Danish poet (1764-1826), stated that the artist ought to treat of every sublime event only *once;* otherwise he will spoil and cheapen it. Such a rule may hold for a creative artist whose product is small, such as that of John Keats, but it cannot be applied legitimately to Haydn, one of the most prolific of artists. Nature, more prodigal than Baggesen, produces her sunrises three hundred and sixty-five times a year. Haydn was content with two—once in *The Creation* and once in *The Seasons,* but the two suns are not the same. In the former work the uppermost significance of the orb lies in its light; in the latter, in its heat. The sun rises out of a hazy twilight; the indistinctness of the scene brings to mind the vague, uncertain period between the departure of winter and the onset of spring. The obscureness lasts but a few bars; then, chromatic, ascending notes suddenly ring out, and solo voices and the chorus blaze across the entire sky: "Hail! Thou glorious sun! Thou source of light and life!"

Now the heat is fully upon us; the sun is like an oriental despot. "It's noon, and vertical the sun darts all his fire, and shoots thro' th' air serene and calm his mighty blaze in torrents down. O'er th' arid grounds and parched fields of gleaming and reflected rays a dazzling deluge reigns." Music like molten metal—crimson, chrome, and fluid—accompanies the recitative. Heat is expressed with comparable fury in only *Mireiò,* the epic by the French poet François Mistral.

Haydn had composed countless thunderstorms since the day when he greeted Nicholas the Splendid with *Le Soir,* in which the flutes shoot zigzag bolts of lightning. But in *The Seasons* he summoned up his powers for the last and greatest of his tempests. With "Hark! The deep tremendous voice," an Egyptian darkness is spread over the sky, making all living creatures tremble. Such a storm is beyond the memory of man and beast; in a fugue of lamentation the creatures attempt to flee this Judgment Day. Then the howling storm, the torrents of rain, end as suddenly as they began, and are succeeded by a mellow, cool evening. The damp, steaming cattle, lowing, return to their barns; in the rain-sweet grass of the mowing the crickets strike up their muted orchestra; the quail calls to her mate, and in the distance the Angelus chimes thanksgiving. The bullfrogs, too, announce themselves; then the summer's day closes in peace with the appearance of the evening star, and the country folk, yawning, retire to their beds.

Spring and summer are treated as a solid mass opposed to the solid mass of autumn and winter. The Number 4, so symbolic, in its squareness, of Haydn the craftsman, is thus divided in twain, for the intermission follows Summer.

With *September* there begin those long stretches of notes which make it almost impossible to perform *The Seasons* in a single night. Haydn's intimate knowledge of country life led him too far afield, and he reveled in the abundance of images he could call to mind. What can we say of a hunting hound who behaves like this:

It is worth noting that all this is not sheer Neapolitan love of ornament. The music renders *literally* a dog running his nose along the ground—but it might well have been done more concisely. Haydn's voluptuous pleasure in hunting, his knowledge of the hunting horn, of the flight, of the stag's dying gaze, of the row of rabbits laid out side by side with the October wind playing in their fluffy fur—all these things he displays for us with genius, but he is too profuse.

There is, however, no good reason why the work should not be performed on two successive evenings. *The Seasons* is a classical composition, and celebrates, after a fashion, the classical agrarian religion, the cults of Ceres and Bacchus, whose year, as the present author has described it in *Six Thousand Years of Bread,* began about September 20 when the seed corn is returned to the earth and the wine is pressed. The second evening of a performance might well begin with the scenes of hunt and vintage. Haydn's peasants are Christians, of course, but the excess and overripeness of autumn links the work of this Austrian composer with the painting of classical vases. Alcohol fills the pipes, the fiddles, and the drums and a drunken polyphony reigns. Beneath the confusion a tight fugue maintains a vertical order; but in the upper section the vintage workers are already sprawled horizontally across their chairs. Haydn objected violently to the text of "Joyful, joyful the liquor flows," and demurred at writing the appropriate bacchanal. It seemed to him unworthy of his pen, and he wrote it only because van Swieten made him toe the line. Apparently, the old sage had forgotten the numerous musical sketches of drunkenness he had written in younger days. There is, for example, the very liquid cantata, *The Election of a Conductor,* or that moist finale to *London Symphony* (No. 102) in which, after the start of a Croatian rustic wedding march, the exuberant, intoxicated instruments make no less than four false starts before they get a grip on themselves.

Bacchanalia is followed by winter, and the music degenerates. It would not be so bad if only the real winter were depicted—the deadly, cosmic winter in which travelers are lost in a blizzard, whose blinding fury is admirably depicted in an aria. But Haydn, that classical realist and devotee of the idyll, found himself confronted by the obvious circumstance "that no peasant works in the later months of fall or in winter." Therefore he had to shift, in the last two parts of *The Seasons,* from his open-air scenes to interiors—and if anything he wrote was ever unworthy of his pen, it was these portraits of domesticity. They are utterly German and utterly dull, if not silly. Their praise of the pretty country maid proves, as Tovey ably puts it, no more than "the superiority of real complexions over lipstick." The whole tone is more like that of Dittersdorf than of Haydn. This "winter" music of *The Seasons* leads us directly to one of the most overrated composers of nineteenth-century Germany, Albert Lortzing (1801-1850) and his philistine comic operas.

Even in this dull "winter," however, there is much splendid music. Every musicologist knows that the spinning scene in *The Seasons* has been the germ of all later spinning music. Haydn well remembered from his father's workshop all the rhythms of a revolving wheel. Without his music to "Set the wheel a going, make it snore a turning,"

Schubert's *Gretchen at the Spinning Wheel* would scarcely have been written, nor is it likely that we should have even Wagner's tremendous "Spinning Chorus" from *The Flying Dutchman.*

However, by subconsciously clinging to his old grudge against van Swieten, he remained unjust against *The Seasons,* almost to his own death. He strongly objected to comparisons between his two oratorios. When, after the success of *The Seasons,* an admirer congratulated him with the words, "This is even greater than *The Creation,*" Haydn retorted, "Don't you realize that in the one *angels* are singing, while in the other merely rustics?" He thought that, after all, sublimity was his métier. How utterly he was mistaken in such an almost senile condemnation of his own powerful realism, no better way of proving it can be found than to visit the old Burgenland in which Haydn and his forefathers lived. It is amazing, even mysterious to scent how the real flavor of Haydn's music lingers on until today in these surroundings—in spite the fact that many musical tides have rolled over it since more than a century.

In 1790, one Leopold Wolf bought the vineyards around Eisenstadt. A descendant of his, Sandor Wolf, an admirer of Haydn, and a great collector of music (until Hitler drove him from the country), showed me, in 1928, around his and Haydn's world. It was a glorious October day. The vineyards, with their masses of fantastically indented leaves, stood against a background of deep-blue sky; rusty, copper, bright yellow, and green hung the heavy masses of grapes. A shot was fired to give the signal for the harvest's start, men and women armed with knives and provided with tubs rushed to the trellises. A flock of starlings had been fluttering about, eager to help with the gleaning, but the shot frightened them off. Brown hands reached for the grapes and lifted them to the rays of the sun; they glittered like gems.

I watched a spider moving deliberately through the tangle of vines. It paid no attention to the movements of human beings; it dwelt in another world—until a girl's hand knocked it into a tub. Was death the vintner here? But then I saw something take hold of a grape; it was the spider, which stood trembling for a moment on its long legs, then cast itself over the edge of the tub, and was safe.

Wolf now led me to the press house, an abattoir for grapes. Violet mounds of pungent crushed husks lay about for the chickens to pick at. These grapes were pressed as they had been for a thousand years, with flat stones moved by wooden levers. The scene was like that of a fairy tale. From above, the grapes were incessantly poured in, and from below the red stream flowed out, day and night.

Close by lay the subterranean Eisenstadt, with its vast catacombs filled with the stores of wine. The Wolf wine cellars ran deep under the whole town, like the galleries of a mine. One might walk for hours —with a lantern in one hand and a glass in the other—through a fragrant, misty labyrinth. Here were stored the vast vats from which Haydn had drunk. He might well have tasted this ancient *Blaufran-*

kischer, this *Mörbischer,* this *Oggauer.* Here were vats of the noble wines of *Rust,* which is grown on the shore of the Steppensee and takes its special quality from the fact that not the sun, but reflected light, ripens the grapes. Here, too, was *Furmint,* white Muscatel. My light fell upon a numbered label: "This vat contains 22,000 gallons." What a monstrous vat! I thought of the phrase from *The Creation:* "In the depths of Ocean writhed Leviathan," and I felt momentarily overcome by all this fermentation. Suppose the cement and the wood should give way? I should be drowned in the flood of wine.

Later, I looked down from the attic window of Wolf's guest cottage, and gazed over the countryside. The first stars winked into the sky, and night came rushing up toward me. Lights blinked out, and sleep settled over the drowsy farmhouses. To the right, a tiny stream gleamed in the gathering mist; to the left, the rocky face of the Esterhazy stone quarry reflected the last, milky light. Everything smelled wet, pungent, and brown. But suddenly it seemed that music was all around me, above or below the ground. It passed through the heart, flowed away and returned. The shrubs stood suddenly like bars of music; the enchanted trees swayed with a sweet melancholy, and slowly the vineyards moved down to the horizon in waves of melody, all *legato.* A chestnut fell to the ground; it was like a single drum-beat. A night-bird croaked like a bassoon, in the garden. Then the breeze put an end to these two *intermezzi* and there remained only the fundamental melody of the cello-brown valley. This was nothing more than the valley of Eisenstadt—but the magic of Haydn's pen had swelled the small scene into the prototype of a complete world, as if God's seasons had all followed the pattern of this place.

"Heyday! Heyday! There flows the wine!" A spectral Thyrsus beat the rhythm for these words. A bunch of grapes lay on the window sill, a gift from my host for my delectation before going to bed. I put one into my mouth; it tasted clear and cool as music.

Book Six

THE CLOUDY NIGHT

Non moriar sed vivam
Et narrabo opera Domini

"Die I shall not, but live
And proclaim the works of the Lord"

FROM THE INSCRIPTION ON HAYDN'S TOMB

TIDYING UP THE WORKSHOP

Haydn's lifework was finished. Now he could sit on the doorstep, and leisurely enjoy the last fading glow of the purple evening. Tradition has it that during 1805 the sunsets were more deeply dyed than ever before. Was this once more a sign of coming war? A man of Papa Haydn's age had outlived many wars; he would survive the next, as well.

An old man finds his greatest pleasure in talking, especially with his own kin. But Haydn's relations were afraid to come to Vienna and visit the town house where their famous kinsman lived. How could they—just ordinary people—talk with such a wonder of the world? They would have come willingly enough if they had realized that the price of cattle and wine, and a well cobbled shoe, never had ceased to interest him. Sometimes, however, Haydn went to see them. He traveled in a rented carriage to Bruck on the Leitha, where the family forgathered in an inn, and there he distributed presents to all the small children. Giuseppe Carpani, the Italian biographer, pretended that this custom was regularized into an annual "Haydn Family Day." *Haydn, rinnovando fra i rustici sinceri abracci l'invito per l'anno susseguente, chiamava questo suo famigliare simposio, il "giorno delle sue grandezza" a ne andava lieto e fastoso.* ("Haydn, exchanging kisses and embraces with these country people, invited them to come again the following year; he declared that this family meal was 'the day of his true greatness' and went away in a mood of elation.") Such an institution was, naturally, pleasing to the warmhearted Italian, but he has, unquestionably, exaggerated it. After Haydn in 1803 gave up his post as kapellmeister in Eisenstadt because of his advancing age (he kept the title, of course, although, in fact, he was succeeded by Hummel), he was no longer able to indulge in such formidable undertakings as annual journeys by carriage from Vienna to Bruck.

After 1803 he really could not compose any longer. He still would not admit this to himself; he assured himself that his uneasiness was merely a nervous condition. The difficulty was not that he lacked ideas; on the contrary, he had too many. He could no longer stop. He could not sleep; music pursued him in his dreams, until, at last, his doctor decided that the French grand piano which had been given him by the Erard ladies would have to be removed from his parlor. Did this mean the end of his creative life? Many persons were reluctant to think so. Among them was the empress, consort of Francis II, who sent emissaries to Haydn. Court circles were toying with the idea of Haydn's composing a third oratorio, *The Last Judgment.* Here was an austere and sober subject that seemed very promising to the empress, a portrayal of heaven and hell and the resurrection of the dead. If Haydn composed on such a subject, the religious empress thought, he would be atoning for a good many of his libertarian sins in *The Creation.* Haydn, too, was enthusiastic; he forgot about his weakness. But who could write the text? Gottfried van Swieten was dead now; not even the success of *The Seasons* had brought about a reconciliation between the two old men. Haydn, therefore, suggested another man who was as old as van Swieten and he—Wieland, the German poet whose work was often marked by frivolity. In making this suggestion the master once again betrayed his utter naïveté in literary matters. Wieland could never have depicted the terrors of the last judgment, nor would he have wished to do so. But since Wieland had once praised Haydn's *Creation,* the composer saw no reason for his unfitness to collaborate on the proposed new oratorio. Naturally, the proposals came to nothing, and this was really fortunate for Haydn. He would not have survived the tremendous strain of bringing forth a third oratorio.

Nevertheless, he could not simply sit idle. What should a neat craftsman, the son of a wheelwright, do with his evening? He must tidy up the workshop, of course, before he goes to sleep; the tools must be put in their place. But Haydn's tools were many, and tidying up proved a laborious task. During almost sixty years he had worked on a vast number of things; the name of Haydn was affixed to a great many compositions. Were they really all his? "*Sunt mala mixta bonis;* some of my offspring have turned out well, some ill, and here and there a changeling has slipped in," he remarked to Griesinger one day. In 1805, therefore, in order to put things in order he dictated to Elssler his *Verzeichnis,* "a catalogue containing the names of all compositions which, as nearly as I can remember, were composed by me between my 18th and 73rd years."

"As nearly as I can remember!" It would be hard to find a more cautious phrase. This precious document, 123 pages long, contains in Elssler's limpid handwriting, a tremendous number of titles, accompanied in many cases by the initial notes of the piece. (The original is in Budapest; the Library of Congress, in Washington, has a copy.) Noted are 118 symphonies, 83 string quartets, 19 operas, 5 oratorios, 24 trios, 163 baritone pieces, 44 piano sonatas, 115 masses, 10 smaller ecclesiastical compositions, 24 instrumental concertos, 42 German and Italian songs, 39 canons, 365 Scotch and Welsh songs, numberless *capriccios* and *divertimenti.* The list seems endless.

Some of these figures look odd. For example, we have come to accept 104 symphonies as the canonical number. This figure derives from Eusebius Mandyczewski (1857-1929), keeper of the archives of the *Gesellschaft der Musikfreunde,* in Vienna, who began publication of the complete works of Haydn; unfortunately, only twelve volumes were finished. What about the other fourteen symphonies that Elssler included in his catalogue?

The explanation is quite simple: The old composer included overtures in his reckoning, or he mistakenly ascribed to himself compositions by others which unscrupulous publishers had put out under the name of Haydn, because the name meant profits. The error in the number of operas can probably be accounted for by assuming that he listed as complete operas certain illustrative stage music which he wrote for Esterhazy.

In an amusing German cabaret sketch, lampooning the pig-headedness of orthodox Goethe philologists, Goethe is shown come back to life and failing in an examination because he does not know the important dates in his own life. In the case of Haydn, however, a stern sort of philology is justified. If we are to choose between Haydn's recollections and the findings of musicologists, the latter unquestionably come off victorious. "Mandy is always right," Mandyczewski's friends used to say. When, in 1909, Mandyczewski asserted that only 104 of the symphonies were really Haydn's, he was directly opposing the Berlin musicologist, Leopold Schmidt, who had raised the figure to 144! Three years after Mandyczewski's death, Adolf Sandberger startled the musical world with the announcement that Haydn had written not 104, but 182 symphonies! But the foremost Haydn scholar of our times, Jens Peter Larsen, of Kopenhagen, asserts that Mandyczewski was correct, in the main.

It is evident that the estimated volume of Haydn's symphonies resembles an accordion which can be expanded or compressed according to the knowledge and opinions of the scholars. This sounds somewhat fantastic, but there are three good explanations for the confusion. The first we have already mentioned—the unscrupulousness of the publishers. Haydn's name was a splendid source of profit. During his lifetime, at least, the master enjoyed an almost legendary fame. We can imagine the astonishment of Adalbert Gyrowetz when, in 1789, in Paris, he found his G-major symphony printed under the name of Joseph Haydn! The second explanation is that counterfeits often emanated from Haydn's own orchestra. We must remember that a tremendous amount of composing was going on during this period, and much of it was excellent. Some violinist or horn player might have a work of his own that he would like to sell. He would know that publishers from perhaps seven countries were circling constantly between Eisenstadt and Vienna. They were like a pack of hungry dogs, eager to snap up a "chunk of Haydn." (A hundred years later there was an equal demand for the music of Johann Strauss.) Consequently, the musician would sell his own work as a genuine composition of the master. Often he could assuage his conscience because Haydn had made, with his unfailing kindliness, a few corrections in the manuscript, of course without dreaming that his good nature would be so abused. Rubens did not paint all the pictures ascribed to him. Without Haydn's knowledge, there may well have arisen a "Haydn atelier," as there arose a "Rubens atelier."

The third explanation, however, outweighs all the others: There was *another* Haydn, "little Michael," the master's favorite brother (1737-1806), who had for years been an ecclesiastical composer in Salzburg. His masses and canons, highly esteemed by Mozart, were well known, but his secular works were less familiar to the public. Now, when some Haydn scholar—Wotquenne in Brussels, Hadow in London, Schmidt in Berlin, or Sandberger in Munich—came across an unprinted symphonic work which bore the name "Haydn," he was quite likely to attribute it to Joseph although it was Michael's. The fact that these works were not included in Elssler's catalogue did not disturb the scholars. They proceeded on the assumption that by 1805 Joseph Haydn was too old to remember accurately; they disregarded the fact that the gap in number between 118 and 182 symphonies is somewhat too large to be explained by a failure of memory. There must have been other factors in the matter.

To complete the confusion, Sir Donald Tovey made the fateful announcement that in the first half of the eighteenth century there had lived an English organist and composer by the name of George Hayden, who wrote many quartets. Who can say that some of George Hayden's works are not in reality Joseph Haydn's, and vice versa?

Perhaps these problems of authorship will never be clarified. Haydn himself would probably not have cared too much, one way or the other. As we have often observed, the modern artist's narrow conception of personality and property was quite foreign to him. To Haydn—and this may give us food for thought—music is, in addition to its spiritual significance, an article of daily use, ordered from an artist and paid for in cash. "True craftsmanship remains anonymous," his contemporary, Herder, had taught.

Thus, the master did not quite succeed in his "tidying up" of his workshop. Nor did he find it easier to arrange for the disposition of his earthly goods than of his spiritual goods. He had already rewritten his testament several times. Anna Aloysia Haydn had died in the spring of 1800, after having suffered for several years from a rheumatic complaint which had compelled her to spend much of her time at a sulphur spa. Thus a half century of unhappy married life came to an end. In justice to Anna Haydn it must be said that her temperament had somewhat softened in the last ten years. She had not only made her husband her principal heir, but also had left almost nothing to her own nephews and nieces. Her death, however, was less important to Haydn than it was to Luigia Polzelli. Would he now marry her? As a widower, Haydn was well cared for by his faithful servant Elssler and his cook, Anna Kremnitzer, and he did not dream of marrying again. In any case, on May 23, 1800, he signed, half under compulsion, half voluntarily, a document in which he promised that if he should marry again he would take no other wife than "the said Luigia Polzelli." "And should I remain a widower, I promise the said Polzelli after my death a pension of 300 gulden for as long as she lives." Luigia, for her part, made no promises at all. With Haydn's agreement in her purse, she promptly married the singer Franchi, and went to Italy with him. Haydn was not at all jealous, but he was evidently somewhat annoyed, after all, for in his testament he brushed aside his promise to Luigia.

Who, then, would be his principal heir? Since Antonio Polzelli, Luigia's second son—and probably his own—had fallen into disfavor together with his mother, the obvious choice was Haydn's brother Michael. The two loved each other dearly, although it often happened that years passed without their seeing each other. In 1800 Michael and his wife, a singer, had their home so thoroughly pillaged when the French invaded Salzburg that they were left with little more than the clothes on their backs. Joseph promptly sent money and a gold watch to his brother. In 1801 Michael visited his brother in Vienna. According to the priest, Werigand Rettensteiner, who had observed the two old gentlemen at their dinner, they outdid each other in expressions of affection. Joseph had enclosed some of his canons in frames, with glass, and had hung them on the wall. He wanted them constantly before him, to remind him "how to write in strict forms." ("I was not wealthy enough to buy fine paintings," he said later to Griesinger, "so I made for myself a wall covering the like of which not everyone can have.") The admiring Michael asked his brother for a few canons, as a gift. "You write better ones yourself," Joseph said, in all earnestness.

However, Michael died before Joseph (on August 10, 1806), and so did Johann Evangelist Haydn (May 16, 1805), the tenor who was called "Hansl Haydn" and who had once been employed by Prince Esterhazy. Haydn's sister, Anna Maria, who had married a smith named Froehlich, had died on August 27, 1802. Her son Matthias therefore became the principal heir, and Haydn distributed many smaller legacies to more distant relatives. His fortune was not small, for Haydn had been earning large sums for several decades, and had always been rather penurious where he himself was concerned. It is touching to note, Geiringer remarks, "that the last will of the world famous composer provided, for the most part, legacies to hardworking artisans. A shoemaker, a blacksmith, a tailor, a saddler's wife, four workmen, and two lacemakers were among the legatees."

A TRIO OF BIOGRAPHERS

ELSSLER was, of course, one of those remembered in the will. His faithfulness was subject to aspersion; it was said that he sold as genuine Haydn manuscripts copies he himself had made. This is scarcely likely, for Elssler had an almost religious awe of his beloved "Papa." Often the servant could be seen at night, long after Haydn had retired, standing reverently, candle in hand, before the master's portrait, "as if he were mentally burning incense to him." The money Haydn bequeathed to Elssler was put to very good use, for the servant drew on it to give his daughters an education. The oldest, Thérèse, born in 1808 while Haydn was still alive, was trained for the ballet. When she left the stage she entered into a morganatic marriage with Prince Adalbert of Prussia. Her younger sister did far better. Fanny Elssler was, as Heine put it, the "dancer of two hemispheres." Her feet, in blue silk dancing shoes, carried her to triumph over the whole world. "She was the most intellectual dancer I have ever seen," Charles Kemble declared of her. The Paris Opera Company paid her an annual salary of almost 50,000 francs. In 1840-1842, when she made her American tour, the critics spoke with admiration of the "Austrian suaveness" that characterized this dancer, in spite of her lofty intellectuality. Perhaps they sensed the "lavender fragrance of the Viennese spirit," that had clung to Haydn himself during his sojourn in England.

Part of Haydn's "tidying up" consisted of his arranging the facts of his life, as nearly as he could recall them. He had the good fortune to be blessed in his lifetime with three biographers, to whom he recounted the story of his life. There were the Saxon Legation Counsellor in Vienna, Georg August Griesinger, who died in 1828; the painter Albert C. Dies, of Hanover (1755-1832), and the writer Giuseppe Carpani (1752-1832), of Villalbese, near Como. Three more various personalities could scarcely have been found, and consequently their versions of Haydn's biography splendidly complement one another.

Griesinger was a diplomat—but, at the same time, he was somewhat more. As a typical diplomat, he might have stuck closely to dry-as-dust documents; but, instead, he went to the people, to the source of creative living and loving. The Saxon looked upon Haydn as that "charming genius of our Austrian neighbors." He was well aware of Haydn's crafty little ways of dealing with the problems of daily life, that boundless Austrian modesty relieved by a slight admixture of Austrian slyness. As an example of that personal modesty Griesinger cited the incident of Haydn's invitation to the coronation ceremonies for the Emperor Leopold, in 1790. Haydn was to ride to Prague with Mozart, but he refused, saying: "Where Mozart is present, Haydn cannot show himself." (It would, of course, have been highly ill advised for any third person to make such a remark—as Griesinger well knew.)

It is to Griesinger that we owe most of our information concerning Haydn's stay in England. The biographer, however, was committed to his own "high-brow" point of view. He remarked, "Scarcely anything in Haydn's London diaries would interest the reader." (Dies is guilty of the same folly, in writing "the small notebooks whose contents Haydn showed me contain little usable material.") Today, we are, of course, most interested in and most deeply moved by precisely these awkward, misspelled notes of Haydn, even where he wrote of entirely non-musical matters.

The warm-hearted Saxon devoted most attention to Haydn's old age, for it was in this period that the biographer came to know the master on an intimate basis. The traces of diminishing strength which Griesinger records arouse deep sympathy in the reader. Perhaps the most touching passage in the book is the one where Griesinger and Haydn sit silently together, and suddenly there flashes into Griesinger's mind certain words of Homer, words spoken by Agamemnon to Nestor:

> Heavy oppresses you the common burden of age. Oh Gods! Might it weigh on another and you walk about in your youth.

Dies, the fifty-year-old painter, was a person of quite another sort. When this gentleman from Hanover, armed with a letter of recommendation from Prince Nicholas Esterhazy, first called upon Haydn and explained his mission, Haydn tried to turn him away, protesting that his life was "not at all interesting." The painter did not perceive that this remark, like so many other of Haydn's remarks, was equivocal. To be sure, there was a direct honesty about it, but, on the other hand, such modesty was also intended to evoke contradiction. In any case, Haydn summoned up all his vivacity for this visitor, in order to make out a good case for his life.

Dies's thirty visits—we might call them "sittings"—were concentrated, in painter-fashion, between April 15, 1807, and August 8, 1808. He kept an account of each visit, and the descriptions of Haydn's appearance and health are especially valuable. Each time that Dies came, he saw the master in a new light, sometimes because of the way the weather affected him, sometimes because of Haydn's reaction to their conversation. Dies observed how successes, and kind or flattering letters from abroad, "electrified" Haydn's vital spirits. Often, however, Dies led the conversation into too abstract a mood. It was almost as hopeless to discuss the "theory of art" with Haydn as it would have been to talk Chinese to him. At such times "he grew weary and ended the conversation." This, however, did not happen often. Dies retained the sharp eyes of the painter, and he reproduced marvelously everything that he saw. He described how Haydn, dressed almost foppishly and wearing elegant shoes in spite of his swollen feet, came forward to greet him. This frail old gentleman with rococo manners belonged, the painter felt, to another age; thus, unlike Griesinger, Dies was prompted to ask many questions about Haydn's youth. He sat with closed eyes and absorbed the images of the places where Haydn had spent his early years—Rohrau, Hainburg, Vienna, Eisenstadt. When Dies began to write his book, he set down *scenes,* images. He even contrived to make the master's music visible. When, for example, he described how Kapellmeister Reuther taught little Haydn to sing a trill, he made the reader see the notes being formed in the boy's mouth, and, in addition, see the glowing crimson of the bowl of cherries before the lad. In this, Dies is a masterful writer.

This biographer zealously upheld the value of Haydn's ecclesiastical music; championship of it did not come hard to him, since he was a North German Protestant. Aware that Haydn's masses were being condemned in Vienna, he took appropriate steps to defend them. He asked permission to publish a letter from Zelter which Haydn had proudly and gladly showed to him. It was the memorable letter of March 16, 1804, in which Zelter, director of the Berlin Liedertafel, begged Haydn to leave Vienna and make his residence in Berlin, "the Haydn city." Zelter had just arranged two of Haydn's songs, *Abendlied,* and *Danklied an Gott,* for mass choruses. "If only I could afford you the pleasure of hearing your choruses sung here! You would find edifying, indeed, the tranquillity, the reverence, purity, and sacredness with which they are sung. The flower of Berlin youth stand here, together with their fathers and mothers, as if in a sky full of angels, celebrating in joyful eulogy the honor of the Almighty and practicing the works of the greatest master of the art of music that the world has ever seen. Oh, come to us, come! *You will be received like a God among men.* We will sing for you a Gloria that will make your venerable gray hair flower into a laurel wreath[!]" The letter would have given greater joy had it come twenty years earlier, when the Berlin critics had been, for the most part, niggardly in their praise of Haydn. But this time he could no longer travel.

The most gifted of the biographers was the Italian, Giuseppe Carpani. He was a professional writer and well grounded in classical tradition. He could, at will, write prose that rang out like that of Caesar or Tacitus. "Like Minerva from the head of Zeus, so instrumental music sprang full blown and beautiful from the mind of a single man." The metaphor is neither original nor accurate, but there is the bestowal of high praise. The author of this and similar sentences wrote in the tradition of the "great eulogists," so that his eloquence far surpassed that of the diplomat and that of the painter. Carpani's characterizations are often excellent. Of Haydn's ancestors he said: *Nacquero, vissero, e morirono: eccovi la loro biographia.* ("They were born, lived, died; such is their biography.") A more trenchant formulation cannot be found. And Carpani could even be witty: *Col Handel in capo, e di molte ghinee de la borsa, usci Haydn dalla fumosa Londra.* ("With Handel on his mind and a good many guineas in his purse, Haydn emerged from the London fog.")

Carpani was the most musical of the three biographers. Although, as he was an Italian, his *point d'appui* was vocal music, he understood that Haydn could make the orchestra "sing." Unquestionably, Haydn's music meant much to him. Thus, for example, he records the remarkable fact that in 1799, when he lay abed with a high fever, he got up, in spite of his weakness, in order to hear a Haydn mass; and the music, he declared, produced such a contraction of his muscles that he broke out into profuse perspiration and became well instantly. (Here Carpani was like van Swieten, the physician's son, who wrote a dissertation on "Music and the Art of Healing." Even the unimaginative Dutchman believed in the mysterious healing powers of music.)

Carpani was shrewd enough as a writer to know that his style had its drawbacks. Since his book is heavily weighted with pathos and rhetoric, he supplied his "Giuseppe Haydn" with a good many bizarre and comical traits. At one time he went so far as to call his subject a *natura di buffone*.

One wishes, however, that Carpani had been a more reliable biographer. It is unfortunate that, as Mendel and Reissmann point out, for many years the Carpani biography served as the chief source book on Haydn's life. The other two biographers are far more dependable. For example, Carpani claims that Haydn had said to him: "I cannot compose at all unless I feel on my finger the ring given me by Frederick William of Prussia. If I forget to put it on in the morning, all my *verve* fades and my thoughts vanish." Who was the snob with whom Carpani confused Haydn?

In another respect, however, Haydn would have been very pleased with Carpani's memorial had he lived to see it. (It was published three years after the master's death.) Carpani spoke of him as if Haydn had been an Italian. The fact that he was born in the North was an insignificant accident; Carpani spirits him away to a typical Italian apotheosis. The biographer sees Handel as the musical Michelangelo. Hasse as another Rubens, Gluck as Caravaggio, Salieri as Annibale Caracci. He compares Mozart with Giulio Romano, and Haydn with Tintoretto! Haydn, certainly, would have been impressed by Carpani's ingenuity in comparing the great masters of music with the great painters.

Curiously enough, Carpani did not gather sufficient material to fill out his book, and, in consequence, engaged in some utterly nonsensical padding. There is one instance in his making an elaborate parallel between Haydn and the Austrian Field Marshal Laudon, with whom the composer had nothing at all in common beyond nationality. Haydn had, to be sure, dedicated a symphony to the famous old soldier, but that meant no more than did Beethoven's dedication of a sonata to Sonnenfels; it was a mere act of politeness. Carpani could not help realizing that this analogy was far fetched. He withdrew it, in a manner as amusing as it was impudent. The passage closes thus: "Haydn was the personification of music, Laudon the personification of war. Otherwise, both of them were profoundly ignorant of all the rest of life. Take them out of their profession and—without affecting their true greatness—you may well call them *two famous idiots*."

But Haydn, so "profoundly ignorant of all the rest of life" and nevertheless a keen observer of human nature, had earlier made fun of Carpani, after his own fashion. Carpani correctly reported that "Haydn invented all sorts of stories to gull the gullible, and if they succumbed to these traps for the unwary, he enjoyed laughing at them, among his friends." But it never occurred to Carpani that he himself had been taken in. For it was for Carpani—for Carpani alone and not for Dies or Griesinger—that Haydn elaborated that "precious" fairy tale about the *America Symphony*—that "famous" bit of program music that he, of course, had never written. "One day I imagined a friend, rich in a large family and poor in wordly goods, setting out for America to improve his circumstances, succeeding in his project, and returning in safety." When Carpani urged him to describe how he had worked out this idea, Haydn went to the piano and explained, with musical illustrations, the "principal vicissitudes of this enormous enterprise." The symphony had a program that described the smallest details: Embarkation of the adventurer; departure of the vessel with a favorable wind, amid the lamentations of the family and the good wishes of the friends on shore; a prosperous voyage; arrival in a strange land; barbarous sounds, dances and voices (about the middle of the symphony); after an advantageous exchange of merchandise the homeward voyage is entered upon; propitious winds blow (return of the first motif of the symphony); then a terrible storm supervenes (a confusion of tones and chords); cries of the passengers, roaring of the sea, whistling of the wind—the melody passes from the chromatic to the pathetic—; fear and anxiety of the wretched voyagers—augmented and diminished chords and semi-tone modulations; the elements become calm again; the wished-for home country is reached; joyful reception by family and friends; general happiness.

It is incredible that Carpani did not observe the twinkle in Haydn's eyes as he unfolded this tale. Later, when the Italian was congratulated by his friends for making such a "find" and was asked for the opus number of the symphony, it appeared that the old master had apparently "forgotten" to mention which symphony it was. The symphonies were examined for some such program material, but nothing was found that remotely resembled it.

Naturally, nothing was found—for Haydn's *America Symphony* had never existed.

THE FRENCH IN VIENNA

Haydn was still busy with his *Verzeychnis,* his inventory, when the French marched into Vienna on November 13, 1805. Never before had a war been begun so swiftly, nor lost more swiftly.

In October, a large part of the Austrian army had surrendered at Ulm. On December 2, Napoleon shattered the rest of the Austrian forces, as well as the Russians who had hastened to their aid, at the battle of Austerlitz. In the meantime, the Emperor Francis, fleeing to Hungary, had declared his capital an open city.

Haydn, peering from his window, saw foreign dragoons, hussars, infantry, artillery and sappers marching by his door. The calamity that had been dreaded for nine years had at last descended upon Vienna, but not in the same dreaded form. It was no Revolutionary army that entered the city, for the remnants of the Jacobins had long since been purged by Napoleon. His was an imperial army, and outwardly a well disciplined one. It was bent on demonstrating to the Austrians the significance of Napoleon's "new order." No one had to fear for his life or property; only the state treasury and the Viennese secret police, the terror of decent citizens, were affected. For nine years the secret police had harried, arrested, and ruined all progressives, everyone tainted with "Josephan" ideas from university professors to the meekest artisans. Now the same police had fled or else (since spying was their profession) had made common cause with the French.

The fact that the French had been hated was advisedly forgotten. The censorship was lifted, or replaced by a new one. The theaters performed whatever they pleased; foreign newspapers poured into the city; the lodges of the Freemasons were reopened.

Almost as soon as the French entered Vienna, old Haydn received an official visit at his home. Two famous men, the heads of Napoleon's military bureaucracy, called upon him. They were Charles Jean-de-Dieu Soult (1769-1859), Marshal of France, who, a few years later became Duke of Dalmatia, and Hughes Bernard Maret (1763-1839), later Duke of Bassano, lawyer, politician and Napoleon's right-hand man, who conducted the French emperor's official correspondence and helped to draw up all the battle communiqués.

What did this pair want of Haydn? Soult, the victor of Austerlitz, was at that time thirty-six. He was a typical trooper, an ill-known "lover of paintings" which he used to snatch away from conquered countries, and altogether unmusical. He probably could scarcely distinguish a flute from a horn. Maret was a person of quite a different sort. Since, in 1793, as a French Ambassador to neutral Switzerland, he had been kidnaped by Austrian agents, chained and carried off to Emperor Francis' country where he had been held in dungeons, infested by malaria, he had sworn terrible vengeance to every Austrian "he would catch." However, when in 1805 he came to Austria as a conqueror, he was prematurely aged, and melancholy in temperament, and he harmed no one. Moreover, he was a very musical man, and wrote poems and plays. We may easily imagine his feelings as he sat facing Haydn—the Haydn who had written *The Creation* and whose music had helped to save his master's life at the time of the explosion in Paris.

To receive these influential foreigners, Haydn had donned his most elegant costume, including a jacket of coffee-brown cloth, embroidered vest and cuffs, and, for cravat, a white scarf with a gold buckle. His breeches were of black silk, which contrasted with his white stockings and the black shoes with large, curved silver buckles. His wig was large and old-fashioned; the white hair fell far down over his high forehead. On a small table beside him lay his hat and the white leather gloves without which no apparel was complete. He sat in an easy chair (he could no longer stand up without help), and turned his head attentively toward the visitors. (Hugo Botstiber, who supplemented Pohl's voluminous biography of Haydn, confused Maret with Marat, the terrorist of the Revolution—who could not have visited Haydn in 1805, for in 1793 he had been assassinated by Charlotte Corday. While he was about it, Botstiber added to the confusion by identifying the other visitor as "a music-loving officer named Soulte." He might easily have found the correct name by reading Griesinger. As a diplomat, Haydn's biographer Griesinger was, of course, professionally interested in this visit, and took note of the names in Haydn's visitors' book.)

We do not know the aim of the visit by the two Frenchmen.

Maret and Soult may have come to inform Haydn that he, as a member of the French Academy, was entitled to armed protection by the French. Or, perhaps, they merely wished to ask after his health and to find out whether he were "really still alive." This was apparently a matter of doubt. In February, 1805, a rumor started in London and reached Paris, to the effect that "Papa Haydn" was dead. It was immediately believed. It was even believed in Vienna, where investigation could not have been very difficult. The Viennese must have known that it was "Hansl," Johann Evangelist Haydn, who had just died. The report had made a deep impression in Parisian musical circles. Luigi Cherubini, with tear-stained face, sat down and composed a cantata of mourning for the *Padre della musica.* With its gloomy, plaintive motifs in the horns and woodwinds, it turned out to be a work on a par with that of Haydn himself. When, in C-major *maestoso,* a female voice conveyed to Haydn an assurance of immortality:

> Nay, this creative fire, this living spark
> Cannot be imprisoned within cold monuments!
> His soul is as immortal as his famous name—
> Both overcome death and time

the modest old man might have nodded melancholically. A memorial meeting was prepared, to be held in Nôtre Dame, the archbishop (who, after Napoleon's reconciliation with the Pope, resided again in Paris) was to read the mass—when the welcome report arrived, that Haydn was living and in good health.

This last assertion was not true. For more than a year, Haydn had been unable to leave his house, except for rare and brief drives in a carriage. Maret reported to his emperor that Haydn was failing. It was, of course, Napoleon who had sent the visitors; he himself resided in Schoenbrunn and came seldom to Vienna. Perhaps Haydn's illness served the master a good turn at this juncture. Otherwise, he might have become Maret's "big Austrian catch" and, above all, a victim of Napoleon's ruthless politics in regard to music.

It was, indeed, an utterly strange world from which these two messengers of Napoleon had emerged, a world in which there was taking shape the first attempt at a totalitarian state in modern times. And this brief endeavor of the French emperor heavily burdened both music and musicians.

It is a mistake to imagine that music does exist in a political vacuum. "Music" Oscar Fleischer declared in his sensational essay (1902) on *Napoleon Bonaparte's Musical Politics,* "was thought of, by the philosophers of old China and by the Greek Pythagoreans, as the cement binding all governmental orders. Music was allegedly the mysterious power which maintained all mobile things, including men, in a satisfying relationship which, without restricting their mobility, excluded disturbing factors." That is to say, music had *always* constituted one of the instruments of politics, and no political system, once it had developed beyond a mere *laisser aller* into a tightly knit organization, could do without its own particular music. In antiquity and in the Middle Ages this fact was accepted as a matter of course. In modern times, Napoleon was the first to recognize the necessity for employing music as an adjunct to his other methods of governing his subjects. From 1800 to 1813, he devoted considerable effort to finding *his* music—that is, to finding a composer who could write it. If he had found such a man, he would unquestionably have conferred upon him an official post comparable to that of a minister of education.

The kind of music Napoleon sought was "Empire" music, embodied in a heroic opera which should be, at the same time an opera extolling "order." Such ideas may smell of Wagner today, but then they really were Napoleon's own. Since he had heard *The Creation,* the dictator had ceased to be a man whose use for music was limited to having something "to whistle while shaving." He needed music now for governing, for integrating his régime, for keeping it running without friction. For if he did nothing, his enemies would take advantage of the power of music. The great success of Grétry's opera, *Guillaume Tell,* telling the story of a tyrannicide, had proved that the hearts of the Parisian populace were still imbued with the republican ideal and Paris was always scheming and plotting!

Napoleon's attempt failed inevitably because he, like most men of violence, was fundamentally unmusical. It is inherent in music that it cannot be seized by violence or obtained by bribery—not even if musicians are kidnapped or seduced with honorific titles and high salaries. If the dictator had had even the slightest understanding of the devout and epic peacefulness of Haydn's music, he would not, during the weeks after the unsuccessful bomb plot, have seriously considered bringing Haydn to Paris. One of the principal reasons for not doing so was the fact that Cherubini, the hated republican, protected Haydn.

So Napoleon had to procure otherwhere his *Musique de l'empire.* Unabashedly, he urged the great Italian composer, Paisiello, to write, in 1804, for his coming coronation a kind of "church music which would suffice for the Catholic ritual and at the same time be thoroughly French and nationalistic." He got it; but, seeing that Paisiello was already too old for being worth the enormous annual salary of 80,000 francs, the emperor turned to Jean François Lesueur, pre-Wagnerian inventor of the *leitmotiv,* and made him the head of the Conservatoire as well as of the Opera. He instructed this composer to write also a heroic work for the Opera, *The Bards.* But Parisians did not like it. They stayed away from the theater, and Lesueur fell into disfavor.

The same thing occurred in the case of the young Italian composer Ferdinando Paër, and his heroic opera, *Achille.* Subsequently, in the last of his dictatorial ventures into the field of music, Napoleon was tamed—or, rather cheated—by the dauntless Gasparo Spontini. When this composer received an *ordre de bataille* to "treat of a Spanish subject" on the eve of the war with Spain, the Chevalier Spontini made a boomerang of the whole project. For the music he wrote to *Ferdinand Cortez* was so grandiose that the war-weary Parisians loudly and provokingly cheered those fiends, the Spanish characters, on the open stage. This was tantamount to high treason!

Nevertheless in those years Napoleon's will was law throughout Europe, Haydn was, therefore, somewhat precariously situated when, in 1805, two of the heads of Napoleon's military bureaucracy put in their surprising appearance at his home. It was during those very months, at the end of 1805, that the French were beginning to seize forcibly singing teachers and instrumentalists, just as they were plundering the museums and libraries of all Europe for the benefit of Paris. Immediately after Austerlitz, Napoleon took possession of the Austrian Empress' singing teacher, Girolamo Crescentini. For not obeying an order of Napoleon, Director Zingarelli of the Vatican Chapel, was seized in Rome and dragged off to Paris.

And what about Beethoven? He—and perhaps he alone—could have fulfilled the emperor's dream of a truly imperial music. But Napoleon did not know of his existence; and if he had, Beethoven's music would have sounded too Teutonic for his ear. With Haydn, however, it was another case. Only the fact that the master was far too old to supply the emperor's needs protected him, we may be sure, from the fate of dying in a "gilded cage."

FAREWELL TO THE WORLD

AFTER the departure of the French and the unhappy peace of Pressburg, in 1806, the master's health deteriorated. His nasal polyp inflicted suffering on him, but it was too late for operation. ("I *shall* have to take my foe to the grave with me," he complained, wryly, quoting Dr. Hunter of London.) In addition, his legs and feet troubled him greatly; they were constantly swollen. In 1807 and 1808, both times on the occasion of the Festival of Saint Peregrinus, the patron of those who suffered from orthopedic afflictions, he had himself carried into the Servite Monastery. The throng of loudly praying cripples, swaying on their crutches, shocked him terribly, and the consciousness that he shared their suffering afflicted him. Both times he returned home in a melancholy mood. It was about this time that he had printed a visiting card bearing the first two lines of his song *Der Greis.* They were *molto adagio: "Hin ist alle meine Kraft; alt und schwach bin ich."* (*"Fled is all my strength; I am old and feeble."*) It bore the name, "Joseph Haydn." And yet, visitors always found him dressed carefully "as if on the point of going out."

There were many visitors. European celebrities, music lovers and virtuosos, left their cards with him. There were famous Frenchmen, such as the violinist Baillot, who embraced Haydn so cordially that he almost crushed him. Pleyel and Cherubini also came. Haydn had not seen Pleyel since the days in London, for the Austrian police had refused to admit Pleyel in 1800, when he entertained the hope of taking Haydn back to Paris with him. As for Cherubini, this was Haydn's first meeting with him, and the master was amazed to find him "such a handsome little man." There were Cherubini Weeks in Vienna which Beethoven, for one, thoroughly enjoyed. The composer of *Fidelio* considered Cherubini the greatest operatic composer of the time. Haydn, however, was unable to attend the performances of Cherubini's operas, *Lodoiska, Faniska,* and *The Water Bearer:* going out was much too tiring for him. Cherubini demurred at dedicating any of these operas to Haydn; it would be presumption, he declared. He called himself a "son of Haydn" who was far from equal to the father. Haydn smiled and presented to the visitor the original manuscript of his *Drum Roll Symphony* (No. 103); Haydn signed himself, *"Padre del celebre Cherubini."*

Russians, Dutchmen, and Swedes also paid their respects. Haydn's music had received many performances in Sweden since the *Kunglike Akademieen,* the Royal Academy in Stockholm, had elected him an honorary member. Even in the Swedish provinces (such as the Baltic Island of Ruegen, which at that time belonged to Sweden), his music was performed frequently. The Swedish author Silverstolpe told, half a century later, how interested Haydn had been in this distant world of the North. Silverstolpe also described an occasion when he had been present to hear Haydn bestow paternal advice upon a young composer—"rests are, of course, the hardest things to write," Haydn had joked. Then he had continued, in a more serious vein, "but if I get hold of an idea that is only half formulated, I try to stick to it for awhile."

The majority of Haydn's callers came from Germany. There, Breitkopf and Haertel, in Leipsic, had published Haydn's major works, while the critic, Friedrich Rochlitz, had commented upon them, extensively and well, in the *Allgemeine Musikalische Zeitung.* As a result, Leipsic had become a city virtually devoted to Haydn. Another visitor from North Germany, was I. F. Reichardt, a popular composer of *Lieder* and a talented author of memoirs. The great stage director, Iffland, also came; and Felix Mendelssohns's aunt, Sara Levi, who arrived from Berlin equipped with a letter of introduction from Zelter. Haydn presented to her the original of the *Heiligmesse.* Another reverent visitor was sixteen-year-old Carl Maria von Weber, whose *Freischutz* was later to outshine the works of all the Cherubinis in the world.

Almost all these visits took the same course. For about half an hour Haydn would chat animatedly; then he would relapse into melancholy. Any small matter, such as the mere mention of Mozart's name, would make him burst into tears. Or else he would begin to weep whenever he opened the box containing his medals, to show them to visitors. An incautious question could start him sobbing—for example, Wenzel Tomaschek, a Czech composer, innocently inquired whose bust it was that stood in the vestibule. "My best friend, the sculptor Fischer," Haydn lamented; "he's dead now. Almighty God, why dost Thou not take me to Thee?"

But these tears frequently sprang from a nobler impulse than self-pity. When Iffland informed him that a charity performance of *The Creation* in Berlin had netted 2,000 taler, Haydn exclaimed, tearfully, "Elssler, do you hear? Two thousand taler for the poor—two thousand taler—my *Creation!*" And he remained agitated for some time. When these visitors took their leave, Haydn offered his hand to be kissed, and he actually sulked if the proferred hand was not instantly taken up. There was in this, evidence of senility; often he seemed to be confusing himself with a princely personage. As a rule, he was quite bewildered about persons. If someone spoke of Prince Esterhazy, Haydn was not sure which one was meant, Paul Anton, his first employer, Nicholas the Splendid, or the latter's son Anton, or the contemporary Esterhazy, the grandson, Nicholas the Second.

Naturally, he received countless visits from Viennese artists. It would be tempting to imagine calls from Beethoven, but, unfortunately, there is no evidence. We should certainly know it if Beethoven had visited Haydn. The two had mutual acquaintances, such as Zmeskall von Domanovicz and the composer Weigl, who might have recorded visits.

There had been no open break between Haydn and Beethoven, but the two composers had been definitely alienated since Beethoven had made deprecatory remarks about the "animal portraits" in *The Creation*—although it was a work which, in general, he sincerely admired. In gossipy Vienna such criticism could not remain secret. Haydn had all the more reason for resentment since the younger composer's first and second symphonies (not to speak of his earlier works) had distinctly demonstrated their great debt, in form and language, to the art of Haydn. In 1801, when the latter met Beethoven at a social gathering, the younger man asked: " 'Papa,' have you heard my ballet, *The Creatures of Prometheus?*" Then, in an access of embarrassment, he added, "Of course, it hasn't exactly turned out to be a *Creation.*" Whereupon Haydn replied, with unusual sharpness, "No one expected it to."

Only resentment could have produced such a remark; otherwise Haydn would never have passed so uncivil a judgment upon *Prometheus* which, although it was a light ballet (Beethoven's only one), contained such significant ideas as:

the one immortal feature which he later incorporated in one of the leading passages of the *Eroica.*

Haydn may also have been astonished and taken aback to learn that this young man, who in point of age might easily have been his grandson, had attempted an oratorio so soon after the overwhelming success of *The Creation.* Beethoven's *Christ on the Mount of Olives* was not received too well. Many religious persons objected to the appearance of Christ Himself on the stage in the oratorio, and even the musical *cognoscenti* did not appreciate the novelty and significance of the work. Cryptically, Beethoven had incorporated his own growing fear of deafness into the passage describing the anxiety of Christ in prayer. It was in 1801 that he first realized what his fate would be, and determined to fight it, to "grip fate by the throat." His only ally in this contest with destiny was his music, and it was this, alas, that was also endangered, for after the summer of 1802 Beethoven could no longer hear high notes. He had already begun to avoid people, in order to conceal his ailment; and this, too, was probably a contributing factor in his failure to call on Haydn.

In any case, the two had parted company in their respective musical aspirations; moreover, their characters were by now even more divergent than they had been when Beethoven was pupil and Haydn teacher. The man who wrote to a disciple, "*Power* is the morality of men who stand out from the rest, and it is also mine," could no longer have anything in common with the old Haydn who bowed to God's will in everything and spent his last years in a mood of lamentation.

And yet all these differences vanished on the day when Haydn bade the world farewell, on that notable twenty-seventh of March, 1808. Then we see Beethoven, the man of power, bowing before a feeble old man.

It had been widely feared that Haydn's death was imminent. In order to rejoice the master's heart once more, a committee of ladies of high society was formed. It consisted of Princess Marie Hermenegildis Esterhazy, the pianist Magdalena von Kurzböck, Baroness Spielmann, and the wife of Baron Pereira, the well known Jewish patron of the arts and sciences. They arranged for another performance of *The Creation* in the University auditorium. The work was to be given in Italian, so that it was, in a sense, a first performance; *Il Creazione del Mondo,* it was called in Carpani's translation.

The devoted women assembled everyone of note in the artistic world of Vienna. Hundreds of persons filled the hall. (The Princess Esterhazy had Balthasar Wiegand paint the gathering; the painting was then affixed to the cover of a chest, and given to the old master. It showed more than two hundred individual heads in portrait.) In order not to excite Haydn needlessly, he was not informed until the last moment before the performance. Then the Princess Esterhazy's carriage called for him. Before the University gates he was met by the rector, Count Herrschan, and a number of musicians. Among them was Beethoven.

Deathly pale, Haydn was seated in a litter and carried into the hall. He shrank, affrighted by the noise, the cheers, the clapping, and the high-pitched flourishes of the instruments. Once again he felt like the eight-year-old boy he had been when he first entered Vienna. (Later, at sixty, the first sight of London had similarly alarmed him.) He trembled all over, and had an impulse to cover his face with his hands. Who were they, this horde of strangers? And yet he knew them all so well. Wasn't that van Swieten over there? But no; van Swieten had been dead five years. Then it must be Sonnenfels, who was his own age; yes, Sonnenfels didn't know how to die. And this beautiful white-haired lady—oh, yes, that was Marianne Martinez, to whom he had given piano lessons sixty years ago. But how was it that his friends from London, Gyrowetz and Clément, were here? How kind of them! If only the crowd did not make so much noise!

At last the audience settled down. Haydn was placed in the first row, directly in front of the orchestra. A wave of awe swept through the hall. The master was not yet eighty—and yet he looked a hundred years old! This man with the waxen face *was* the eighteenth century—the flutes, the silver candelabra, the elegant diplomacy—he embodied an age scarcely conceivable in these early days of the nineteenth century. When Haydn was born, Charles VI had still been alive—that Charles who was the almost legendary emperor of the late baroque age, and at whose Austrian court Spanish had been spoken. Then Maria Theresa had come; she had lost three wars to Prussia, but had conquered the heart of the world. Her daughter, Marie Antoinette, had been married to the French dauphin, and had later lost her throne and head. Joseph II, too, the humanitarian, the rationalist emperor, the contender with the papacy and the monks, had passed away. Leopold II was also dead, and now *der gute Kaiser Franz* had been reigning for a full sixteen years. All these things Haydn, with his supernatural vitality, had survived. Must he not really be a hundred years old?

The performance began. Salieri conducted an orchestra of fifty; Konradin Kreutzer played the piano; the solo parts were sung by three singers from the Court Theater—Fischer, Weinmueller, and Radichi. When the audience interrupted the passage, "Let there be light," with enthusiastic applause, as was the custom, Haydn pointed a trembling hand upward. "Not I, but a power above, created that!" he exclaimed. There was such tumult in the hall that the performance could scarcely continue.

At the end of the first part, when those standing near came forward to congratulate the composer, they found that he had fainted. Hummel and Gyrowetz hurried out to fetch water. According to some accounts, it was wine that was given to Haydn. He recovered at once, and began speaking in a feeble voice. "Don't you see that he's shivering with cold?" the French ambassador exclaimed. Going closer, he saw with deep emotion that the sole decoration worn by the old man was that of the French Academy. "You deserve to possess all the decorations in the world!" the ambassador said, as he clasped Haydn's hand. At his cry that the master was cold, ladies standing near took off their shawls and furs and covered Haydn's feet.

The intermission was nearing its end, and it was almost time for the second part to begin. But Cappelliani, an Italian physician, sternly insisted that Haydn must not stay any longer. The litter bearers therefore raised him, to carry him out. This proved difficult, however. There now ensued a "tumult of love" which has been eloquently described by Heinrich von Collin, in a long poem. The people would not let Haydn go; they fought to keep him. Beethoven thrust his way through the throng. Overcome with emotion, he knelt beside Haydn's litter, and covered the master's limp hand with kisses.

What a moment this was! The old man, who had given so much, no longer had anything to give to this man who knelt beside him. Beethoven had already composed three *Leonore* overtures, *Fidelio,* the opera of liberation, the Fourth and the Fifth Symphonies, the *Waldstein Sonata,* and *Coriolanus*—truly Promethean creations in which only a few signs of Haydn's heritage were left. Beethoven had begotten these works in a mystical marriage with the *élan terrible* of the Revolution. And yet he knelt before Haydn as a man might kneel before the portraits of his ancestors, or in taking leave of his own youth.

Enough! The litter bearers at last made their way to the exit. "Farewell, 'Papa,' God bless you!" people on all sides sobbed. They felt that Haydn was among them for the last time—and they felt as if "Austria's good spirit" were departing with him. As the litter reached the door, Haydn turned around once more, and, with a painful gesture, stretched out his hand in blessing.

DEATH

Now there remained only the process of dying—but, almost incredibly, Haydn lived on for fourteen months. A hardy offspring of Mother Earth, he resisted dissolution. It seemed as if Haydn could die only in time of war. And another war was in the making.

The war of 1809 was like an unequal combat between a wholly untrained man and a healthy pugilist who had behind him, moreover, the backing of all the world. Besides Austria's little army also burghers, peasants, and students revolted against Napoleon, only to experience a defeat worse than that of four years before.

This time the French army did not march peacefully to the heart of the capital. Street fighting broke out, but the French—bleeding, hot, and furiously embittered—pushed their way in, through the suburbs. Haydn's modest dwelling was situated near the Gumpendorf Church. Neighboring houses were already afire, and Viennese militia, guns in hand, tramped through Haydn's garden.

The old man had steadfastly refused to leave his imperiled home and move into the city apartment of Fräulein von Kurzböck. His feeling for order revolted against such a step. He was now completely helpless, and had to be lifted from his bed in the morning, by his servant and the cook. Was he to allow strangers—strange women, no less—to witness the misery of his old age? His pupil Neukomm, a Frenchman, who had cared for him during the winter, had been forced to leave when the war broke out. For weeks now Haydn had seen only two men, I. C. Rosenbaum, son-in-law of his old friend the deceased composer Gassmann, and Prince Esterhazy's personal physician, Doctor von Hohenholtz. Haydn had bidden a tender good-bye to G. A. Griesinger, the Saxon Consul, who had also had to leave Vienna, for the King of Saxony was fighting on the side of Napoleon. War between those good old neighbors, Saxony and Austria, seemed truly to prefigure the end of the world. Haydn wept when Griesinger departed; if Leipsic, the city of publishers, were now to be enemy territory, he would receive no money—perhaps not for a long time. Haydn became obsessed by the delusion that he would starve; although his money was secure with Fries and Company and other banks, he sent Johann Elssler to a pawnshop to pawn rings and watches.

On May 10 the French took Schoenbrunn. On May 11, at nine at night, the bombardment of Vienna began; all night long, shot and shell poured into the city. The following morning grapeshot fell in Haydn's garden, "just as we were busy getting our good 'Papa' out of bed," Elssler wrote to Griesinger. "The air pressure of the explosion forced open the bedroom door, and all the windows shook. Our good 'Papa' started in alarm at this, but then he cried out in a loud voice, 'Don't be afraid, children; where Haydn is, nothing can happen.' " Fear belied his words; he was trembling violently.

On the following morning, when Vienna surrendered, Haydn was very weak, but Elssler administered tonics which revived him. Weak as he was, he had them carry him, thrice daily, to the small piano in the living room, so that he might play the imperial anthem. As he played he murmured earnestly, "God preserve my Emperor Francis!" He played the anthem for the last time at one o'clock in the afternoon on May 26—three times in succession, and with wonderful expressiveness. "It's a long time since I played the song like that," he said, apparently astonished and with joy in his eyes.

At two o'clock the household was sent into a flurry of alarm, when a French officer came prancing up, hitched his horse to the post, and knocked on the door with the handle of his dagger. Elssler's child, who was visiting, began to cry; Haydn's English parrot shrieked piercingly; and the din awoke Haydn from his afternoon nap. Elssler and Anna Kremnitzer, the cook, decided not to open the door. The mounted man might be a pillager, and there were many valuables in the house. However, the foreign officer continued to knock, more and more vehemently. Finally, the trembling servant opened the door to him. A tall, handsome man, with deeply tanned face and wavy chestnut hair, stood at the portal; his green and red uniform glistened with medals and ornaments. "Why didn't you open sooner?" the Frenchman asked in some perplexity. "We speak no French," Elssler mumbled. Scarcely had he finished his sentence before he heard, "Sono amico." The stranger asked in Italian whether *il celeberrimo Haydn* lived here.

The heavenly Italian language! Nothing could have been more

reassuring, at so anxious a moment, than the mellifluous Italian. The servants stepped aside as the visitor hastened past them toward Haydn's door. "I just want to glance through the keyhole," he explained, humbly.

"Come in," Haydn called out, in Italian.

The stranger opened the door, and introduced himself as Captain of Hussars Clément Soulémy, singer and music lover. He was not an Italian, but he came from a region of Southern France in which much Italian was spoken. He asked, as the greatest favor the master could grant, for permission to perform the aria from *The Creation,* "In native worth and honor clad." Would Haydn accompany him? Delighted and seemingly reinvigorated, Haydn agreed. Although he was in his night shirt, he had the servants carry him to the piano in the adjoining room. In a fine, resonant voice the stranger began:

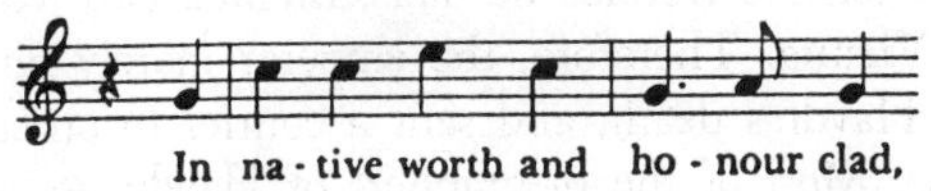

"And in his eyes with brightness shone the soul, the breath and image of his God!" The two men burst into tears as both thought of the humiliation of the soul of man—now, created to rule the earth, he abused his power by killing his fellows. Haydn and the Frenchman embraced and kissed each other. Then Soulémy hurried away. According to the record, he fell at Wagram.

This visit was Haydn's last great pleasure. The rest is matter for legends. One of these recounts how two days before his death he was visited by Friedrich Staps, the son of a North German preacher. The young man had planned to assassinate Napoleon, and, it is said, told his plan to Haydn. The dying old composer is said to have told him the story of the Paris performance of *The Creation,* and to have warned him not to sully the cause of national liberation by base murder—even the demon of evil must go unharmed until God appoints the time of his defeat. This argument is supposed to have persuaded Staps to give up his plan. The story is a fabrication; half a year later Friedrich Staps actually attempted the assassination in the Palace of Shoenbrunn, and at the trial, where he was condemned to death, no mention was made of Haydn. The latter never saw Staps—but the minds of men enjoy recapitulations. Although Heraclitus insisted that no moment can be lived twice, the symphonic movement of world history requires reprises of themes; Haydn's contemporaries liked to believe that the master had decisively intervened in Napoleon's fate a second time.

At one o'clock in the morning of May 31, 1809, Haydn died; he passed away peacefully in his sleep while Anna, the cook, held his hand. On the day before, two doctors, Hohenholtz and Boehm, had decided that he was very weak, but not in danger.

In the morning, Elssler went to the police station to report the death. The police at once sent word to the French occupation authorities; Maret, Duke of Bassano, was immediately informed, and he, in his turn, told Napoleon.

This day was sad for Napoleon. A few hours after Haydn's decease the emperor's old comrade in arms, Marshal Lannes, had succumbed to the terrible wounds he had sustained two weeks earlier in the battle of Vienna. Therefore, the emperor merely nodded silently when told of Haydn's death, and sent a courier to order a guard for Haydn's house. Most of the biographers of Haydn assert that Napoleon had earlier placed a guard of honor before the composer's house, as a gesture of respect. This is not likely. However, in guarding the house after Haydn's death, Napoleon was sensibly safeguarding Haydn's valuables and invaluable manuscripts.

When Elssler saw the guard approaching—mustachioed grenadiers, fur hats strapped to the chin—he was apparently overcome by panic. Up to this moment he had been quite level headed; he had laid out the body and had sent for a sculptor to take the death mask (or perhaps had done this himself). But now his nerves gave way completely and he, the only man in the house, left it in charge of the cook, the servant maid and one of Haydn's nieces, and vanished for three days. He was found at last by Andreas Streicher, a friend of Haydn's old age, who managed to extract from the servant the story of what had actually happened. Meanwhile, Haydn had been buried in the Hundsthurm Cemetery.

Vienna knew nothing of his death. The poor, confused Elssler took refuge with his wife; he had informed no one at all. The foreign soldiers frightened away the neighbors, and only a handful of persons followed Haydn's coffin to its resting place. We do not even know the name of the priest who conducted the services. One of Haydn's closer friends, the ubiquitous Rosenbaum, was there and wrote in his diary,

"Not a single conductor in Vienna was in the funeral train." As we shall see, we have good reason to wish that Rosenbaum himself had been journeying to hell, rather than following Haydn's casket.

Paris heard of Haydn's death while Vienna remained in ignorance of it. The *Moniteur* reported that *Joseph Haydn, le célèbre compositeur, membre de l'Institut Français,* had departed this life. When, in Vienna, Maret, Napoleon's Minister of Publication, saw in black and white the announcement he himself had earlier given out, he felt that the occupation authorities ought to conduct some kind of memorial service. But Maret had on his mind some complicated political problems; he therefore turned over the arrangements to Baron Vivant Denon.

BIZARRE AFTERMATH

VIVANT DENON (1747-1825), *littérateur fameux*—and even more notorious as an *homme à femmes*—was a painter and an engraver on copper. In 1797 he joined Napoleon's Egyptian expedition, and he catalogued French archaeological findings in the valley of the Nile. From archaeology he turned to politics. In 1804 he became Director General of French Museums, and in this capacity accompanied the emperor on all his campaigns. Wherever he went he plundered the treasuries of the art of Europe, for the benefit of the Louvre. His presence in Vienna boded no good to that city.

In the matter of honoring Haydn, however, Denon acted with good taste. He called upon a musicians' society of which Haydn had been a member to assist him in preparing the memorial service. The outcome was the receipt by many Viennese of printed invitations to a service to be held at ten o'clock in the morning on June 15, in the *Schottenkirche*.

The church was draped in black and illuminated by many candles. Denon had had placed in the center an artistically arranged cenotaph—an empty coffin heaped with laurel wreaths. On it were displayed eight of Haydn's medals; those from France, Russia, Austria, and Holland. England was represented solely by a small ivory trinket which had been very dear to Haydn; it had served him as a pass to the London concerts. Around the bier stood the French guard—as though guarding Haydn against the Viennese. The soldiers, presenting their bayonets, stood like a wall of steel. Denon had hesitantly consented to the presence of the Vienna city militia, who guarded the entrances to the church; it bristled with arms. Napoleon was expected, but he did not come; he was busy with dispatches that morning, for on the previous day his stepson, Eugène de Beauharnais, had won a battle in Western Hungary and had taken ten thousand Austrian prisoners.

In lieu of the emperor were Marmont, Davoust, and other generals—majestic, bewhiskered men wearing stiff high collars, and carrying sabers under their arms. The clank of swords unnerved the poor Viennese. Word of the most recent defeat passed around the church in whispers. In spite of the playing of Mozart's *Requiem*—music which induces a mood of serene introspection—everyone was nervous and distracted. We have an account of the service, in a letter written by Andreas Streicher, a maker of pianos. He aptly summed up the general feeling: "Since May 9, when the battle for Vienna began, we have heard sounds so penetrating, so urgent, that the ordinary tones of music can scarcely make any impression upon us. I find it still harder to think of any one individual, even though he be the great Haydn; for at present we are not in the orchestra or in remote boxes, but *upon the stage itself*, and we have our own parts to play in a drama that will decide the destinies of twenty million people."

Present in the church was one of the most hated French officials —Napoleon's "Iron Daru," Count Pierre-Antoine Daru, chief of the French commissariat. Back of him stood a sallow, uniformed young man with dreamy eyes. To this young commissary agent, a native of the city of Grénoble, was entrusted the unwelcome task of obtaining provisions for the embattled army. His was the responsibility of wresting food and fodder from the angry peasants, of setting up a hospital for one division, an artillery park for another. Sometimes he went without sleep for three days; when he could finally permit himself an interval of rest, he would lie down on the straw-covered floor of a poor Austrian inn and sleep almost as soundly as the dead who sprawled only a few yards away.

Strangely, a man drunk with fatigue is often more receptive to experiences than one who is wide awake and alert. In his mind's eye this young man could still see "the queer disorder that war produces," all the relics of yesterday's battle; helmets, shoes, and broken carriages scattered in all directions. "The battlefield had not yet been cleared," he had written, on May 3, from Wels, in Upper Austria, "and I saw my wagon wheels churning through the half-burned intestines of an entire regiment of French chasseurs." What a scene of horror is compressed into that one detail! And now, five weeks later, this same man stood listening to the music of Mozart, staring at Haydn's cenotaph, and witnessing the honors accorded to a humble man who had belonged to a previous, more gracious age—a man who was a great artist, a great Christian, and a great reconciler of all mankind. "Glory!" the young man murmured to himself. And, shuddering, he realized that the glory of Haydn was not the same as the *gloire Napoléenne*. Then he went home and decided to write a book about Joseph Haydn.

He had never yet written a book—and how was he to write about Haydn? To be sure, he was a music lover, but he had had no education whatsoever in theory. And yet, for some years after that June 15, 1809, this remarkable young man was haunted by the idea that he must write a book about a man he had never seen—about the man's music, his daily life, his friends, habits, and whims. But how was he to carry out so wild an intention?

In 1812, Carpani's book, *Le Haydine, Lettere sulla Vita e Morte di Giuseppe Haydn,* was published in Milan. The young French quartermaster was as familiar with Italian as with French. He liked Carpani's book, but he did not content himself with using it for source material. Rather, he stole every word of it, published it in French, and put on the title page his name, Louis Auguste César Bombet. This was literary theft on a unique scale. Was the man mad? Or had love for the subject, and the ambition to be somehow linked with Haydn, transformed him into a plagiarist? Or was the young man merely carrying out the Napoleonic policy of pillage which he had learned in the army? But he himself had only recently blamed the emperor for taking booty from all over Europe, and for corrupting the moral character of the army "by encouraging all kinds of looting."

Men are rarely aware of the reasons for their own actions, even when—as was the case with young Bombet—they are psychologists by avocation. Carpani immediately denounced the French work, and heaped invective upon the plagiarist. But Carpani's rage beat only the empty air, for Bombet, with the haughty first names of Louis, César and Auguste, was only a pseudonym. Shame did not attach itself to the real author of the spurious book—for the true name of the chap whom love drove to plagiarism was Henry Beyle. But the reader has already guessed that Beyle was, again, not the true name—the name which was to go down to immortality. We know the man now, and shall know him for all time, by the name of Stendhal. Thus he made his entry into literature by means of a highly contemptible deed. Yet we who see the misdemeanor from afar realize that it was prompted irrationally by an immense admiration for Haydn and a sense of personal inadequacy, and we cannot help forgiving it.

Amid the confusion of the times the daring could possess themselves of other things besides art treasures, riches, or literary fame. At the time of Haydn's death, the princely house of Esterhazy experienced its greatest hour. From Schoenbrunn, where he was holding court, Napoleon sent a message to Nicholas II of Esterhazy; he offered to him the crown of Hungary.

The war was still raging. Emperor Francis had already lost the Tyrol, Upper Italy, and Galicia. The states of West and Central Germany—Bavaria, Wuerttemberg, Baden, and Saxony—wore the enemy's chains, and were fighting in the pay of Napoleon. France stood at the apex of her power. If Hungary should now have been torn away from the realm of the Emperor Francis, the last bastion would have crumbled, and 1809—rather than 1918—would have seen the dissolution of the might of the Hapsburgs.

The French were in Vienna. Napoleon's stepson was besieging Pressburg. In a few days' march Marshal Davoust could take Budapest. Simultaneously with his alluring offer to Esterhazy, Napoleon published his proclamation to the Hungarians:

> "People of Hungary! The moment has come! You can now win back your hereditary independence. Accept the peace that I offer you . . . Your land and your constitution shall remain inviolable. I desire nothing from you and wish only that you may become a free nation." He sang the siren song of political psychology: "The union with Austria is the principal cause of your misfortunes . . . Your land was the most beautiful part of the Empire—and yet you have always been ruled by principles alien to you. Now is the time to fulfill the law of your nature: choose a national king for yourselves, a king who will live in your midst. Hungarians, this is what Europe asks of you! Assemble on the field of Rakos after the custom of your ancestors—and inform me of your decision!"

Before the nation came to be governed by the Viennese emperors, the Hungarians had traditionally elected their kings on the field of Rakos. Napoleon's scheme was to have his agents present at the field of Rakos and nominate Nicholas II of Esterhazy. Nicholas was a conservative landowner, not too clever, not too ambitious, and the French were convinced that he could provide Napoleon with 100,000 soldiers. But more important was the shattering impression the coup would produce upon all of eastern Europe—defection of Hungary would signify the downfall of the Hapsburgs.

Napoleon had developed his plan with great astuteness, but it failed at the eleventh hour because of an unforeseen factor, the character of Nicholas Esterhazy. He had wider allegiances than that to Hungary; he held the rank of Austrian field marshal. For him to take the crown of Hungary away from the Emperor of Austria, even though it were accorded to him by a popular election, would be high treason, obviously punishable by death. The man under whose patronage Haydn had written his *"Gott erhalte"* shrank from this crime of crimes. Thus he did his best to help God save Emperor Francis. His loyalty proved to be wise politics, for four years later the French hegemony was shattered—and by 1815 the great usurper was on his way to St. Helena.

The victorious powers never forgot Esterhazy's loyalty in that historic hour. In 1820, when peace had reigned for a few years, Adolphus Frederick, Duke of Cambridge and brother of the King of England, traveled through the Continent. In a visit to the palace at Eisenstadt he heard a performance of *The Creation*. Afterward he toasted Nicholas, and linked with the name of the loyal prince the name of Haydn, the immortal composer whom England as well as Austria considered one of her own. Turning toward Nicholas, he gallantly concluded: "Happy the man who had a Haydn in his life—and who now possesses the body of that departed immortal."

Nicholas pricked up his ears; his cultural conscience was stung. For eleven years a void iron coffin had stood in the Viennese palace of the Esterhazys. It had been intended for the bringing of Haydn's body to Eisenstadt, but the matter had been overlooked, in the turbulence of wartime. Haydn still lay in the Hundsthurm Cemetery, at the gates of Vienna. The grave was known, because Sigismund Neukomm, who had since returned to Vienna in the French diplomatic service, had, with a disciple's piety, ordered a modest memorial to be erected over it.

The remark of the English prince roused Esterhazy to action in the matter of transferring the body from Vienna to Eisenstadt. After obtaining permission from the Viennese authorities, Esterhazy's men set about exhuming the body. The prince was present. When Haydn's remains came to light, all saw that the master's bones, clothes, and well known wig were there—*but the head was missing!* Where could it be? The prince, indignant at what he considered to be an affront to himself, turned the matter over to the police.

It was discovered that, on the night following the burial, ghouls had opened the grave, cut through the cervical vertebra with a sharp instrument (in effect, guillotining Haydn!) and made off with the head. Who could these inhuman monsters have been? This had happened during a time of terror, and war commonly brutalizes men and corrupts morals. But the heathenish French, who were at first suspected, had not committed this atrocity.

The culprit was an otherwise pious Catholic, I. C. Rosenbaum, Haydn's friend and admirer; he had bribed a gravedigger to exhume the body for him. Rosenbaum had probably made the acquaintance of the gravedigger through Johann Nepomuk Peter, a prison warden who was also involved in the affair. It is not often that we hear of the personal friends of the grim wardens of men. Peter and Rosenbaum were good friends. Two Viennese tax collectors, Ullmann and Jungmann, were, apparently, also involved.

Questioned as to their motives, all of them replied that "they had acted out of reverence."

It was developed that Rosenbaum and Peter were both fanatical believers in phrenology, the "science" which Franz Joseph Gall (1758-1828) had recently founded in Paris. Based on the dubious idea that the external shape of the head corresponded precisely to that of the brain—that is to say, to the contents of the skull—Gall's theory asserted that the contour of the cranial bones governed the intellectual gifts of every human being. For decades, phrenologists conducted treasure hunts in the effort to locate the seat of the organs of speech, of music, of mathematics, of spatial sense, and the sense of color, of memory and recall. Many years elapsed before modern encephalology, singling out a few serviceable traits, put an end to Gall's theory. Peter and Rosenbaum seriously believed that in preserving Haydn's skull they were "saving from destruction a palace of musical art." What a peculiar instance this was of materialism, compounded with traits of idealism and the compulsive possessiveness of love! And how bizarre the aftermath to a great man's death! Stendhal had stolen the "life of Haydn"; these other two stole his skull.

The two men had made a wooden box, had polished it highly in black, had shaped it like a sarcophagus, and had ornamented it with a golden lyre. Within it the head rested on a white silk cushion. When the stir Nicholas made over the theft reached the ears of the Viennese public, popular sentiment turned, with remarkable vulgarity, to the side of the ghouls. The Viennese populace concluded that Peter and Rosenbaum had been "smart" in "cheating the worms," and still smarter in refusing to surrender the skull to Esterhazy. Legally nothing could be done to them; the cemetery where the ghoulish act had taken place no longer lay within the territory of Vienna, and the Viennese local authorities could not lodge a complaint against the men. Extra-legally, of course, the police could confiscate the skull and give it to Esterhazy. This they attempted—but it was easier said than done. Rosenbaum and Peter each, alternately, insisted that the other had the skull; then it was alleged that the skull was lost. Searches of their homes proved fruitless. (At one time the "relic" was hidden in the bed of Rosenbaum's wife, the singer Therese Gassmann, and thus escaped the eyes of the Viennese police.) In the meanwhile, the populace of Vienna appeared to have quite forgotten that the skull appertained to Haydn himself. They rejoiced because Esterhazy did not have it, for Esterhazy was a Hungarian and a haughty nobleman who had kept *their* Haydn, their good, old Haydn, to himself for so many years.

After all, why should not Peter and Rosenbaum worship their Haydn after their own fashion? Worshiping bones might seem morbid; on the other hand, it was not too remote from the practices of the Church—by this time the deceased man had become virtually a saint. At the auction in 1810 of his effects, which provided the heirs with an incredible sum in gulden—today the amount would be twenty-seven thousand dollars—the common people of Vienna had bid wildly for Haydn's linen and underwear as if these things were precious relics. Prince Johannes von Liechtenstein had bought for one thousand five hundred gulden the live parrot which the master had brought from England—it was an inconceivable price for those days. Froehlich, the smith, who was the principal heir, had, according to Carpani, "been on the point, the day before, of swapping the apparently useless bird for an eatable Styrian capon."

In the matter of the scandal over the skull, Prince Esterhazy hoped for assistance from the Emperor Francis or from the Minister of Police, Count Sedlnitzki, but neither would aid him to recover the skull and take it to Eisenstadt where the rest of the body now lay. Then the prince acted stupidly; he sent his personal physician to Peter to *buy* the head from him. Peter did exactly what might have been expected of him—he sent *another* skull. This one was placed in the grave at Eisenstadt with Haydn's remains. The *real* head is still in Vienna, in a glass cabinet, and belongs to the Society of the Friends of Music (*Gesellschaft der Musikfreunde*); on his deathbed, Rosenbaum bequeathed it to this organization. A Viennese anatomist, Professor Julius Tandler, has testified that it is indeed Haydn's skull; his careful measurements admit of no doubt.

Since Haydn had spent almost his entire life between Vienna and Eisenstadt, perhaps it is fitting that each city should possess a part of him; nevertheless, the fate of the body of this quiet man is peculiar and gruesome. It is noteworthy, too, that Prince Esterhazy was too distracted and too haughty, even after he did fetch home the body of Haydn, to provide a solitary grave for him! This is a fact. Haydn rests in the Bergkirche, together with six other Esterhazy servants. The poor people who are associated in immortality with Haydn are: Theresa Schmidt; the Pavlowskys, man and wife; Johann Szentgaly, Magdalena Juhaszs, and Johann Fuchs. They were servants, as was Haydn himself—perhaps they were silver polishers, butlers, or teamsters for the princely house.

But that does not matter. As these lines are being written, a chestnut tree flutters in the breeze, above the steps of the church, and scatters gold over the ground. Autumn leaves drift over the threshold and over the pavement beneath which Haydn lies. With closed eyes, we still see deep into far-away central Europe.

We see also, not at the grave itself but nearby, a tablet bearing the titles and accomplishments of which the master was proudest: *Doctor Oxoniensis* is graven there—"Doctor of Oxford." *Vir pius, probus, mansuetus*—"a pious, just, and peaceable man." *Fugandi curas artifex, mulcendi pectora primus*—"Artistic dispeller of cares, and foremost soother of our hearts." Reading these words, we feel a sense of awe. For here is the assertion of something that has long been lost to us—the Aesculapian meaning of music; music as a healing art. It can heal no longer, today.

But we are affected most of all by two lines from the Psalms which are also engraved upon the stone tablet. They proclaim the covenant that was made between Haydn the artist and his Almighty Creator, a covenant to which both adhered:

"DIE I SHALL NOT, BUT LIVE
AND PROCLAIM THE WORKS OF THE LORD"

EPILOGUE: THE HAYDN RENAISSANCE

SCARCELY two decades after his death, Haydn was, as an instrumental composer, virtually defunct. When Robert Schumann wrote, in 1835, "Today it is impossible to learn anything new from Haydn. He is like a familiar friend of the house whom all greet with pleasure and with esteem, but who has ceased to arouse particular interest," he was speaking euphemistically. Haydn had so little to say to the rising, creative spirits in music that young Berlioz walked out of a concert in Paris to avoid hearing the Haydn quartets on the program. Well, he had just heard Beethoven!

But the founders of romanticism had taken a different view. To them Haydn was a well that never ran dry. For example, Schubert followed one of Haydn's doctrines, never to abandon a theme until everything possible had been got out of it, so slavishly, in his early symphonies, that, before he found his true vein, his writing was more Haydnesque than Haydn's. Even more astonishing was the instance of young Carl Maria von Weber's fidelity to Haydn. From Weber's *Peter Schmoll and His Neighbors* (written when Weber was sixteen), with its orchestrated Haydn-subject at the beginning of the overture, there is a direct line of descent to the period of his greatest mastery and the peasant scenes in the *Freischutz.*

The later romantics, however, could not abide Haydn. His "outdated humor," his "tedious regularity," the artfulness with which he prolonged his themes, his assurances, so unlike those of Beethoven, that heaven and earth stand solidly established—above all, the vast herds of beasts that populate his music—to all these things the middle of the nineteenth century vigorously objected. Haydn's art was considered to be both childish and superannuated, at once. Even so good a poet as Mörike declared that, essentially, all that remained vital of Haydn was "the pig-tail of humor swinging at the back of his neck."

In the meantime, Haydn's art—though only the vocal side of it—had conquered other continents. In 1815 the Handel and Haydn

Society was founded in Boston; all honor to that city! "It did not spring suddenly into life, like the mythic olive tree at the bidding of Athena," wrote Charles C. Perkins, historian of the society. The first Haydn symphonies heard in America had probably been performed in 1782 in New York. Four years later, Reinagle, the Austrian music teacher of Washington's stepdaughter Nelly, began actively the promotion of Haydn's work. And in 1793, Hewitt and Bergman, two musicians from London, presented in America the Haydn symphonies that they had heard conducted by the composer himself, only the previous year, at Salomon's concerts. Thus there was little loss of time before a lively Haydn tradition was established in America, and in 1811 a significant contribution to this tradition was made by the choir and instrumentalists of the Moravian Brethren, in Bethlehem, Pennsylvania, who gave an uncut performance of *The Creation* for the first time on this continent.

The most enduring propagation of Haydn's music, however, came from the Handel and Haydn Society, a choral association which was to make accessible for more than a hundred years the work of the two great masters. A society bearing such a name could hardly have come into being in Europe, for there religious differences outlawed any such bidenominational grouping of Handel and Haydn. In America, however, the Protestant Handel, "the sword of God," and the mild and universalistic Catholic Haydn could form, without objection from any religious group, two pillars of a house of sacred song.

South America, too, paid tribute to Haydn. His *Seven Words of the Saviour* early took its place among the most frequently performed works of church music in the Spanish-speaking countries. *The Creation,* however, was not heard in South America until one of Haydn's most grateful disciples came to Brazil in 1816. He was Sigismund Neukomm, himself a composer of Biblical oratorios, who had been in the French diplomatic service and had been ennobled, through the influence of Talleyrand. The Chevalier de Neukomm organized a Haydn Festival in Rio de Janeiro.

In the nineteenth century, however, the New World forgot, more or less, that Haydn had composed great symphonies. In Germany there was a similar lapse of interest. Germans were so familiar with *The Creation* that sometimes they did not bother to put the composer's name on the program announcement of that work, but they no longer knew anything about the rest of Haydn's vast production. This state of affairs was to continue until Johannes Brahms (1833-1897) undertook, in his own works, to amalgamate romanticism and classicism; in the course of this effort, he rediscovered the greatness of Haydn as a symphonic composer and orchestrator. The modern—which, we may hope, is the permanent—evaluation of Haydn dates from Brahms and his friend Josef Joachim, the Jewish violinist who was one of the foremost exponents of chamber music of his time. A similar evaluation was reached by one of the opponents of Brahms; this was the great Lieder composer Hugo Wolf (1860-1903). Wolf's *avant-garde* temperament understood the eternally *avant-garde* character of Haydn's Chaos music; his essay on the Chaos music of *The Creation* is of moving grandeur and uniqueness unequalled in all previous criticism of Haydn.

However, the reverence of Brahms for Haydn's quartets and symphonies did not affect other composers for some time, until Gustav Mahler (1860-1911), in his First and Fourth Symphonies, drew heavily upon the Austrian elements in Haydn's work and upon the old master's practice of parody. Somewhat earlier, young Richard Strauss (born 1864) had spoken with admiration of the realism in Haydn's animal portraiture; in hearing such music, he said, "His own heart would burst forth in happiness and laughter." As a mature composer, Strauss, in 1912, imitated the principal effect of the Haydn *Clock Symphony;* this he did in the very first pages of his *Bourgeois Gentilhomme* (in the prelude to *Ariadne*). This might be interpreted as genre painting, since Haydn so perfectly exemplified the eighteenth-century mood. But more than that was in question: The twentieth century witnessed a swing away from that subjectivistic romanticism which had rejected Haydn. The creative musicians of the new era were impelled to delve out more in the foundations of classicism and that true objectivism that was already sorely missed. Heinrich Schenker, the Viennese aesthetician, went so far as to declare, in 1925, that "only now can we properly grasp the greatness of Haydn (and of classical artists in general)"—only now, when the "often foolish enthusiasm of his contemporaries has faded away as completely as has the equally foolish scorn of the generations immediately following." Sir Donald Tovey, as musical representative of the English-speaking world, seconded this opinion. He stressed the fact that Haydn's work belonged in the sphere of the unique, and was as little susceptible to the sway of friendly or hostile fashions as had been Michelangelo or Shakespeare.

The influence of searching, scientific musicology upon the actively musical life of the present is, unfortunately, slight. One of our best scholars has, sadly, dubbed his whole profession *muscologists.* But when men like Guido Adler and Eusebius Mandyczewski began in 1909, on the hundredth anniversary of Haydn's death, to speak of a "Haydn Renaissance," they meant more than the publication of "complete works" and the enlistment of the interest of learned societies. In that same year Claude Debussy, *pointillist* and impressionist, wrote his *Homage à Haydn* for the piano.

Debussy's work seemed, for a long time, to have hewn to the line implicit in Dante Gabriel Rossetti's declaration that he painted beings who do *not* exist on earth. But at the time of Debussy's death, in 1918, he seemed about to enter an era of neo-classicism strongly marked by Haydn's influence. And, indeed, while Mozart's lilting manner has remained the bugbear of modern expressionism, the Haydn tone, with its incomparable mixture of bluntness and tenderness, underlies, really, not a few passages in present-day music. This is perhaps most striking in the later works of Paul Hindemith (born 1895) and in the productions of some of the young French composers. Since 1918, when the poet Jean Cocteau proclaimed that French music had to be once more *"une fille robuste, saine, franche,"* French creative composers have turned wholeheartedly to Haydn. In the works of Darius Milhaud (born 1899), Arthur Honegger (born 1892) and Francis Poulenc (born 1899) we catch, frequently, glimpses of old Haydn peering out—but his aspect is not at all old, and his pig-tail is missing! Haydn once more functions as the founder of a solid sonata-form structure and the guiding spirit of music that is turning back to the land.

The most modern of all compositions in the Haydn manner was, however, written in Rome rather than in Paris. It is the orchestral suite *The Birds,* by Ottorino Respighi (born 1879). This is truly composed in a manner "worthy of the creatures." Moreover, we sense that Haydn, the realist and positivist, would himself have done something similar if he had had at his disposal the orchestral resources and experience of the present day.

But the real Haydn Renaissance revolves about Haydn's own symphonic works, and in this field America is predominant, as England was in recognition of the master, in the last decade of the eighteenth century. America's leadership is based on greater wealth and the fact that the nation has been spared the calamities of warfare on its home soil. In times like these, the sheltered community can afford more culture than one affected directly by the disasters of an entire continent.

Even as late as 1932, the two hundredth anniversary of Haydn's birth, wielders of the baton tended to give Haydn a rather left-handed treatment. But in 1938, the year in which Hitler dealt the death-blow to Austrian culture, this situation was radically changed. The refugees in America—and not they alone—brought Haydn with them, and his works are now presented with a frequency unheard of even in Europe. On the New York radio, Haydn has moved up to eighth place, and for the past ten years he has ranked at symphony concerts next to Mozart and Beethoven—as is only proper.

Not only the quantity, but the quality, of these performances must be stressed. To see a great American or guest conductor leading one of the many splendid American orchestras in a Haydn symphony —the 98th, with its Mozartian *adagio,* conducted, say, by Toscanini, or the *Surprise,* by Koussevitzky—and to hear such performances, is to learn many things about Haydn. There is, for example, Hermann Scherchen's performance of the *Toy Symphony,* in which the conductor is concerned less with "animal sounds" than with his realistic discovery of "how short children's breath is." But it is doing an injustice to single out individuals. Fritz Stiedry, Felix Weingartner, Fritz Reiner, Artur Rodzinsky, Erich Kleiber, Eugene Ormandy, Fabian Sevitzky, Leonard Bernstein, and many others, have done great service to Haydn and to the radio audience. It must mean a great deal to our modern Everyman to leave his home in the morning with the harmonies of Haydn still in his ears.

Ours is the era of recorded music. The spinning disk spreads knowledge of music faster and farther than music that is not "canned." At the same time, there is a concomitant loss in acquaintance with the real depths of music. To have magnificent music offered for the mere pushing of a button may be discouraging to those who would like to learn to play the piano or the violin themselves—for what is the use? Amateur quartet playing has become an almost forgotten art. (However, on the professional level, Haydn's quartets are receiving their just due.)

The Haydn Renaissance in this country shows one strange omission—that is *The Creation.* Formerly perhaps overdone, it is never performed today. Has it become too expensive to assemble large choruses and orchestras for so grand a purpose? Occasionally, *The Creation* can still be heard in small, remote churches. The solo singers are good, but in place of an orchestra an organ vainly attempts to reproduce the beauties of Haydn's accompaniment. The organ goes well with Handel, and Bach, the baroque giants, but it drowns out Haydn's delicate coloration.

It is to be hoped that *The Creation* will be rescued from neglect; otherwise, we shall have to add a question mark to the heading "Haydn Renaissance." (We did so originally, but wrote it so small that it has become invisible in print.)

FINIS LIBRI

BIBLIOGRAPHY

Abert, Hermann: Joseph Haydns Klavierwerke (Zeitschrift für Musikwissenschaft, Vol. II-III), 1920-21

Abert, Hermann, und Jahn, Otto: Mozart, Berlin 1920

Adler, Guido: Festrede über Joseph Haydn, Vienna 1909

———: Die Wiener klassische Schule (Handbuch der Musikgeschichte), Leipzig 1920

Altenburg, W.: Versuch einer Anleitung zur heroischmusikalischen Trompeter- und Paukenkunst, Leipzig 1795

Altmann, Wilhelm: Handbuch für Streichquartettspieler, Berlin 1928

Amoroso, Ferruccio: Haydn, Torino, 1933

Anders, Guenther: Philosophische Untersuchungen über musikalische Situationen, Berlin 1929. Thesis (unprinted).

Antos, E.: Ungarische Magnatenhäuser, Pesth 1886

Arnold, Ignaz Th. F. C.: Joseph Haydn, Erfurt 1810

Artaria, F.: Verzeichnis der musikalischen Autographen von Joseph Haydn, Vienna 1893

Artaria und Botstiber: Joseph Haydn und das Verlagshaus Artaria, Vienna 1909

Audrey et Bellegarde: Napoléon I. et la musique, Paris 1889

Barone, Iole Maria: La lirica musicale dì Pietro Metastasio (Rivista musicale Vol. XII), Torino 1905

Beau, Albin: Das Verhältnis Stendhals zur Musik, Thesis, Hamburg 1930

Bekker, Paul: The Story of the Orchestra, New York 1936

Bernet Kempers, K.Ph.: Haydn en het strijkkwartet (Muziek Vol. VI), Amsterdam 1931-32

Bie, Oskar: Die Oper, Berlin 1913

Blume, F.: Haydns Persönlichkeit in seinen Streichquartetten (Jahrbuch Peters, XXXVII), Leipzig 1931

Bobillier, Marguerite: see Brenet, Michael

Bombet, César-Auguste-Louis: see Stendhal

Botstiber, Hugo: Geschichte der Ouverture, Leipzig 1913

Brand, Carl Maria: Die Messen von Joseph Haydn, Würzburg 1941

Brenet, Michael: Haydn, Paris 1909

———: Histoire de la Sinfonie, Paris 1913

Bücken, Ernst: Der heroische Stil in der Oper, Leipzig 1924

Buerkli, Johann Georg: Biographie von Joseph Haydn, Zürich 1830-31
Burney, Charles: General History of Music, Vol. I-IV, London 1776-89
———: Memoir of the Life and Writings of Metastasio, London 1796
Carpani, Giuseppe: Le Haydine, ovvero lettere su la vita e le opere del celebre maestro Giuseppe Haydn, Milano 1812
Carse, Adam: The History of Orchestration, London 1925
Cherbuliez, Antoine E.: Joseph Haydn, Zürich 1932
Chrysander, Friedrich: G. F. Haendel, Leipzig 1919
Conrat, H.: Joseph Haydn und das Kroatische Volkslied (Die Musik, Vol. XIV), Leipzig 1904-05
Cowen, Sir Frederic: Haydn, New York 1912
Coxe, Howard: Stranger in the House (A Life of Caroline of Brunswick), New York 1940
Cramer, Carl Friedrich: Magazin der Musik, Kopenhagen 1789
Csatkai, André: Aus dem Haydnzimmer der Sammlung Wolf, Eisenstadt 1932
Dale, Kathryn: Schubert's Indebtedness to Haydn (Music and Letters), 1921
Dankert, W.: Mozarts Menuettypen, Leipzig 1932
Dent, Edward I.: Mozart's Operas, London 1913
Deutsch, Otto Erich: Franz Schubert, München 1913-14
———: Mozart und die Wiener Freimaurerlogen, Wien 1932
Diemand, A.: Joseph Haydn und der Oetingen-Wallersteinsche Hof, Augsburg 1922
Dies, Albert Christoph: Biographische Nachrichten über Joseph Haydn, Vienna 1810
Dittersdorf, Karl Ditters von: Lebensbeschreibung, seinem Sohn in die Feder diktiert (New Edition, Leipzig, without year.)
Eichhorn, Hermann: Die Trompete in alter und neuer Zeit, Leipzig 1881
Einstein, Alfred: Gluck, London 1936
———: Mozart, His Character, His Work, New York 1945
Engel, H.: Ueber den Begriff der Klangfarbe, Berlin 1886
Engl, Johann Evangelist: Haydns handschriftliches Tagebuch aus der Zeit seines zweiten Aufenthaltes in London, Leipzig 1909
Esterhazy, Miklos: Tratai, Budapest 1930-32
Fétis, E.: Biographie universelle des musiciens, Brussels 1839
Fischer, Wilhelm: Zur Entwicklungsgeschichte des Wiener klassischen Stils (Studien zur Musikwissenschaft, Vol. III), 1915
———: Instrumentalmusik von 1750-1828 (Adlers Handbuch der Musikgeschichte), Berlin 1929
Fleischer, Oskar: Napoleon Bonapartes Musikpolitik (Zeitschrift der Internationalen Musikgesellschaft, Vol. III), Leipzig 1901-02

Flueler, Max: Die norddeutsche Sinfonie zur Zeit Friedrichs des Grossen und die Werke Philipp Emanuel Bachs. Thesis. Berlin 1908
Fox, Douglas Gerard Arthur: Joseph Haydn, London 1929
Framery, N.: Notice de Joseph Haydn, Paris 1810
Friedlaender, Max: Van Swieten und das Textbuch zu Haydns "Jahreszeiten" (Jahrbuch Peters), Leipzig 1909
Froehlich, J.: Joseph Haydn, Regensburg 1936
Gal, Hans: Die Stileigentümlichkeiten des jungen Beethoven (Studien zur Musikwissenschaft Vol. IV.)
Galli: Estetica della Musica, Torino 1900
Geiringer, Karl: Joseph Haydn, Potsdam 1932
———: Haydn's Sketches for "The Creation" (Musical Quarterly, Vol. XVIII), London 1932
———: Haydn, a Creative Life in Music, New York 1946
Gerber, Ernst Karl: Neues Lexikon der Tonkunst, Leipzig 1790-92
Graf, Max: Composer and Critic, New York 1946
Greilsamer, L.: Le Baryton du Prince Esterhazy (Sammelband der Internationalen Musikgesellschaft, Vol. VI), Leipzig 1910
Griesinger, Georg August: Joseph Haydn, Leipzig 1810
Gyrowetz, Albert: Biography (New Edition by Alfred Einstein), Leipzig 1915
Hadden, I. C.: George Thomson, His Life and Correspondence, London 1898
———: Haydn, London 1934
Hadow, William Henry: A Croatian Composer, London 1897
Hase, H. von: Joseph Haydn und Breitkopf und Haertel, Leipzig 1909
Heuss, Alfred: Die Kaiserhymne (Zeitschrift für Musikwissenschaft, Vol. I), Leipzig 1918
———: Die Dynamik der Mannheimer Schule (Zeitschrift für Musikwissenschaft Vol. III), Leipzig 1919-20
Hinderberger, Adolf: Die Motivik in Haydns Streich quartetten, Thesis, Bern 1933
Hohenemser, R.: Joseph Haydn als Instrumentalkomponist (Die Musik, Vol. VIII) Berlin 1909
Hughes, R. S. M.: Dr. Burney's Championship of Haydn (Musical Quarterly Vol. XXVII), London 1941
Jacob, H. E.: Die Weinlese an Haydns Grab (Berliner Tageblatt), Berlin 1928
———: Die Grösse Haydns (Die Neue Rundschau), Berlin 1932
———: Johann Strauss, Father and Son, New York 1940
Josephson, Matthew: Stendhal, New York 1946
Karajan, Theodor von: Joseph Haydn in London, Vienna 1861

Klafsky: Michael Haydn als Kirchenkomponist (Studien zur Musikwissenschaft Vol. III)
Kobald, Carl: Joseph Haydn, Vienna 1932
Kolb, Annette: Mozart, Vienna 1937
Krehbiel, H. E.: Music and Manners in the Classical Period, New York 1896
Kretzschmar, Hermann: Führer durch den Konzertsaal, Leipzig 1887-1921
——: Haydns Jugendsymphonien (Jahrbuch Peters, Vol. XV) Leipzig 1908
Kuhac, F.: Josip Haydn i Hrvatske Narodne Popievke, Zagreb 1880
Kurth, Ernst: Musikpsychologie, Berlin 1931
Lang, Paul Henry: Haydn and the Opera (Musical Quarterly, Vol. XVIII) New York 1932
——: Music in Western Civilization, New York 1941
Larsen, Jens Peter: Die Haydn-Ueberlieferung, Kopenhagen 1938
——: Drei Haydn-Kataloge in Faksimile, Kopenhagen 1941
Lambkin, John: Haydn (Dublin Review), London 1932
Le Breton, Joachim: Notice historique sur la vie et les ouvrages de Joseph Haydn, Paris 1810
Lewis, L.: Geschichte der Freimaurerei in Oesterreich, Vienna 1861
Lorenz, F.: Haydns, Mozarts und Beethovens Kirchenmusik, Breslau 1866
Ludwig, Emil: Beethoven, New York 1943
Mitrofanow, Paul von: Josef der Zweite, Vienna 1910
Mohl, Adolf: A Horvatok bevándorlása 1533–ban (The Croatic Migration of 1533) Budapest 1915
Moore, Douglas: From Madrigal to Modern Music, New York 1942
Müller, Robert F.: Joseph Haydns letztes Testament (Die Musik, Vol. XXIV), Berlin 1932
Neukomm, Sigmund: Dix-huit mois de la vie de Haydn (Revue et Gazette musicale de Paris, Vol. XXI), Paris 1854
Niemann, Walter: Brahms, New York 1945
Nohl, Ludwig: Haydn, Leipzig 1931
Norton, Mary D. Herter: Haydn in America until 1820 (Musical Quarterly, Vol. XVIII), New York 1932
Orel, Alfred: Katholische Kirchenmusik (In Adlers Handbuch der Musikgeschichte), Berlin 1929
Parke, W. T.: Musical Memoirs, London 1830
Paumgartner, Bernhard: Mozart, Zürich 1945
Photiadès, Constantine: En l'honneur de Joseph Haydn (Revue de Paris), Paris 1932
Pirker, Max: Rund um die Zauberflöte, Vienna 1920
Pohl, Carl Ferdinand: Mozart und Haydn in London, Vienna 1867

———: Joseph Haydn, Berlin 1875 and 1882 (3rd volume completed and edited by Hugo Botstiber, Leipzig 1927)

Pourtalès, Guy de: Richard Wagner, Berlin 1933

Reichardt, Johann Friedrich: Vertraute Briefe von einer Reise, Amsterdam 1810

Reissmann, A.: Joseph Haydn, Berlin 1880

Riehl, Wilhelm Heinrich: Haydn (In: Musikalische Charakterköpfe), Stuttgart 1862

Riemann, Heinrich: Handbuch der Musikgeschichte, Leipzig 1922

Rochlitz, Johann Friedrich: Für Freunde der Tonkunst, Leipzig 1824-32

Rosenbaum, I. C.: Unedited Diaries, 1797-1822 (kept in the Manuscript Collection of the Wiener Nationalbibliothek)

Rywosch, Bernhard: Beiträge zur Entwicklung in Joseph Haydns Symphonik, 1759-80, Thesis, Zürich 1934

Sandberger, Adolf: Zur Geschichte des Haydnschen Streichquartetts (In Gesammelte Aufsätze), Munich 1921

———: Zur Entwicklungsgeschichte von Haydns "Sieben Worten" (In Gesammelte Aufsätze), Munich 1921

Schemann, Ludwig: Cherubini, Stuttgart 1925

Schenker, Heinrich: Die Chaos-Musik der "Schöpfung" (In Das Meisterwerk in der Musik, Vol. II) München 1925-30

Schering, Arnold: Geschichte des Oratoriums, Leipzig 1911

Schmid, Ernst Fritz: Joseph Haydn. Ein Buch von Vorfahren und Heimat des Meisters, Kassel 1934

———: Joseph Haydn in Eisenstadt (Burgenländische Heimatblätter) Eisenstadt 1932

Schmidt, Leopold: Haydn, Berlin 1907

Schnerich, Alfred: Joseph Haydn und seine Sendung, Vienna 1926

———: Messe-Typus von Haydn bis Schubert, Vienna 1893

Schrade, Leo: Beethoven in France, New Haven 1942

———: Das Haydn-Bild in den ältesten Biographien, Königsberg 1932

Scott, Marion M.: Haydn in England (Musical Quarterly Vol. XVIII), London 1932

———: Haydn Relics and Reminiscences in England (Music and Letters Vol. XIII), London 1932

Seeburg, Fr. von: Joseph Haydn, Regensburg 1912

Stendhal: Lettres écrites de Vienne en Autriche sur le célèbre compositeur Joseph Haydn, Paris 1814

Stollbrock, Ludwig: Karl Georg Reutter (Vierteljahrsschrift für Musikwissenschaft, Vol. VIII), Berlin 1892

Strunk, O. W.: Haydn's Divertimenti for Baryton, Viola and Bass (Musical Quarterly, Vol. XVIII), New York 1932

Tappert, Wilhelm: Wandernde Melodien, Berlin 1889
Tenschert, Roland: Joseph Haydn, Berlin 1932
———: Frauen um Haydn, Vienna 1946
Thackeray, William M.: The Four George, Boston 1883
Thayer, A. W.: The Life of Beethoven, New York 1921
Tietze, Hans: Wien, Vienna 1933
Tolnai, Gabriel: Le Style des Esterhazy (Revue de Hongrie) Budapest, 1938
Tovey, Sir Donald Francis: Haydn's String Quartets (In Cobbett's Cyclopedic Survey of Chamber Music), London 1929
———: Haydn's "Creation" and "Seasons" (In Essays in Musical Analysis), London 1935-44
———: Beethoven (uncompleted), London 1945
Townsend, Pauline D.: Joseph Haydn, New York 1884
Tschuppik, Karl: Maria Theresia, Amsterdam 1934
Valentin, Berthold: Napoleon, Berlin 1913
Waldkirch, Fr.: Die Konzertanten Sinfonien der Mannheimer im 18 Jahrhundert, Heidelberg 1921
Weczercza, Walter: Das koloristisch-instrumentale Moment in Haydns Sinfonien, Thesis (unprinted) Vienna 1923
Zarek, Otto: History of Hungary, London 1940

INDEX